QUALITY MANAGEMENT IN FORENSIC SCIENCE

QUALITY MANAGEMENT IN FORENSIC SCIENCE

Author

SEAN DOYLE

Linked Forensic Consultants Ltd, Wellington, New Zealand

ELSEVIER

ACADEMIC PRESS

An imprint of Elsevier

Academic Press is an imprint of Elsevier
125 London Wall, London EC2Y 5AS, United Kingdom
525 B Street, Suite 1650, San Diego, CA 92101, United States
50 Hampshire Street, 5th Floor, Cambridge, MA 02139, United States
The Boulevard, Langford Lane, Kidlington, Oxford OX5 1GB, United Kingdom

Library of Congress Cataloging-in-Publication Data
A catalog record for this book is available from the Library of Congress

British Library Cataloguing-in-Publication Data
A catalogue record for this book is available from the British Library

ISBN: 978-0-12-805416-1

For information on all Academic Press publications visit our website at https://www.elsevier.com/books-and-journals

Publisher: Stacy Masucci
Acquisition Editor: Elizabeth Brown
Editorial Project Manager: Tracy Tufaga
Production Project Manager: Bharatwaj Varatharajan
Cover Designer: Christian Bilbow

Typeset by TNQ Technologies

Copyright and Permissions

To my wife Dianne and my two daughters Alisha and Rhianna who made the real sacrifices in the preparation of this work.

CONTENTS

FOREWORD

O hateful Error, Melancholy's child,
Why dost thou show to the apt thoughts of men
The things that are not?

Shakespeare, "Julius Caesar"

We all want to get things right. But how do we know when we are right, and perhaps more importantly, how might we know when we are getting things wrong? And if something is not quite right, what do we do about it? The subject is rarely trivial for any aspect of human endeavor but is particularly crucial for work within the forensics sciences. In the forensic sciences, where the well-being of many people is involved, a professional obligation exists to avoid error. Arguably, the obligation is an ethical one as well. An error could ruin a person's life. In some instances, it could end it.

Within the forensic sciences, the processes with which we are concerned are the application of science and the furtherance of what we term a rational "system of justice." A fundamental tenet of this process is that science, devoted to the establishment of justice, be reliable and be fair. Science in the service of justice is a powerful tool, but only if it is trustworthy. This book is not intended to treat the lofty subject of how any justice system ensures fairness. It is a book rather on how the system, having embraced science, ensures reliability and through reliability and ensures trust. Science improperly applied can only result in a perversion of justice.

Without science there can be no forensic science, and regardless of whether we focus on disciplines, or methodologies, or physical evidence types, we have an obligation to deliver fair, accurate, and trustworthy science. It is a big task. Those of us who practice these tasks must do so responsibly. We must strive for correctness in all that we do. Society expects us to do so. An error in the analysis or interpretation of physical evidence could lead to the conviction of an innocent person or the acquittal of a culpable one. While the former is universally seen as the more egregious error, both do violence to the administration of justice.

Everyone expects the forensic sciences to consistently display a high quality ethic. In a way, this expectation is peculiar. It is also unrealistic. In most things around us, we tolerate some range of quality. We make judgments, but while we want good quality, we will accept less than the ideal if the product is serviceable. If we are manufacturing ball bearings, for example, we want most to fall within a particular range, but we acknowledge that a few will crowd the upper end of this range and a few will crowd the lower, and we will accept that. Even with a system of justice, we expect justice will be served if those guilty of a crime are convicted and those innocent will be acquitted. But at the same time we know, and accept, that some guilty people will go free, and a number of innocent people are convicted. If the latter were not true, there would be no need of appeal processes. But society expects infallibility in the work of a forensic laboratory. Although this may be a lurid ideal, it is the expectation with which forensic laboratories must conduct their work.

So we must strive to get things *right*. If we do not get it right, will we get it *wrong*? How will we know? In the literature on quality assurance, the word *wrong* is rarely if ever seen. This is somewhat curious because it is a word with which all of us are quite familiar. We place a call to a wrong number. I made a wrong turn and got lost. What is the capital of New Zealand? Auckland. Wrong! Most of us would agree that the opposite of wrong is *right*. But again, in the literature on quality assurance, the word right is never seen. We use right, however, in everyday speech and writing with the same comfort and familiarity as the word wrong. Right on! I'm looking for Mr. Right. Who knows the right answer?

Is there anything actually improper in using the terms right and wrong in a discussion of the work of a forensic laboratory? Probably not. (It was an effort not to use the word *wrong* in the penultimate sentence instead of *improper*. The sentence would have been just as sensible.) But in any rigorous treatment of quality assurance, we are forced to abandon our old friends, right and wrong, in favor of other terminology.

The new landscape of terminology is vast. The horizon stretches as far as we can see, with a bewildering assortment of concepts—error, measurement, nonconformance, protocols, quality assessment, quality assurance, quality control, accreditation, certification, and so on. Must we acquaint ourselves with these concepts? No. Actually, we must master them.

This should be a journey commensurate with our professional obligations, not a reluctant march through enemy territory. How may we be guided? To begin with, we should listen to Sean Doyle, who has a profound and indelible grasp of quality management within the forensic sciences. He is well poised to share with us his understanding of the subject, and we would be well advised to hearken to what he has to say.

Worldwide, the work conducted by forensic laboratories is reliable. It is not infallible, however, and for anyone who needs to be reminded, this is not a perfect world. New methods have been introduced, accreditation and certification have been institutionalized as professional norms, and proficiency testing has contributed to the quality ethic that forensic laboratories are expected to achieve. But forensic laboratories are not infallible, just as clinical laboratories are not, or winery laboratories, or sausage quality laboratories. The spectre of human error is always present. Forensic examinations always involve humans, even when the human is utilizing a dispassionate instrument. Many forensic examinations are subjective in nature, where the interpretation of data is greatly dependent on the perceptions and beliefs held by the analyst, and this is an area that requires particular attention. Random error is often measureable, but human error is often much more difficult to assess. Whatever the source of error, it must first be recognized, then measured, and then dealt with. Whatever the source of error, an effort must be made to manage the unavoidable and to avoid the unmanageable. An appreciation of the material presented in this text will assist greatly in this effort. This effort cannot be ignored. Listen to Sean Doyle. He has much to offer.

John I. Thornton
Emeritus Professor of Forensic Science
University of California, Berkeley

ACKNOWLEDGMENTS

First, I am grateful to Max Houck and John Thornton for providing me with the opportunity to prepare this book.

I am grateful to many who have knowingly or unknowingly helped me. I am particularly grateful to Sheila Willis, Ian Evett, and my former colleagues at the Forensic Explosives Laboratory (FEL). At FEL, we witnessed at first hand the journey from the depths of reputational damage to the heights of becoming one of the best forensic science laboratories in the world aided by the adoption of quality standards and embracing an ethos of continuous improvement. For the success of that journey, Maurice Marshal and Robin Hiley should be acknowledged. I am also grateful to Penny Gamaché, Stephen Ellison, and Dyon Deckers. Any errors or omissions are mine alone.

This is the first edition of a work which is also the first of its kind and, therefore, there are bound to be errors and omission which should be communicated to the author. If the book is well received and found to be of benefit, then there may be a second edition which will provide an opportunity for errors and omissions to be addressed.

ACRONYMS AND ABBREVIATIONS

A2LA American Association for Laboratory Accreditation
AAFS American Academy of Forensic Sciences
AB Accreditation body
ACPO Association of Chief Police Officers (E&W)
AFFSAB Australasian Forensic Field Sciences Accreditation Board
AFIS Automated fingerprint identification system
AFRAC African Accreditation Cooperation
AFSN Asian Forensic Sciences Network
AFSP Association of Forensic Science Providers (UK and Ireland)
AG Attorney General
AICEF Academia Iberoamericana de Criminalística y Estudios Forenses
ANAB ANSI/ASQ National Accreditation Board
ANSI American National Standards Institute
ANZ Australia and New Zealand
ANZFEC Australia and New Zealand Forensic Executive Committee
ANZFSS Australia and New Zealand Forensic Science Society
ANZPAA Australia New Zealand Policing Advisory Agency
APLAC Asia Pacific Laboratory Accreditation Cooperation
AQC Analytical quality control
ASB American Academy of Forensic Sciences Standards Board
ASCLD American Society of Crime Laboratory Directors
ASCLD/LAB American Society of Crime Laboratory Directors/Laboratory Accreditation Board
ASQ American Society for Quality
ATF Bureau of Alcohol Tobacco and Firearms (US)
ATFE Association of Firearms and Tool Mark Examiners (US)
AUD Australian dollars
BIPM Bureau international des poids et mesures/International bureau of weights and measures
BPA Bloodstain pattern analysis
BPM Best practice manual (Europe)
CAB Conformity assessment body
CABL Compositional analysis of bullet lead
CAC California Association of Criminalists
CAI Case Assessment and Interpretation
CASCO ISO Committee of Conformity Assessment
CCP Code of Criminal Procedure (Netherlands)
CCQM Consultative Committee for Amount of Substance: Metrology in Chemistry and Biology
CDR Cartridge case discharge residue, synonymous with FDR and GSR
CEN Comité Européen de Normalisation/European Committee for Standardization
CENLEC European Committee for Electrotechnical Standardization
CEPOL The European Union Agency for Law Enforcement Training
CERTICO ISO Certification committee, CASCO predecessor
CHF Swiss Franks
CIPM Comité international des poids et mesures/International Committee for Weights and Measures

CITAC Eurachem/Cooperation on international traceability in analytical chemistry
CODIS Combined DNA index system (US)
CPD Continuous professional development
CPS Crown prosecution service (E&W)
CRFP Council for the registration of forensic practitioners (UK)
CrimPD Criminal practice directions (E&W)
CrimPR Criminal procedure rules (E&W)
CRM Certified reference material
CSFS Chartered society of forensic sciences
DAB DNA Advisory Board (US)
DEA Drugs Enforcement Agency (US)
DEVCO ISO committee on developing countries
DIS ISO Draft International Standard
DNA Deoxyribonucleic acid
DOJ Department of Justice (US)
DPS Department of Public Safety (US TX)
E&W England and Wales
EA European cooperation for accreditation
EC European Council
EFTA European Free Trade Association
ENFSI European Network of Forensic Science Institutes
ESR Institute of Environmental Science and Research (NZ)
EU European Union
EUROPOL European Police Office
EWG Expert Working Group (Europe)
FBI Federal Bureau of Investigation (US)
FDR Firearms discharge residue, synonymous with CDR and GSR
FFSAB Forensic Field Sciences Accreditation Board (Australia)
FISH Forensic Information System for Handwriting (US)
FQS Forensic Quality Services (US)
FSAB Forensic Specialties Accreditation Board (US)
FSAC Forensic Science Advisory Council (UK)
FSR Forensic Science Regulator (E&W)
FSS Forensic Science Service (E&W)
FSSB The Forensic Science Standards Board of OSAC (US)
GBP Great British Pounds
GRIM Glass refractive index measurement instrument
GSR Gunshot Residue, synonymous with CDR and FDR
GUM Guide to the Expression of Uncertainty
HFC Human Factors Committee of OSAC (US)
HLS High Level Structure of ISO9001
IAAC Inter-American Accreditation Cooperation
IAEA International Atomic Energy Authority
IAF International accreditation forum
IAI International Association of Identification
ICSU International Council for Science
IEC International Electrotechnical Commission
IFSA International Forensic Science Alliance
ILAC International Laboratory Accreditation Cooperation

INTERPOL International Criminal Police Organization
ISO International Organization for Standardization
ITU International Telecommunication Union
IUPAC International Union of Pure and Applied Chemistry
JCGM Joint Committee for Guides in Metrology
LA-ICP-MS Laser ablation—inductively coupled plasma—mass spectrometry
LCN Low copy number DNA
LGC LGC Group, formerly the Laboratory of the Government Chemist
LIMS Laboratory information management system
LOD Limit of detection
LR Likelihood ratio
LTDNA Low template DNA
MLA Multilateral recognition arrangement
MRA Mutual recognition arrangement an agreement between national
MRD IFSA minimum requirement document
NAMAS National Measurement Accreditation Service (UK)
NATA National Association of Testing Authorities (Australia)
NATLAS National Testing Laboratory Accreditation Scheme (UK)
NCFS National Commission on Forensic Sciences (US)
NDIS National DNA index system (US)
NDNAD National DNA database (UK)
NFPA National Fire Protection Association (US)
NIFS National Institute of Forensic Science (ANZ)
NIST National Institute of Standards and Technology (US)
NMI National Measurement Institute
NOS National Occupational Standards (UK)
NRC National Research Council of the National Academies (US)
NRGD Nederlands Register Gerechtelijk Deskundigen/Register of Court Experts
NZ New Zealand
NZD New Zealand Dollar
OBP ISO online browsing platform
OCME Office of the Chief Medical Examiner (US NY)
OIG Office of the Inspector General (US)
OIML Organisation Internationale de Métrologie Légale/International Organization of Legal Metrology
OSAC Organization of Scientific Area Committees (US)
OSTP Office of Science and Technology Policy (US)
PCAST President's Council of Advisors on Science and Technology (US)
PCR Polymerase chain reaction
PDQ Paint data query database
QAS Quality Assurance Standards for Forensic DNA Testing Laboratories (US)
QMS Quality management system
RCA Root cause analysis
RCMP Royal Canadian Mounted Police
REMCO ISO Committee on reference materials
RI Refractive index
RLFP Restriction length fragment polymorphisms
RM Reference material
RMP Random match probability
SADCA Southern Africa Development Community in Accreditation

SAFE Scientific Association of Forensic Examiners (US)
SAG Specialist Advisory Group (Australasia)
SARFS Southern Africa Regional Forensic Science Network
SDO Standards Development Organizations
SEM-EDS Scanning electron microscope—energy dispersive X-ray spectroscopy
SFJ Skills for Justice (UK)
SFR Streamlined forensic reporting (E&W)
SI Système international. International system of units, e.g., the kilogram
SIDS Sudden infant death syndrome
SMANZL Senior Managers of Australian and New Zealand Forensic Science Laboratories
SOFT Society of forensic toxicologists
SOP Standard operating procedure
STR Short tandem repeat
SWG Scientific Working Group (US)
SWGDAM SWG on DNA analysis methods (US)
SWGFAST SWG on friction ridge analysis, study and technology (US)
SWGGUN SWG for firearms and toolmarks (US)
SWGMAT SWG for materials analysis (US)
SWGSTAIN SWG on bloodstain pattern analysis (US)
SWGTOX SWG for forensic toxicology (US)
TMB ISO Technical Management Board
TWGDAM Technical Working Group on DNA analysis methods (US)—SWGDAM predecessor
TWGFEX Technical Working Group for Fires and Explosions (US)
UK United Kingdom of Great Britain and Northern Ireland
UKAS UK accreditation service
UKFSLG United Kingdom Forensic Science Liaison Group
UKIAFT United Kingdom and Ireland Association of Forensic Toxicologists
UNIDO United Nations Industrial Development Organization
UNODC United Nations Office on Drugs and Crime
USD US dollars
VAM Valid analytical measurement
VNTR Variable number tandem repeats
WHO World Health Organization
WTC World Standards Cooperation

TERMS AND DEFINITIONS

Term	Definition or Explanation
Abduction	An inferential method which starts from an observation/result/finding then seeks to find the simplest and most likely explanation, it is effect-to-cause reasoning. As there will be more than one explanation, the hypothesized explanation must be evaluated. See also induction and deduction.
Accreditation	Third-party attestation related to a conformity assessment body conveying formal demonstration of its competence to carry out specific conformity assessment tasks (ISO). Accreditation is the independent evaluation of forensic science providers against recognized standards to carry out specific activities to ensure their impartiality and competence. Through the application of national and international standards, stakeholder can have confidence in the calibration and test results, inspection reports, and certifications provided.
Accreditation cycle	The time between (re-) accreditations that varies according to the accreditation body. Is often 4 years during which time the entire QMS should be audited.
Accrediting body	An authoritative body that performs accreditation. The authority of an accreditation body is generally derived from government.
Accuracy	The closeness of agreement between a test result and the accepted reference value or the "true" result.
Activity level proposition	See hierarchy of propositions.
Analytical test	Analytical testing, performed inside a laboratory under well-controlled environmental conditions and using sophisticated equipment or testing procedures, is a laboratory activity and therefore does not fall within the scope of ISO/IEC 17020.
Audit	A systematic, independent, documented process for obtaining records, statements of fact, or other relevant information and assessing them objectively to determine the extent to which specified requirements are fulfilled.
Bayes' rule	Posterior probability = prior probability × likelihood ratio (the rule can be expressed in other ways).

Continued

Term	Definition or Explanation
Bayesian	The Bayesian notion of probability is as a degree of belief. Probability is defined by the strength of belief in a given proposition. The degree of belief is updated by applying Bayes' rule in the light of new information or data. See also Frequentist.
Blinding	A means of reducing the risk of cognitive bias by withholding information from the examining forensic scientist.
Calibration	A means of establishing the relationship between the response of an instrument and the quantity of the measurand using measurement standards.
Case assessment and interpretation	A forensic examination strategy utilizing the likelihood ratio.
Categorical opinion	An opinion selected from a limited range, and usually fixed number, of possible opinions, often of the type match/no match/inconclusive.
Certification	The provision by an independent body of written assurance (a certificate) that the product, service, or system in question meets specific requirements.
Cognitive bias	An error in reasoning that may lead to a mistake.
Common law jurisdiction	A legal system derived from English common law in which decisions are reached using an adversarial process.
Comparison disciplines	Those based on comparing questioned and reference, or known, materials and determining the degree of resemblance for the purpose of source attribution.
Competence	The ability to apply knowledge and skills to achieve intended results (ISO).
Conformity assessment	An activity undertaken to determine, directly or indirectly, whether a product, process, system, person, or body meets relevant standards and fulfills specified requirements.
Critical finding	Observations and results that have a significant impact on the conclusion reached and the interpretation and opinion provided. In addition, these observations and results cannot be repeated or checked in the absence of the exhibit or sample and/or could be interpreted differently.
Deduction	An inferential method which starts from a general statement or hypothesis and reaches a specific logical conclusion. In science, deduction is used to test hypotheses or theories. If the theory is true, then predictions based on the theory must also be true. It is cause-to-effect reasoning. See also abduction and induction.
Discipline	A subset of a field, e.g., handwriting examination, is a discipline within the field of document examination.

Term	Definition or Explanation
Evaluative opinion	An opinion of evidential weight expressing the strength of evidence and based on a likelihood ratio.
Fact-finder	Also termed trier-of-fact, the member of a court or tribunal charged with deciding questions of fact, for most criminal trials in common law jurisdictions this will be a jury.
Flexible scope accreditation	A means of extending the scope of accredited methods to deal with novel situation without reference to the accreditation body.
Frequentist	In the frequentist model, probability is defined in terms of the relative frequency of occurrence. The estimation of probabilities is based solely on statistical sampling. See also Bayesian.
Functional test	Functional tests are used to check conformance with specification. Such tests include comparing recovered latent prints with those of a suspect.
Harmonization	The process of conforming to common standards.
Hierarchy of propositions	In assessing the strength of evidence using a likelihood ratio, a pair of propositions is considered. They are ordered in a hierarchy; Offense, Activity, Source, and now Subsource. At source level, the pair are related to the source of the evidence, e.g., semen. At activity level, propositions are related to the alleged activity, e.g., sexual intercourse, and at office level the alleged crime, e.g., rape. Forensic scientists do not evaluate offense level propositions. When a DNA profile is obtained from an unknown source of cellular material, the propositions are at subsource level.
Individualization	Assigning an item of evidence to a class of one, one source is attributed to the exclusion of all others.
Induction	An inferential method by which a conclusion is drawn based on observations made accepting that the conclusion may be wrong. In science this is moving from experiment to theory. See also abduction and deduction.
Inferential reasoning	A process of gaining knowledge by means of abduction, induction, and deduction.
Informative element (of a standard)	An element intended to assist the understanding or use of the document or provides contextual information about its content, background, or relationship with other documents.
Inspection	Examination to determine conformity with specific requirements.
International Standard	An International Standard provides rules, guidelines, or characteristics for activities or for their results, aimed at achieving the optimum degree of order in a given context. It can take many forms. Apart from product standards, other examples include test methods, codes of practice, guideline standards, and management systems standards.

Continued

Term	Definition or Explanation
Investigative opinion	One that offers a rational and logical explanation for findings/results/observations. See also evaluative opinion.
Likelihood ratio	A ratio of conditional probabilities, the value of which updates prior beliefs. The value assigned by a forensic scientist is a measure of the strength of his or her evidence.
Limit of detection	Is the lowest quantity or concentration of a substance that can be reliably detected with a given analytical method.
Low template and low copy number	DNA analysis in which profiles are obtained from vary small quantities of DNA often of unknown source.
Measurand	The quantity intended to be measured.
Measurement	The assignment of a number to a characteristic of an object, which can be compared with other objects.
Measurement error	The difference between the result of a measurement and the "true" or accepted value of the measurand.
Measurement uncertainty	A parameter associated with the result of a measurement that characterizes the dispersion of the values that could be attributed to the measurand based on the information used, i.e., gives the range in which the "true" result might lie.
Method	A technical procedure, analytical or functional.
Method performance characteristics	Include accuracy, precision, limit of detection, and measurement uncertainty.
Metrological traceability	The property of a measurement result whereby the result can be related to a reference through a documented unbroken chain of calibrations, each contributing to the measurement uncertainty.
Normative element (of a standard)	The element that describes the scope of the document or sets out provisions.
Occupational standards	Outcome-based standards against which the competence of the individual can be assessed.
Opinions	See evaluative, investigative, and categorical.
Orthogonality	Obtaining the same result by two independent methods.
Perfect test	A "match" test with a zero false positive and zero false negative rate.
Precision	The closeness of agreement between measurements or test results obtained under given conditions.
Probabilistic genotyping	Mathematical modeling of a mixed DNA profile to find single profiles and giving weight to the results.
Professional judgment	Decision-making that is supported by a body of rigorous and objective analysis.
Proficiency test	A means of measuring performance for specific tests or measurements, used to monitor a provider's continuing performance. Proficiency testing is also called interlaboratory comparison.

Term	Definition or Explanation
Prosecutors fallacy	A logical fallacy of the transposed conditional in which, to put it crudely, the probability of the evidence given guilt becomes the probability of guilt given the evidence: mathematically $pX\|Y \neq pY\|X$.
Provision	An expression in the content of a normative document that takes the form of a statement, an instruction, a recommendation, or a requirement.
Prüm decisions	Decisions that facilitate cross-border police cooperation within the European Union granting access to DNA database and fingerprint data.
Qualitative	Qualitative properties are properties that are observed and can generally not be measured with a numerical result. A test method can result in qualitative data about something. This can be a categorical result or a binary classification (e.g., match/no match, is or is not an illicit substance).
Quality	The degree to which a set of inherent characteristics of an object fulfills requirements (ISO). In this work, the object is forensic science and the requirements are primarily those of law enforcement and justice.
Quality assurance	Part of quality management focused on providing confidence that quality requirements will be fulfilled (ISO).
Quality control	Part of quality management focused on fulfilling quality requirements (ISO).
Quality management	Coordinated activities to direct and control an organization with regard to quality.
Quality management system	Part of a set of interrelated or interacting elements of an organization to establish policies and objectives and processes to achieve those objectives with regard to quality (ISO).
Random error	Errors that cause results to differ in an unpredictable way.
Random match probability	The probability that the "match" occurred by chance. It is usually the denominator of the likelihood ratio.
Reference materials	Materials, sufficiently homogeneous, and stable with respect to one or more specified properties, which has been established to be fit for its intended use in a measurement process.
Reliable evidence	Of sufficient quality to be used by a tribunal to reach a safe decision by a fair process.
Requirement	An expression in the content of a document conveying objectively verifiable criteria to be fulfilled and from which no deviation is permitted if compliance with the document is to be claimed.

Continued

Term	Definition or Explanation
Robustness	A measure of a method's capacity to remain unaffected by small but deliberate variations in method parameters and provides an indication of its reliability during normal usage.
Root cause analysis	Root cause analysis is a method of problem-solving used for identifying the root causes of faults or problems. A factor is considered a root cause if removal thereof from the problem—fault sequence prevents the final undesirable event from recurring.
Ruggedness	The extent to which an analytical method can be modified without significant loss of performance.
Selectivity	The degree to which a method can detect and measure the substance of interest without interference from other components of the sample.
Sensitivity	The relationship between amount of substance and the size of signal or response. A more sensitive method will generate a bigger signal.
Sequential unmasking	A means of reducing the risk of cognitive bias by requiring questioned material to be characterized prior to sight of and comparison with the reference material.
Source level proposition	See hierarchy of propositions.
Standard	A document established by consensus and approved by a recognized body that provides for common and repeated use, rules, guidelines, or characteristics for activities or their results, aimed at the achievement of the optimum degree of order in a given context; i.e., a documented statement of requirements and other provisions (ISO).
Standard method	Methods published in international, regional, or national standards, or by reputable technical organizations, or in relevant scientific texts or journals, or as specified by the manufacturer of the equipment employed.
Standard operating procedure	A method or procedure that has been validated or verified as fit-for-purpose by the forensic science provider and falls within the scope of accreditation.
Standardization	The process of creating common standards.
Standards, types of	Professional (ethics, codes of practice), occupational (what should be done), and procedural (how it should be done).
Systematic error	Error arising from some effect of the method, the operator, the environment, or combinations of thereof which cause results to differ from the expected result in a predictable way either always higher or always lower. Systematic error remains constant or may vary in a predictable way over a series of measurements and cannot be reduced by making replicate measurements.

Term	Definition or Explanation
Trueness	The closeness of agreement between the average of an infinite number of replicate measurements and a reference or "true" value.
"True" value	The true value of a measurand is unknowable. However, measurement uncertainty can be determined providing a range of values in which the measurands value probably lies.
Unique	The state of being the only member of a class.
Validation	Confirmation by the provision of objective evidence, such as a validation study, that a method is fit for its intended purpose.
Verification	Confirmation by the provision of objective evidence that the method performance parameters established during method validation can be met (ISO).

INTRODUCTION

This book is intended to be of practical use to all forensic science stakeholders: practitioners, scholars, managers, lawyers, judges, law enforcement officers, prosecuting authorities, legislators, students, and interested members of the public.

It is an exposition of the current [December 2017] quality standards frameworks existing in the regions of Australasia, Europe, and North America in support of the main stakeholders, law enforcement, and justice, and against which conformance can be assessed.

This work is one of reference and is not intended to be read "from cover to cover." Each section is designed to stand alone and therefore there is necessary repetition.

The aim of quality management is to ensure conformance with quality standards. By conforming to quality standards, a forensic science provider demonstrates competence and the ability to produce science of sufficient quality that it might be relied on by stakeholders.

Since the first publication of ISO/IEC 17025 "General requirements for competence of testing and calibration laboratories" in 1999 and its adoption by forensic science providers as a means of independently demonstrating competence and the ability to generate reliable science, a forest of other standards has sprung up. Most are guidance documents that are aimed at ensuring forensic science providers conform to ISO/IEC 17025 or more recently ISO/IEC 17020 "Conformity assessment—Requirements for the operation of various types of bodies performing inspection." The object of this book is to guide the reader through that forest.

Given the breadth of the potential readership, the first section aims to provide all readers with a sufficient understanding of the basics to benefit from the remaining of this book. The basics are science, quality, metrology, or measurement and cognitive bias or errors in thinking. As this book is intended to be of practical use, none of the subjects in Section 1 is introduced in depth. Section 1 is science for the nonscientist and quality for those not engaged in quality management, etc.

Having provided an understanding of the basics, Section 2 introduces organizations that, to varying degrees, exercise responsibility for quality management. They are many and varied and are classified by primary function: standards development and setting, accreditation, regulation, and networking. Many of these organizations exercise more than one function making classification difficult. To aid classification, the concept of a hierarchy of standards is introduced later, in Section 3. The objects of these organizations and their governance, funding, and interrelationships are outlined. The risk of conflicts of interest is highlighted.

Section 3 introduces the standards themselves and with Section 6 [Discipline-Specific Quality Management] constitutes the major part of this book. As mentioned above, the concept of a hierarchy of standards is introduced to more easily classify standards and better navigate through the forest. The hierarchy has four levels with international generic standards such as ISO/IEC 17025 at the top and procedural standards, those setting out what must be done, at the bottom. The requirement of a competent organization staffed with competent personnel employing valid methods and procedures is stated. In addition, a typical quality standards framework is described.

In planning the route ahead, it is important to know the path already taken. Section 4 records and charts the historical development of quality management and argues that it was, and continues to be, miscarriages of justice that drive improvements in quality management. This reactive process is a weakness. The adoption of quality management systems by forensic science providers and the development of quality standards frameworks in response to judicial and government review are described. The duties and responsibilities of the forensic scientist acting as an expert witness are set out, distinguishing a forensic scientist from other types of scientist. The important role of the forensic exploitation of the DNA molecule is examined. The historical development of quality management in general is also discussed.

Having looked back in Section 4, Section 5 sets out the current position describing quality management as it currently operates. The two International Standards ISO/IEC 17025 and 17020 are more closely examined. The elements of a quality management system are specified, and the process of obtaining and maintaining accreditation to ISO/IEC 17025 or 17020 is described. Flexible scope accreditation is introduced, and its advantages described. Finally, an incident that highlights the risks in the current system is reported.

Standards that apply to the nuts and bolts of forensic science are the subject of Section 6 which, together with Section 3, constitutes the major part of this book. Section 6 details discipline-specific standards. The disciplines are classified by field: feature-comparison, forensic chemistry, forensic biology, and scene examination. The quality standards framework applying to each discipline in the regions of Australasia, Europe, and the United States are recorded and most are tabulated. The frameworks are found to differ markedly between disciplines. It is argued that the plethora of standards militates against standardization and harmonization.

Section 7 catalogues and discusses current issues, that is, challenges and risks to the quality of forensic science. The list is not exhaustive. The issues are classified as external and internal. Among the external issues are the impact of politics and economics and the use of Bayesian reasoning in the practice of forensic science. Among the internal issues is that of independence, particularly between law enforcement/prosecution and forensic science providers, a recurring theme in this book. Fragmentation in quality standards frameworks, the impact of scientific and technological developments, transparency, and streamlined forensic reporting are also discussed.

TABLE OF CASES REFERRED TO IN THE TEXT

Case	Section
Clemons v State [2006] 389 Maryland CA	4.3.2.2.2
Frye v United States [1923] 293 F 1013 DC Cir	1.4.2, 4.3.3.1.2
Daubert v Merrell Dow Pharmaceuticals [1993] 509 US 579	1.4.2, 3.4.7.1, 4.3.3.1.1, 4.3.3.1.2
Davie v Magistrates of Edinburgh [1953] SC 34	4.3.3.2.1, 7.7
General Electric Co. v Joiner [1997] 522 US 136	4.3.3.1.2
Ikarian Reefer [1993] 2 Lloyds Law Rep 68	4.3.3.2.1
Kumho Tire Co v Carmichael [1999] 526 US 137	4.3.3.1.2
Melendez-Diaz v Massachusetts [2009] 129 S Ct	4.3.3.1.2
People v Hector Espino [2009] NA076620 LACSC	4.4.4
People of New York v Castro [1989] 545 NYS 2d 985 SC	4.4.2
People of New York v Hemant Megnath [2010] 20037 SC	4.4.4
Preece v H M Advocate [1981] 783 Crim LR	4.3.3.2.1
R v Abraham Ghebre-Amlak [2014] 1670 EWCA	7.8
R v Deen CA (Crim Div) 21/12/1993	7.2.2.2
R v Broughton [2010] Crim 549 EWCA	4.3.1.2.2, 4.4.4
R v Clark [2003] Crim 1020 EWCA	3.4.2.4.4
R v Cooper [1998] 2258 EWCA	1.2.4.1
R v Doheny and Adams [1997] 1 Cr App R 369 CA	4.3.3.2.1, 4.4.5, 7.2.2.2
R v Hoey [2007] 49 NICC	4.4.4
R v J.L.J. [2000] 51 SCC	3.4.7.1.5
R v Lawrence (Nyira) [2013] Crim 1054 EWCA	7.8
R v Mohan [1994] 2 SCR 9	3.4.7.1.5
R v Reed and Reed and Garmson [2009] Crim 2968 EWCA	1.4.2, 4.3.1.2.2, 4.4.4
R v T [2010] Crim 2439 EWCA	3.2.5, 4.3.1.2.1, 4.4.5, 7.2.2.5, 7.4.1
State v Schwartz [1989] 447 NW 2d 422 428 Minn	4.4.2
Turner [1975] 834 QB	1.2.4.1
US v Morgan [2014]	4.3.3.1.2, 4.4.4
White Burgess Langille Inman v Abbott [2015] SCC 23	3.4.7.1.5

SOME IMPORTANT EVENTS IN THE DEVELOPMENT OF QUALITY MANAGEMENT IN FORENSIC SCIENCE

Year	Month	Event
1923		Los Angeles forensic science laboratory founded
1932		FBI laboratory founded
1966		British Calibration Service (BCS) formed
1974		ASCLD founded (US)
1974		Birmingham (UK) Pub Bombings
1975		Birmingham six convicted of Birmingham Pub Bombings
1977		CIPM asked BIPM with national standards laboratories to address the problem of a lack of consensus on measurement uncertainty
1977		ILAC established
1981		UK National Testing Laboratory Accreditation Scheme (NATLAS) introduced
1985		NAMAS formed from NATLAS and BCS
1986		SMANZFL founded
1986		First use of DNA "fingerprinting" in E&W
1987		ISO 9001 first edition published
1987		First use of DNA "fingerprinting" in the USA
1989		New York v Castro—DNA challenged for the first time
1989		Release of the Guidelines for a Quality Assurance Program for DNA Analysis by the Technical Working Group on DNA Analysis Methods (TWGDAM) (US)
1989	Oct	Enquiry by Sir John May begins into the case of the Guildford Four and Maguire Seven (E&W)
1990		FBI's CODIS begins as a pilot software project
1991	Mar	Royal Commission on Criminal Justice established (E&W)
1991	Mar	Birmingham six released after convictions quashed
1991	Apr	Forensic Science Service (E&W) becomes an executive agency
1991		NIFS founded (Australasia)
1992	July	First NRC report on DNA
1992		Innocence Project created
1993	Apr	House of Lords Select Committee Report on Forensic Science published
1993	July	Royal Commission on Criminal Justice Report published
1994		Netherland Forensic Institute accredited to EN45001 based on ISO/IEC Guide 25
1994		US DNA Identification Act (Codis)
1995	Apr	FSS establishes the world's first DNA Database
1995	Oct	ENFSI founded

Continued

Year	Month	Event
1995		ISO/IEC Guide 98-3 replaces GUM (guide to uncertainty of measurement)
1995		UKAS formed from NAMAS and National Accreditation Council for Certification Bodies
1995		US DNA Advisory Board (DAB) established
1996	Apr	FSS and the Metropolitan Police Forensic Science Laboratory merge
1996	Dec	Caddy report published on centrifuge contamination at the British Forensic Explosives Laboratory
1996	Dec	Second NRC Report on the evaluation of DNA evidence
1996		Finland National Bureau of Investigation accredited to EN45001
1996		New Zealand national DNA Databank established, second in the world
1996		ILAC formalized as a cooperation with 44 Accreditation Bodies signing a Memorandum of Understanding
1999	Jan	First "live" LCN DNA case by FSS
1999	Aug	UK Council for the Registration of Forensic Practitioners (CRFP) incorporated
1999		ISO/IEC 17025 first published
2000	Oct	CRFP register opened
2000	Nov	Damilola Taylor murdered in London, UK
2000		CFSO formed
2001	Oct	Association of Forensic Quality Assurance Managers established
2001		SMANZFL restructured
2002	Jan	Paper on cognitive bias by Risinger, Saks, Thompson, and Rosenthal published in the California Law Review
2004	Jul	FBI issues standardized DNA audit guide
2005	Mar	UK House of Commons report "Forensic Science on Trial" published
2005	Sep	FBI Laboratory Announces Discontinuation of Bullet Lead Examinations
2005	Dec	FSS changes from Executive Agency with a trading fund to a Government-owned company Gov Co and is effectively privatized creating a market in forensic science
2006	Jun	ENFSI and EA select ISO/IEC 17020 as the standard for crime science examination
2006	Sep	UKFSLG becomes Forensic Science Providers' Group
2006		ENFSI becomes a member of ILAC
2007	Apr	Damilola Taylor review published—registration of assistants recommended
2007	Jul	The creation of the post of Forensic Science Regulator in E&W announced
2007	Jul	Trial of Sean HOEY (Northern Ireland), validity of LT DNA method questioned, work suspended
2008	Jan	The FSAC established (UK)
2008	Feb	Full-time Forensic Science Regulator appointed (E&W)

Year	Month	Event
2008	May	FSR Response to the Caddy LTDNA review—LT DNA science valid
2008	Jun	EU Council decision 2008/615/JHA stepping up cross-border cooperation
2008	Dec	EA-5/03 Guidance on the implementation of ISO/IEC 17020 for crime scene examination published
2008		NIFS becomes a directorate within ANZPAA
2009	Jan	FSR publishes a review of the options for the accreditation of forensic practitioners
2009	Feb	NRC report on strengthening US forensic science published
2009	Mar	CRFP ceases trading and the register is closed
2009		Forensic Science Subcommittee created by the US White House
2010	Jan	Expert Witness in Criminal Cases Act (Netherlands)
2010	Oct	R v T judgment
2010	Nov	Publication of the 1st of 4 Royal Statistical Society Practitioner Guides
2010	Dec	Proposed start date for UKAS ISO/IEC 17020 pilot
2010	Dec	Closure of the FSS announced by the UK government
2011	Nov	ANSI-ASQ ANAB acquires Forensic Quality Services
2011		First experts (DNA) registered with the Nederlands Register Gerechtelijk Deskundigen
2012	Feb	Proposed finish date for UKAS ISO/IEC 17020 pilot
2012	Mar	FSS closed
2012		Australian Standard 5388.1—4 "Forensic Analysis" published
2013	Feb	US NIST and DOJ sign an MOU creating the NCFS
2013	Mar	NCFS (DOJ and NIST) established
2013	Apr	Streamlined forensic reporting introduced in E&W
2013	Jul	NATA agrees to assess conformance to AS5388 in addition to the current standard for forensic science ISO/IEC 17025:2005.
2014	Feb	OSAC established
2014	Mar	Expert witness opinion based on experience banned by Canadian Supreme Court
2014	Jul	Publication of the "Independent Review of NIFS"
2014	Aug	ANZFSS replaces Code of Ethics for all members with a Code of Professional Practice
2014	Aug	FSR publishes Codes of Practice and Conduct v2.0, an extension to scope of ISO/IEC 17025
2015	Apr	NCFS charter renewed for 2 more years
2015	Aug	UKAS published guidance for ISO/IEC 17020
2015	Sep	Durham PD (NC USA) accredited to ISO/IEC 17020 for crime scene activities
2015	Sep	Publication of ISO 9001:2015
2015	Oct	FSR publishes guidance on cognitive bias FSR-G-217
2015	Nov	CSFS Code of Conduct published

Continued

Year	Month	Event
2015	Nov	NCFS issues draft recommendation/suggestions
2016	Feb	FSR publishes the latest edition, Issue 3, of the Forensic science providers codes of practice and conduct
2016	Apr	ASCLD/LAB merges into ANAB
2016	Oct	ANAB to administer the American Board of Forensic Toxicology (ABFT) accreditation program
2016	Sep	US AG directs DOJ agencies, e.g., FBI, to adopt code of professional responsibility and post QMS documents online within 18 months
2016	Nov	Guiding Principles of Professional Responsibility for Forensic Service Providers and Forensic Personnel published by ANAB
2017	Apr	13th and final meeting of US NCFS
2017	Oct	LGC Forensics sold to Eurofins
2017	Nov	ISO/IEC 17025:2017 published

SECTION 1

Brief Introduction to Some Important Concepts and Key Terms

1.1 INTRODUCTION

Quality management, to varying degrees, affects all aspects of forensic science. Thus, the readership for this work is expected to be broadly based, ranging, for example, from lawyers requiring an understanding of quality management to quality managers needing to know something of the law as it relates to the practice and delivery of forensic science. The aim of this book is to be of practical benefit to that wide readership.

To fully benefit from this work, a practical understanding of some of the concepts underlying forensic science and quality management is required. The purpose of this section is to introduce those concepts and ensure all readers, irrespective of background, have a sufficient knowledge and understanding to gain benefit.

Some of the more fundamental concepts, such as "science," will be introduced and discussed briefly with sufficient detail to afford an understanding that is of practical use but not further developed. Other concepts, particularly those related to quality, will be introduced here and developed in some detail prior to a comprehensive treatment later in the work. Key terms will be defined and explained. In addition, some important issues will be mentioned in passing and returned to later in the work.

In describing and discussing the concepts, the aim has been to be as precise as possible without clouding the meaning for the nonspecialist reader. Readers specializing in a particular field may well have issues with the precision of some of the explanations offered and definitions given. However, a degree of leeway must be permitted to ensure that the nonspecialist gains an understanding. In later sections the terminology will be more precise.

This section covers the following four areas:

- Science,
- Quality,
- Metrology, and
- Cognitive bias.

However, before proceeding, the concept of a "standard" needs to be introduced. Dictionary definitions include an accepted or approved example of something against which others are judged or measured or an authorized model of a unit of measure or weight. Simple examples are the standard kilogram or meter in metrology. In science the standard would be the scientific method and in quality the quality management standard, ISO 9001:2015. The quality management definition of a standard is given later in Section 1.3.2.

Quality Management in Forensic Science
ISBN 978-0-12-805416-1, https://doi.org/10.1016/B978-0-12-805416-1.00001-3

1.2 SCIENCE

1.2.1 Science

What science is and is not has been and remains the subject of debate among philosophers (Rosenberg, 2000). However, the philosophy of science is of little relevance in a work intended to be of practical assistance. Nevertheless, a practical and precise understanding of the concept is required so that the subject of quality management in forensic science might be better set out and understood.

The word "science" has two basic meanings:

1. a body of knowledge; e.g., the science of chemistry, and
2. a method of enquiry; to find out about the universe.

Science, as a method of enquiry, relies on observation, theory, and experiment (in no particular order), the so-called observational and experimental procedures of science. Theories, or hypotheses, usually arise from observations made, experiments conducted, or, more generally, data gathered. The resulting theory (an explanation for the observations made or results obtained) is tested by further observations, experiments, or the gathering of more data and, if necessary, revised accordingly. This definition of science is useful as all forensic disciplines, including those based on comparison and largely relying on skill, such as marks and impressions, involve observation (i.e., making measurements and obtaining results or, more generally, gathering data) formulating hypotheses and often testing those hypotheses.

As scientific knowledge is often counterintuitive, scientific enquiry must be characterized by rationality, logic, and the avoidance of bias. The inferential methods of induction, deduction, and abduction all play a part. A detailed discussion of inference is beyond the scope of this work, but it does affect the interpretation of results obtained and this is discussed in Section 3.4.2.4. Jon Nordby (1999) in his book "Dead Reckoning: The art of Forensic Detection" gives a practical and easily understood description of each inferential method in a forensic science context.

To the above elements and characteristics of enquiry peer review should be added. There are different forms of peer review, but review by an expert of at least equal standing is a minimum requirement for the enquiry to qualify as scientific.

All these properties taken together constitute what is often termed the Scientific Method, the precise definition of which is also a matter of debate among philosophers, e.g., Karl Popper (1959) rejected the notion and Francis Bacon (1620) is credited with being its father.

For the purpose of this book, science is both a body of knowledge and a method of enquiry with the properties outlined above and as represented in Fig. 1.1.

It is worth noting in passing that the Law, particularly in judicial proceedings, is also a method of enquiry. However, where science admits no final conclusion the Law must. The "certainty" of the Law and the "uncertainty" of science are often at the root of issues in forensic science.

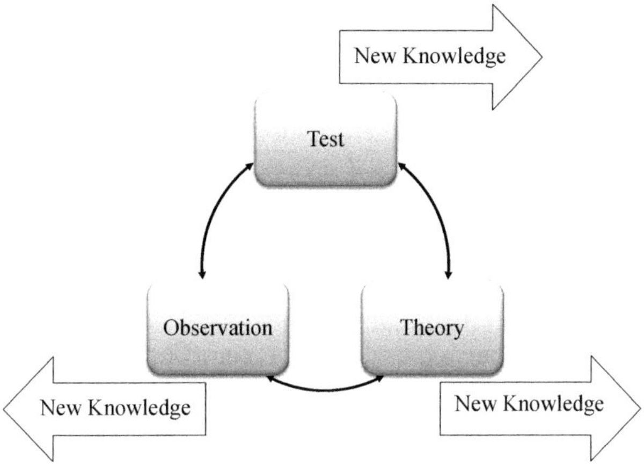

Figure 1.1 Scientific processes.

1.2.2 Forensic Science

Quite simply, forensic science is the use of science, or the scientific method, to help resolve disputes in civil or criminal law or, at a greater degree of abstraction, prove facts in issue. In comparison, law enforcement agencies tend to see the role of forensic science as aiding incident reconstruction, i.e., determining what happened at a crime scene and piecing together the story of events (UK Home Office, 2016). However, incident reconstruction is essentially another evidence type to be placed before a tribunal of fact. At the philosophical level, and to some extent at the practitioner level, there has been much debate regarding the processes by which the objective of forensic science might be achieved. Three of these processes are individualization, identification, and classification (Broeders, 2006).

Individualization is a type of classification and is the process of assigning an item of evidence to a class of one; examples might include DNA typing and fingerprint examination. In these disciplines, the aim is to identify an individual to the exclusion of all others.

DNA evidence is presented probabilistically and fingerprints, at the time of writing (2017), categorically[1], i.e., "match," "no match," or "inconclusive". The difference in the way these evidence types are reported can be explained, in part, by the fact that fingerprints, and similar feature-comparison disciplines, are mainly the province of skilled examiners rather than scientists.

The concept of individualization has fueled much debate and scholarship with the consensus emerging that it may not be helpful (Saks and Koelhler, 2008; Cole, 2009; Kaye, 2010). Individualization is now considered an unachievable aim.

[1] A categorical opinion is one with a limited and fixed number of categories. The weakness of this approach is discussed in Section 6.3 and Chapter 7.

The quality issues raised by this debate will be explored more fully in Section 6.3. It is worth noting in passing that for decades many scholars considered forensic science to be the science of individualization (Kirk, 1963; Inman and Rudin, 2001).

Identification is simply answering the question, what is it? Quantitation answers the question, how much? These processes are mainly the province of forensic chemistry. A plethora of analytical chemical techniques and technologies are employed to identify illicit substances such as drugs of abuse and explosives and quantify in terms of weight, as in drug seizures, or concentration, as in blood alcohol. Quantitation involves measurement which is introduced and discussed further in Section 1.4.

A fundamental process in forensic science is classification. Although individualization, the attempt to assign evidence to a class of one, may not be helpful, classification is. Classification involves reducing the size of the class to which the item of evidence belongs. The smaller the class size, the greater the value of the evidence. To give a practical example, drugs of abuse may be manufactured in a number of different ways. Chemical profiling might indicate the method of manufacture and the starting materials used. Recovered materials might then be classified by method and starting material.

With regard to quality management, the objective of forensic science is achieved by conducting tests of two basic types: analytical and functional. Analytical tests can be further subdivided into qualitative and quantitative. Qualitative tests support the process of identification and address the question, what is it? Quantitative tests support the process of quantitation and address the question how much? Functional tests might also be termed comparative tests. Comparative tests address the question do the patterns match? The relationship between the tests and processes is set out in Table 1.1. Analytical and functional tests are discussed more fully in Section 3.3.2.2 and Section 6.

Although the distinction between these types might seem clear, they are not, as comparative tests might support analytical tests and vice versa. However, comparative tests are the main type used in feature-comparison disciplines, such as fingerprint examination. Comparative testing is an activity that falls within the scope of one of the two major standards applying to forensic science, ISO/IEC 17020 for forensic inspection agencies. The other standard is ISO/IEC 17025, which applies to laboratories carrying out analytical tests. These standards are introduced in Section 3.

Table 1.1 Tests and Processes in Forensic Science

Test	Type	Process	Question	Typical Test Result
Analytical	Qualitative	Identification	What is it?	An explosive
	Quantitative	Quantitation	How much?	Blood alcohol concentration
Functional	Comparative	Classification	Do items "match"?	Questioned and reference fingerprints "match"

In conclusion then, forensic science can be most simply be described as science employed to assist in the resolution of legal disputes, to help the fact-finder determine facts in issue in judicial proceedings. To achieve this aim, scientific information must be reliable, i.e., to be of sufficient quality that the fact-finder may rely on it in determining the facts in issue. A more prosaic definition of forensic science might be science at the service of the Law.

1.2.3 Forensic Scientist

A forensic scientist is a person who relies on a body of scientific knowledge or the application of the scientific method (or part thereof) or both to help resolve legal disputes.

The use of the title "forensic scientist" by those who have little or no scientific training, which may include those in disciplines based on comparison such as marks and impressions, can be problematic. These examiners are not scientists in the ordinary sense of the word, e.g., a chemist, physicist, or biologist. To avoid difficulties the title "forensic practitioner" is sometimes used as a generic term to cover all those who rely on a body of scientific knowledge and/or the scientific method to help resolve legal disputes. However, anyone involved in a judicial process may be termed a forensic practitioner and therefore those offering expert evidence of a scientific nature often prefer to be called forensic scientists and indeed in this work are.

As stated in the section on conventions, the title "forensic scientist" in this work will include examiners and others employing the scientific method, or part therefore, but lacking formal scientific training and qualifications.

Forensic scientists are usually considered to have two basic roles: one as an investigator and secondly as an evaluator (Jackson et al., 2006). At this point the introduction of a model of forensic science as a three stage process might be of benefit. The process is represented in Fig. 1.2.

The role of investigator dominates the early stages of the forensic process in which the forensic scientist provides forensic information. The role of evaluator is necessary at the stage at which the forensic information becomes evidence.

This investigator/evaluator model applies generally but is particularly important as a guarantor of independence where the forensic scientist is employed by state organizations, which are part of, or closely related to, law enforcement. Applying this model helps to ensure the necessary degree of independence, impartiality, and objectivity required of good forensic practice.

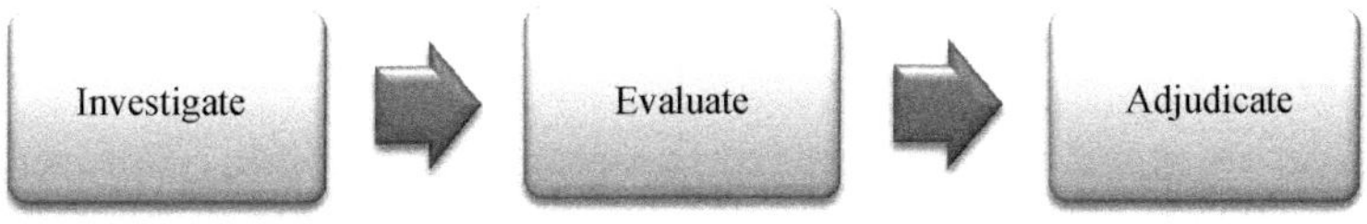

Figure 1.2 A model of the forensic science process.

As the vast majority of forensic scientists are state or government employees, the investigator/evaluator model is particularly important and will be explored in greater depth in Section 3.4.2.4.

1.2.3.1 Forensic Information: Intelligence and Evidence

One helpful outcome of this duality of roles is to highlight the use to which forensic science outputs are put. As not all forensic science outputs are adduced as evidence, the term scientific information is used rather than scientific evidence, except where the forensic science output will certainly be adduced as evidence. Forensic science outputs will always be used to some extent to aid an investigation or provide forensic intelligence but may not be adduced as evidence in judicial proceedings, i.e., at the adjudication stage. To be clear, the term scientific information includes both forensic scientific intelligence and evidence.

1.2.4 Expert Witness: Role, Responsibilities, and Duties

An expert witness is a witness called to assist a tribunal of fact (usually a court of law) on matters within the expert's area of expertise which lie outside the expertise of the tribunal. Expert witnesses are allowed, and are usually required, to give evidence of opinion (as opposed to evidence of fact) and rely on hearsay (of a specialist nature—usually research) in arriving at that opinion.

As a witness of opinion, an expert is considered to be in a privileged position and therefore must comply with legal standards in addition to the standards of science and any standards set by the expert's profession or employer.

In addition to giving evidence of opinion, expert witnesses can also assist the court by giving expert evidence of fact, e.g., explaining technical processes and the meaning of technical terms, and providing the court with the benefit of their expertise in the assessment of other evidence. A catalogue of expert evidence types, both of opinion and of fact, is given in Expert Evidence: Law and Practice (Hodgekinson and James, 2014).

Jurisdictional variations are considered later in Section 1.2.4.1 but, as stated above, the principal role of an expert witness is to assist a tribunal of fact on matters within the expert's area of expertise. Every forensic scientist must be prepared to give expert evidence if called on to do so. For many it is a regular part of their job. This raises an important point; a forensic scientist is a professional expert witness. This must be recognized by having in place an appropriate regulatory framework. Apart from forensic pathologists and forensic scientists, many expert witnesses are not employed as such. A higher standard is required and expected of forensic scientists than of expert witnesses who earn their living in other ways.

The duty of an expert witness is not to the instructing party or employer but to the court. The expert must neither usurp the role of the fact-finder (e.g., the jury) nor act as an advocate. The expert's evidence must be independent, unbiased, impartial, and objective. This list of dos and don'ts seem clear and, on the face of it, easy to comply with. However, despite the professional standing of forensic scientists, this is not the case in practice and standards have been developed to help ensure conformance to good practice.

Giving expert evidence is perhaps the most important task undertaken by a forensic scientist. To ensure that evidence is fit-for-purpose and meets the needs of the court a number of legal, scientific, and quality standards must be complied with. These standards constitute the regulatory framework for forensic science. Detailing this framework of quality standards is the major part of this work.

1.2.4.1 Expert Witness: Some Jurisdictional Variations

In the United States, the qualifications for an expert witness are set out in Federal Rule 702. A witness who is qualified as an expert by knowledge, skill, experience, training, or education may testify in the form of an opinion or otherwise if:

1. the expert's scientific, technical, or other specialized knowledge will help the trier of fact to understand the evidence or to determine a fact in issue;
2. the testimony is based on sufficient facts or data;
3. the testimony is the product of reliable principles and methods; and
4. the expert has reliably applied the principles and methods to the facts of the case.

In England and Wales, and other similar common law jurisdictions, who qualifies as an expert is founded mainly on case law and amounts to a person who is able to furnish the court with information likely to be outside the experience and knowledge of the fact-finder or judge (Turner, 1975; R v Cooper, 1998).

In continental Europe, where an inquisitorial system operates, medical experts tend to be registered and there is a move toward registering competent scientific experts, e.g., the Dutch Besluit Register Deskundige in Strafzaken (2009).

Despite these jurisdictional variations in determining who qualifies as an expert, it is in most, if not all, jurisdictions the judge (or the judicial authority) who decides.

It is worth noting in passing that in England and Wales, and other similar common law jurisdictions, the "qualification" bar is set quite low.

In each jurisdiction, there will be procedural rules to follow and even codes of conduct, however named, that expert witnesses must comply with. These legal standards will be discussed in greater detail in Section 3.

1.3 QUALITY MANAGEMENT

For ease, the standards referred to in this section are listed in Table 1.2 in the order in which they are referred to. Copies of the ISO standards may be purchased from ISO. The ILAC guides are free.

ISO is another name for the International Organization for Standardization. ISO is an SDO (Standards Development Organization) introduced and discussed in Section 2.2.2.

Table 1.2 Standards Listed in the Order Discussed

Standard	Edition	Title
ISO 9000	2015	Quality management systems—Fundamentals and vocabulary
ISO/IEC 17025	2017	General requirements for the competence of testing and calibration laboratories
ISO/IEC 15189	2012	Medical laboratories—Requirements for quality and competence
ISO/IEC 17020	2012	Conformity assessment—Requirements for the operation of various bodies performing inspection
ISO 9001	2008	Quality management systems—Requirements
ISO 9001	2015	Quality management systems—Requirements
ISO/IEC 17024	2012	Conformity assessment—General requirements for bodies operating certification of person
ISO/IEC 17011	2004	Conformity assessment—General requirements for accreditation conformity assessment bodies
ILAC Guide 19	2002	Guidelines for Forensic Science Laboratories
ILAC Guide 19	2014	Modules in a Forensic Science Process

Note: ISO/IEC 17025 and ISO/IEC 15189 are also conformity assessment standards.

ILAC is an abbreviation for International Laboratory Accreditation Cooperation. ILAC is also an SDO, among other things, and is introduced and discussed in Section 2.2.3.

1.3.1 Quality

ISO, in the standard ISO 9000:2015(E) "Quality management systems—Fundamentals and vocabulary," defines quality as

> *[T] he degree to which a set of inherent characteristics of an object (i.e. a product, service, process, person, organization, system or resources) fulfils requirements. ©ISO/IEC 2015 — All rights reserved*

As quality can be qualified by degree, objects (e.g., scientific information) may be, for example, of poor, high, or excellent quality. However, the most important measure is whether or not the object is of sufficient quality to meet requirements, most importantly, those of law enforcement and justice, and hence whether or not the object is fit for its intended purpose.

In the context of forensic science those inherent characteristics are essentially the competence of the organization, the competence of the individual, and the validity of the methods and procedures employed. These characteristics help ensure the fitness-for-purpose of outputs and hence the reliability of forensic scientific information provided to law enforcement and justice stakeholders.

The ultimate requirement is simply that the forensic scientific information provided is of sufficient quality that it can be relied on to help ensure that the judicial process is fair and that the outcome is safe. The inherent characteristics of forensic science and its practice are a major part of this work.

1.3.2 Standards: Requirements

ISO defines a standard as

> *[A] document established by consensus and approved by a recognized body that provides for common and repeated use, rules, guidelines or characteristics for activities or their results, aimed at the achievement of the optimum degree of order in a given context. ©ISO/IEC 2004 — All rights reserved*
>
> ***(ISO Guide 2:2004 3.2)***

This may be briefly paraphrased as a statement of requirements and other provisions.

The international standards ISO/IEC 17025 and ISO/IEC 17020 specify the requirements for forensic science providers to enable them to demonstrate that they operate competently and are able to generate valid results that might be relied on. These standards, and others, also contain elements in addition to requirements such as information and recommendations which aid conformance to the standard. Together with the requirements, these are collectively termed provisions. Requirements are identified by the use of the verbal form "shall". To conform to a standard the provider need only meet the requirements specified. In this work the adjective "mandatory" is sometimes used to classify requirements.

1.3.3 Standards: Purpose and Fitness

As catalogued in Section 3, standards are many and varied including legal, scientific, and quality standards. For the most part they can be categorized as follows:

- professional (e.g., a code of conduct),
- occupational (detailing what needs to be done), or
- procedural (setting out how tasks should be completed).

Nevertheless, all standards are essentially quality standards as they all play some part in determining whether or not scientific information meets stakeholder needs, whether or not it is fit-for-purpose. To determine whether or not an object is fit-for-purpose, the purpose must first be clearly defined and an appropriate measure of fitness found and applied. It follows that if the purpose changes, then so must the standard (or at least the means by which the standard is met). An example is the use of DNA typing in criminal proceedings, which falls under the standard ISO/IEC 17025:2017 for forensic science laboratories and the use of DNA typing for the purpose of disease diagnosis which falls under ISO/IEC 15189:2012 for medical laboratories.

1.3.4 Competence: Individual and Organizational

ISO defines competence as:

> *[T]he ability to apply knowledge and skills to achieve intended results. ©ISO 2015 — All rights reserved*

In the context of forensic science, the intended result is reliable information. The knowledge and skills required, to which must be added behaviors, should be documented as the key competencies required by the individual to achieve the intended result. Compliance with ISO/IEC 17025 and ISO/IEC 17020 (for organizations providing crime scene-based services) requires both the organization and the individual to be competent.

For the individual, competence will be demonstrated by appropriate qualifications, training, continuous professional development, and behaviors. Competence is measured by performance monitoring, testing and compliance with the relevant professional, occupational, and procedural standards.

For an organization, competence will be demonstrated and assessed by conformance and continuing accreditation to ISO/IEC 17025:2017 or ISO/IEC 17020:2012.

A lack of competence by forensic science providers and forensic scientists has contributed to numerous miscarriages of justice over many decades[2] and continues to do so today. Insufficient competence is perhaps the single most important barrier to meeting stakeholder needs and ensuring forensic information is fit-for-purpose.

1.3.5 Certification and Accreditation

Many commentators take the view that organizations are accredited and individuals are certified. In the United States individuals are certified by a number of organizations as qualified to practice in certain disciplines. The Forensic Field Sciences Accreditation Board performs a similar role in Australia.

Accreditation is defined by ISO as:

> *[T]hird-party attestation related to a conformity assessment body conveying formal demonstration of its competence to carry out specific conformity assessment tasks. ©ISO/IEC 2004 — All rights reserved*

Accreditation is the independent, or third party, evaluation of conformity assessment bodies, such as forensic science providers, against recognized standards, such as ISO/IEC 17025, to ensure their impartiality and competence. For ISO/IEC 17020 independence is an additional requirement.

In quality management 'certification' has a technical meaning. Certification is the confirmation that an organization or individual operates in conformance to a standard. The Certifying Body, which is technically a conformity assessment body, is accredited. Hierarchically accreditation is one step higher than certification. Accredited bodies certify, and accreditation bodies accredit. For example, LRQA (Lloyds Register of Quality Assurance now known as Lloyd's Register) certifies organizations as conforming

[2] Each jurisdiction will have its celebrated cases. In the United States that might be the case of Brandon Mayfield's false fingerprint identification and in England and Wales the "Birmingham 6" is another example.

to the standard ISO 9001 and an accrediting body such as UKAS (United Kingdom Accreditation Service) accredits LRQA to do so.

Although the use of the term "certification," for practitioners who are, as it were, licensed to practice by nonaccredited bodies, can be accommodated in a quality management framework, there is a real underlying issue. For example, in the case of ISO/IEC 17025 accredited laboratories, it is the management that are responsible for ensuring the competence of forensic scientists, in effect certifying them as competent to practice, and not external organizations. This issue is problematic and will be explored further in Section 3.

It should be noted that in quality management persons can be certified by external organizations, provided the organization is accredited to ISO/IEC 17024 "Certification of Persons." The US FSAB (Forensic Specialties Accreditation Board), mentioned in Section 2.3 and Section 3.4.4.3, at the time of writing [Decembers 2017], is in the process of adopting this standard.

It should also be noted that ISO/IEC 17020:2012 "Conformity assessment—Requirements for the operation of various types of bodies performing inspection" has been adapted for application to forensic science (ILAC[3] Guide 19:08/2014). Organizations responsible for crime scene examination have recently tended to seek and obtain accreditation to ISO/IEC 17020 rather than ISO/IEC 17025. ISO/IEC 17020 is a standard applicable to organizations undertaking inspection where the inspector relies on personal judgment to some degree. At the time of writing [December 2017], the position is that organizations exclusively providing laboratory-based tests are accredited to ISO/IEC 17025 and organizations exclusively providing crime scene-based services and/or those relying on comparisons, such as marks and impressions, should be accredited to ISO/IEC 17020. Some organizations provide a comprehensive service. Accreditation is costly in time, effort, and money and making a business case to fund accreditation to two standards a challenge. Many forensic science providers offering both laboratory and scene based services obtained ISO/IEC 17025 accreditation before ISO/IEC 17020 became available have retained accreditation to the one standard. Accrediting bodies are responding flexibly to customer needs and appropriate permitting providers to gain or retain accreditation to a single standard or managing accreditation to a second standard as an extension to scope of the first. Issues regarding the utility and choice of standards, and indeed the choice of accrediting body, will be discussed in Section 3.

In any event, the key point is that whichever ISO accrediting standard applies it is the employing organization that "certifies" the forensic scientist. This calls into question the need for certification by an external body of individuals employed by an accredited forensic science provider. This issue will occur again in later sections.

[3] ILAC—International Laboratory Accreditation Cooperation.

1.3.6 Quality Management

Quality management is defined by ISO as

> *[C]oordinated activities to direct and control an organization with regard to quality ©ISO/IEC 2015 — All rights reserved*
>
> ***(ISO 9001:2015 3.3.4)***

To be clear, "management" refers to a process and not to a group of individuals. ISO mandates that where "management" refers to a person or group of persons a qualifier such as "top" is used to make the distinction clear.

Quality management includes quality control (QC), a reactive process, and quality assurance (QA), a proactive process, terms introduced later in Section 1.3.7 and Section 1.3.8.

Quality management is about direction, and the latest version of the quality management system (QMS) standard ISO 9001:2015 emphasizes the responsibility of senior management to take account of stakeholders in addition to the customer in ensuring conformity of products and services (objects) to meet stakeholder needs and expectations. The standard promotes risk-based management. It uses the PDCA (plan—do—check—act) cycle and the interaction of those processes as a system with risk-based thinking identifying those processes that have highest impact on the organizations ability to deliver conforming products and services, i.e., reliable scientific information.

It should be noted that ISO 9001:2015 is far less prescriptive than its 2008 predecessor. There is no specifically prescribed documentation or procedures. Stakeholder requirements and regulatory frameworks define the needs for documentation to manage the organization and comply with the standard. One aim of ISO 9001:2015 is to provide a stable set of requirements for regulators to build onto.

Conformity assessment standards such as ISO/IEC 17025 and ISO/IEC 17020 are essentially a combination of ISO 9001 (management requirements) and technical requirements. The significant changes in the latest edition of ISO 9001 are reflected in the latest edition of ISO/IEC 17025 and will be in the next edition of ISO/IEC 17020. ISO aims to review and issue revised versions of standards every 5 years.

1.3.7 Quality Control (QC)

QC is that part of quality management focused on fulfilling quality requirements. The main feature of QC is monitoring processes with the aim of detecting nonconforming product. QC involves measuring, testing, and inspection. It is a reactive process.

1.3.8 Quality Assurance (QA)

QA is that part of quality management focused on providing confidence that quality requirements will be fulfilled. The aim of QA is prevention, ensuring nonconformances do not occur. This is achieved through planning. Thus, the process is proactive.

1.3.9 Quality Management System (QMS)

The historical development of quality management is covered in depth in Section 4. However, it is of benefit to note here that what began as QC, a reactive process relying on inspection, has developed into a proactive and high-level management tool to ensure the interests of all stakeholders, including regulators, are served and that nonconforming product is a rare event. These developments have resulted in greater efficiency, improved performance, higher customer satisfaction, and, of course, greater profits for commercial organizations. Regarding lowering risk and the rareness of nonconforming product, the phrase "6 sigma" is sometimes used in quality management; this equates to no more than 0.34 nonconforming product per 1000.

ISO defines a QMS as

> *[P]art of a set of interrelated or interacting elements of an organization to establish policies and objectives, and processes to achieve those objectives with regard to quality. ©ISO/IEC 2015 — All rights reserved*
>
> ***(ISO 9001:2015 3.5.4)***

Quality management is considered to be a distinct management discipline akin to financial, project, and health and safety management, etc. The management system elements establish the organization's structure, roles and responsibilities, planning, operation, policies, practices, rules, beliefs, objectives, and processes to achieve those objectives. Through quality management, forensic science providers are able to offer a service compliant with a recognized international standard, which in turn can assure the reliability of scientific information. Quality management also encourages an ethos of continuous improvement. QMSs include practical drivers to establish and maintain that ethos for the benefit of the organization and stakeholders.

1.3.10 Quality System Levels

The older 2008 edition of the QMS standard ISO 9001 will be replaced by the latest version (ISO 9001:2015) in 2018. As mentioned earlier, the 2015 edition is far less prescriptive in terms of documenting the QMS than the 2008 edition. However, the prescription in the 2008 edition was helpful in offering a model QMS. The structure of a documented QMS based on the 2008 edition and the purpose of the different levels are represented in Fig. 1.3.

As the figure demonstrates, a documented policy sets out the intent (aims and objectives) and the quality manual sets out how what is intended will be achieved. The completed records and forms provided the objective evidence of conformance.

The 2015 edition is less prescriptive and may be adapted more easily for the benefit of the certified organization, resulting in less documentation. It is perhaps important to note that it was never ISO's aim to encourage an over-documented QMS. Indeed, quality auditors were instructed to look out for and combat over documentation. Conformity

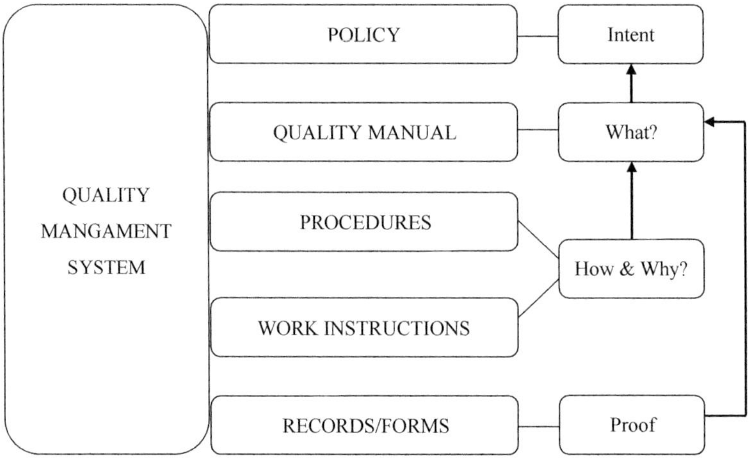

Figure 1.3 The quality management system—according to ISO 9001:2008.

assessment and certifying bodies recommended that in smaller organizations the manuals, procedures, and instructions should be combined into one document. The aim of satisfying an auditor rather than the customer might result in detailing every small detail of a process or procedure, which should be avoided.

Controlling the size and complexity of the QMS is an optimal policy objective. Procedures are at the heart of the documented QMS and describe its operation. The amount of detail in a procedural standard should be dependent on the

- complexity of the task,
- competence of the operator, and
- frequency of use.

To be clear, a simple task performed frequently by a competent operator should require little detail and documentation.

As demonstrated in Section 3, many of the non-ISO standards tend to be at the procedural level. Were those non-ISO standards originate in isolation from a QMS, they tend to be over prescriptive and over detailed risking being ignored by competent operators.

It is likely that ISO 9001:2015, ISO/IEC 17025:2017, and, in due course, ISO/IEC 17020 revised in line with ISO 9001:2015 will result in a documented QMS that is simpler than at present and more focused on the needs of the organization and its stakeholders rather than satisfying quality auditors.

As is clear from the terminology, quality management has its origin in manufacturing where products are the primary object. It is important to note that quality management is not about a flawless or perfect product or service merely meeting the needs of a customer. The needs of the customer will dictate the degree of deviation from "perfect" that can be tolerated.

1.4 METROLOGY

Metrology is the science of measurement. This section introduces that part of the QMS which deals with measurement. Measurement is at the heart of ISO/IEC 17025 "General requirements for the competence of testing and calibration laboratories."

1.4.1 Accuracy and Trueness

Accuracy is the degree to which a result (observation, finding, datum, etc.) obtained by applying a particular method differs from the "true"[4] value or accepted reference value. A highly accurate method is capable of producing a result very close to the "true" value. No method is capable of returning a result that is accurate in the sense of being exactly the same as the "true" value, i.e., no method is perfect. As stated earlier, the degree (or sufficiency) of accuracy required of a method will be determined by stakeholder needs. To offer a practical example, it might not be necessary to quantify the amount of illicit substance in a sample to a nearest unit of measurement merely to establish its presence and order of magnitude, e.g., not how many grams but is it hundreds, thousands, etc.?

Strictly, trueness is the closeness of agreement between the average value obtained from a large series of results and the true value or an accepted reference value. However, in this work trueness and accuracy will be used synonymously.

1.4.2 Validation

According to ISO 9001:2015 validation is:

> *[T]he confirmation through the provision of objective evidence that the requirements for a specific intended use or application have been are fulfilled. ©ISO/IEC 2015 — All rights reserved*

In forensic science, this might be rewritten as objectively confirming that scientific information can be relied on by investigators and tribunals of fact, e.g., courts of law, for the purpose of ensuring a fair process and a safe decision, that the information is fit-for-purpose and meets the needs of stakeholders.

The use of valid methods is one of the three key requirements to ensure that scientific information is of sufficient quality to be relied on. The two others being a competent organization and competent individuals.

ILAC Guide G19[5]:2002 5.4.5.1 requires all technical procedures used by a forensic science laboratory to be fully validated before being used in casework. ILAC Guide G19:2014 at 3.10 also mandates validation prior to use.

[4] Logically the true value is unknowable. The measurement result obtained is reported with a range in which the true value may lie (Vosk, 2015).

[5] This guide is effectively the standard against which accrediting bodies assess the compliance of forensic science laboratories with ISO/IEC 17025.

For analytical methods, validation involves determining performance characteristics[6], e.g., the limit of detection. The scope and type of validation will depend on customer needs. However, validation is essential for any forensic scientific method.

Determining the performance characteristics of an analytical procedure, or indeed any forensic science procedure, may be termed a validation study. As inferred above, a validation study is essential for compliance with ISO/IEC 17025 and ISO/IEC 17020.

Arguably, the most important performance characteristic of a method is its accuracy; how far the test result is likely to be from the "true" result. This needs to be determined. In analytical science as specified in ISO/IEC 17025 this is achieved by estimating measurement uncertainty, which is conveyed as a range of values between which the "true" value may lie. Where the method returns a categorical result[7], e.g., "match," "no match," or "inconclusive," the uncertainty of the test result might be conveyed as the likelihood of a false positive or negative. However, as will be argued in Sections 6 and 7 categorical results and error rates are widely considered suboptimal in forensic science.

Without a validation study objectively demonstrating that the method employed produces scientific information that might be relied on (of known and sufficient accuracy), the results of the method cannot be considered reliable. Whether or not the method meets stakeholder needs and is fit-for-purpose cannot be known.

In the United States, the Frye ruling (Frye v. United States, 1923) and particularly the Daubert ruling (Daubert v. Merrel Dow Pharamceuticals, 1993) require methods to be "valid"[8].

However, in England and Wales the Forensic Science Regulator in evidence to the Court of Appeal (R v Reed and Reed and Garmson, 2009) stated that

> *... he did not consider validation a necessary pre-condition for the admission of scientific evidence, provided the obligations under Rule 33.3(1) of the Criminal Procedure Rules were followed.*

The Criminal Procedure Rule referred to requires the expert to provide the court with an assessment of scientific validity of the method used to allow the fact-finder to attach the correct weight to the scientific evidence.

There seems to be a trend, of which this may be a part, toward admitting scientific evidence of uncertain reliability and leaving it to the fact-finder to determine weight.

The position of the Regulator and the appellate court on the requirement for validation is of concern. In the absence of an objective assessment of the degree to which a test

[6] ILAC Guide 19:2002 5.4.5.1 lists several performance characteristics.

[7] As will be discussed in Section 7.3, the days of categorical opinions should be numbered to be replaced with a probabilistic approach to classification in disciplines relying on comparison such as fingerprints.

[8] This is essentially an admissibility rule requiring methods used to produce scientific evidence to be accepted as valid by the relevant scientific community. The Daubert ruling is discussed in more detail in Section 4.3.3.1.2.

result (observation, finding, etc.) might differ from the "true" result, i.e., a validation study, it would be inappropriate for a fact-finder to attach any weight to a result so obtained. Indeed, it could also be argued that it would be unethical for a forensic scientist to offer such a result as evidence.

It may be that at the heart of this issue is a difference in understanding between quality experts, scientists, forensic scientists, and lawyers as to what "validation" and "valid" mean. Alternative meanings for these and related terms will be explored more fully in Section 3.

However, the more recent guidance published by the Regulator has reestablished the requirement for validation (Forensic Science Regulator, 2014).

1.4.3 Reliability (and Pedigree)

The meaning of reliability varies by discipline. It has no quality/metrologically specific definition. In some usage it seems to be synonymous with precision, i.e., the closeness of agreement between successive test results obtained using the same method and the same material. Such a "reliable" method may consistently return an inaccurate or untrue result. This is distinguished from a "valid" method which returns a result of known accuracy.

The term "pedigree" should also be mentioned. In some usage the pedigree of a method refers to the acceptance by courts of law of evidence produced by that method over a period without challenge. However, there is a risk here as tribunals are not competent to assess the validity of scientific methods.

In this work "reliable" has its normal meaning of sound, trusted, and dependable. Reliable evidence will mean evidence that might be used by a fact-finder to reach a safe decision and a court to provide a fair trial.

1.4.4 Measurement

A measurement tells us about a property of something. It might tell us how heavy an object is, its volume, concentration, or how hot or how long it is. A measurement gives a number to that property. The technical name for the quantity to be measured is "measurand"[9].

Measurements are always made using an instrument of some kind. Rulers, stopwatches, weighing scales, and thermometers are all measuring instruments. The result of a measurement is normally in two parts: a number and a unit of measurement, e.g.,

> *"What was the total mass of drugs seized? … 2 kg."*

There are some processes in forensic science that might seem to be measurements but are not. For example, comparing two fingerprints is not really a measurement. Counting

[9] The "true" value of the measurand is unknowable (Vosk, 2015).

is not normally viewed as a measurement. Often, a test is not a measurement. Tests can return a "yes/no" answer or a "pass/fail" result and that is not measurement. However, measurements may be part of the process leading up to a test result. For example, determining the amount of alcohol in the breath of an individual is a measurement, which leads to a pass/fail breath test result.

In quality management knowing what is and is not a measurement is important. Measurements must always be reported with an estimate of uncertainty, introduced later in Section 1.4.6, and the basis for the uncertainty estimate needs to be stated. An example of how a measurement should be reported with an estimate of uncertainty is given below for blood alcohol concentration where the ± figure gives the range in which the true result may lie.

$$0.021 \pm 0.001 \text{ g/100 mL of blood}$$

1.4.5 Error (Measurement Error)

The term error in metrology does not refer to a mistake. Error means the difference between a "true" value, or an accepted reference value, and the result, or measured value. Errors can be the result of random variations affecting the method or be systematic arising from some biasing effect of the method, the operator, the environment, or combinations thereof. Random error does not render a method inaccurate and can be accommodated if the error is not too great or can be reduced. It is not possible to correct for a random error. Systematic errors do render a method inaccurate because they result in a constant and predictable departure from the true result. Ideally, the cause of a systematic error should be identified and the source removed. A method that returns a result with a systematic error of unknown source is unlikely to have forensic utility. However, as discussed in Section 7 a different probability model can account for systematic error in measurement uncertainty.

The term bias is often used to describe systematic error. As explained in the section on conventions, in this work bias will only refer to cognitive bias, which is introduced in Section 1.5 further.

1.4.6 Uncertainty of Measurement

Uncertainty of measurement is the doubt that exists about the result of any measurement. Uncertainty is a measure of dispersion, a parameter that characterizes the range of values within which the "true" value of the quantity being measured is expected to lie taking into account all sources of random and systematic error. All measurements made are subject to uncertainty and any reported measurement result must include a statement of the uncertainty associated with that result. The confidence interval given in Section 1.4.4 earlier is a measure of uncertainty.

"Error" and "uncertainty" should not be confused. To be clear, error is the difference between the measured value and the "true" value of the measurand or the quantity being measured. Uncertainty is a measure of the doubt about the measurement result.

1.4.7 Comparability (Metrological Traceability, Commutability, and Harmonization)

1.4.7.1 Metrological Traceability

The fifth principle of Valid Analytical Measurement published by the UK's National Measurement Institute, LGC, in 2006 is

> *Analytical measurements made in one location should be consistent with those [made] elsewhere.*

Obtaining the same measurement result irrespective of method, instrument, operator, or laboratory is an important aim of analytical science and is essential in the investigation of transnational crime: illegal migration, international terrorism, and drug trafficking. In such investigations, results obtained in one jurisdiction need to be reliably compared with those obtained in another for the purpose of the investigation and subsequent prosecution or other legal action.

At the heart of comparability, being able to compare results confident of their accuracy or trueness, is metrological traceability.

According to ISO, traceability is the ability to trace the history, application, or location of an object. In the current context the object is a measurement result.

Metrological traceability is the property of the measurement result whereby it can be related to a standard reference material (RM) through an unbroken chain of comparisons all having stated uncertainties.

A relevant example will better elucidate the point. The traceability of breath alcohol measurements made with evidential breath testing instruments is required to provide an assurance that the result is "true" and can be relied on by courts of law. Measurements made at different times or in different places using different instruments are directly related to a common reference breath alcohol standard. It is the closed traceability chain from each breath alcohol measurement to the reference breath alcohol standard that assures reliability and comparability.

A reference standard is usually termed an RM or a certified RM. The function of an RM is to act as a calibrator or trueness control with a known uncertainty.

The ISO definition of RM/trueness control is as follows:

> *[A] material, sufficiently homogeneous and stable with reference to specified properties, which has been established to be fit for its intended use in measurement or in examination of nominal properties. ©ISO 2015 — All rights reserved*
>
> **(ISO/IEC Guide 30:2015 2.1.1)**

Nominal properties are qualitative properties.

A calibrator establishes the relationship between the response of an instrument and the quantity being measured, e.g., the instrument used for the measurement reads 10 units and the calibrator(s) equates that to a weight of 10 g. This process is termed "calibration" and is essential in the establishment of the metrological traceability and its corresponding metrological traceability chain of the measurement result.

An RM reveals and measures systematic error, the difference between the measured result and the "true" result.

Use of an RM allows a result to be obtained from a measurement and to know how far the result obtained might lie from the "true" or expected result.

1.4.7.2 Commutability

To ensure that different methods, instruments, etc., produce the same or a comparable measurement result for a given quantity, the RM used must be commutable. In simple terms, a commutable RM is one that will return the same measurement result irrespective of method, instrument, etc. Producing a commutable RM for evidential breath testing is quite straightforward. In contrast, producing a commutable RM for measuring the concentration of delta-9-tetrahydrocannabinol, the psychoactive ingredient, in cannabis is more challenging (UNODC, 2009).

Indeed, it is worth quoting from the UNODC (United Nations Office on Drugs and Crime) manual (UNODC, 2009) to highlight both the need for comparability and commutable RMs.

> *All of this [gaining intelligence from the variation in production methods of cannabis] requires analytical data which are comparable between laboratories and over time. However, most countries do not require by law the detailed analysis of the THC content of the different products, and where such analyses are carried out, they use a variety of approaches and experimental designs, reducing the comparability of results … On the technological side, the analysis of cannabis products is further complicated by the relatively restricted availability of pure or well defined reference material of THC and other cannabinoids.*
>
> **UNODC (2009)**

To better meet customer needs, measurement results must be comparable ideally among different measurement procedures, different locations, and different times. Comparability will improve forensic utility. Harmonization, in the broad sense, is the overall process of achieving comparability of results among forensic laboratory measurement procedures that measure the same quantity or measurand.

Use of noncommutable RMs increases variability among analytical methods. Investigators, fact-finders, and judges are not aware of the variability that might exist in results obtained from different measurement procedures. Those parties may well attach the same weight to results obtained using methods of low accuracy as to those obtained using highly accurate methods. Variability might result in wrong decisions being made or conclusions drawn and, in turn, miscarriages of justice. This issue in discussed in detail in Section 7.

Using the same method to produce a result in the same set of circumstances, on the face of it, would seem like a sensible objective. However, in certain disciplines forensic scientists have successfully defended the right to select whatever method seems appropriate; hence, the need for commutable RMs.

The issues arising from the lack of a common approach among forensic scientists to analysis and detection will be discussed more fully in Section 3.

When measurement results are to be compared, metrological traceability is essential. If the measurement results are obtained from different methods, then commutable standards are also essential. Without traceability and commutability there is no objective evidence that the same result can be obtained using different methods or instruments.

For the sake of completeness, the ISO definition of commutability is given. However, it is quite technical, and the reader should already have grasped the essentials of commutability. Commutability defines whether an RM is fit-for-use as calibrator and trueness control for more than one method.

According to ISO,

> *Commutability is a property of a reference material (RM)), demonstrated by the equivalence of the mathematical relationships among the results of different measurement procedures for an RM and for representative samples of the type intended to be measured.*
>
> ***(ISO/IEC Guide 30:2015 2.1.20)***

1.4.7.3 Harmonization and Standardization

Harmonization seems to be a particularly European concept. Harmonization of forensic science methods and practices is one of the principal aims of the European Network of Forensic Science Institutes and its Expert Working Groups[10]. Indeed harmonization in general is an aim of the European Union (EU). Harmonization might be broadly defined as creating common standards. Harmonization facilitates transnational cooperation in the investigation and prosecution of crime.

In this work, standardization is the process of creating common standards and harmonization the process of conformance.

In terms of the investigation and prosecution of crime, the desire for harmonization within the EU was manifested most clearly in the Prüm treaty and subsequent decision.

The Prüm Decision[11] is part of EU legal framework regulating transnational exchange of bioinformation (fingerprints and DNA profiles) for the purpose of fighting transnational crime: illegal migration, international terrorism, and drug trafficking.

In 2005 Prüm treaty was signed by a number of EU member states, which provided that each country would be allowed to search national databases containing DNA profiles and fingerprints. In 2008, the treaty was signed into EU law. This was followed in 2009

[10] Harmonization is included in the aims and objectives of most, if not all, Expert Working Groups.

[11] EU Council Decision 2008/615/JHA.

by EU council framework decision 2009/905/JHA requiring forensic service providers carrying out laboratory activities to be accredited to ISO/IEC 17025.

As the impact and implementation of the Prüm Decision and later EU Council Decisions relate directly to quality standards in forensic science, and therefore quality management, they will be explored in greater depth in Section 3.

It is of interest to note that the United Kingdom (UK) opted out of the Prüm Decision in December 2014 offering concerns about differences in quality standards as one of the reasons. Despite pressure from many quarters to rejoin, the UK remains opted out at the time of writing [December 2017]. Given the decision by the UK to leave the EU, the issue is perhaps moot.

The widespread adoption of ISO/IEC 17025 by laboratory-based forensic science providers might be considered part of the process of harmonization and, to an extent, it is. However, the aim of the standard is to ensure stakeholder needs are met and the stakeholders and their needs tend to differ by jurisdiction. In addition, accrediting bodies tend to interpret ISO/IEC 17025 in different ways. These are very important issues in quality management and forensic science and will be addressed in Section 5.

1.4.7.4 Data Basing

The issue of comparability has its greatest potential impact in data basing, constructing and populating databases to store and process data for the purpose of providing forensic intelligence. In addition to the obvious example of DNA databases, another example is in the investigation of international drug trafficking where chemical profiling might help to track and trace drugs of abuse.

To populate databases, measurement results need to be generated by fully validated methods. The measurements obtained need to be traceable, comparable, and, ideally, the product of a standardized method. Databases populated with data of questionable reliability are not fit-for-purpose.

1.5 COGNITIVE BIAS

Cognitive bias, in the context of forensic science, is an error in reasoning that may lead to a mistake. Cognitive bias is also referred to as observer effects. The conclusions drawn by a forensic scientist are not only a product of findings/observations/results/measurements but also of the state of the individual and the context of the observations made. Bias, if not recognized and managed, contributes to miscarriages of justice whereby a judicial process might be unfair and the outcome unsafe.

There are many forms of cognitive bias. The three most likely to affect the quality of forensic information are as follows:

- Context—biasing extraneous (nonscientific) information gained from case involvement,
- Confirmation—bias arising from the well-established desire of human beings to seek evidence in support of held hypotheses, or beliefs, and avoid that which does not[12], and
- Expectation—bias arising from expected findings/observations/results.

The first major study of the effects of bias in human reasoning was conducted by Tversky and Kahneman (1974). It is of interest to note that Francis Bacon (1620) recognized the risk of bias and accepted that the proper application of the scientific method will include bias avoidance measures. However, it was not until the early years of this century that the effects of cognitive bias on the quality of forensic information were first recognized at the practitioner level (Saks et al., 2003; Risinger et al., 2002); since then there has been a major effort in scholarship and research, which has created a beneficial body of knowledge. Providers of forensic science are now beginning to incorporate bias avoidance measures into their QMSs.

Cognitive bias and its effects are now fully recognized. The next step is for forensic science providers to reach consensus as to how to effectively mitigate bias in the forensic process. Cognitive bias is discussed further in Sections 4 and 7.

1.6 SUMMARY AND CONCLUDING REMARKS

The purpose of this section was to ensure that all readers have a common understanding of the following: what forensic science is; what a forensic scientist does; the fundamental concepts and terms of quality management and metrology; and, in addition, to recognize the existence and potential effects of cognitive bias.

With this understanding in place, readers should be better placed to understand the detail in later sections particularly that which lies outside their own specialist area.

Quality was defined as the inherent characteristics required to fulfill customer requirements and ensure forensic information is fit-for-purpose. At the highest level these inherent characteristics are the

- competence of the organization,
- competence of the individual, and
- validity of methods employed.

The way in which these characteristics are assessed and regulated by QMSs in general and ISO/IEC 17025 in particular, and to a lesser extent ISO/IEC 17020, has been briefly explained and will be expanded on throughout the remainder of this work.

[12] Some assert that seeking contrary evidence is the proper scientific approach. This has been raised to a philosophical principle by Karl Popper (1959) as falsifiability.

One of the major benefits of quality management has also been introduced, promoting and supporting an ethos of continuous improvement. If used as intended, quality standards can help identify opportunities for improved performance and risks to be managed. Thereby benefiting the organization, the individual practitioner and all the stakeholders particularly law enforcement and justice.

This section has also identified a number of important issues which will be explored more widely throughout this work.

REFERENCES

Bacon, F., 1620. Novum Organum.

Broeders, A.P.A., 2006. Of earprints, fingerprints, scent dogs, cot deaths and cognitive contamination—a brief look at the present state of play in the forensic arena. Forensic Sciecne International 148–157.

Cole, S.A., 2009. Forensics without uniqueness, conclusions without individualization: the new epistemology of forensic identification. Law, Probability and Risk 233–255.

Daubert v. Merrel Dow Pharamceuticals. 1993. 509 (US).

Forensic Science Regulator, 2014. "Guidance – Validation." FSR-G-201 Issue 1. The Forensic Science Regulator, Birmingham.

Frye v. United States. 1923. 293 F (D.C.Cir.).

Hodgekinson, T., James, M., 2014. Expert Evidence: Law and Practice. Sweet & Maxwell, London.

Inman, K., Rudin, N., 2001. Principles and Practice of Criminalistics: The Profession of Forensic Science. CRC Press, Boca Raton.

Jackson, G., Jones, S., Booth, G., Champod, C., Evett, I.W., 2006. The nature of forensic science opinion – a possible framework to guide thinking and practice in investigations and in court proceedings. Science & Justice 46 (1), 33–44.

Kaye, D.H., 2010. Probability, individualization, and uniqueness in forensic science evidence: listening to the academies. Brooklyn Law Review 1163–1185.

Kirk, P.L., 1963. The ontogeny of criminalistics. The Journal of Criminal law, Criminology, and Police Science 235–238.

Nordby, J.J., 1999. Chapter 2. In: Nordby, J.J. (Ed.), Dead Reckoning: The Art of Forensic Detection. CTC Press LLC, Boca Raton, pp. 42–43.

Popper, K., 1959. The Logic of Scientific Discovery. Routledge, London and New York.

R v Cooper. 1998. 2258 (EWCA).

R v Reed and Reed and Garmson. 2009. Crim 2698 (EWCA).

Risinger, M.D., Saks, M.J., Thompson, W.C., Rosenthal, R., 2002. The Daubert/Khumo implications of observer effects in forensic science: hidden problems of expecatation and suggestion. California Law Review 1–56.

Rosenberg, A., 2000. The Philosophy of Science. Routledge, London and New York.

Saks, M.J., Risinger, D.M., Rosenthal, R., Thompson, W.C., 2003. Context effects in forensic science: a review and application of the science of science to crime laboratory practice in the United States. Science & Justice 77–79.

Saks, M.J., Koelhler, J.J., 2008. The individualization fallacy in forensic science evidence. Vanderbilt Law Review 199–219.

Turner. 1975. 834 (QB).

Tversky, A., Kahneman, D., 1974. Judgement under uncertainty: heuristics and biases. Science 1124–1131.

UK Home Office, 2016. Forensic Science Strategy: A National Approach to Forensic Science Delivery in the Criminal Justice System. HMSO, London. Cm9271.

UNODC, 2009. Recommended Methods for the Identification and Analysis of Cannabis and Cannabis Products. UN, New York.

Vosk, T., 2015. Measurement uncertainty. In: Houck, M.M. (Ed.), Professional Issues in Forensic Science. Elsevier, San Diego, pp. 65–76.

SECTION 2

Organizations Exercising Responsibility for Quality Management in Forensic Science

2.1 INTRODUCTION

In this section, organizations exercising some degree of responsibility for quality management in forensic science are introduced. Their objectives, governance, funding, interrelationships, and relevance to quality management are outlined. These bodies are many and varied but, in terms of their primary function, they tend to fall into one of the categories listed below:

- standards development/setting,
- accreditation[1],
- regulation/oversight, and
- networking.

Some organizations exercise more than one role which renders precise categorization difficult. Combining the roles of service provision, standards development, and/or regulation, as discussed in Section 7, is suboptimal and can risk conflicts of interest.

The categories reflect the roles required to assure the quality of forensic science in meeting the needs of all stakeholders, particularly those of law enforcement and justice. The separation and independence of these roles supports that assurance.

Many of these organizations develop and set standards which apply to the same activities, e.g., the interpretation of results. In addition to duplication of effort, different standards for the same activity militates against the very concept of standardization by which objects tested or measured once are accepted everywhere. If standards in forensic science vary, so might the quality of justice.

2.2 STANDARDS, DEVELOPMENT AND SETTING ORGANIZATIONS

2.2.1 Introduction

These bodies are collectively termed Standard Development Organizations (SDOs). In categorizing SDOs, a hierarchical model of standards is useful and employed in this work. The model is further developed in 3.1.1. Generic standards applying to organizations performing particular activities are at the highest level, Level 1. The most

[1] It should be noted that accreditation is a regulatory function.

Quality Management in Forensic Science
ISBN 978-0-12-805416-1, https://doi.org/10.1016/B978-0-12-805416-1.00002-5

appropriate example is ISO/IEC 17025:2017 "General requirements for the competence of testing and calibration laboratories." One step below is standards that adapt and interpret the highest level standards to meet the needs of a particular industry or field of application; in this work, forensic science, an appropriate example is the ILAC (International Laboratory Accreditation Cooperation) Guide 19:2002 "Guidelines for Forensic Science Laboratories." These standards are designated Level 2. Lower in the hierarchy are standards that address the specifics of the forensic science process. An appropriate example is the Australian Standard AS5388:2012 "Forensic Analysis," introduced in 3.4.2. These are Level 3 standards.

The process of standards development and setting involves a number of steps. The need for a standard is first identified by a community of stakeholders and a development body tasked with drafting a standard to meet the need. With input from stakeholders, the draft is revised until it is deemed fit-for-purpose. The standard, essentially a list of requirements or more technically provisions, is then published and adopted by organizations wishing to demonstrate conformance. The standards development process of International Organization for Standardization (ISO) is shown in Fig. 2.1 as an example.

Figure 2.1 Standards development process of the International Organization for Standardization.

2.2.2 Level 1 Standard Development Organizations

2.2.2.1 International Organization for Standardization

ISO was established in 1947 and has its headquarters in Geneva, Switzerland. According to ISO, ISO is not an abbreviation for the name of the organization, but it is instead a play on the Greek word isos (ἴσος) meaning equal.

ISO is an independent, nongovernmental, worldwide federation of national standards bodies (ISO member bodies[2]). It is funded by membership subscription and the sales of published standards. In addition, members undertake voluntary work in support of ISO's activities. ISO is the primary international standard setting body and often relies on other standard setting bodies, such as IUPAC (International Union of Pure and Applied Chemistry), in developing consensus standards.

The work of preparing International Standards is normally carried out through ISO technical committees (TCs). Each member body interested in a subject for which a TC has been established has the right to be represented on that committee. International organizations, governmental and nongovernmental, in liaison with ISO, also take part in the work.

Draft International Standards (DISs) adopted by TCs are circulated to the member bodies for voting. Publication as an International Standard requires approval by at least 75% of the member bodies casting a vote. There is usually a delay between publication and implementation by national standards bodies. The process is represented in Fig. 2.1.

TCs are managed by the Technical Management Board, which is governed by the ISO Council. The General Assembly of members and officers is the ultimate authority for the organization. The Council includes the Committee on Conformity Assessment (CASCO), which has particular relevance to quality management in forensic science. CASCO is the ISO committee that develops, publishes, and revises conformity assessment standards such as ISO/IEC 17025 and liaises with the relevant ISO TCs to ensure a consistent and harmonized approach to conformity assessment.

According to ISO, International Standards ensure that products and services are safe, reliable, and of good quality. For business, they are strategic tools that reduce costs by minimizing waste and errors and increasing productivity. Conformance to International Standards help companies access new markets, level the playing field for developing countries, and facilitate free and fair global trade.

The commercial focus of ISO standards is an important factor in understanding quality management in forensic science, which will be considered in greater depth in Section 5.

ISO standards applying to forensic science are discussed in the next Section 3. As stated earlier, the most important and most widely adopted ISO standard in forensic

[2] http://www.iso.org/iso/about/iso_members.htm.

science is ISO/IEC 17025 "General requirements for the competence of testing and calibration laboratories." Another important ISO standard is ISO/IEC 17020 "Conformity assessment—Requirements for the operation of various types of bodies performing inspection" applicable to crime scene examination and feature-comparison disciplines such as fingerprints. A forensic science provider accredited to ISO/IEC 17025 or ISO/IEC 17020 also conforms to the quality management standard ISO 9001.

Working in partnership with ISO is a number of other international standards development bodies. Of particular relevance are the International Electrotechnical Commission (IEC) and the European Committee for Standardization (Comité Européen de Normalisation or CEN).

The IEC develops and sets International Standards for all electrical, electronic, and related technologies. Together with ISO, it forms the specialized system for worldwide standardization; hence the inclusion of "IEC" in the full title of standards, e.g., ISO/IEC 17025.

Together with ISO and the International Telecommunication Union, IEC comprise the World Standards Cooperation alliance.

CEN is a public organization, the purpose of which is to develop and set standards for the benefit of the European Union (EU). CEN is officially recognized by the EU as being responsible for developing and defining voluntary standards at the European level. Conformance with CEN prepared standards is sometimes mandated in EU legislation. CEN works closely, and often in partnership, with ISO in standards development. The "parallel processing" of the latest edition of ISO/IEC 17025 is an example of that close cooperation.

CEN TC on Forensic Science Processes (CEN/TC 419) was developing a set of standards that define procedures for forensic science processes, starting at the scene of crime—through the recognition, recording, recovery, transportation, and storage of material—followed by the examination and analysis of material, the interpretation of results, reporting, and data exchange. This is a similar approach to that undertaken by Australia, which resulted in AS5388 discussed in Section 3.4.2. Responsibility for these work items has been transferred to the ISO TC 272 on forensic sciences. At the time of writing [December 2017], ISO standards based on AS5388 are in development.

2.2.3 Level 2 Standard Development Organizations

2.2.3.1 International Laboratory Accreditation Cooperation (ILAC) and International Accreditation Forum (IAF)

ILAC is the international organization for accrediting bodies operating in accordance with the International Standard ISO/IEC 17011 "Conformity assessment—General requirements for accreditation bodies accrediting conformity assessment bodies" and involved in the accreditation of conformity assessment bodies, including forensic science providers, to the standards ISO/IEC 17025 and ISO/IEC 17020.

Accreditation is defined by ISO in ISO/IEC 17011 as follows:

> *[T]hird-party attestation related to a conformity assessment body conveying formal demonstration of its competence to carry out specific conformity assessment tasks.*

In forensic science, accreditation is the independent evaluation of providers against the standards ISO/IEC 17025 and/or ISO/IEC 17020 to ensure the impartiality and competence of the organization.

An accrediting body is defined as "[A]n authoritative body that performs accreditation," with a note that the authority of an accreditation body is generally derived from government.

Accreditation bodies, therefore, are authoritative bodies that provide independent oversight of conformity assessment bodies such as forensic science providers. Authority is gained by peer evaluation of the accreditation body to demonstrate competence and signing regional and international arrangements. These accrediting bodies then assess and accredit conformity assessment bodies such as forensic science providers to the relevant standards, e.g., ISO/IEC 17025 and ISO/IEC 17020.

Accrediting bodies that are full members of ILAC are signatories to a Mutual Recognition Arrangement (ILAC MRA). In effect this means that reliable forensic information produced by an accredited provider in one jurisdiction can be considered equally reliable in another, applying the principle "Tested or inspected once, accepted everywhere."

The purpose of the arrangement is to ensure mutual recognition of accredited certification and inspection bodies and laboratories between signatories to the MRA, and subsequent acceptance of accredited certification and inspection bodies and laboratories in many markets based on one accreditation.

The ILAC MRA is a form of regulation and oversight for accrediting bodies and is discussed further in 2.4.3.

The arrangements are managed by ILAC in the fields of calibration, testing, medical testing, and inspection accreditation and by the International Accreditation Forum (IAF) in the fields of management systems, products, services, personnel, and other similar programs of conformity assessment. Both organizations, ILAC and IAF, work together and coordinate their efforts to enhance accreditation and conformity assessment worldwide.

The regional arrangements are managed by the recognized regional cooperation bodies that work in harmony with ILAC and IAF. The recognized regional cooperations are also represented on the ILAC and IAF Executive Committees and ILAC works closely with those bodies. Regional cooperations are listed in Table 2.1.

At the time of writing [December 2017], Southern Africa Development Community Cooperation in Accreditation (SADCA) and African Accreditation Cooperation

Table 2.1 International Laboratory Accreditation Cooperation Regional Cooperations in Alphabetical Order of Acronym

Acronym	Regional Cooperation
AFRAC	African Accreditation Cooperation
APLAC	Asia Pacific Laboratory Accreditation Cooperation
ARAC	Arab Accreditation Cooperation
EA	European Accreditation
IAAC	Inter-American Accreditation Cooperation
SADCA	Southern Africa Development Community Cooperation in Accreditation

(AFRAC) are in the process of developing their respective MRAs and their associated evaluation procedures before seeking recognition with ILAC. These regional corporations have yet to reach the standard necessary for recognition by ILAC.

ILAC is currently [December 2017] in the process of developing the necessary peer evaluation documents to allow for the extension of ILAC MRAs to include the accreditation of proficiency testing providers (ISO/IEC 17043 discussed in 3.2.2.3) and reference material producers (ISO/IEC 17034 discussed in 3.2.2.2).

In support of standardization and harmonization, ILAC produces guides for use by accrediting bodies and accredited organizations: the G-Series documents. These guides, introduced and discussed in Section 3, provide information on the interpretation of accreditation criteria for specific applications such as forensic science and enable an assessment of conformity to be made. They are used as interpretive documents by both accrediting bodies and forensic science providers. These guides include ILAC G:19 08/2014 "Modules in a Forensic Science Process," which offers guidance to forensic science providers on conforming to ISO/IEC 17025 and/or ISO/IEC 17020. A full list of ILAC G-Series documents can be found on ILAC's website (ILAC n.d.).

ILAC also produces a P-Series of policy documents for the operation of the ILAC MRAs and forms part of the criteria for ILAC MRA evaluations. Of particular relevance is ILAC P15:07/2016 "Application of ISO/IEC 17020:2012 for the Accreditation of Inspection Bodies," which provides information for use by both accrediting bodies and inspection bodies on the application of ISO/IEC 17020 and enables an assessment of conformity to be made. A full list of ILAC's P-Series documents can be found on ILAC's website (ILAC n.d.).

2.2.4 Level 3 Standard Development Organizations (SDO)

2.2.4.1 Introduction

Level 3 standards are those that apply to the "nuts and bolts" of the forensic science process. The process is variously described but generally involves crime scene examination, recovery of evidence, laboratory examination, interpretation of findings, and presentation of conclusions, all to meet stakeholder needs, particularly those of law enforcement and justice. As always, the quality of forensic science is dependent on competent organizations, competent individuals, and valid methods.

In Section 3, Level 3 standards are categorized according to application. However, such categorizing is difficult for the SDOs themselves. As pointed out in the introduction, organizations may exercise a number of roles; e.g., networks of providers, discussed later in 2.5, also develop and set standards as do regulators such as the Forensic Science Regulator of England and Wales (E&W). In addition, Level 3 SDOs might develop and set standards for the entire forensic science process, a part of it, or both; they may be international, regional, national, or just discipline-specific. In an effort to employ a systematic approach, in this section SDOs are considered under the following headings:

- the forensic science process (or part thereof)
- methods
- discipline-specific
- professional bodies

Where a Level 3 SDO exercises a primary role in another category, and many do, the organization will be more fully discussed under the non-SDO heading.

2.2.4.2 The Forensic Science Process (or a Part Thereof)

2.2.4.2.1 Evidence Interpretation—The Association of Forensic Science Providers (AFSP)

As the name implies, this is an association of forensic science providers (AFSP), and its role as an association is discussed in detail later in 2.5.2. Its membership includes all the major providers of forensic science in the United Kingdom and Ireland, both private companies and those that are part of government. One of the AFSP's aims is to improve the quality of forensic science and to that end it has developed and published the AFSP Standard (Association of Forensic Science Providers, 2009), an important standard which applies to the evaluation of scientific evidence based on a likelihood ratio approach. This standard is discussed in 3.4.2.4.2.

2.2.4.2.2 The American Academy of Forensic Sciences Standards Board (ASB)

As discussed in 4.3.2.2.3 and later in this section at 2.7, the US Organization of Scientific Area Committees (OSAC) is populating a registry of standards to be used by US accrediting bodies for accrediting forensic science providers to either ISO/IEC 17025 or ISO/IEC 17020.

To this end, the ASB was created in 2015 and accredited by the American National Standards Institute (ANSI) as an SDO providing consensus-based standards for forensic science. Its purpose is to develop American National Standards. Since its inception, the 13 new Consensus Bodies (CBs) of the ASB have begun to develop more than 33 standards, most of which in consultation with the OSAC which is hosted by the National Institute of Standards and Technology (NIST). CBs are intended to be balanced to ensure that no stakeholder dominates. CBs include experts, users, government representatives, forensic science providers, academics, law enforcement agents, and lawyers. All of the meetings are held online and observers are welcome, but cannot vote.

According to the most recent update [May 2017], the Toxicology CB is close to producing the first finalized standard, "Standard Practices for Measurement Traceability in Forensic Toxicology." The DNA CB has two documents at the editing stage that will soon be submitted for public comment, "Validation Standards for Probabilistic Genotyping Systems" and "Standards for Validation Studies of DNA Mixtures for the Development and Verification of a Laboratory Mixture Interpretation Protocol."

The initiative is funded by charitable donation which will allow work to continue until 2019. The work is supported by voluntary effort. For the initiative to continue beyond 2019, further donations are required. The plan is for ASB standards to be freely available.

The American Academy of Forensic Sciences (AAFS) is also a professional body and is discussed later in 2.2.4.5.1.

2.2.4.2.3 ASTM International

ASTM Int. is an SDO headquartered in Pennsylvania, USA, with offices in Belgium, Canada, and Peru. It is a not-for-profit organization funded by sales and services and voluntarily supported by its members. It began life in 1898 as the American Society for Testing Materials.

ASTM Int. has an entire section devoted to forensic science, Committee E30. That committee has two relevant subcommittees, E30.1 on Criminalistics and E30.11 on Interdisciplinary Forensic Science Standards. Between them, these committees publish 45 active standards which cover the entire scope of the forensic science process and many specific disciplines.

ASTM Int.'s discipline-specific forensic science standards are listed in Tables 3.11 and 3.12 and on its website (ASTM International n.d.). Each is available for purchase as a PDF for around 40USD.

As mentioned earlier, OSAC is populating a registry of standards to be used by US accreditation bodies for accrediting forensic science providers to either ISO/IEC 17025 or ISO/IEC 17020. As part of this process, ASTM Intl. standards are being used as a starting point for standards' development.

In addition, ASTM Int. is a proficiency test provider accredited to ISO/IEC 17043: 2010 "Conformity assessment—General requirements for proficiency testing," discussed in 3.2.2.3, by the American Association for Laboratory Accreditation (A2LA), discussed later in 2.3.3. The proficiency tests currently available [December 2017] relate to automobile fuels and lubricants.

2.2.4.2.4 European Network of Forensic Science Institutes

The European Network of Forensic Science Institutes (ENFSI) is essentially a network of European and near-Asian forensic science providers and as such it is discussed in detail later in 2.5.4. However, one of its stated aims is to improve the quality of forensic science and, to that end, the organization has developed and published a number of discipline and activity-specific standards, which are discussed in Section 3. These are published as Best Practice Manuals and Forensic Guidelines and listed in Tables 3.8 and 3.9, respectively; of particular note is the ENFSI Guideline for Evaluative Reporting in Forensic Science (ENFSI, 2015) discussed in 3.4.2.5.1.

2.2.4.2.5 Standards Australia

Standards Australia (SA) is an Australian public, not-for-profit, company, limited by guarantee and registered as a charity for taxation purposes. It is recognized by the Australian Commonwealth Government as the "peak non-government" SDO. SA also facilitates Australian participation in international standards' development.

The company is governed by a board of directors which is monitored by a council and run by an executive officer. Members of the company are legal entities recommended by the board. In 2016, there were 75 members of the company. It is funded through sales and investments.

Standards' development is undertaken by Technical Committees, which include relevant stakeholders. Through a process of consensus, these committees aim to develop standards for Australia's net benefit.

Of particular relevance is AS5388-2012 "Forensic Analysis" developed and published by SA and discussed in 3.4.2.

SA is the national member, and Australia's ISO representative. This role is recognized in a Memorandum of Understanding (MOU) between the Commonwealth Government of Australia and SA. Consequently, SA is responsible for coordinating Australia's participation in ISO standardization activities.

2.2.4.2.6 Competence—UK Skills for Justice

Skills for Justice (SFJ) is a not-for-profit organization, a registered charity and a UK government licensed Sector Skills Council. SFJ develops and publishes National Occupational Standards (NOS) for the UK forensic science sector, among others. Its headquarters are in Bristol, England, and it is funded through membership fees and sales. It is operated by an executive team accountable to a board representing stakeholders.

NOS are statements of the standards of performance that individuals must achieve when carrying out functions in the workplace, together with specifications of the underpinning knowledge and understanding. Access to the standards is via paid membership which is open to organizations that might benefit. The relevant standards are discussed in 3.4.4.5.2.

Skills for Justice offers assistance in helping organizations meet the requirements for training and competencewhich are part of ISO/IEC 17025 and ISO/IEC 17020, particularly for organizations preparing for accreditation with employees lacking essential skills.

2.2.4.2.7 Evaluation and Validation—National Institute of Forensic Science Australia and New Zealand

The National Institute of Forensic Science (NIFS) is an Australasian organization, which exercises a variety of roles and as such falls into all categories. It is a complex organization and warrants its own section 2.6. It has recently published a number of Level 3 standards, including a guide to evaluative reporting (ANZPAA NIFS, 2017), which is very much a recasting of the ENFSI Guide (ENFSI, 2015) discussed in 3.4.2.4.3. NIFS has also published a guide to the validation of feature-comparison methods (ANZPAA NIFS, 2016) drawing on guidance offered by the E&W Forensic Science Regulator (Forensic Science Regulator, 2014), recommendations in the 2009 NRC Report (National Research Council, 2009), and the 2016 PCAST Report (Presidents Council of Advisors on Science and Technology, 2016), which are all discussed in Section 3.

2.2.4.2.8 Crime Scene Examination, DNA, and Drugs of Abuse—International Forensic Strategic Alliance

The International Forensic Strategic Alliance (IFSA) is a multilateral partnership of six autonomous regional organizations, which is discussed more fully in 2.5.

IFSA is documenting a quality management framework comprising a set of Minimum Requirement Documents (MRD) (IFSA, 2016) for the benefit of emerging forensic science providers. The framework covers the following areas:

- competence of personnel;
- equipment and consumables;
- collection, analysis, interpretation, reporting;
- procedures, protocols, validation; and
- quality management.

At the time of writing [December 2017], MRDs for the analysis of drugs, DNA profiling, and crime scene examination were available with others in preparation.

2.2.4.3 Method Validation

2.2.4.3.1 AOAC International

AOAC Intl. is an SDO with headquarters in Gaithersburg, Maryland, USA, and incorporated in the District of Columbia, USA. It is a not-for-profit organization governed by a board of directors elected by the membership and managed by an executive director.

Its stated aim is to promote method validation and quality measurements in the analytical sciences. It publishes standardized, chemical analysis methods designed to increase confidence in the results of chemical and microbiologic analyses.

Membership is open to appropriately qualified individuals, including those representing an organization, and is obtained by application.

The AOAC is funded by membership fees and sales. It began life as an abbreviation for the Association of Official Agricultural Chemists, a body established by the US

Department of Agriculture in 1884. AOAC is no longer an abbreviation. The legal name of the organization is AOAC International. According to the AOAC, it is a globally recognized, independent, third party, not-for-profit association and voluntary consensus standards developing organization. Its main focus is on foodstuffs and therefore has relevance in food forensics.

It develops consensus-based analytical method performance requirements that might be adopted and adapted by forensic science providers. AOAC standards are published in the "Official Methods of Analysis of AOAC International." In addition, AOAC Intl. is a proficiency test provider accredited to ISO/IEC 17043:2010 "Conformity assessment-General Requirements for Proficiency testing" discussed in 3.2.2.3, by the accrediting body A2LA, discussed later in 2.3.3. The proficiency tests currently available [December 2017] relate to foodstuffs.

In addition to its Official Methods of Analysis, AOAC Intl. publishes a number of other documents related to the quality of foodstuff measurements (AOAC International n.d.) including a guide for laboratories seeking accreditation to ISO/IEC 17025 by A2LA. It also publishes a peer-reviewed scientific journal: the Journal of AOAC International.

It is of interest to note that in method development, stakeholder requirements and method performance parameters must be specified early in the process in conformance with good practice as discussed in 3.4.5.2. In contrast, forensic science providers often begin with the methods available.

Although AOAC Official Methods may be fit-for-purpose at the time of publication, there seems to be no mechanism for periodic review to ensure that they remain fit-for-purpose.

2.2.4.3.2 Eurachem/Cooperation on International Traceability in Analytical Chemistry (CITAC)

Eurachem is an SDO that focuses on analytical chemistry and the quality-related issues of measurement and traceability.

Eurachem is a network of organizations. Membership is open to countries within the EU and the European Free Trade Association (EFTA), the European Commission and European countries recognized by the EU and EFTA as accession states. Other European countries and organizations with an interest in the quality of analytical measurements may participate in Eurachem as Associate or Observer members. Eurachem currently has 32 member countries.

Eurachem's main objectives are to establish a system for the international traceability of chemical measurements and promote good quality practices in analytical science.

Eurachem promotes good practice in analytical measurement by producing authoritative guidance within its expert working groups, publishing guides on the web and supporting workshops to communicate good practice. Guidance covers technical issues of relevance in forensic science such as measurement uncertainty evaluation, method validation, and proficiency testing. Copies of these guides are freely available on the Eurachem website, some of which are applicable to forensic science practice.

In 2014, Eurachem released the second edition of its guide on method validation, devised to help laboratories demonstrate the fitness-for-purpose of test methods, taking into account developments in terminology, standards, and analytical practice. Method validation is an essential requirement in forensic science. The guide is discussed in 3.4.5.4.

Another output of practical benefit is the Eurachem reading list which is updated annually (Eurachem, 2017).

Eurachem also collaborates with accreditation bodies and other organizations, such as Cooperation on International Traceability in Analytical Chemistry (CITAC), with interests in measurement quality to help ensure practical accreditation policies and promote sensible technical provisions in regulation.

CITAC has similar aims and objectives as the UK Valid Analytical Measurement program discussed in 3.4.5.1 but with an international basis. Its focus is on chemical measurement comparability and traceability. CITAC works closely with other international organizations such as BIPM (Bureau International des Poids et Mesures/International Bureau of Weights and Measures), ISO/REMCO (Committee on Reference Materials), IUPAC, ILAC, and regional and national professional chemistry societies and institutions, such as Eurachem and IUPAC, in meeting its objective of promoting and facilitating good metrological practice. From time to time it publishes guidance documents in conjunction with Eurachem; examples include the following:

"Quantifying Uncertainty in Analytical Measurement," third Edition (2012)

The second is an excellent guide for forensic science laboratories wishing to ensure that they are operating in accordance with good practice in analytical science.

2.2.4.3.3 International Union of Pure and Applied Chemistry (IUPAC)

IUPAC is an international federation of National Adhering Organizations that represents chemists in individual countries. It is a member of the International Council for Science. The international headquarters of IUPAC is in Zürich, Switzerland, with an office in Chicago, Illinois, USA. The administrative office, known as the "IUPAC Secretariat", is in Research Triangle Park, North Carolina, USA. The administrative office is headed by IUPAC's executive director.

Its members, the National Adhering Organizations, can be national chemistry societies, national academies of sciences, or other bodies representing chemists. There are 54 National Adhering Organizations and 3 Associate National Adhering Organizations. IUPAC's Inter-divisional Committee on Nomenclature and Symbols (IUPAC nomenclature) is the recognized world authority in developing standards for the naming of the chemical elements and compounds.

IUPAC's Analytical Chemical Division is of particular importance in forensic science. The goal of the Analytical Chemistry Division is the promotion of the principal branches of analytical chemistry. This includes the critical and comparative evaluation of established and emerging analytical methods, to enable analytical chemists to choose those best suited for specific applications.

The activities of the Analytical Chemical Division of particular relevance in forensic science include the following:

- harmonization and proposal of rules for interlaboratory comparisons;
- recommendations for sample collection, preparation, storage, and handling;
- the compilation of data used in analytical chemistry and their critical evaluation; and
- the definition of recommended methods and proper application of QC and QA procedures.

IUPAC has an interdivisional working party on the harmonization of quality assurance. The aims of the working party are to

- harmonize the general approaches on the quality assurance requirements for analytical laboratories between different IUPAC Divisions and Commissions;
- collect information on all aspects of quality assurance, quality management, quality systems, total quality management and conformity assessment of quality systems currently in practice in analytical laboratories;
- harmonize requirements on quality assurance and quality management systems in analytical laboratories set out by other international, regional or national organizations (ISO, WHO, FAO, IAEA, CEN, AOAC International, NATA, EURACHEM, CITAC, etc.);
- provide a channel of communication between IUPAC and ISO/REMCO concerning availability, needs, production and use of reference materials; and
- assist analytical laboratories in developing countries to achieve their desired quality of work through the proper application of international standards and guides related to the fields above.

This work is carried out in close cooperation with other international organizations, especially ISO/DEVCO (ISO Committee on Developing Countries).

2.2.4.4 Discipline-Specific Standard Development Organizations

This category mostly comprises the specialist working groups such as that on DNA analysis methods SWGDAM. Most US discipline-specific SDOs are now Scientific Area Committees (SACs), see 2.7, and these together with ENFSI Expert Working Groups are discussed in Section 6, where their identities, operations, and outputs are detailed. One discipline-specific SDO that does not fall within these groupings is the United Nations Office on Drugs and Crime (UNODC), discussed next.

2.2.4.4.1 United Nations Office on Drugs and Crime

According to the UNODC, it is a global leader in the fight against illicit drugs and international crime. It operates in all regions of the world through an extensive network of field offices and relies on voluntary contributions, mainly from governments, for 90% of its budget which was around 760 million USD for the 2014–15 biennium. UNODC is mandated to assist UN Member States in their "struggle" against illicit drugs, crime, and terrorism.

Its headquarters are in Vienna, Austria. The organization is run by an executive director appointed by the UN Secretary General. It employs around 500.

In terms of quality management, UNODC has developed and published a number of standards/guides, those of particular note are listed below.

"Staff skill requirements and equipment recommendations for forensic science laboratories" (2011)

"Drug Characterization/Impurity Profiling—Background and Concepts" (2001)

"Methods for Impurity Profiling of Heroin and Cocaine Manual for use by National Drug Testing Laboratories" (2005)

"Guide for the development of forensic document examination capacity" (2010)

"Guidelines for the Forensic analysis of drugs facilitating sexual assault and other criminal acts" (2011)

2.2.4.5 Professional Bodies

2.2.4.5.1 American Academy of Forensic Sciences (AAFS)

The Academy is a society of individuals professionally engaged in "the forensic enterprise." Its membership is not restricted to forensic scientists or US-based individuals. It is incorporated as a not-for-profit legal entity in Illinois, USA, with headquarters in Colorado, USA. It is funded by membership fees and donations.

The objectives of the Academy are

> *[T]o promote professionalism, integrity, and competency in the membership actions and associated activities; to promote education for and research in the forensic sciences; to encourage the study, improve the practice, elevate the standards and advance the cause of the forensic sciences; to promote interdisciplinary communications; and to plan, organize and administer meetings, reports and other projects for the stimulation and advancement of these and related purposes.*

The Academy is, in part, a professional body that has developed and published professional standards that apply to its membership. Its Code of Ethics and Conduct, conformance with which is a condition of membership, encourages good practice, professional competence, and protects the reputation of the organization. The standards are discussed in 3.4.4.4.1.

The AAFS is also a learned society and publishes the Journal of Forensic Sciences.

2.2.4.5.2 Australia and New Zealand Forensic Science Society (ANZFSS)

The Society is a society of individuals with a "bona fide" interest in forensic science. Membership is not restricted to those professionally or otherwise engaged in forensic science. Its membership is drawn from the region which is reflected in its structure, having branches in each state and territory managed by an elected council/executive committee.

It is a not-for-profit, legal entity incorporated in Victoria, Australia. It is funded by membership fees, sponsorship, and sales.

The objects of the society are variously stated as:

To advance the study and application of forensic science.

To facilitate association of, and collaboration and interchange of information between, [members].

[T]o enhance the quality of forensic science.

The Society recently decided to become, in part, a professional body. Those members who may act as expert witnesses agree to be bound by a Code of Professional Practice which is discussed in 3.4.4.4.2.

2.2.4.5.3 California Association of Criminalists (CAC)

The California Association of Criminalists is a professional membership organization of forensic scientists. Membership is restricted to forensic science practitioners or students pursuing, or intending to peruse, a career as a forensic scientist.

The Association is a private foundation and a legal entity incorporated in California, USA. It is funded by membership fees and sales.

The objects of the Association are many and are listed on its website (CAC n.d.), they include to

- foster an exchange of ideas and information within the field of criminalistics,
- promote wide recognition of the practice of criminalistics as an important phase of jurisprudence,
- promote a high level of professional competence among criminalists, and
- establish, maintain, and enforce a Code of Ethics for criminalists.

The CAC has a Code of Ethics that binds all its members. There are effective conformity assessment and enforcement mechanisms in place. The CAC has the most detailed, learned, and comprehensive of the extant codes applying to individual forensic scientists and is discussed in 3.4.4.4.3.

2.2.4.5.4 Chartered Society of Forensic Science (CSFS)

The Society is a charity registered in England and headquartered in Yorkshire, UK. Its main purpose is to serve the interests of its members.

Chartered status is issued by the UK Crown. The Society is incorporated under a Royal Charter with the permission of the Privy Council of the United Kingdom.

It is governed by a council elected by the membership and run by a chief executive officer. It is funded by membership fees and sales.

The Society has four "overarching" objectives which are to

- promote and develop regulation in forensic science and practice,
- provide opportunities for education, training, and development for forensic practitioners,
- support and encourage research and development in forensic sciences, and
- strive to continuously improve its internal structure and finances.

The Society has several categories of membership which includes individuals with a general interest and professional members who are, in the main, forensic science practitioners. All members are bound by part of the Code of Conduct. Professional members are additionally bound to comply with Forensic Science Regulator's Code of Practice and the Criminal Procedure Rules Part 19, both of which only have effect in E&W. The Society's code is discussed in 3.4.4.4.4 and those of the Regulator in 3.4.6.2. The Forensic Science Regulator is introduced later in 2.4.4.

In addition to developing and publishing standards that apply to members, the Society also accredits university courses within the United Kingdom, Europe, and Australia to its own standards. At the time of writing [July 2017], 70 courses at 20 universities are accredited. It should be noted that in the United States the Forensic Science Education Programs Accreditation Commission performs a similar standards development, accreditation, and regulatory role.

Combining the roles of standards development, accreditation, and regulation introduces the potential for conflicts of interest. The Society itself does not conform to any quality standards such as ISO 9001.

The Society is also a learned society and publishes the journal Science and Justice.

2.2.4.5.5 International Association of Identification (IAI)

The International Association for Identification is a professional membership organization comprising individuals who work in the field of forensic identification which includes those that employ so-called feature-comparison disciplines and crime scene examination, which are appropriately covered by the inspection standard ISO/IEC 17020, discussed in 3.2.3. It should be noted that the validation of feature-comparison methods was examined in the 2016 PCAST Report (Presidents Council of Advisors on Science and Technology, 2016), which is discussed in 6.3.2.

The IAI is a not-for-profit corporation registered in Delaware, USA. It is governed by a board of directors, elected by the membership, and run by a chief operations officer. It has a variety of membership categories ranging from forensic practitioners to students.

It is funded by membership fees, sales, and revenue generated by its exclusive training partner Tritech Training Forensics.

The Association's aims and objectives are mainly serving members' interests, providing training and education, and certifying practitioners as competent.

In common with other US forensic science bodies, it combines the roles of standards development/setting, accreditation/certification, and regulation which introduce the potential for conflicts of interest.

It also publishes a Code of Ethics and Standards of Professional Conduct which binds members. The code is divided into sections on professionalism, competency and proficiency, communications, and organizational responsibility. It is closely similar to other codes discussed in 3.4.4 and is reproduced as Appendix A for information.

2.2.4.5.6 Society of Forensic Toxicologists (SOFT)

The Society of Forensic Toxicologists Inc. is a not-for-profit professional organization headquartered in Mesa, Arizona, USA. The Society is composed of practicing forensic toxicologists and those interested in the discipline for the purpose of promoting and developing forensic toxicology. Through its annual meetings, the Society provides a forum for the exchange of information and ideas among toxicology professionals.

Membership is restricted to suitably qualified individuals actively engaged in forensic toxicology. The Society is governed by a board of directors. It is funded through membership fees and sales.

The stated mission of the Society is as follows:

> *The Society of Forensic Toxicologists, Inc. is an organization composed of practicing forensic toxicologists and those interested in the discipline for the purpose of promoting and developing forensic toxicology.*

It publishes a Code of Ethics, which binds its members, and a complaints procedure to be followed. The code is based on documents prepared by the former accreditation body ASCLD/LAB (American Society of Crime Laboratory Directors/Laboratory Accreditation Board) circulated to numerous forensic science organizations. This fact might explain the close similarity between codes.

The Society has published laboratory guidelines (SOFT/AAFS, 2006), which apply to the competence of the organization and individual, and the validity of methods. The document is light on the requirements for validation as set out, for example, in the Eurachem and IUPAC guides, discussed in 3.4.5, and the Codes and Guidance of the Forensic Science Regulator discussed in 3.4.6.2. This weakness is probably a reflection of the age of the SOFT guidelines that were published in 2006.

Calibration seems to be the main tool for ensuring a method's fitness-for-purpose. The guidelines are vague on quality control and assurance which do not correspond to the definitions provided by ISO (2015).

SOFT is also a learned society and publishes the Journal of Analytical Toxicology.

2.2.4.5.7 The United Kingdom and Ireland Association of Forensic Toxicologists (UKIAFT)

The United Kingdom and Ireland Association of Forensic Toxicologistsis a professional body. Its membership comprises forensic toxicologists in the United Kingdom and Ireland who are representatives of each of the main laboratories in the region offering forensic toxicology services. It was formed to provide a forum for practicing forensic toxicologists to share knowledge, discuss the development of new analytical techniques, and advocate a high level of professionalism among its members. Membership of the UKIAFT is open to all practicing or trainee forensic toxicologists working in the region. It is funded by membership subscriptions. The Association is managed by a council. Its legal status is unclear.

The organization has a Code of Conduct that binds members and is closely similar to that of the Forensic Science Regulator discussed in 3.4.4.1. Investigation of an alleged breach and sanctions are mentioned in the Association's constitution but no complaints procedure is documented.

The code does provide some helpful detail on potential conflicts of interest and the avoidance of poor practice in general.

The Association recommends conformance to the following standards: ISO/IEC 17025, the E&W Association of Chief Police Officers/Crown Prosecution Service guidance for experts on disclosure (ACPO/CPS, 2010), and the Association's own practice guidelines on the forensic process for forensic toxicology laboratories (Cooper et al., 2010). The guidelines are an adaptation of the laboratory guidelines of the US SOFT and the AAFS, mentioned earlier in 2.2.4.5., to better reflect toxicology standards within the United Kingdom and Ireland. The UKIAFT guidelines have little to add on method validation but at 8.3.3 seem to argue against the need for validation in certain circumstances which is at variance with standard practice. Arguing against the need for validation might be due to the wide range of potential target substances/analytes encountered in the discipline and the infrequency with which a particular method might be used. In addition, specificity and not selectivity is a designated performance measure; see 3.4.2.3 for a discussion on selectivity and specificity.

The parts of the guidelines that relate to quality management appear to have been copied directly from the SOFT/AAFS guidelines discussed above in 2.2.4.5.6 and therefore suffer from similar weaknesses.

SOFT and UKIAFT guideline documents need revision to take account of the current quality standards framework that exists in both the United States and the United Kingdom.

2.3 ACCREDITING BODIES

2.3.1 Introduction

With the near universal adoption of ISO/IEC 17025 as the standard for forensic science laboratories and the growing adoption of ISO/IEC 17020 for crime scene examination and feature-comparison disciplines, there are now bodies that accredit forensic science providers in every jurisdiction/territory of the developed world.

Those that accredit forensic science providers in the English language are the focus in this work and taken as a proxy for all other accrediting bodies. This is not as limited as it might seem at first as two of those bodies, the UK Accreditation Service (UKAS) and the US National Accreditation Board (ANAB), accredit providers beyond their national borders.

Accrediting bodies list accredited organizations and those under sanction on their websites. This provides an opportunity for interested parties to check claimed accreditation for a particular forensic science discipline.

Bodies that accredit forensic science providers should be signatories to ILAC's MRA discussed earlier in 2.2.3.1. Signatories have been peer evaluated as competent and compliant with ISO/IEC 17011. In this way, ILAC brings together all competent accrediting bodies.

Accreditations granted by ILAC MRA signatories are recognized worldwide based on their equivalent accreditation programs and achieve the objective of "tested or inspected once accepted everywhere."

All the accrediting bodies discussed in this section conform to ISO/IEC 17011 "Conformity assessment—General requirements for accreditation bodies accrediting conformity assessment bodies" and are signatories to the ILAC MRA. As reported earlier in Section 2.2.3.1 at the time of writing (July 2017) accrediting bodies in the regions covered by SADCA and AFRAC are not yet MRA signatories.

It should be noted that bodies that appear to be discipline-specific accrediting bodies such as the Australasian Forensic Field Sciences Accreditation Board (AFFSAB), managed by the NIFS Australia and New Zealand, mentioned later in 2.6, and the US Forensic Specialities Accreditation Board (FSAB) are actually certifying bodies in terms of quality management. These and similar bodies, directly or indirectly, certify individuals as competent. However, at the time of writing [Decembers 2017], they are not accredited conformity assessment bodies. The appropriate standard is ISO/IEC 17024:2012 "Conformity assessment—General requirements for bodies operating certification of persons" discussed in 3.2.5. As discussed in 3.4.4.3, the FSAB is working towards becoming accredited to ISO/IEC 17024, a significant advance. The AFFSAB is dicussed in 3.4.4.5.1.

2.3.2 ANSI-ASQ National Accreditation Board

ANSI-ASQ National Accreditation Board (ANAB) is a US-based, private sector, standards organization. Its headquarters are in Milwaukee, Wisconsin, USA.

ANAB is jointly owned by ANSI (American National Standards Institute) and ASQ (American Society for Quality) ANSI is the ISO representative for the US government.

The stated mission of ANAB is to be a leader in guiding the international development of accreditation processes that build confidence and value for stakeholders worldwide and providing high quality and reliable accreditation services with the most professional value-added services for customers and end users.

ANAB is governed by a board of directors which represents the stakeholder community, including industry and government, and is operated by an executive board. It is funded mainly by accreditation and training fees. ANAB governance includes an Accreditation Council for Forensics which is a standing committee of technical specialists acting in an advisory capacity.

ANAB has grown to become the major accrediting body for forensic science providers in the United States particularly since the American Society of Crime Lab Directors/Laboratory Accreditation Board (ASCLD/LAB[3]) merged into ANAB in 2016. As discussed in 4.5, ANAB acquired Forensic Quality Services (FSQ) in November 2011, which enabled ANAB to offer accreditation under the FSQ brand to ISO/IEC 17020 for crime scene examination and feature-comparison disciplines and ISO/IEC 17025 for forensic science laboratories.

2.3.3 American Association for Laboratory Accreditation

The name of this accrediting bodie is abbreviated to A2LA. A2LA is a not-for-profit, private sector, public service, membership society, and accrediting body. It has its headquarters in Frederick, Maryland, USA. It distinguishes itself from ANAB as being "independent" meaning that it is not owned by a "parent" organization. As reported above, ANAB is jointly owned by ANSI and ASQ.

The Association is governed by a board of directors, which is elected by the Association membership which comprises individuals and organizations. It is funded by membership subscriptions and accreditation fees.

A2LA offers accreditation to ISO/IEC 17025 and ISO/IEC 17020 and a range of options for organizations conducting activities that might fall under either or both standards.

2.3.4 National Association of Testing Authorities, Australia

National Association of Testing Authorities (NATA) is a not-for-profit company, limited by guarantee, operating as an association owned, and governed by its members and representatives from industry, government, and professional bodies. NATA is "largely self-funded" by accreditation fees and sales but relies heavily on unpaid volunteers[4], which are likely to be employees of the accredited entities in which case the organization may be conflicted. NATA only accredits Australian entities.

[3] Not to be confused with ASCLD.

[4] The 2016 Annual Report states that 3359 technical assessors were used.

All NATA accredited organizations are members of the company, and membership is mainly restricted to organizations accredited by NATA.

NATA is governed by a board elected by and from the membership and stakeholders and is managed by an executive. Its registered office is in Rhodes, New South Wales.

NATA has memoranda of understanding (MOU) with the Commonwealth, State, and Territory governments of Australia that recognize its key role in Australia's technical infrastructure. The Commonwealth Government uses NATA accredited facilities wherever possible and encourages State and Territory governments to do likewise.

NATA is the authority responsible for the accreditation of laboratories, inspection bodies, calibration services, producers of certified reference materials (CRMs), and proficiency testing scheme providers throughout Australia.

One MOU with the Commonwealth Government recognizes NATA as the sole national accreditation body for establishing and maintaining competent laboratory practice.

NATA offers accreditation to ISO/IEC 17025 for forensic science providers. It does not offer accreditation to ISO/IEC 17020 for crime scene examination or feature-comparison disciplines.

As suggested earlier, the fact that the company is funded and governed by organizations it accredits and relies on for support may give rise to conflicts of interest.

2.3.5 The United Kingdom Accreditation Service

The United Kingdom Accreditation Service (UKAS) is a not-for-profit company limited by guarantee. Its registered office is in Staines-upon-Thames, England. It claims to be independent of government, operating in the public interest under a MOU with the UK government, through the Secretary of State for Business, Energy and Industrial Strategy. UKAS is appointed as the national accreditation body by Accreditation Regulations 2009 (SI No 3155/2009) and the EU Regulation (EC) 765/2008. It is the sole national accreditation body recognized by the UK government to assess the competence of certification, testing, inspection, and calibration services together with producers of CRMs and proficiency testing scheme providers. It is funded by accreditation fees.

Members of the company represent those who have an interest in all aspects of accreditation: national and local government, business and industry, purchasers, users, and quality managers. In contrast to NATA, members of the company are not the accredited organizations/entities.

The company is managed by a board of nonexecutive and executive directors. The board is supported in the day-to-day running of the company's activities by an executive drawn from senior UKAS staff.

UKAS offers accreditation to forensic science providers to both ISO/IEC 17025 and ISO/IEC 17020. It has also incorporated compliance with the Forensic Science Regulator's Codes of Practice and Conduct into its requirements for UK-based forensic science providers. UKAS accredits forensic science providers outside the United Kingdom.

2.4 BODIES PROVIDING REGULATORY OR OVERSIGHT FUNCTIONS

2.4.1 Introduction

As stated in the introduction to Section 2, many bodies exercise more than one of the key roles: service provision, standards development, accreditation/certification, and regulation. Bodies exercising regulation and oversight tend to combine the roles with standards development. The bodies discussed here do not act in their own interest and seek to engage with the broadest range of stakeholders.

At the time of writing [December 2017], most regulation is voluntary. However, the trend is toward enforced compliance with quality standards. As discussed later in 2.4.4, in the United Kingdom the Forensic Science Regulator is seeking statutory powers, and in the United States the forensic science providers within the Department of Justice must maintain accreditation to ISO/IEC 17025 and conform to a Code of Practice.

2.4.2 National Measurement (or Metrology) Institutes

National Measurement Institutes (NMIs) develop and maintain primary measurement standards such as the kilogram. They also offer certified or standard reference materials that help forensic science providers calibrate instruments, validate methods, and ensure the accuracy of test results. Measurement standards underpin the infrastructure of traceability throughout the world, which ensures accuracy and consistency of measurement.

As discussed in 2.7, the US NMI, NIST, hosts the Organization of Scientific Area Committees (OSAC) which are discipline-specific working groups.

Accurate measurements or the identification and quantitation of illicit substances are essential in forensic science. Traceability and the availability of certified calibrants and reference materials with an estimate of uncertainty are requirements for fit-for-purpose forensic science. Without traceability and an estimate of uncertainty reported results are of unknown quality and reliability.

NMIs provide reference materials of forensic utility, e.g., DNA quantitation standard, ethanol for blood and breath alcohol measurements, drugs of abuse, their precursors, intermediates, metabolites, profiling impurities, manufacturing identifiers, and surrogates.

The BIPM, based in Sèvres, France, is the intergovernmental organization through which member states act together on matters related to measurement science and measurement standards.

Each state has its own metrology infrastructure; that for selected English-speaking countries is shown in Table 2.2. In most cases, the BIPM interacts principally with one NMI per state, as nominated through the state's foreign affairs department. The nominated NMI is responsible for coordinating with any other institutes (NMIs or others) that comprise that nation's metrology system.

Table 2.2 Some Quality Infrastructure Information From Selected English-Speaking Countries (Comprehensive Information Can Be Found at Bureau International des Poids et Mesures (BIPM n.d.)

Country	Metrological Institute	Accrediting Body	Standards Body
Australia	National Measurement Institute	NATA	Standards Australia
Canada	National Research Council of Canada	Canadian Association for Laboratory Accreditation (among others)	Standards Council of Canada
Ireland	NSAI National Metrology Laboratory	Irish National Accreditation Board	National Standards Authority of Ireland (NSAI)
NZ	Measurement Standards Laboratory	International Accreditation New Zealand (IANZ)	Standards New Zealand
RSA	National Metrological Institute of South Africa	South African National Accreditation System	South African Bureau of Standards
UK	LGC (among others)	UKAS	British Standards Institute
USA	National Institute of Science and Technology (NIST)	ANAB (among others)	American National Standards Institute (among others)

ANAB, ANSI-ASQ National Accreditation Board; *NATA*, National Association of Testing Authorities Australia; *NZ*, New Zealand; *UKAS*, United Kingdom Accreditation Service.

The CIPM (Comité international des poids et mesures) MRA is the international framework through which the NMIs demonstrate the equivalence of their measurement standards and the calibration and measurement certificates they issue. Participation in the CIPM/MRA provides for the mutual recognition of national measurement standards and of calibration certificates issued by national metrology institutes worldwide. The CIPM/MRA is the means by which NMIs are overseen and regulated.

The MRA has been drawn up by the CIPM, under the authority given to it in the Metre Convention. NMIs from 57 member states are signatories to the MRA.

In the field of chemical and biological measurements, CRMs and reference measurement methods provide stated references on which analytical laboratories can anchor their measurement results. The traceability of measurement results to internationally accepted stated references, together with their stated measurement uncertainties, provide the basis for their comparability and global acceptance. Global activities to develop a system for the international equivalence of chemical and biological measurements are led by the Consultative Committee for Amount of Substance: Metrology in Chemistry and Biology.

2.4.3 International Laboratory Accreditation Cooperation

As reported earlier in 2.2.3, this organization, through its regional cooperations, regulates and oversees accrediting bodies through MRAs which are entered into by accreditation bodies that have been peer evaluated and conform to ISO/IEC 17011. The ILAC MRA helps to ensure that accreditation bodies are interpreting and applying standards consistently in the manner intended by ISO. The guides issued by ILAC discussed in 3.3.2 assist in this matter.

The ILAC MRA is an internationally recognized "stamp of approval" and supports the aim of "tested or inspected once, accepted everywhere."

Bodies accrediting forensic science providers should conform to ISO/IEC 17011 and be ILAC MRA signatories.

2.4.4 The Forensic Science Regulator

The Forensic Science Regulator is a public appointee. The appointing minister is the UK Home Secretary and the funding department is the Home Office, which is the UK police/internal security ministry. Public appointees are expected to be independent of government. Although this link with the UK police ministry is not ideal, the independence of the Regulator is not in doubt.

The stated objective of the Regulator is to ensure that the provision of forensic science services across the criminal justice system in E&W is subject to an appropriate regime of scientific quality standards.

Although the remit of the Regulator is limited to E&W, forensic science providers in Scotland and the province of Northern Ireland have volunteered to comply with the Regulator's quality standards framework. Providers from those jurisdictions are represented on the Forensic Science Advisory Council (FSAC) which is in this section.

At the time of writing [December 2017], the provision of forensic services to the UK's criminal justice systems is regulated on a voluntary basis with the exception of populating the national DNA database, which requires the provider to be ISO/IEC 17025 accredited. The Regulator is concerned that without statutory powers of enforcement, standards may fall in response to cost pressures or never be adopted at all. In order to avoid these risks, the Regulator is seeking statutory powers of enforcement.

The Regulator can and does consider complaints of breaches of the Codes of Practice and Conduct. However, sanctions for breaches are currently [December 2017] limited to censure. Nevertheless, accrediting bodies can act in response to the Regulator's findings and, in the extreme, suspend and withdraw accreditation from the provider.

After a controversial start: facilitating the closure of the Council for the Registration of Forensic Practitioners, discussed in 4.3.1.2.1, and thereby removing the independent assessment of practitioner competence from the quality standards framework; and standing by while the Forensic Science Service (the highly regarded national forensic science provider) was also closed by the UK government, considerable progress has been made. The Regulator has moved quality management up the agenda of all forensic science stakeholders and significantly increased the awareness of quality and the need for an adequate quality standards framework to ensure forensic science meets the needs of the criminal justice systems of the UK.

The Regulator is supported by the FSAC which advises the Regulator on

- setting and monitoring compliance with quality standards in the provision of forensic science services,
- arranging the accreditation of those supplying forensic science services to the police, including in-house police services,
- procedures for validating and approving new technologies and applications in the field of forensic science,
- setting and monitoring compliance with standards relating to national forensic science databases, including the National DNA Database,
- the quality of academic and educational courses in forensic science, and
- international developments relevant to forensic science quality standards.

The membership of the FSAC, taken from its Terms of Reference, is shown in Table 2.3. It is clear that the document is out of date, e.g., the Forensic Science Society is now the Chartered Society of Forensic Sciences and no member for Northern Ireland is listed.

As can be gleaned from the membership list, the Regulator liaises closely with most stakeholders identifying gaps in the quality standards framework and ensuring suitable standards are developed in response.

In comparison with, for example, the late US National Commission Forensic Science, the FSAC seems light on academic and independent membership. The 2009 NRC Report (National Research Council, 2009) identified the need for a body of peer-reviewed research to support forensic science, a call which has been echoed in the more recent 2016 PCAST report (Presidents Council of Advisors on Science and Technology, 2016). Thus, academic representation is warranted and certainly justified by the pioneering work by UK universities such as King's College London, the Scottish Universities of Strathclyde and Dundee, and of course the University of Leicester.

2.4.5 International Organization of Legal Metrology

OIML (Organisation Internationale de Métrologie Légale) is an international treaty organization, based in Paris, with the responsibility of promoting harmonization of legal metrology procedures, defined by OIML as:

> *Legal metrology comprises all activities for which legal requirements are prescribed on measurement, units of measurement, measuring instruments and methods of measurement, these activities being performed by or on behalf of governmental authorities, to ensure an appropriate level of credibility of measurement results in the national regulatory environment.*

Table 2.3 Membership of the Forensic Science Regulator's Forensic Science Advisory Council

Area of Expertise	Person Description	Nominating Authority
Accreditation	A person experienced in accrediting forensic science laboratories and processes to recognise international and domestic standards.	UKAS
Forensic science	A fully qualified forensic scientist who has achieved eminence in the practice of forensic science, including holding a senior management position in a forensic science laboratory or a police service forensic science department.	CSFS
Pathology	A senior practising, or recently retired, Home Office registered pathologist.	BAFM, in consultation with Royal College of Pathologists
Academic training and qualification	A person from the academic field with experience in, and responsibility for, feeder training for the forensic science and crime scene examination professions. The responsibilities to be national rather than local.	Skills for Justice
Forensic science providers	A senior manager from a commercial or Government-owned forensic science laboratory.	AFSP
CJS	A senior manager or lawyer with experience of prosecuting, or managing the prosecution of, cases in which forensic science has been at issue; or a senior manager with responsibility for setting policy in this area.	CPS
	A member of the judiciary with responsibilities relevant to forensic science in the courts, or a particular interest in this area.	LCJ
	A member of the Bar with significant experience of acting for both the prosecution and the defence.	CBA

Table 2.3 Membership of the Forensic Science Regulator's Forensic Science Advisory Council—cont'd

Area of Expertise	Person Description	Nominating Authority
Scotland	A senior forensic manager with extensive knowledge of the Scottish legal system and the provision of forensic services in Scotland.	SPSA
Police	A senior police officer or member of police staff with responsibilities in relation to the provision of forensic science services to the police, or a closely related field, and with knowledge of the application of forensic science in the investigation of major crime.	ACPO
Lay Member	A person, not a member of a government department or organisation within the CJS, with experience of operating at an influential level alongside the CJS on behalf of the public. This might, for example, involve working on behalf of victims and witnesses. Knowledge of relevant legislation would be an advantage.	OCJR

ACPO, Association of Chief Police Officers of E&W; *AFSP*, Association of Forensic Science providers; *BAFM*, British Association of Forensic Medicine; *CBA*, Criminal Bar Association of E&W; *CJS*, Criminal Justice System of E&W (England and Wales); *CPS*, Crown Persecution Service of E&W; *CSFS*, Chartered Society of Forensic Science; *LCJ*, Lord Chief Justice's Department of E&W; *OCJR*, Office of Criminal Justice Reform; *SPSA*, Scottish Police Services Authority; *UKAS*, UK Accreditation Service.

OIML publishes guidelines for requirements pertaining to the use of measuring instruments. According to OIML, its guidelines apply to 88% of the world's population and 98.5% of the world's economy. It publishes guidelines for the manufacture, performance, and use of evidential breath machines, analytical balances, and spectrophotometers among many other measurement instruments.

2.5 NETWORKS OF FORENSIC SCIENCE PROVIDERS

2.5.1 Introduction

Networks of forensic science providers were created and continue to exist for the purposes of information exchange and benchmarking, i.e., evaluating and comparing performance, identifying and sharing good practice, and thereby improving performance, however it is measured.

The outcomes of benchmarking are variously described by the Networks such as "achieving excellence" but, in essence, the aim is always to improve the quality of forensic science to better meet the needs of law enforcement and justice.

2.5.2 The Association of Forensic Science Providers (AFSP)

As is discussed in 4.2.3, the AFSP began life as the UK Forensic Science Liaison Group. Membership is restricted to the major forensic science providers of the United Kingdom and Ireland. Members are accredited to ISO/IEC 17025 and agree to comply with the Forensic Science Regulator's Codes of Practice and Conduct. The AFSP offers support to the Regulator's Specialist Working Groups and has a seat on the FSAC.

The stated aims and objectives of the Association include facilitating the effective delivery of justice and promoting public confidence in forensic science. Its mission and vision statements are reproduced below.

> *Mission*
>
> *To represent the common views of the providers of independent forensic science within the United Kingdom and Ireland with regard to the maintenance and development of quality and best practice in forensic science and expert opinion in support of the justice system, from scene to court.*
>
> *Vision*
>
> *To be the unified, objective, informed voice of practical forensic science provision to best support the interests of the criminal justice system through a partnership approach.*

According to the AFSP, membership of the Association encourages and facilitates;

- best practice sharing among members,
- development and upholding of standards within the forensic community,
- assistance with Forensic Strategy, where it affects the quality of forensic service provision, and
- improving the provision of forensic science to the Criminal Justice Systems of the Great Britain and Ireland.

The Association comprises senior managers of the member organizations. Those currently represented [December 2017] are as follows:

Cellmark Forensic Services

Dstl (Defence Science and Technology Laboratory)

Environmental Scientifics Group
Forensic Science Ireland
Forensic Science Northern Ireland
Key Forensic Services
LGC Forensics
Scottish Police Authority Forensic Services

The Association is governed and funded by its members. It is informally managed by means of periodic meetings chaired by members in turn and calls on the expertise available in the member organizations when needed. The AFSP supports a collaborative exercises group which manages proficiency tests to monitor and improve performance. The AFSP also includes the Body Fluids Forum (Allard and Rankin, 2010) as a subgroup.

As recorded in 3.4.2.4.2, the AFSP developed and published a standard for the formulation of evaluative forensic science expert opinion (Association of Forensic Science Providers, 2009). This standard has been adapted and published as an ENFSI Guideline detailed in 3.4.2.4.3 and discussed briefly in the next section.

The Association does not publish its records, e.g., the minutes of its meetings or proficiency test results.

2.5.3 The American Society of Crime Laboratory Directors (ASCLD)

ASCLD is a not-for-profit professional society of the 'directors'[5] of mostly US local (as opposed to federal/national) forensic science laboratories. It is essentially a society of laboratory managers which serves their needs and interests. Its headquarters are in Garner, North Carolina, USA. Membership is open to current and former laboratory managers and educators/trainers. The list of members is not publically available.

ASCLD should not be confused with ASCLD/LAB, which was an accrediting body that has now "merged into" ANAB as reported in 2.3.2.

The Society is governed by a board of directors drawn from eligible members and elected by those members. The board numbers 14 and serves for a period of 4 years. It is funded by membership subscription and sales.

Its mission statement is

> *To promote the effectiveness of crime laboratory leaders throughout the world by facilitating communication among members, sharing critical information, providing relevant training, promoting crime laboratory accreditation, and encouraging scientific and managerial excellence in the global forensic community.*

ASCLD particularly focuses on enhancing leadership and management skills and knowledge in a forensic science laboratory. The main way in which ASCLD serves its

[5] Senior managers or laboratory heads not necessarily exercising the legal responsibilities of a company director.

members is through an annual members' conference, in which management training is given and networking is encouraged. The website provides news and information.

It publishes a Code of Ethics that applies to laboratory managers. Conformance is voluntary. The Code includes a complaints procedure. The sanctions of censure, suspension, and expulsion are available. It also publishes an official journal: "Forensic Science Policy and Management Journal."

The Association administers and chairs the United States Technical Advisory Group to the ISO TC 272 on Forensic Science for the development of international standards for forensic science.

ASCLD is a member of the Consortium of Forensic Science Organizations (CFSO). The other members are AAFS; International Association for Identification; International Association of Forensic Nurses; National Association of Medical Examiners; and SOFT/American Board of Forensic Toxicology. The CSFO is essentially a lobbying group which seeks to advance the interests of its member organizations. It is fair to say that like ASCLD, CFSO represents the interests of smaller forensic science providers. The CFSO has no particular relevance in quality management.

The Association is also a member of IFSA discussed later in 2.5.5.

2.5.4 The European Network of Forensic Science Institutes (ENFSI)

ENFSI, as the name implies, is a network of forensic science providers. It was founded in 1995 with the purpose of improving the mutual exchange of information in the field of forensic science. Membership is drawn mainly from major providers in Council of Europe member states. It is a large and complex organization. At the time of writing [December 2017], it claims 68 member institutes in 36 countries and 17 discipline-specific Expert Working Groups. It has achieved a great deal since its inception. It has created its own quality standards framework to which members must conform, as discussed at length in 3.4. In developing its framework it has done much to improve the quality of forensic science and ensure forensic science within Europe meets the needs of law enforcement and justice. Through its projects, initiatives, and training and development, the Network continues to do so. In 2009, ENFSI was recognized by the European Commission as the monopoly forensic science organization within the EU.

The Network is a not-for-profit association, registered in Wiesbaden, Germany, and is therefore subject to German law. It is funded mainly by membership subscription. It has published a number of foundational documents including a constitution (ENFSI, 2016) which, among other things, sets out membership criteria. Much of its documentation, which includes an annual report, is published and in the public domain, the exclusions being meeting minutes and financial reports.

ENFSI is governed by a five-member board elected by, and accountable to, the membership and serves for a period of 3 years. The board and membership are supported by a permanent secretariat, which is a separate legal entity registered as a charity in Wiesbaden, Germany. The secretariat is accountable to, and operates under the supervision of, the board. ENFSI has two standing committees, a Quality and Competence Committee and a Research and Development Committee, which advise the board on matters within their remit.

The ENFSI mission statement expresses the main purpose of the Network and that is to

> *… share knowledge, exchange experiences and come to mutual agreements in the field of forensic science.*

One of its stated aims is of particular relevance in quality management and that is to

> *… encourage all ENFSI laboratories to comply with best practice and international standards for quality and competence assurance.*

ENFSI is also a member of the IFSA discussed next.

2.5.5 International Forensic Strategic Alliance (IFSA)

The IFSA is a multilateral partnership established by a MOU between five autonomous regional networks of operational forensic laboratories and NIFS Australia and New Zealand. The five regional networks are as follows:

- Academia Iberoamericana de Criminalística y Estudios Forenses (AICEF),
- Asian Forensic Sciences Network,
- ASCLD,
- ENFSI, and
- Southern Africa Regional Forensic Science Network

Each of the partners has slightly different aims and objectives. For example, as explained earlier, ASCLD focuses on laboratory management and promotes good practice in that area. ENFSI has a far broader remit, and AICEF is an association of research institutes. In addition, as detailed next in 2.6, NIFS is different again.

The IFSA vision is

> *[T]o create opportunities for strategic collaboration across the global forensic science community.*

and its purpose is to

> *Represent the global operational forensic science community dedicated to the improvement of forensic science in all jurisdictions.*

IFSA is not a legal entity. The partnership is headed by a rotating "presidency," and representatives aim to meet at least annually. It has two strategic partners: the UNODC and INTERPOL.

IFSA works closely with the UNODC developing forensic good practice guidelines, such as the MRD (Minimum Requirement Documents) discussed earlier in 2.2.4.2.8, which apply to a range of forensic science disciplines for developing countries and emerging forensic science providers in those countries. IFSA also offers technical assistance to emerging providers. By these means, IFSA helps the UNODC ensure that all Members States conform to internationally accepted standards.

IFSA has agreed to adopt, review, and promote the use of minimum standards that guarantee an acceptable level of quality and interoperability. It seeks to address crime scene examination and evidence management as the starting point of all forensic processes. IFSA claims to recognize the importance of a quality management framework in forensic science laboratories to provide quality and standardized results, be it procedures undertaken in the field or in the laboratory.

IFSA also provides a focus on emerging technologies, forensic science service models, and tracking of key research and development activities within the Networks.

One beneficial aim that IFSA could adopt is to coordinate the development of Level 3 standards to avoid duplication of effort.

2.6 NATIONAL INSTITUTE OF FORENSIC SCIENCE AUSTRALIA AND NEW ZEALAND (NIFS)

NIFS is a directorate within the Australian and New Zealand Policing Advisory Agency (ANZPAA NIFS).

NIFS claims to have no counterpart and indeed does not fit easily into any of the above categories having accreted a diversity of roles and responsibilities since its foundation in 1991/2 as a National Common Police Service. NIFS, therefore, has its own section in this work.

As discussed in Section 4, NIFS was created in response to the wrongful convictions of Edward Charles Splatt and Alice Lynne Chamberlain in 1984 and 1987, respectively (Morling, 1987).

NIFS is ultimately governed by the Police Commissioners of Australia and New Zealand as the ANZPAA Board but has a second governance body that comprises all the agencies that fund NIFS, called the Australia New Zealand Forensic Executive Committee (ANZFEC). The membership of ANZFEC comprises the government forensic science providers of Australasia including police and nonpolice agencies. Its "strategic intent" is to "promote and facilitate excellence in forensic science."

NIFS provides a very broad range of products and services in support of ANZFEC members. These include sponsoring and supporting research, developing and coordinating forensic science services, facilitating information exchange, training and quality management, and developing and publishing standards. In essence, NIFS provides common products and services which are better managed, coordinated, and/or delivered by one central organization than by individual providers and police forces.

Among the products and services provided by NIFS, those that relate directly to quality management include the management of the AFFSAB, developing and publishing standards such as "A Guideline to Forensic Fundamentals" (ANZPAA NIFS, 2016), the management of a proficiency testing program, membership of SA committee CH041—Forensic Analysis and also being a member of NATA's Forensic Science Accreditation Advisory Committee.

As discussed in Section 4, the independence of NIFS itself is an issue which was considered in the Vincent review (Vincent, 2014). The Honourable Frank Vincent recommended that NIFS become an independent agency. In addition, the existence of NIFS as a police directorate is contrary to recommendation 4 of the 2009 NRC Report (National Research Council, 2009), which calls for a separation between the administration of forensic science and law enforcement. However, it is fair to say that the Australasian authorities are not alone in ignoring that recommendation. The idea of NIFS as an independent agency has not been discounted and may be considered in the future (Wilson-Wilde, 2017). At the time of writing [December 2017] there is no plan in place for NIFS to become an independent agency.

2.7 ORGANIZATION OF SCIENTIFIC AREA COMMITTEES (OSAC)

OSAC, like NIFS, is an organization that is not easy to categorize and is given its own section in this work. In essence, its aim is to construct a sustainable quality standards framework to improve the quality and consistency of work in the forensic science community by populating a registry with suitable standards for use by accreditation bodies. Among its roles is the management of standards development.

The 2013 MOU between NIST and the US Department of Justice (DOJ) that created the National Commission of Forensic Sciences[6], discussed in Section 4, also created OSAC which is administered by NIST.

OSAC is a collaborative body of around 600 forensic science practitioners and other experts who represent local, state, and federal agencies, academia, and industry.

According to OSAC, its aim is to identify, promote, and populate a register of scientifically sound, consensus-based, fit-for-purpose documentary standards that can be used to strengthen the practice of forensic science. A standard that is posted on the OSAC Registry demonstrates that the methods it contains have been assessed to be valid by forensic practitioners, academic researchers, measurement scientists, and statisticians through a consensus development process that allows participation and comment from all relevant stakeholders.

[6] The commission ended in April 2017 when its charter was not renewed.

OSAC is governed by the Forensic Science Standards Board (FSSB). The FSSB establishes governance rules to ensure that quality standards are properly developed and to encourage their use in the provision of forensic science services. The FSSB supports the organization by overseeing operations of all resource committees, SACs, and subcommittees; approving standards for listing on the OSAC Registry of Approved Standards; and facilitating communication within OSAC and between OSAC and the forensic science community. The Board resolves disputes and appeals on developed standards and engages in international developments relevant to forensic science quality standards.

The FSSB is composed of 16 members initially appointed by NIST-DOJ leadership and membership selection committee comprising 5 SAC chairs, 5 representatives of professional organizations (e.g., AAFS, IAI, and SOFT), 5 members at large from the research and measurement science communities, and 1 NIST ex officio.

The structure of OSAC and the role of the FSSB and the resource committees are shown in Fig. 2.2 or 2.3 and line management is shown in Fig. 2.3.

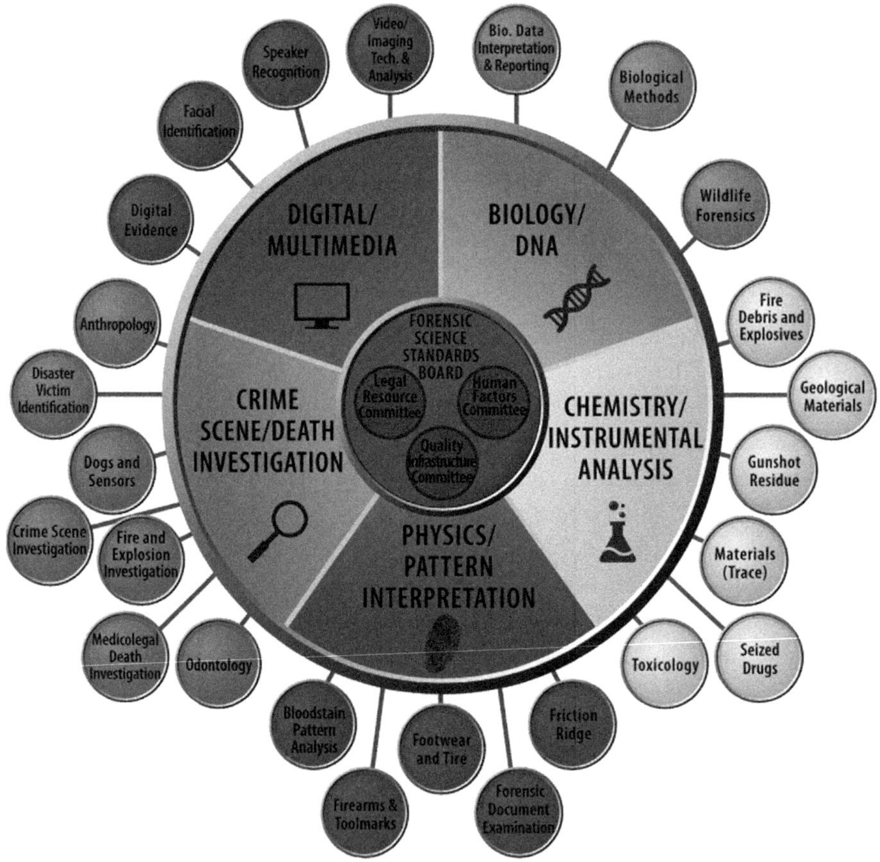

Figure 2.2 Organization of Scientific Area Committees.

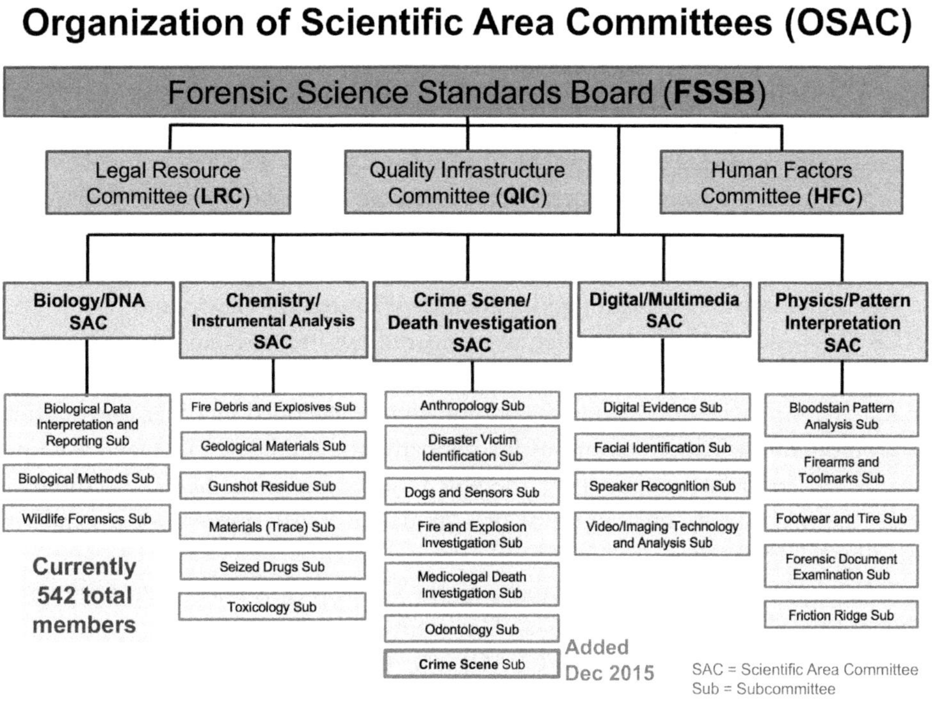

Figure 2.3 OSAC line management.

OSAC consists of five SACs that report to the FSSB. Each of the five SACs oversees discipline-specific subcommittees. The five SACs cover broadly defined forensic science topic areas: biology/DNA; chemistry/instrumental analysis; crime scene/death investigation; information technology/multimedia; and physics/pattern.

A Human Factors Committee, Legal Resource Committee, and Quality Infrastructure Committee provide input to the FSSB, SACs, and SAC subcommittees on standards being developed within OSAC infrastructure and are responsible for specific duties in their resource committee content area.

The Resource Committees play a critical support role for the entire OSAC by providing their expertise during reviews and development of standards within the OSAC.

The Legal Resource Committee reviews and provides a legal perspective on standards within OSAC. The Committee is composed of up to 10 judges, lawyers, and legal experts who provide guidance on the legal aspects of forensic standards under development and input on presentation of forensic results to the legal system.

The Quality Infrastructure Committee provides guidance on quality issues throughout OSAC and will interface with standards development organizations as needed. The Committee is composed of up to 10 standards experts, quality systems managers, and accreditation and certification specialists who are responsible for writing and updating the Forensic Science Code of Practice.

The Human Factors Committee provides guidance on the influence of systems design on human performance, on ways to minimize cognitive bias, and on ways to mitigate errors in complex tasks. The Committee is composed of up to 10 psychologists, quality systems managers, and usability experts who provide guidance on the influence of systems design on human performance and on ways to mitigate errors in complex tasks.

The SACs approve standards and guidelines identified by the subcommittees and provide coordination when standards and guidelines span multiple disciplines.

The SACs and subcommittees identify standards, test methods, and requirements for laboratory accreditation appropriate to the scientific area and discipline. The SACs and subcommittees may identify standards and guidelines developed by other organizations, may promote the development of needed standards and guidelines, or may create new standards and guidelines themselves, thereby functioning as an SDO. According to OSAC, the SAC grants final approval of a guideline. Final approval of a standard is granted by the FSSB after approval by the SAC.

OSAC approved documents will make up the OASC Registry. The Registry will be freely available online through NIST and/or OSAC websites.

Based on the early work of the OSAC, it seems that the ASTM forensic practice standards will serve at least as a starting point for the development of documented standards.

Oddly, as ISO standards seemed to lie outside the remit of the OSAC, the International Standard ISO/IEC 17025 has recently [September 2016] been added to the OSAC Registry. The fact that forensic science providers have been accredited to this standard since the late 1990s is perhaps a measure of the progress required.

REFERENCES

ACPO/CPS, May 2010. Disclosure Manual. Crown Prosecution Service. http://www.cps.gov.uk/legal/d_to_g/disclosure_manual/annex_k_disclosure_manual/.

Allard, J., Rankin, B., 2010. Body fluids conference jointly hosted by the forensic science society & the centre for forensic investigation, university of teeside. Science and Justice 100−109.

ANZPAA NIFS, 2016. Strategic Plan 2016−2019. ANZPAA NIFS, Plan, Melbourne.

ANZPAA NIFS, 2017. Publications. ANZPAA. http://www.anzpaa.org.au/forensic-science/our-work/products/publications.

AOAC International. Publications. AOAC. http://www.aoac.org/AOAC_Prod_Imis/AOAC/PUBS/AOAC_Member/PUBSCF/PUBSA.aspx?hkey=0feb64dc-a23a-4c67-81c9-bf11bceb01d8.

Association of Forensic Science Providers, 2009. Standards for the formulation of evaluative forensic science expert opinion. Science and Justice 49, 161−164.

ASTM International. Forensic Science Standards. https://www.astm.org/Standards/forensic-science-standards.html.

CAC. About Us. http://www.cacnews.org/membership/purpose.shtml.

Cooper, G.A.A., Paterson, S., Osselton, M.D., 2010. The United Kingdom and Ireland association of forensic toxicologists forensic toxicology laboratory guidelines (2010). Science and Justice 166−176.

ENFSI, 2015. ENFSI Guideline for Evaluative Reporting in Forensic Science. Guide. ENFSI, Wiesbaden.
ENFSI, September 27 , 2016. European Network of Forensic Science Institutes: Bylaws, Policy. ENFSI. http://enfsi.eu/wp-content/uploads/2016/09/151021_enfsi_constitution.pdf.
Eurachem, April 24, 2017. Publications. Eurachem. https://www.eurachem.org/index.php/publications/mnu-rdlst.
European Network of Forensic Science Institutes, 2017. Home: European Network of Forensic Science Institutes. http://enfsi.eu/.
Forensic Science Regulator, 2014. "Guidance – Validation." FSR-g-201 Issue 1. The Forensic Science Regulator, Birmingham.
IFSA, 2016. Minimum Requirements Documents. http://www.ifsa-forensics.org/minimum-requirements-documents/.
ILAC. ILAC Guidance Documnets (G-Series). http://ilac.org/publications-and-resources/ilac-guidance-series/.
ISO, September 15, 2015. "Quality Management Systems – Fundamentals and vocabulary." ISO 9001: 2015(E). ISO, Geneva.
ISO, 2004. "ISO/IEC 17011:2004(en)." Conformity assessment — General requirements for accreditation bodies accrediting conformity assessment bodies. ISO.
Morling, T.R., 1987. Royal Commission of Inquiry into Chamberlain Convictions. Royal Commission Report. Government Printer, Canberra.
National Research Council, 2009. Strengthening Forensic Science in the United States: A Path Forward. Committee Report. The National Academies Press, Washington DC.
Policy Documents *(P-Series)*. http://ilac.org/publications-and-resources/ilac-policy-series/.
Presidents Council of Advisors on Science, Technology, 2016. Forensic Science in Criminal Courts: Ensuring Scientific Validity of Feature-comparison Methods. Washington, D.C..
SOFT/AAFS, 2006. Forensic toxicology laboratory guidelines 2006 version. Society of Forensic Toxicologists. http://www.soft-tox.org/files/Guidelines_2006_Final.pdf.
Vincent, F., 2014. Independent review of the national institute of forensic science. Review.
Wilson-Wilde, L., 2017. The future of the national institute of forensic science – implications for Australia and New Zealand. Australian Journal of Forensic Sciences 1–8.

SECTION 3

An Introduction to the Standards Applicable to the Management, Practice, and Delivery of Forensic Science

3.1 INTRODUCTION

This section introduces, briefly describes, and sets out the relationships between all the standards that might apply to the provision of forensic science of sufficient quality to meet stakeholder needs, in particular, those of law enforcement and justice. Conformance to these standards assures that one or more of the following requirements are met:

- a competent organization
- a competent individual
- valid procedures

To recap, ISO (ISO, 9000) defines quality as:

> *[T]he degree to which a set of inherent characteristics of an object fulfills requirements. ©ISO 2015 — All rights reserved*

In this work the quality is degree to which forensic science is fit-for-purpose and meets the needs of its stakeholders particularly law enforcement and justice. Those inherent characteristics lie within the competence of the organization, the competence of the individual, discussed in 1.3.4, and the validity of the methods and procedures employed, discussed in 1.4.2.

Again, ISO defines competence as

> *[T]he ability to apply knowledge and skills to achieve intended results. ©ISO 2015 — All rights reserved*

in the context of forensic science, the intended result is scientific information that might be relied on by law enforcement and justice.

In very general terms, standards set out the competencies required and how those competencies might be demonstrated.

The standards introduced in this section collectively constitute the quality standards framework, which needs to be reflected in the documented quality management system (QMS) of a forensic science provider.

Most of these standards are consensus standards. As detailed in Section 2, standards development and setting take place as follows: the need for a standard is first identified

Quality Management in Forensic Science
ISBN 978-0-12-805416-1, https://doi.org/10.1016/B978-0-12-805416-1.00003-7

by the stakeholder community and a development body is tasked with drafting a standard to meet the need. With input from stakeholders, the draft is revised until it is deemed fit-for-purpose. The standard, essentially a list of requirements, is then published and adopted by organizations wishing to demonstrate conformance. To avoid potential conflicts of interest, standards development, conformity assessment, and service provision should be undertaken by separate and independent bodies.

3.1.1 Hierarchy of Standards

In categorizing standards, a hierarchical model is useful and employed in this work. Generic standards applying to organizations performing particular activities are at the highest level. The most appropriate example is ISO/IEC 17025:2017 "General requirements for the competence of testing and calibration laboratories." One step below is standards that adapt and interpret the highest-level standard to meet the needs of a particular industry or field of application; in this work, forensic science. An appropriate example is International Laboratory Accreditation Cooperation (ILAC) Guide 19:2002 "Guidelines for Forensic Science Laboratories." Lower in the hierarchy are standards that address the specifics of the forensic science process (scene examination, laboratory examination, interpretation, and reporting). An appropriate example is the Australian Standard AS5388:2012 "Forensic Analysis," introduced later in 3.4.1. At the lowest level are procedural standards. These standards detail the actual methods and procedures employed by a forensic science provider which conform to the higher-level standards and in so doing produce scientific information that meets stakeholder needs. Procedural standards are the subject of accreditation. For the purpose of this work, in order to provide a systematic framework and more clearly reveal relationships, the standards have been classified into four levels as set out in Table 3.1.

The following example illustrates the hierarchy. A higher-level standard might state that in recovering samples, contamination should be avoided without specifying the contamination avoidance procedures to be employed in a particular set of circumstances. The standard at the next level of detail might specify that barrier clothing must be worn, and that the clothing must be quality assured as contamination free. The final procedural level might be instructions as to how to don the barrier clothing. A further example is given in Fig. 3.1.

Level 1 standards discussed in this section are listed in Table 3.2.

Table 3.1 Hierarchy of Standards

	Level	Example	Activity
1	Activity	ISO/IEC 17020:2012	Crime Scene Examination
2	Interpretation	UKAS RG201	Guidance on accreditation
3	Forensic Process	AS 5388.1	Sample Recovery
4	Procedure	Accredited method	Recovery

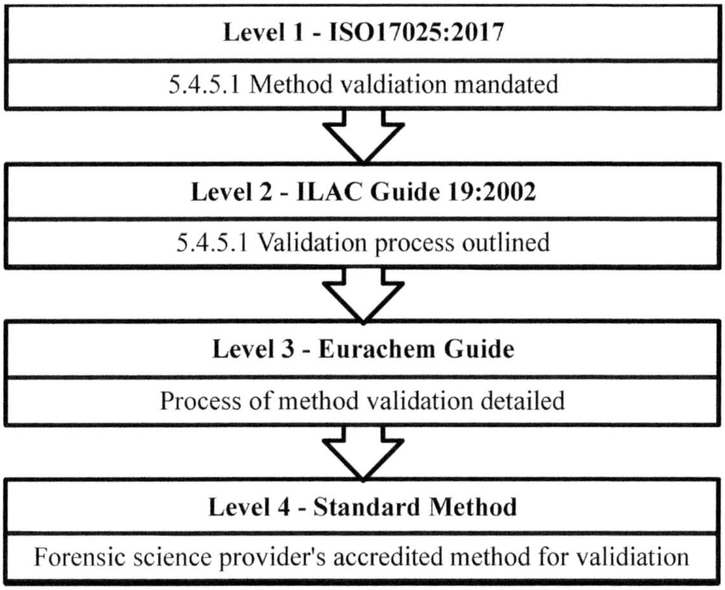

Figure 3.1 Hierarchy of standards with examples.

Table 3.2 Level 1 Standards

Standard	Title	Pages
ISO 9001	Quality management systems—requirements	19
ISO/IEC 17025	General requirements for the competence of testing and calibration laboratories	36
ISO/IEC Guide 98-3	Uncertainty of measurement—Part 3: Guide to the expression of uncertainty in measurement (GUM:1995)	120
ISO/IEC 17034	General requirements for the competence of reference material producers	24
ISO/IEC 17043	Conformity assessment—General requirements for proficiency testing	39
ISO/IEC 17020	Conformity assessment—Requirements for the operation of various types of bodies performing inspection	18
ISO/IEC 17011	Conformity assessment—General requirements for accreditation bodies accrediting conformity assessment bodies	21
ISO/IEC 17024	Conformity assessment—General requirements for bodies operating certification of persons	21
ISO 15189	Medical laboratories—Requirements for quality and competence	53

3.1.2 The Risks and Impact of Overdocumentation

Although all standards above the procedural level aim to be nonprescriptive and outcome-based, the amount of detail needed to be included in a standard is such that prescription tends to increase as the hierarchy is descended. Higher-level standards set out what needs to be done (aims and objectives) and lower-level standards increasingly set out how it should be done (how those aims and objectives can be achieved).

With increasing level of detail comes increasing complexity which, in turn, increases the risk of nonconformance. The objective, introduced in 1.3.10, of reducing unnecessary detail and simplifying quality management, which is reflected in the 2015 edition of ISO 9001, is lost in the plethora of overdocumented standards that exist today, many of them covering similar ground.

Since its introduction in 1999, ISO/IEC 17025 "General requirements for the competence of testing and calibration laboratories" has become the most widely adopted standard by forensic science providers. Although principally a standard for laboratories, it is also used to accredit organizations undertaking crime scene examination, particularly in Australasia.

To better interpret and adapt ISO/IEC 17025 for application in forensic science, a number of organizations have produced guides and supplements. These documents will be introduced in this chapter.

At the time of writing [December 2017] ISO, through technical committee (TC) 272, is developing a set of standards, based on the Australian forensic science standard AS5388, discussed later in 3.4.2, as a supplement which presumably will replace or at least obviate the need for some of the various supplements and guides currently in place.

3.1.3 ISO/IEC 17025 and/or ISO/IEC 17020

Although ISO/IEC 17025 was and, to some extent—particularly in Australasia, remains the standard for crime scene examination, the critical role of crime scene examination in the forensic science process and the consequent risks associated with this step, discussed in 6.6, was considered such that a more appropriate standard was sought by European providers. In 2006, the European Network of Forensic Science Institutes (ENFSI) and European Co-operation for Accreditation (EA) jointly selected ISO/IEC 17020:1998 "Conformity assessment—requirement for the operation of various types of bodies performing inspection" as the most appropriate standard. For the purpose of interpreting and applying this standard to crime scene examination, EA published EA-5/03 "Guidance for the implementation of ISO/IEC 17020 in the field of crime scene activity" in 2008 and in 2014 ILAC published Guide 19:08/2014 "Modules in a Forensic Science Process".

Accreditation of crime scene examination to ISO/IEC 17020 has been available since 2011; but at the time of writing [December 2017], there has been little uptake.

In summary then, the standard to which forensic science providers offering mainly laboratory-based activities involving tests should be accredited is ISO/IEC 17025: 2017. Forensic science providers offering crime scene examination involving inspections should be accredited to ISO/IEC 17020:2012. However, even at a crime scene if an instrument is used to make a measurement the appropriate standard for that activity is ISO/IEC 17025. Accrediting bodies will accredit to a mixture of the two standards where required but ISO/IEC 17025 has greater utility than ISO/IEC 7020 and this might partly explain the low number of forensic science providers currently [December 2017] accredited to ISO/IEC 17020 for crime scene examination.

Both these standards include a management section which broadly meets the requirements of ISO 9001 and a section or sections that set out the requirements for a calibration or testing laboratory and an inspection body.

3.1.4 Use of Methods Outside the Scope of Accreditation

Stakeholders should look carefully at the scope of any claimed accreditation to ensure the methods and procedures employed by the provider lie within that scope. The scope of accreditation is defined by the methods accredited. A provider may properly make a general claim to be accredited. However, that accreditation will be for specific methods used for a specific purpose, e.g., a test to determine the amount of alcohol in blood. Using a test method that lies outside the scope of accreditation renders the claim to accreditation false. Circumstances may arise in the practice of forensic science that requires the use of a method which lies outside the scope of accreditation. In that case, the method must be fully validated. The use of a method outside the scope of accreditation should be disclosed. This requirement for disclosure is discussed in the responsibilities and duties of an expert witness in 3.4.7.

Determining the scope of accreditation is sometimes difficult. Some publicly available scopes, particularly those of ANAB (ANSI-ASQ National Accreditation Board) and NATA (National Association of Testing Authorities) accredited providers, are vague. In which case the only way of determining whether or not the method used to produce the evidence adduced lies within the scope of accreditation is to ask the provider or the forensic scientist presenting that evidence. This issue is further discussed in 9 [Current issues].

Thus, accreditation may not guarantee conformance of scientific evidence with the standard. In addition, fourth party, independent assessment of conformity may reveal nonconformances that the accreditation body is not aware of.

3.1.5 Interpretation and Application

A standard may be considered simply as a list of requirements to be met, technically "provisions". However, ISO distinguishes between the contents of a standard and defines "requirement" as follows:

> *[An] expression in the content of a document conveying objectively verifiable criteria to be fulfilled and from which no deviation is permitted if compliance with the document is to be claimed.*
>
> ***ISO/IEC (2016). ©ISO/IEC 2016 — All rights reserved***

In simple terms, "requirements" are mandatory; they must be met for conformity and are identified by the verbal form "shall." According to ISO, the contents of a standard are collectively termed "provisions" and include "statements," "instructions," "recommendations," and "requirements." Only requirements are mandatory. Nonmandatory provisions are identified by the verbal forms "should," "may," and "can."

In ISO/IEC 17025 and ISO/IEC 17020

- "shall" indicates a requirement
- "should" indicates a recommendation
- "may" indicates a permission, and
- "can" indicates a possibility or a capability. ©ISO/IEC 2017 — All rights reserved

The interpretation and application of standards, in general, and ISO/IEC 17025 and ISO/IEC 17020, in particular, depends on how the mandatory requirements are met and the degree to which the accrediting body "enforces" the nonmandatory provisions of the standard.

It should be noted that in the case of ISO/IEC 17025 and ISO/IEC 17020, most of the provisions are requirements and are therefore mandatory.

At this juncture, it is convenient to introduce and explain the terms normative and informative. According to ISO, a documented standard is composed of elements (ISO/IEC, 2016). Among those elements are normative and informative elements. A normative element is one

> *... that describes the scope of the document or sets out provisions ©ISO/IEC 2016 — All rights reserved*

and an informative element is

> *... intended to assist the understanding or use of the document or provides contextual information about its content, background or relationship with other documents." ©ISO/IEC 2016 — All rights reserved*

It is important to emphasize that among the normative elements are nonmandatory provisions. However, in the case of "normative references" these are, to some specified degree, "requirements" and mandatory.

3.1.6 Access to Standards

Readers should be aware that standard development and publishing bodies tightly control copyright. All quotations and other materials reproduced in this work are published with the permission of the copyright holders. Readers wishing to quote from this work will need to obtain permission to do so. Those wishing to inspect standards may need to purchase copies. The fact that many of the standards applicable to forensic science lie behind a pay wall is an issue which will be explored in Section 7.

ISO provides an online browsing platform which allows free access to an abstract, the introductory sections, and the table of contents for each standard. This information may be sufficient to meet the needs of most readers.

3.2 LEVEL 1 STANDARDS—ISO (INTERNATIONAL ORGANIZATION FOR STANDARDIZATION) STANDARDS (SEE TABLE 3.2)

3.2.1 ISO 9001:2015—The Competence of Organizations

ISO 9001:2015 "Quality management systems—Requirements" is a fundamental standard, conformance to which demonstrates an organization's ability to meet stakeholder needs and to continually improve. As mentioned in the introduction and explained in 3.2.2 and 3.2.3, organizations accredited to ISO/IEC 17025:2017 or ISO/IEC 17020: 2012, or both, conform to the quality management standard ISO 9001.

ISO 9001 is the basis for the management requirements of ISO/IEC 17025 the most widely adopted standard in forensic science and ISO/IEC 17020, the requirements are specified in section 8 of both standards.

When considering the quality of forensic science provided, ISO 9001:2015 offers more detail for conformity assessment, i.e., assessing whether or not the forensic science provider is sufficiently competent to meet the needs of its stakeholders, particularly law enforcement and justice.

This standard has been recently revised and the latest edition, ISO 9001:2015, is now in force. The previous edition 2008 will be withdrawn in 2018.

The standard has 28 pages and is available for purchase from ISO at a cost of 138 CHF[1] [December 2017]. The structure of the 2015 edition differs significantly from its predecessors. The so-called high-level structure, set out below, will gradually be applied by ISO to all management system standards:

1. Scope
2. Normative references
3. Terms and definitions
4. Context of the organization
5. Leadership
6. Planning
7. Support

[1] The cost of purchase from ISO HQ in Swiss Francs (CHF) is given. ISO standards are also available for purchase from national ISO bodies in local currency where a local sales tax might apply.

8. Operation
9. Performance evaluation
10. Improvement

ISO has not demanded that QMSs compliant with the 2008 edition be changed to conform to the new structure. However, the greater flexibility afforded by the 2015 edition will encourage organizations to transition as speedily as resources permit. Indeed certifying bodies have been instructed to audit against the new standard at the earliest opportunity.

It is important to be aware that ISO 9001 is part of the so-called ISO 9000 "family" listed below:

- ISO 9001:2015—sets out the requirements of a quality management system
- ISO 9000:2015—covers the basic concepts and language
- ISO 9004:2009—focuses on how to make a quality management system more efficient and effective
- ISO 19011:2011—sets out guidance on internal and external audits of quality management systems.

ISO 9001:2015 specifies the criteria for a QMS and is the only standard in the "family" that an organization can be certified[2] to. According to ISO, this International Standard is based on the quality management principles described in ISO 9000. The quality management principles are as follows:

- customer focus,
- leadership,
- engagement of people,
- process approach,
- improvement,
- evidence-based decision-making, and
- relationship management.

According to ISO:

> *Using ISO 9001:2015 helps ensure that customers get consistent, good quality products and services, which in turn brings many business benefits. ©ISO/IEC 2015 – All rights reserved*

"The potential benefits to an organization of implementing a QMS based on this International Standard are:

1. the ability to consistently provide products and services that meet customer and applicable statutory and regulatory requirements;
2. facilitating opportunities to enhance customer satisfaction;

[2] Organizations are certified as conforming to ISO 9001 and not accredited. The difference between certification and accreditation is explained in 1.3.5.

3. addressing risks and opportunities associated with its context and objectives;
4. the ability to demonstrate conformity to specified quality management system requirements." ©ISO/IEC 2015 — All rights reserved

3.2.2 ISO/IEC 17025:2017 "General Requirements for the Competence of Testing and Calibration Laboratories"

ISO/IEC 17025 is not a standard which specifically applies to forensic science providers, hence the need for interpretive documents such as ILAC Guide 19:2002, which is introduced later in 3.3.

Since it was first published ISO/IEC 17025 has become the most widely adopted standard in forensic science. Most forensic science providers in the developed world are now accredited to ISO/IEC 17025. The development of this standard is charted in Section 4.

The first edition of this international standard was published in 1999. It was reviewed without a change in 2010 and in line with ISO's policy of five yearly reviews it was recently reviewed and revised. The latest edition was published on the 29th of November 2017. It will now be for member states to implement the standard and there will be a transition period of around 3 years to allow accredited providers to conform to the new edition.

The 2017 edition differs from the previous edition in structureand follows the pattern of ISO/IEC 17020:2012, discussed next. It introduces sections on impartiality and confidentially. The requirement for impartiality is given particular importance; in addition to competence impartiality is required.

Impartiality is defined in Section 3.1 of the standard as the "presence of objectivity" and the notes further explain

> *Objectivity is understood to mean that conflicts of interest do not exist or are resolved so as not to adversely influence subsequent activities of the laboratory*

and

> *Other terms that are useful in conveying the element of impartiality are freedom from conflicts of interests, freedom from bias, lack of prejudice, neutrality, fairness, open-mindedness, even-handedness, detachment and balance. ©ISO/IEC 2017 — All rights reserved*

Given the close relationship between some forensic science providers and law enforcement agents/prosecuting authorities, meeting this requirement might be a challenge. Extra safeguards might be needed to demonstrate impartiality.

The new edition introduces the "risk-based thinking" approach of ISO 9001:2015. ISO/IEC 17025:2017 requires the provider to plan and implement actions to address risks and opportunities aimed at improving the effectiveness of the organization.

The standard now has four main sections. The first sets out general requirements with a focus on impartiality and confidentiality. The remaining sections are listed in the structure below.

The standard contains the requirements for laboratories to enable them to demonstrate that they operate competently and can generate valid results.

The standard is available for purchase from ISO at a cost of 138 CHF [December 2017], has 36 pages, and its structure is as follows:

1. Scope
2. Normative references
3. Terms and definitions
4. General requirements
5. Structural requirements
6. Resource requirements
7. Process requirements
8. Management requirements

Annexes

A. Metrological traceability (informative)
B. Management system (informative)

Bibliography

ISO/IEC 17025:2017 specifies the general requirements for the competence, impartiality, and consistent operation of laboratories.

It covers testing performed using standard methods, nonstandard methods, and laboratory-developed methods.

The standard is for use by forensic science providers in developing their management system for quality and administrative and technical operations. Customers, regulatory authorities, and accreditation bodies may also use it in confirming or recognizing the competence of forensic science providers.

Accreditation to ISO/IEC 17025 not only provides authoritative assurance of the technical competence of a laboratory to undertake specified analyses but also reviews particular aspects relevant to forensic science, for example, continuity of evidence, management of case files, and storage of exhibits. Accreditation determines the competence of staff, the validity and suitability of methods, the appropriateness of equipment and facilities, and the ongoing assurance and confidence in outcomes through internal quality control.

The validation of test methods, and procedures for sampling, handling, and transportation, is a key component of the technical requirements of ISO/IEC 17025 and one of the three top-level requirements: a competent organization, competent individuals, and valid methods.

The standard itself provides much informative detail on how methods might be validated. The previous edition included a definition of validation, now given in ISO 9000: 2015 at 3.8.13:

> *[T]he confirmation through the provision of objective evidence that the requirements for specific intended use or application are fulfilled ©ISO/IEC 2015 — All rights reserved*

i.e., the method or procedure meets stakeholder needs, particularly those of law enforcement and justice.

Validation is always a balance between costs, risks, and technical possibilities. A highly accurate result may not be required by the customer. Law enforcement agencies are often satisfied with a categorical result[3]: "yes," "no," or "inconclusive." The standard requires validation to be as extensive as necessary to meet the needs of the given application.

Sections 6 and 7 of the standard document the requirements for competent personnel, method selection and validation, measurement uncertainty, and metrological traceability. Section 7 cover sampling and reporting.

Providers accredited to ISO/IEC 17025 require a means of demonstrating the technical competence of personnel (6.2), procedures for ensuring that all measurements are traceable to the SI system of units (6.5), the validity of methods (7.2.2), and for evaluating the uncertainty of measurement (7.6). ISO provides standards which can help providers meet these requirements: ISO/IEC Guide 98, ISO/IEC 17034, and ISO/IEC 17043. These standards might be considered a subdivision of Level 1 and are introduced later in 3.2.2.1 to 3.2.2.3.

Conforming to ISO/IEC 17025 is a challenge and continual improvement is expected and essential to maintain conformance. Conformance is also demanding on resources. Major forensic science providers estimate that quality costs around 15% of turnover (House of Commons Science and Technology Committee, 2011).

Accreditation is granted for a period that varies with the accrediting body but should be no more than 4 years. During that period, the accrediting body should conduct a risk-based audit once a year and aim to cover the entire QMS within the accreditation cycle. In addition to annual external audits, sometimes called surveillances, accredited organizations are required to conduct internal audits according to a plan agreed with the accrediting body. Through these audits, which invariably identify both risks and opportunities for improvement, together with management review and customer feedback, continual improvement is promoted and achieved. An accredited provider must record risks and opportunities for improvement together with any actions taken. Root cause analysis might be required when the nonconformance could result in the issue of nonconforming produce or service; in forensic science that would be unreliable or misleading scientific information.

Accrediting bodies can and do withdraw accreditation when a major nonconformance is discovered and corrective actions have not been implemented (The Detail, 2011). Accrediting bodies list organizations that have had accreditation withdrawn or are otherwise under sanction.

[3] The weakness of this form of reporting is explained in Section 7.

Most forensic science providers now consider accreditation essential. However, accredited providers that do not use quality management as a means of continually improving performance and adopt a minimalist approach to maintaining conformance are at risk of underperforming. Therefore, accreditation is not an absolute guarantee of competent performance and the use of valid methods. Organizations might be accredited but not conform to the standards.

Accreditation bodies must conform to their own standard ISO/IEC 17011, considered later in 3.2.4. However, it is clear that the competence of accrediting bodies varies (Schecter, 2011; Alexander, 2015) as does their interpretation as to how to apply the provisions of ISO/IEC 17025 to forensic science providers. These factors militate against the aims of standardization and harmonization.

As mentioned above, a number of other ISO standards support accreditation to ISO/IEC 17025; ISO/IEC Guide 98-3, ISO/IEC 17034, and ISO/IEC 17043. These standards are discussed next.

3.2.2.1 ISO/IEC Guide 98—3:2008 "Uncertainty of Measurement—Part 3: Guide to the Expression of Uncertainty in Measurement (GUM, 1995)[4]"

An estimate of measurement uncertainty provides a range in which the true result is believed to lie. When reporting the result of a measurement, some quantitative indication of the quality of the result must be given so that those who use it can assess its reliability. Without such an indication, measurement results cannot be compared, either among themselves or with reference values given in a specification or standard. Evaluating and expressing uncertainty is the generally accepted procedure for characterizing the quality of a result of a measurement.

ISO/IEC Guide 93-3 is a fundamental standard in metrology, introduced in 1.4, and the importance of this standard merits some background information. Recognizing the lack of international consensus on the expression of uncertainty in measurement, the world's highest authority in metrology, the Comité International des Poids et Mesures (CIPM), tasked the Bureau International des Poids et Mesures (BIPM) with addressing the problem in conjunction with the national standards laboratories and to make a recommendation.

The task of developing a detailed guide was referred by the CIPM to ISO, as ISO better reflected the needs arising from the broad interests of industry and commerce.

The group responsible for coordinating development of a guide led by ISO were the International Electrotechnical Commission (IEC), the partner of ISO in worldwide standardization; the CIPM and the International Organization of Legal Metrology (OIML), the two worldwide metrology organizations; the International Union of

[4] For a less technical introduction to uncertainty of measurement see the UKAS Guide M3003 introduced in 3.3.3.2.

Pure and Applied Chemistry (IUPAC) and the International Union of Pure and Applied Physics, the two international unions that represent chemistry and physics; and the International Federation of Clinical Chemistry.

A working group composed of experts from BIPM, IEC, ISO, and OIML were given the following terms of reference:

To develop a guidance document based upon the recommendation of the BIPM Working Group on the Statement of Uncertainties which provides rules on the expression of measurement uncertainty for use within standardization, calibration, laboratory accreditation, and metrology services;

The purpose of such guidance is

— to promote full information on how uncertainty statements are arrived at;

— to provide a basis for the international comparison of measurement results.

That guidance document is ISO/IEC Guide 98–3:2008 "Uncertainty of Measurement—Part 3: Guide to the expression of uncertainty in measurement (GUM 1995)"

Most forensic science providers at some stage of the forensic science process will use an instrument to make a measurement. As explained above and in 1.4.6, no measurement result is complete without an estimate of uncertainty. Conformance to ISO/IEC 17025 requires at least a reasonable estimation of uncertainty (7.6.2). Measurements in forensic science include blood and breath alcohol, the quantity and concentration of illicit substances and their metabolites, the dimensions of items such as the length of the barrel of a firearm, and the refractive index and density of glass. Uncertainty of measurement is also important in forensic science when thresholds have a significant impact, e.g., in blood or breath alcohol, in certain DNA mixture deconvolution algorithms and more generally detection limits.

ISO/IEC 17025 (7.6.2) does make clear that the rigor of estimation of uncertainty depends on the method, stakeholder needs, and the impact of the result. The full rigors of ISO Guide 98-3:2008 will not apply in all circumstances. Where a qualitative result is all that is required, e.g., of chemical identity, an estimate of uncertainty might not be necessary. The uncertainty associated with qualitative results is discussed in Section 7.

Contributors to uncertainty include:

- sampling—selecting a representative sample of a population;
- sample preparation effects—extraction, digestion;
- the measuring instrument—drift, systematic error, random error, noise;
- the item being measured—homogeneity, stability, matrix;
- operator effects—precise but inaccurate or vice versa;
- environment—temperature, pressure, humidity; and
- "imported" uncertainties—of calibrants and reference materials (RMs).

Where there is a need to estimate uncertainty with a degree of accuracy, ISO/IEC Guide 98-3:2008 provides assistance in a complex subject area. Reflecting that complexity, the ISO/IEC Guide 98 comes in five parts; only Part 3 is of relevance in this section of the work.

The standard has 120 pages and its structure is as follows:

1. Scope
2. Definitions
3. Basic concepts
4. Evaluating standard uncertainty
5. Determining combined standard uncertainty
6. Determining expanded uncertainty
7. Reporting uncertainty

Annexes

- **A.** Recommendation for working group and CIPM
- **B.** General metrological terms
- **C.** Basic statistical terms and concepts
- **D.** "True" value, error, and uncertainty
- **E.** Motivation and basis fro Recommendation INC-1 (1980)[5]
- **F.** Practical guidance on evaluating uncertainty components
- **G.** Degrees of freedom and levels if confidence
- **H.** Examples
- **J.** Glossary of principle symbols[6]

Bibliography

ISO/IEC Guide 98-3:2008 is a reissue of the 1995 version of the GUM, with minor corrections. The earlier document now revised and published as JCGM 104:2009 is freely available for download (JCGM, 2009). ISO/IEC Guide 98-3:2008 is available for purchase at a cost of 198 CHF at the time of writing [December 2017].

The ISO/IEC guide establishes general rules for evaluating and expressing uncertainty in measurement that can be followed at various levels of accuracy. The principles of this guide are intended to be applicable to

- maintaining quality control and quality assurance in production;
- complying with and enforcing laws and regulations;
- conducting basic research, and applied research and development, in science and engineering;
- calibrating standards and instruments and performing tests throughout a national measurement system to achieve traceability to national standards; and
- developing, maintaining, and comparing international and national physical reference standards, including RMs.

[5] Expression of experimental uncertainty (BIPM, 1980).

[6] The guide records this as Annex J.

The titles of the other parts of ISO Guide 98 are as follows:

Part 1 Introduction to the expression of uncertainty in measurement

Part 2 Concepts and basic principles

Part 4 Role of measurement uncertainty in conformity assessment

Readers wishing to learn more about these other parts of ISO Guide 98 should use ISO's online browsing platform.

3.2.2.2 ISO/IEC 17034:2016 "General Requirements for the Competence of Reference Material Producers"

This is the second of the three standards that support accreditation to ISO/IEC 17025. This standard applies to the production of all RMs (reference materials)\, including certified RMs, for metrological traceability and comparability. The standard specifies general requirements for the competence and consistent operation of RM producers. It specifies general requirements in accordance with which an RM producer has to demonstrate that it operates. It is intended to be used as part of the general quality assurance procedures of the RM producer.

RMs are used in all stages of the measurement process, including validation, calibration, and quality control. They are also used in interlaboratory comparisons for method validation and for assessing laboratory proficiency. Forensic science providers accredited to ISO/IEC 17025 should be using RMs produced in conformance to ISO/IEC 17034 where these are available. The scientific and technical competence of RM producers is a basic requirement for ensuring the quality of RMs.

The standard is available for purchase from ISO at a cost of 118 CHF. It has 24 pages, and its structure conforms to that now required by ISO Committee of Conformance Assessment (CASCO) which is as follows:

1. Scope
2. Normative references
3. Terms and definitions
4. General requirements
5. Structural requirements
6. Resource requirements
7. Technical and production requirements
8. Management system requirements

The use of RMs enables the transfer of the values of measured or assigned properties between testing and measurement laboratories. Such materials are widely used, e.g., for the calibration of measuring equipment, such as evidential breath testing instruments and for the evaluation or validation of measurement procedures. In certain cases, RMs enable properties to be expressed conveniently in arbitrary units.

3.2.2.3 *ISO/IEC 17043:2010 "Conformity Assessment—General Requirements for Proficiency Testing"*

This is the third of the three standards which support accreditation to ISO/IEC 17025. It applies to the providers of proficiency test (PT) schemes. The successful participation in PTs is an important demonstration of competence and conformance to ISO/IEC 17025. Optimally, PT providers should be accredited to ISO/IEC 17043.

According to ISO, ISO/IEC 17043:2010 specifies general requirements for the competence of providers of proficiency testing schemes and for the development and operation of proficiency testing schemes. This is a generic standard applying to all types of proficiency testing schemes. It can be used as a basis for specific technical requirements for particular fields of application.

In forensic science, proficiency testing involves the use of interlaboratory comparisons to evaluate the performance of providers for the determination of performance for specific tests or measurements or inspections and to monitor continuing performance. Interlaboratory comparisons are an essential element in evaluating the performance characteristics of a method, i.e., method validation. PTs may also be used to identify areas for improvement in staff training.

The standard is available for purchase from ISO at a cost of 158 CHF [December 2017]. It has 39 pages and the following structure:

1. Scope
2. Normative references
3. Terms and definitions
4. Technical requirements
5. Management requirements

Annexes

- **A.** Types of proficiency testing
- **B.** Statistical methods for proficiency testing
- **C.** Selection and use of proficiency testing

The management requirements are those of ISO 9001:2008. The standard was reviewed in 2015 without revision.

The need for ongoing confidence in laboratory performance is not only essential for laboratories and their customers but also for other stakeholders, such as regulators, laboratory accreditation bodies, and other organizations that specify requirements for laboratories. ISO/IEC 17011, discussed later in 3.2.4, requires accreditation bodies to take account of provider's participation and performance in proficiency testing.

ISO/IEC 17025:2017 (7.7) requires quality control procedures to be in place for monitoring the validity of tests and suggest that such monitoring might include participation in interlaboratory proficiency testing programs. PTs conforming to this standard would be a means of demonstrating that validity.

ISO/IEC 17020:2012, discussed later in 3.2.3, makes no mention of PTs but the ILAC Guide:19 08/2014 (3.9), discussed in 3.3.2.2, suggests PTs as an ongoing means of monitoring performance.

ILAC Guide:19:2002 (5.9.1B), discussed in 3.3.2.1, recommends participation in proficiency testing programs as a means of monitoring performance.

While not always enforced, participation in appropriate PTs is an essential element in demonstrating competence and in fully validating methods prior to use, as set out in ILAC Guide 19:2002 and prior to reporting as in ILAC Guide 19:08/2014.

Proficiency testing involving the use of interlaboratory comparisons is essential for the full validation of methods. Where a method has not been the subject of interlaboratory comparisons then it cannot be considered fully validated.

Litigators should ensure that where an expert relies on a result or measurement, the method employed has been validated using a PT optimally provided by an accredited PT scheme provider.

3.2.3 ISO/IEC 17020:2012 "Conformity Assessment—Requirements for the Operation of Various Types of Bodies Performing Inspection"

In forensic science, this standard applies to and assures the competence of organizations providing crime scene examination, their employees, and the validity of their methods. It is perhaps the second most important standard in forensic science after ISO/IEC 17025.

According to ISO, ISO/IEC 17020:2012 specifies the requirements for the competence of bodies performing inspection and for the impartiality and consistency of their inspection activities. It applies to inspection bodies of type A, B, or C,[7] as defined in the standard, and it applies to any stage of inspection.

Inspection is defined in ISO 9000:2015 at 3.11.7 as

[The] determination of conformity to specified requirements. ©ISO 2015 – All rights reserved

Inspection might be more broadly defined as to examine closely, to test an individual activity against established standards for that activity, and/or to make a comparison. Inspection involves examination, measurements, testing, and comparison of materials or items. The process includes examination of an object and determination of its conformity with specific requirements on the basis of professional judgment. The reliance on professional judgment is a distinguishing feature of ISO/IEC 17020. In these respects, ISO/IEC 17020 is also considered suitable for application to feature-comparison disciplines such as fingerprints and toolmarks.

[7] An explanation of these categories is given in Annex A of the standard. "A" is the most independent of inspection bodies and "C" the least. Crime scene examination units under the direct operational control of law enforcement fall into category "C" and require special measures to meet the requirements of independence and impartiality. This is discussed later in 3.3.3.1 [UKAS Guide RG201].

Crime scene, fingerprint, footwear, and firearms examination, etc., are all types of inspection activities in which comparisons are made against defined criteria or a specification, and a conclusion is drawn based on professional judgment. Using fingerprints as an example, an unknown print is compared against a suspect's print and then a judgment is made as to the degree of resemblance between the two.

The standard has 18 pages and is available for purchase from ISO at a cost of 88 CHF [December 2017]. The structure of the standard conforms to that now required by ISO/CASCO which is as follows:

1. Scope
2. Normative references
3. Terms and definitions
4. General requirements
5. Structural requirements
6. Resource requirements
7. Process requirements
8. Management System Requirements

Annex A Independence requirements for inspection bodies

Annex B Optional elements of inspection reports

Bibliography

Among the general requirements of this standards are the impartiality and independence of the inspection body. The standard requires a documented record of conformance.

Impartiality is defined in 3.8 of the standard and is the same as ISO/IEC 17025; the "presence of objectivity" and again the notes further explain:

> *Objectivity means that conflicts of interest do not exist or are resolved so as not to adversely influence subsequent activities of the inspection body.*

and

> *Other terms that are useful in conveying the element of impartiality are: independence, freedom from conflict of interests, freedom from bias, lack of prejudice, neutrality, fairness, open-mindedness, even-handedness, detachment, [and] balance. ©ISO/IEC 2012 – All rights reserved*

In simple terms, an inspection body and the inspector employed must be demonstrably and unequivocally free of undue influence when conducting an inspection and reporting results. Where crime scene examination bodies are under operational control of law enforcement agencies, extra safeguards are needed to demonstrate independence and impartiality.

The standard recognizes that inspection activities can overlap with testing and calibration activities. Measurement is considered in 6.2.6ff of the standard. Measurement equipment having a significant influence on the result of an inspection must be calibrated.

Calibration is discussed in 1.4.7.1 of this work under metrological traceability. Calibration is a process that establishes the relationship between the response of an instrument and the quantity being measured and relies on measurement standards or calibrants for accuracy. Including measurement in ISO/IEC 17020 might suggest that this standard can accredit measurements. This is not the case as the ILAC Guide P15:07/2016 makes clear in 6.2.7; where metrological traceability is required and testing is performed, ISO/IEC 17025 is the applicable standard.

Accreditation to ISO/IEC 17020 for crime scene activities has been available since 2011. At the time of writing [December 2017], the only accredited provider in the United Kingdom is a private company and in the United States some local police units. Therefore, the operational effectiveness of crime scene inspection bodies in conformance to this standard is difficult to assess as is the effect on performance and meeting stakeholder needs.

A reason that might partly explain the poor take up is that in Australasia organizations conducting crime scene inspections are, and have been for some time, accredited to ISO/IEC 17025 and there is no plan to introduce ISO/IEC 17020. With the introduction of the Australian Standard AS5388 that applies to the forensic science process, discussed later in 3.4.1, and its likely conversion to an ISO standard, there may be even less incentive to adopt ISO/IEC 17020. In addition, any activity that requires a measurement to be made at a crime scene will need to be accredited ISO 17025. Finally, accreditation bodies have accredited crimes scene activities to ISO/IEC 17025 and, if the customer requires it, will continue to do so.

3.2.4 ISO/IEC 17011:2017 "Conformity Assessment—General Requirements for Accreditation Bodies Accrediting Conformity Assessment Bodies"

This standard applies to accrediting bodies that accredit forensic science providers. In terms of quality management, forensic science providers are conformity assessment bodies (CABs) providing the following conformity assessment services: testing, inspection, personnel certification, product certification, and calibration.

Conformance with this standard meets the requirements for the accrediting body to be evaluated for Mutual Recognition Arrangements (MRAs) through ILAC.

The standard is available for purchase from ISO at a cost of 138 CHF [December 2017]. It has 29 pages, and the structure of this latest edition is similar to that of ISO/IEC 17025 and 17020 and is as follows:

1. Scope
2. Normative references
3. Terms and definitions
4. General requirements
5. Structural requirements

6. Resource requirements
7. Process requirements
8. Information requirements
9. Management system requirements

Annex A—Knowledge and skills for performing accreditation activities

Bibliography

Accreditation bodies having an MRA with ILAC agree to maintain conformity with the current version of ISO/IEC 17011 and to regularly submit themselves and their own QMSs to peer review and evaluation. By complying with ISO/IEC 17011, accreditation bodies demonstrate that they are capable of accreditation testing and/or calibration laboratories to the ISO/IEC 17025 standard and inspection bodies to ISO/IEC 17020. In essence, the ILAC arrangement guarantees that test results are mutually acceptable between different governmental and regulatory organizations on regional, national, and international levels, and that these test results meet the same **minimum** standards for quality regardless of the provider's accreditation body. Each member of the agreement recognizes other members' accredited laboratory as if they themselves had performed the test, calibration, or inspection because the MRA ensures that each laboratory is actually complying with the same **minimum** standards. [emphasis added]

The practical effect of an MRA is that a forensic science provider accredited to ISO/IEC 17025 in one jurisdiction is providing services to the same standard as a similarly accredited provider in another jurisdiction, supporting the aim of "tested or inspected once, accepted everywhere". This aids the cross-border cooperation in crime investigation as discussed in 1.4.7.3.

3.2.5 ISO/IEC 17024:2014 "Conformity Assessment—General Requirements for Bodies Operating Certification of Persons"

This standard applies to organizations that certify individuals as competent. One of the characteristic functions of a certification body for persons is to conduct an examination which uses objective criteria to measure competence.

As this standard has yet to be adopted by the forensic science industry, it is mentioned in passing and for information. However, given the number of bodies that certify individuals as competent, particularly in the United States (see 3.4.3), it is perhaps surprising that this standard has yet to be adopted. It does seem odd that as the regulatory framework supporting forensic science has been assembled this standard has been overlooked. Although, at the time of writing [December 2017], the situation is about to change with the US FSAB (Forensic Specialities Accreditation Board), discussed later in 3.4.4.3, in the process of adopting the standard.

According to ISO, ISO/IEC 17024:2012 contains principles and requirements for a body certifying persons against specific requirements and includes the development and maintenance of a certification scheme for persons.

The standard has 21 pages and is available from ISO at a cost of 118 CHF. The structure of the standard is as follows:

1. Scope
2. Normative references
3. Terms and definitions
4. General requirements
5. Structural requirements
6. Resource requirements
7. Records and information requirements
8. Certification schemes
9. Certification process requirements
10. Management system requirements

Annex A—Principles for certification bodies for persons and their certification activity

Bibliography

Bodies certifying individual forensic scientists as competent to practice should be accredited to this standard.

According to this standard, and in contrast to other types of CABs such as management system certification bodies, a characteristic function of a certification body for persons is to conduct an examination which uses objective criteria to measure competence. While it is recognized that such an examination, if well planned and structured by the certification body, can substantially serve to ensure impartiality of operations and reduce the risk of a conflict of interest, additional requirements have been included in this International Standard.

To recap, the situation as it now stands [December 2017] is that most forensic science providers rely on the staff competence requirements of ISO/IEC 17025 to ensure the competence of staff. This is problematic. As will be discussed in Section 7 as exemplified by *R v T* (R v T, 2010), ISO/IEC 17025 has a systemic weakness in this area; the independent and objective accreditation body does not assess the competence of the individual forensic scientist but the competence of the provider to ensure the competence of its staff (ISO/IEC 17025 6.2). The provider itself assures the competence of its staff and essentially certifies them as "fit-to-practice" (ISO/IEC 17025 6.2.5 e). Whether this is sufficient is a matter of debate, as discussed in 7.4.1, *R v T* suggests not. It may be that a scheme accredited to ISO/IEC 17024 is a necessary addition to the quality standards framework and would strengthen forensic science. This weakness may be of greater significance in ISO/IEC 17020 where the opportunity for subjective judgment to influence inspection results is greater.

3.2.6 ISO/IEC 15189:2012 "Medical Laboratories—Requirements for Quality and Competence"

As the title implies, this standard applies to medical laboratories. It is essentially an adaptation of the 2005 edition of ISO/IEC 17025 to allow for the primacy of the patient as the principle stakeholder.

According to ISO, ISO 15189:2012 specifies requirements for quality and competence in medical laboratories. The standard can be used by medical laboratories in developing their QMSs and assessing their own competence. It can also be used for confirming or recognizing the competence of medical laboratories by laboratory customers, regulating authorities and accreditation bodies.

At the time of writing [December 2017], the structure of the standard mirrors the 2005 edition of ISO/IEC 17025 and so needs revision. At 53 pages it is considerably longer than ISO/IEC 17025:2017. It is available from ISO for 178CHF. The structure of the standard is as follows:

1. Scope
2. Normative references
3. Terms and definitions
4. Management requirements
5. Technical requirements

While the standard is based on ISO/IEC 17025:2005, and consequently ISO 9001: 2008, it is a unique document that takes into consideration the specific requirements of the medical environment and the importance of the medical laboratory to patient care. The customer, i.e., the medical practitioner who commissions the work and receives the product or service, is not the most important stakeholder in the process, it is the patient. This aspect of ISO/IEC 15189 anticipates the recent changes to ISO 9001, which requires the needs of all stakeholders to be considered.

Although this standard is not applicable to forensic science, it is helpful in deepening an understanding of quality management and contrasting and comparing this standard to ISO/IEC 17025 as it applies to forensic science providers. It recognizes the particular requirements of medical laboratories, the purpose of which are essentially disease prevention, diagnosis, and patient care. Comparison of this standard with ISO/IEC 17025 reveals that in certain respects it is a higher standard, e.g., in terms of the educational and training requirements for staff.

The most significant differences are in 4.7 "service to the customer" and 4.9 "identifying and controlling non-conforming product." There is a far higher reliance on professional judgment in ISO/IEC 15189 compared with ISO/IEC 17025. The relationship between medical laboratory staff and their customers must be far stronger, e.g., medical laboratory staff are expected toprovide advice on the choice of examinations and services. ISO/IEC 15189 requires regular meetings between medical laboratory staff and clinical staff. Medical laboratory staff are also required to participate in clinical rounds to advise on the use of the laboratory services and for the purpose of consultation on scientific matters.

ISO/IEC 15189 indicates that the professional staff in a medical laboratory must have the competence to consider the medical significance of their work when dealing with nonconforming examinations. It, therefore, provides specific direction that the referring clinician is informed where the nonconformity may have an impact on patient management.

ISO/IEC 15189 may provide a model for a single standard for forensic science incorporating both measurement and the exercise of professional judgment.

3.3 LEVEL 2 STANDARDS—GUIDANCE DOCUMENTS ON THE INTERPRETATION AND APPLICATION OF LEVEL 1 STANDARDS

3.3.1 Introduction

The purpose of these standards is to provide guidance for both organizations and accrediting bodies on the application of the Level 1 standards and their interpretation in relation to the management, practice, and delivery of forensic science. The most important guides, therefore, are those that apply to ISO/IEC 17025 and ISO/IEC 17020. These guides are intended to be used by accrediting bodies for assessing conformity and by organizations seeking to manage operations in a manner conforming to the requirements for accreditation. They are freely available for download.

3.3.2 International Laboratory Accreditation Cooperation (ILAC) Guides

The main publisher of guidance documents is ILAC, and ILAC guides are the subject of this section. ILAC guidance documents relevant to the quality management of forensic science are listed in Table 3.3.

Table 3.3 International Laboratory Accreditation Cooperation Guidance Documents

Guide	Edition	Application
15	2001	Accreditation to 17025
17	2002	Uncertainty of Measurement
19	2002	Forensic Science Laboratories
A4	2004	Application of ISO/IEC 17020[a]
P15	07/2016	Accreditation to ISO/IEC 17020: 2012
13	2007	Competence of PT Providers
19	08/2014	Modules in a Forensic Science Process

[a]This guide was issued jointly with the International Accreditation Forum.

These documents are all freely available for download and they provide comprehensive guidance on the application of the relevant standard. However, in this section the focus is on those directly related to the application of ISO/IEC 17025 and ISO/IEC 17020 to the provision of forensic science: ILAC G19:2002 (which has been withdrawn but remains a useful guide and is available online) and ILAC G19:08/2014 supported by P15 07/2016 and EA05/03, which are introduced in 3.3.2.

3.3.2.1 ILAC Guide 19:2002 "Guidelines for Forensic Science Laboratories"[8]

ISO/IEC 17025 is a standard for the accreditation of testing and calibration laboratories. It, therefore, requires interpretation for application to forensic science providers. That guidance was originally provided by ILAC Guide 19:2002. The structure of the guide corresponds to the original 1999 edition of ISO/IEC 17025 and is as follows:

1. Scope
2. References
3. Terms and definitions
4. Management requirements
5. Technical requirements

The guide sets out the scope of forensic science:

- examination of scenes of crime,
- recovery of evidence,
- laboratory examinations,
- interpretation of findings, and
- presentation of the conclusions reached for intelligence purposes for court use.

It lists the activities undertaken by forensic science laboratories under the following headings:

- Controlled substances
- Toxicology
- Hairs, blood, body fluids, and tissues
- Trace evidence
- Firearms and ballistics
- Handwriting and document examination
- Fingerprints
- Marks and impressions
- Audio, video, and computer analysis

[8] At the time of writing the status of this ILAC Guide is unclear. It is not on ILAC's list of withdrawn documents yet does not appear in ILAC's list of current guides. ILAC G19:08/2014 is based on ILAC G19:2002 but does not claim to replace it. Given the length and unwieldy nature of ILAC G19:08/2014, ILAC G19:2002 remains a fit-for-purpose guide for assessing conformity to ISO/IEC 17025. ILAC G:19 2002 is available online at sadcmet.org.

- Accident investigation
- Scene investigation, and
- Forensic pathology, entomology, and odontology

Reproduced with permission ©ILAC

It should be noted that accident investigation and scene investigation are not laboratory-based activities.

In Section 1, of the guide concedes that some forensic examinations, particularly comparisons,[9] have a subjective element but are nevertheless considered objective for the purpose of compliance with the standard.[10] In Section 3, of the guide defines an objective test as one that produces the "same" result when applied by "appropriately trained staff."

In Section 3, the guide defines an objective test as

A test which having been documented and validated is under control so that it can be demonstrated that all appropriately trained staff will obtain the same results within defined limits.[11]

This effectively includes comparison disciplines within the scope of ISO/IEC 17025 obviating the need for ISO/IEC 17020 accreditation, except perhaps in the case of crime scene examination.

In Section 4, the guide expands on the control of records in ISO/IEC 17025:1999 and, among other things, requires laboratories to have in place documented procedures for the review of case reports prior to issue. Without defining the term it refers in particular to "critical findings."[12] Checks on critical findings must be thoroughly recorded.

In Section 5, the guide provides more detail on the competence of individuals, i.e., how the necessary competencies should be developed, maintained, and recorded.

A laboratory should have clear statements of the competencies required for all jobs and records should be maintained to demonstrate that all staff are competent for the jobs they are asked to carry out.

The environmental conditions necessary to meet forensic requirements are also set out in the guide including the need for clean rooms for trace work and access control and specialist storage to protect the integrity of evidence.

The guide describes the documentation required for validation and in 5.4.5.1 mandates that:

[9] For example, handwriting, fingerprints, and marks and impressions generally.

[10] It should be emphasized here that ISO/IEC 17020 specifically addresses comparisons undertaken as part of inspections.

[11] These defined limits relate to expressions of degrees of probability as well as numerical values.

[12] A definition is given in ILAC Guide 19:08/2014 "Observations and results that have a significant impact on the conclusion reached and the interpretation and opinion provided. In addition, these observations and results cannot be repeated or checked in the absence of the exhibit or sample and/or could be interpreted differently."

All technical procedures used by a forensic science laboratory must be **fully** validated before being used in case work. [emphasis added]

Full validation is usually taken to mean that an interlaboratory comparison exercise is part of the method validation process. Validation is defined and discussed in 1.4.2 of this work. It follows that full validation is a fundamental requirement for all methods used to produce results that contribute to scientific information.

The guide also provides forensic science-specific requirements for equipment maintenance, traceability records, the recovery and management of evidence, a record of continuity (also termed chain-of-custody record), laboratory quality control, and interlaboratory comparisons in the form of PTs.

The guide also requires that the testimony of forensic scientists should be monitored for

appearance, performance and effectiveness.

Finally, the guide recognizes that forensic scientists may not be able to issue reports that comply precisely with the requirements of ISO/IEC 17025:1999 (5.10) and lists some alternatives.

Compared to its successor, discussed next, ILAC Guide 19:2002 may be more easily used to assess conformance to ISO/IEC 17025 and lists requirements. If forensic science providers are not compliant with any of those requirements, then they cannot claim to conform to ISO/IEC 17025.

3.3.2.2 ILAC Guide 19:08/2014: Guidance for Both ISO/IEC 17025 and ISO/IEC 17020

The ENFSI Expert Working Group (EWG) on crime scene investigation concluded that ISO/IEC 17025 was not entirely suitable for application to crime scene examination. Given the laboratory testing and measurement focus of ISO/IEC 17025, there is some merit in that position.

In response to the perceived gap, the ENFSI EWG decided that ISO/IEC 17020 was the most appropriate standard for application to crime scene examination. An ENFSI and European Cooperation for Accreditation (EA), introduced in 2.2.3.1, joint working group tasked the Swiss Accreditation Service to prepare an interpretive standard and in 2008 EA published EA-5/03 "Guidance for the Implementation of ISO/IEC 17020 in the field of crime scene investigation."

In October 2007, the International Accreditation Federation (IAF) and ILAC Joint General Assembly resolved that a single top-level document that approaches the forensic science process as a whole and provides common guidance for both ISO/IEC 17020 and ISO/IEC 17025 **in areas where the activities overlap** be drafted, and that the guidance be based on EA-5/03, for crime scene investigation, and on ILAC G19:2002 for laboratory-based forensic science. [emphasis added]. The resulting document is ILAC Guide 19:08/2014 "Modules in a Forensic Science Process."

The stated purpose of the document is to provide guidance for forensic science providers in the application of ISO/IEC 17025 and ISO/IEC 17020 "in areas where the activities overlap."

The structure of the guide departs from that of both standards which, at the time of publication in 2014, also differed from each other. This lack of correlation presents a challenge to interpretation and application. In an attempt to overcome the difficulty, a chart correlating Sections 3 and 4 of the guide with the corresponding sections of ISO/IEC 17025:2005[13] (the edition current at the time) and ISO/IEC 17020:2012 is given as Annex C of the guide. The comparative structures are given in Table 3.4. The guide covers structural, resource, and process requirements but says little about management requirements or the general requirements of impartiality and independence. As discussed in 5.2, achieving, maintaining, and demonstrating impartiality and independence can be a challenge for crime scene inspection bodies under the direct control of law enforcement agencies. To some extent and as applied to crime scene inspection, the guide is more a new Level 1 standard than a Level 2 guidance document and this point is supported by its scope.

The guide also redefines the forensic science process set out in the scope of ILAC G19:2002. Table 3.5 compares the forensic science processes of G19:2002 and G19:08/2014. This table makes it clear that ILAC G19:08/2014 mostly applies to crime scene inspection.

The main section is 4, and its structure is as follows:

4 Activity modules in the forensic science process
4.1 Initial discussion regarding scene of crime attendance
4.2 Undertaking initial actions at the scene of crime
4.3 Developing a scene of crime investigation strategy
4.4 Undertake scene of crime investigation
4.5 Assess scene of crime findings and consider further examination
4.6 Interpret and report findings from the scene of crime
4.7 Examination and testing
4.8 Interpretation of the results of examinations and tests
4.9 Report from examinations and tests including interpretation of results

Apart from Section 4, which covers crime scene examination at considerable length and in seemingly exhaustive detail, this guide contains little that is not found in the other guides. The length is the result of the level of detail. The detail is such that the guide could also serve as a Level 3 standard, in addition to 1 and 2. This guide comprises 37 pages, for comparaison; ISO/IEC 17020:2012 totals 18 pages, ISO/IEC 17025:2017 36 pages, and ILAC G19:2002 15 pages.

[13] ISO/IEC 17025:2017 differs in structure and therefore Annex C is in need of revision.

Table 3.4 Comparative structures of the guides with section numbers

ILAC G19:08/2014[a]	EA-5/03[b]	ILAC G19:2002 ISO/IEC 17025	ILAC P15:07/2016 ISO/IEC 17020[c]
1 Scope	1 Scope	1 Scope	1 Scope
		2 Normative references	2 Normative references
2 Terms and definitions	2 Definitions	3 Terms and definitions	3 Terms and definitions
	4 Independence, impartiality, and integrity		4 General requirements
	3 Administrative requirements		5 Structural requirements
	6 Personnel, 7 Facilities and Equipment, 12 Subcontracting		6 Resource requirements
	8 Inspection methods and procedures, 9 Handling inspection samples and items, 10 Records, 11 Reports, 13 Complaints.		7 Process requirements
	5 Quality system	4 Management requirements	8 Management system requirements
		5 Technical requirements	
	14 Cooperation		
3 General guidance common to all activities in the forensic science process			
4 Activity modules in the forensic science process			

[a]This guide includes a correlation chart, Annex C, listing the correspondences between Sections 3 and 4 and the relevant sections of ISO/IEC 17025:2005; 4 and 5, and ISO/IEC 17020:2012; 4, 5, 6, 7 and 8.
[b]This guide was based on ISO/IEC 17020:2004 which was structured differently to the 2012 edition. The numbers do not correspond to ILAC P15:07/2016 and ISO/IEC 17020:2012 but the subjects do.
[c]This is the structure of ISO/IEC 17020:2012.

Table 3.5 The forensic science process redefined

ILAC G19:2002	ILAC G19:08/2014
Examination of scenes of crime	4.1 Initial discussion regarding scene of crime attendance 4.2 Undertaking initial actions at the scene of crime 4.3 Developing a scene of crime investigation strategy 4.4 Undertaking initial actions at the scene of crime 4.5 Assess scene of crime findings and consider further examination 4.6 Interpret and report findings from the scene of crime
Recovery of evidence	
Laboratory examinations	4.7 Examination, testing and presumptive testing (including appropriate case assessment)
Interpretation of findings	4.8 Interpretation of the result of examinations and tests
Presentation of the conclusions reached	4.9 Report from examinations and tests including interpretation of results

The guide introduces the concept of a "forensic unit" being the collective term for any entity providing forensic science but on occasion also uses the term "laboratory" (4.7.3 and 4.9). In this work, the term "forensic science provider" or just "provider" will continue to be used. Section 2 of the guide, "Terms and definitions," provides a helpful glossary which, among other things, defines "Critical findings" as follows:

> *Observations and results that have a significant impact on the conclusion reached and the interpretation and opinion provided. In addition, these observations and results cannot be repeated or checked in the absence of the exhibit or sample, and/or could be interpreted differently.* (2.5)

It defines "testing" as "an activity including measurements and analytical techniques" and as such "should" meet the requirements of ISO/IEC 17025 as stated in 4.4.4 of the guide. As with all ISO/ILAC documents "should" is used to indicate a recommendation that is generally accepted practice which if not adopted must be replaced by an equivalent or something better. It is difficult to conceive of a situation where a method requiring metrological traceability and an evaluation of measurement uncertainty would not be accredited to ISO/IEC 17025. As metrological traceability and the evaluation of uncertainty are requirements of ISO/IEC 17025, the mandatory "shall" should, perhaps, have been used.

According to IAF/ILAC-A4:2004 "Guidance on the Application of ISO/IEC 17020,"[14] testing performed by an inspection body may fall into one of two categories,

[14] This ILAC guide has been withdrawn and replaced by ILAC P15:07/2016. This later guide does not include the concepts of functional and analytical testing which are useful in distinguishing between the application of ISO/IEC 17025 and ISO/IEC 17020.

functional and analytical. These test types were introduced in 1.2.2. Functional testing forms a normal part of the activities of an inspection body and is therefore within the scope of ISO/IEC 17020. Analytical testing, which should be performed inside a laboratory under well-controlled environmental conditions and using more sophisticated equipment or testing procedures, is a laboratory activity and therefore does not fall within the scope of ISO/IEC 17020. Inspection bodies wishing to undertake such laboratory type analytical testing as part of an inspection activity must do so in accordance with the relevant requirements of ISO/IEC 17025. Such bodies may be accredited to ISO/IEC 17020 with ISO/IEC 17025 requirements as an extension to scope.

The increased portability of equipment does permit what were once laboratory activities to be conducted at the crime scene. However, the uncontrolled environmental conditions at the scene and the increasing sophistication of laboratory-based equipment particularly in improved selectivity and limit of detection (LOD) weigh against ISO/IEC 17025 accredited activities being conducted at the crime scene, except perhaps for initial screening.

Under 3.4, "Additional considerations relating to personnel," the guide recommends conformance with a code of conduct. The code should address

> *[E]thical behaviour, confidentiality, impartiality, personal safety, relationship with other members of the forensic unit and any other issues needed to ensure appropriate conduct of all staff.*

According to Annex C, this requirement does not correlate with any part of ISO/IEC 17025 or ISO/IEC 17020, and yet these are some of the competency requirements of personnel. The competence of personnel falls under Section 6, Resource requirements.

Section 3.10 of the guide concerns method validation which is defined and discussed in 1.4.2 of this work. This guide does not mandate validation of methods prior use as required by ISO/IEC 17025 and ILAC Guide19:2002. As stated earlier in 3.3.2.1, ILAC Guide G19:2002 includes the requirement that methods are "fully validated before being used on case work." (5.4.2). This guide introduces the condition of "where practicable." and gives the example of the detection of a novel substance not within the scope of the method used and mandates that validation must take place before "any results are reported." The "tentative" detection of the substance at a crime scene will be reported to someone by some means which introduces the risk of the release of nonconforming product, i.e., scientific information of uncertain quality and questionable reliability. In addition, relying on a nonvalidated method which might later be found to be invalid does not seem to be a sensible strategy. A better approach would be to anticipate the situation and have in place a method within flexible scope accreditation as discussed in Section 5 .

Section 4 of the guide focuses on the "forensic science process." It introduces the title of "forensic investigator" without explaining its meaning; sets detailed requirements following the redefined forensic science process; and, under "Critical Findings Check" (4.7.5), the guide introduces the concept of "blind" review, i.e., blind to the extent that the reviewer is unaware of the original result.

The authors claim that the guide was developed

> *[T]o provide additional guidance for specific sections within ISO/IEC 17020 and ISO/IEC 17025 and does not repeat the requirements of these standards, where the given explanations are sufficient. It endeavours to provide interpretation or clarification and should be read in parallel with ISO/IEC17020 and ISO/IEC 17025 as appropriate.*

Given the guide's lack of alignment with either standard, finding the sections in the standards to which the guidance applies is a challenge. As reported earlier, a correlation chart is given at Annex C of the guide. The size of the guide suggests the requirements, or more broadly provisions, documented in ISO/IEC 17025 and 17020 are insufficient to a marked degree. In terms of ISO/IEC 17025 at least, this is not borne out by the experience of forensic science providers which have been accredited to ISO/IEC 17025 since the late 1990s.

The guide is *de facto* the standard for crime scene examination and sets out the requirements for conformance at some length. For more accessible and concise guidance on assessing conformance to ISO/IEC 17025 by forensic science laboratories, readers should refer to ILAC Guide 19:2002 discussed earlier in 3.3.2.1. For similar guidance on assessing conformance to ISO/IEC 17020 by crime scene examination bodies, readers should refer to the United Kingdom Accreditation Service (UKAS) guide RG201, which mirrors the structure of the standard and is, therefore, easier to apply. RG201 is discussed next in 3.3.3. There is also a very concise ANAB guide GD 3002 discussed subsequently in Section 3.3.4.

Despite the attempt to synthesize the activities of inspection bodies, offering crime scene examination, and forensic testing laboratories the fact is that the process of inspection on the one hand and testing and measurement on the other are seen very differently by ISO and accreditation bodies. If testing and/or measurement are conducted at a crime scene and the results affect the outcome of an inspection, then those activities must conform to the requirements of ISO/IEC 17025.

In conclusion then, ISO/IEC 17020:2012 is the most appropriate standard for crime scene examination and comparison disciplines, such as fingerprints, where judgment rather than tests or measurements form the basis of the forensic information provided to stakeholders. However, where tests and measurements contribute to the judgments made then the process must conform to the requirements of ISO/IEC 17025. Providers currently accredited to ISO/IEC 17025 for inspection activities are likely to remain so accredited. Where crime scene inspection bodies are seeking accreditation for the first time, ISO/IEC 17020 would seem to be the most appropriate standard. Where inspection activities rely on the results of tests or measurements accreditation to ISO/IEC 17025 as an extension to scope should be obtained.

Finally, it is beyond the scope of this work to consider all the strengths and weaknesses of this guide. However, there are three main weaknesses. The first is that the "forensic science process" it covers mostly takes place at the crime scene and in support of criminal justice. While not wishing in any way to diminish the critical importance of quality management at the crime scene, the fact is that a lot of forensic science takes place after the crime scene is closed and outside the criminal justice system.[15] The second is the fact that there is no "overlap" between ISO/IEC 17020 and ISO/IEC 17025. Activities that are essentially inspection and rely on professional judgment should conform to ISO/IEC 17020, and activities that involve test and measurement should conform to ISO/IEC 17025. Thirdly, the guide is overdocumented, a condition that should be avoided as discussed in 1.3.9, this makes conformance more difficult than it needs to be and increases the risk of nonconformance.[16]

Recalling points made in Section 1.3.109. the level of detail in a standard is a function of:

- the complexity of the task,
- the competence of the operators, and
- the frequency of the operation.

The level of detail in the guide is a reflection, not only of the undoubted complexity of crime scene examination, ranging from a simple break-in to a multiscene terrorist incident, but also limited operator competency and low frequency of operation in the range of scenes that need to be covered by the standard.

It could be argued that ILAC Guide G19:08/2014 should have focused exclusively on ISO/IEC 17020:2012 and crime scene examination.

To restate what was concluded earlier, what seems clear is that forensic science providers offering laboratory, crime scene services, and feature-comparison and currently accredited to ISO/IEC 17025 may remain accredited to that standard, which Australasian providers are doing. Providers offering crime scene examination alone and currently unaccredited may be better accredited to ISO/IEC 17020 as interpreted by ILAC Guide 19 08/2014 or better still UKAS RG201, see 3.3.3.1, which in effect is the standard for crime scene examination. Providers offering feature-comparison may choose either, it would seem.

[15] For example, health and safety/accident investigation, paternity/familial testing, provenance/authentication, regulation, environmental pollution, etc.

[16] The risk is a disconnect between actual processes and documented procedures, standards are set higher than can be achieved and maintained.

In any event, this ILAC guide, at the time of writing [December 2017], is in need of revision to take account of ISO/IEC 17025:2017, ISO 9001:2015, and ISO 9000:2015.

3.3.3 United Kingdom Accreditation Service Guides

3.3.3.1 UKAS RG201 "Accreditation of Bodies Carrying Out Scene of Crime Examination"

The second and at the time of writing [April 2017] current edition of RG201 was published by UKAS in 2015. It updated the first edition by replacing references to EA 5/03 with ILAC Guide 19:08/2014 discussed above in 3.3.2.2. As already stated in that section the structure of RG201 aligns with that of ISO/IEC 17020:2012 and makes this guide easy to use for identifying requirements and assessing conformance.

This guide is of course only applicable to UKAS accredited organizations and those seeking UKAS accreditation. But it is of wider utility. It is freely available for download and comprises 10 pages.

It is a guide clearly aimed at the application of ISO/IEC 17020 for organizations that offer crime scene examination under the operational or administrative control of law enforcement agencies.

The structure, aligned to ISO/IEC 17020, is as follows:

4 General requirements
- **4.1** Impartiality and independence
- **4.2** Confidentiality

5 Structural requirements
- **5.1** Administrative requirements
- **5.2** Organization and management

6 Resource requirements
- **6.1** Personnel
- **6.2** Facilities and equipment
- **6.3** Subcontracting

7 Process requirements
- **7.1** Inspection methods and procedures
- **7.2** Handling inspection items and samples
- **7.3** Inspection records
- **7.4** Inspection reports and inspection certificates
- **7.5** Complaints and appeals
- **7.6** Complaints and appeals process

8 Management system requirements
- **8.1** Options
- **8.2** Management system documentation
- **8.3** Control of documents
- **8.4** Control of records
- **8.5** Management review

8.6 Internal audits
8.7 Corrective actions
8.8 Preventive actions

The UKAS guide recommends reading it in conjunction with the standards ISO/IEC 17020:2012 and the ILAC Guide 19: 08/2014. However, the document ILAC P15:07/2016 should also be referred to for a better understanding of the application of the standard. The guide sets out the conformance requirements for organizations carrying out scene of crime examination and how conformance assessment will be conducted. It defines two scopes, volume and major crime (2.1).

Where appropriate, conformance to ISO/IEC 17025 is expected. The guide makes clear that the QMS of an accredited organization can meet the requirements of both ISO/IEC 17025 and ISO/IEC 17020. For example, laboratories accredited by UKAS to ISO/IEC 17025 that undertake crime scene examination can obtain accreditation to ISO/IEC 17020 by extension to scope.

The requirements for impartiality, independence, and confidentiality are set out. The risk to these requirements being met by crime scene units under the control of law enforcement agencies is recognized, and in such cases, demonstrable safeguards must be in place.

The guide includes a novel requirement (6.1.7).

> *If any of the services offered by the organisation are not covered by UKAS accreditation, then this shall be made clear to the customer.*[17]

As far as can be determined this is not a requirement specified by other accreditation bodies or indeed the standards themselves. In practice, providers often declare and disclose organizational accreditation but do not inform stakeholders whether or not the methods or procedures used fall within scope. This is further discussed in 3.4.7.1.3, where the requirement for such disclosure is contained within the legal guidance offered by the Forensic Science Regulator. The need for such transparency and the ethical duty to provide it is discussed Section7.

3.3.3.2 UKAS M3003 "The Expression of Uncertainty and Confidence in Measurement"

The third and current edition was published in November 2012. It is freely available for download. It has 82 pages, and the structure is as follows:

1. Introduction

[17] Unhelpfully "customer" is not defined. Reading of the document suggests that "customer" is the commissioner of the service. The justice system is one of the main stakeholders and its needs must be met. If a method outside the scope of accreditation has been used then that fact should be communicated to the justice system through disclosure.

2. Overview
3. More detail
4. Type A evaluation of standard uncertainty
5. Type B evaluation of standard uncertainty
6. Reporting of results
7. Step by step procedure for evaluation of measurement uncertainty

Appendix A Calibration and measurement capability
Appendix B Deriving a coverage factor for unreliable input quantities
Appendix C Dominant non-Gaussian Type B uncertainty
Appendix D Derivation of the mathematical model
Appendix E Some sources of error and uncertainty in electrical calibrations
Appendix F Some sources of error and uncertainty in mass calibrations
Appendix G Some sources of error and uncertainty in temperature calibrations
Appendix H Some sources of error and uncertainty in dimensional calibrations
Appendix J Some sources of error and uncertainty in pressure calibration using DWTs
Appendix K Examples of application for calibration
Appendix L Expression of uncertainty for a range of values
Appendix M Assessment of compliance with specification
Appendix N Uncertainties for test results
Appendix P Electronic data processing
Appendix Q Symbols
Appendix R References

The scope of the guide is uncertainty of measurement in calibration and testing laboratories accredited to ISO/IEC 17025, and its normative references are as follows:

- ISO/IEC 17025:2005
- ISO/IEC Guide 98-3:2008 "Uncertainty of Measurement—Part 3: Guide to the expression of uncertainty in measurement (GUM 1995)"

The purpose of the guide is to provide policy on the evaluation and reporting of measurement uncertainty for testing and calibration laboratories.

The guide is an excellent introduction to uncertainty of measurement for the nontechnical reader but goes on to provide sufficient technical depth and detail for the skilled practitioner, as the introduction states the guide is for both the beginner and expert.

The document is based on GUM/ISO/IEC Guide 98 and is consistent with GUM but does not preclude the use of other methods of uncertainty evaluation, for example, using Bayesian reasoning which is discussed in 7.2.2.

3.3.4 ANAB GD 3002 "Guidance on ISO/IEC 17020 Accreditation for Forensic Inspection Agencies"

The guide was published in 2016 and is freely available for download. Its purpose is essentially to explain the difference between ISO/IEC 17025 and ISO/IEC 17020 and to clarify the requirements for accreditation. The normative reference is IAF/

ILAC-A4:2004 "Guidance on the Application of ISO/IEC 17020," which has been withdrawn by ILAC and replaced by ILAC P15:07/2016 "Application of ISO/IEC 17020:2012 for the Accreditation of Inspection Bodies". It is noteworthy that there is no reference to ILAC Guide 19:08/2014 or ILAC P15:07/2016.

The guide comprises 9 pages and is structured as follows:

1. Purpose
2. Introduction
3. Definitions
4. Accreditation process guidance
  4.1. Guidance for proficiency testing/interlaboratory comparisons
  4.2. Guidance for measurement traceability
  4.3. Guidance for ISO/IEC 17020 Clauses 5.1.4 and 6.4.3
  4.4. Guidance for the on-site assessment
  4.5. Guidance for document and record needs for the assessment
  4.6. Guidance on the accreditation requirements of ISO/IEC 17020
5. Reference documents.

Under "Purpose," the need for ISO/IEC 17020 accreditation is explained and offers a US perspective. The explanation is the move from "crime lab" provision of crime scene services to provision by "police forensic agencies". These agencies perform crime scene examination, latent print analysis, tenprints, foot and tire prints examinations, firearms examinations, handwriting, digital media, and anthropology, most of which are inspection activities.

In passing, the need for this standard should be considered in the light of recommendation 4 of the NRC Report (National Research Council, 2009), which called for removing forensic science provision from the administrative control of law enforcement. In this case, forensic science is not only administered but also delivered by the police.

The guide explains that ANAB's ISO/IEC 17020 forensic accreditation program is for police organizations that do not do testing using laboratory instrumentation and equipment but perform inspections. The process accredited is one in which a comparison against a defined criterion or specification and then draws conclusions based on professional judgment. ISO/IEC 17020 accreditation is deemed appropriate for most police agencies that perform comparisons between a piece of evidence and a known specification (e.g., an unknown print against a suspect print) and then make a professional judgment as to whether the two items are similar or not.

The guide defines the "forensic science process" as

> *Gathering, evaluation, and assessment of all types of evidence using scientific procedures, as well as the location, documentation, and preservation of evidence.*

It is also of interest to note that the guide states that comparison can lead to individualization. As discussed in Section 1 individualization is an unachievable aim.

The guide, in an effort to distinguish between the scope of ISO/IEC 17020 and ISO/IEC 17025, uses the concepts of functional and analytical tests discussed earlier in 3.3.2.2 and introduced in IAF/ILAC—4:2004 "Guidance on the Application of ISO/IEC 17020."

Functional tests are used to check conformance with specification. Such tests include inspection activities at a crime scene, e.g., measurement, screening, presumptive testing, and comparisons such as those between recovered latent prints and those of a suspect. The guide states that these procedures lie within the scope of ISO/IEC 17020. However, the rider is added that where a functional test result requires metrological traceability and an estimate of uncertainty, it may still be covered by ISO/IEC 17020, provided the technical requirements of ISO/IEC 17025 are met. As with UKAS, it will be up to the accrediting body to resolve the quality management issues raised by this set of circumstances and decide which parts of the QMS are accredited to which standard.

Analytical tests are those methods of analysis and detection (tests and measurements) employed by laboratories and, as should be clear by now, must be accredited to ISO/IEC 17025.

This guide is concise and offers some easily understood explanations of the differences between ISO/IEC 17020 and ISO/IEC 17025 accreditation. The guidance in Section 4 is helpful. It repeats the point that ISO/IEC 17020 is for application to crime scene activities and comparison disciplines. To a certain extent, it can be used to assess conformance to either standard.

3.3.5 Other Application/Interpretation Guides

The reader should be aware that, in addition to those introduced above, accrediting bodies also publish other application guides for ISO/IEC 17025 and ISO/IEC 17020. Some are generic and some forensic science specific. They are all freely available for download and may be used to better understand those standards and assess the conformance of forensic science providers to those standards. The generic guides include

- NATA ISO/IEC 17020:2012 Inspection Standard Application Document, August 2015
- NATA ISO/IEC 17025:2005 Standard Application Document for accreditation of testing and calibration facilities, March 2015
- UKAS LAB series relating to ISO/IEC 17025:2005

The specific guides include two published by ANAB:

- ISO/IEC 17025:2005—Forensic Science Testing Laboratories—Accreditation Requirements, 2017/08/22, #AR 3028
- ISO/IEC 17020:2012—Forensic Inspection Bodies—Accreditation Requirements, June 2017, #AR 3055

And one published by NATA:

- Forensic Science ISO/IEC 17025 Application Document, July 2015

In addition to providing helpful guidance on application and interpretation, the specific guides include supplemental requirements applicable to forensic science providers in the pertaining jurisdiction.

It should be noted that the guides to the application of ISO/IEC 17025 relate to the 2005 edition and not the 2017 edition. Therefore, these guides require revision at the time of writing [December 2017].

3.4 LEVEL 3 STANDARDS—RELATED TO THE "NUTS AND BOLTS" OF THE FORENSIC SCIENCE PROCESS

3.4.1 Introduction

In this section, the plethora of standards relating directly or indirectly to the forensic science process, from crime scene to court room, will be introduced and briefly discussed. Those that relate to the process, in general, will be discussed first in 3.4.2, followed by standards that relate to the competence of the organization, the competence of the individual, and valid analytical measurement (VAM). Standards that are discipline specific will be introduced next. They are many in number and some will be discussed in some detail in Section 6. Finally, standards that relate to the legal process will be introduced and discussed.

3.4.2 Standards That Apply to the Forensic Science Process in General

3.4.2.1 Introduction

In this section the forensic science process is as follows:

1. Scene examination/sample collection,
2. Laboratory examination/analysis,
3. Interpretation, and
4. Reporting.

3.4.2.1.1 AS5388-2012 "Forensic Analysis"

Included in this section is the Australian Standard AS5388 "Forensic Analysis." It has been published and is available for purchase as four separate parts,[18] each one applicable to a step in the forensic science process as enumerated above. Each part is sold and marketed as a separate standard. It includes the discipline of forensic pathology which is not within the scope of this work. These standards contain many Australian-specific

[18] At the time of writing [April 2017] the cost of purchasing a single license PDF was as follows: Part 1—147.74AUD; 2—147.74AUD; 3—91.09AUD, and 4—72.66AUD. ILAC guides are free.

requirements particularly in relation to occupational health and safety; these requirements lie outside the scope of ISO/IEC 17025. AS5388 is silent on ISO/IEC 17020.

Health and safety apart, this set of standards specify in considerable detail the requirements for the conformity of a forensic science provider to ISO/IEC 17025. The level of detail assists in the process of conformity assessment but, as with ILAC Guide 19:08/2014 mentioned earlier in 3.3.2.2, increased detail corresponds to an increased risk of nonconformance. Collectively AS5388 might be considered an equivalent of ILAC Guide G19:08/2014, certainly there is much common ground. If they are equivalent, then one or other may be redundant, at least to a degree.

However, it is probably fairer to say that AS5388 is more applicable to a laboratory-based provider offering crime scene examination and ILAC G19:08/2014 more applicable to an organization providing crime scene examination that conducts analytical testing and measurement as part of that service. What can be concluded is that between them these documents make clear the complexity of the entire forensic science process, a complexity that puts at-risk conformance to quality standards. Indeed, it would be reasonable to conclude that no provider could be fully compliant with the requirements set out in these documents. In practice, they offer a detailed list of potential nonconformances.

In Australia, AS5388 is considered a core standard from which discipline-specific standards can be developed. For an account of the development and application of these standards from an Australian perspective see Robertson et al. (2014) and the editorial by J. Robertson (2013).

Standards Australia is seeking to have these standards adopted by ISO through TC 272 Forensic Sciences (ISO n.d.). At the time of writing [December 2017], it is unclear how ISO/IEC 17020 and ILAC Guide 19:08/2014 will be accommodated in a new standards framework.

In 2013, the Australian accrediting body NATA published a gap analysis comparing the requirements described in AS5388 against the current NATA accreditation criteria for ISO/IEC 17025 (NATA, 2013). NATA concluded that the majority of requirements described in these documents are currently expected to be undertaken to gain NATA accreditation. Thus, AS5388 adds few, if any, new requirements. It just provides more detail and, as a guidance document, facilitates conformance with ISO/IEC 17025.

The plethora of standards at this level works against the objects of standardization and harmonization. The law varies by jurisdiction; the standard of forensic science should not.

3.4.2.1.2 US Federal Judicial Center Reference Manual

Another comprehensive guide applicable to the forensic science process is the Reference Manual on Scientific Evidence published by the US Federal Judicial Centre (Federal Judicial Centre & National Research Council, 2011). Its purpose is to aid US judicial authorities better exercise their role as gatekeepers as required by the Federal Rule of

Evidence 702, which is discussed later in 3.4.7. It provides an excellent nontechnical guide to the science in forensic science.

3.4.2.2 Scene Examination and Sample Collection

3.4.2.2.1 ILAC G19:08/2014

Although ILAC Guide 19:08/2014 is correctly classified as a Level 2 standard, discussed earlier in 3.3.2.2, it can also be classified as a Level 3 standard for the following reasons: crime scene examination constitutes most of its scope and it documents the requirements in great detail.

3.4.2.2.2 AS 5388.1—2012 Forensic Analysis, Part 1: Recognition, Recording, Recovery, Transport, and Storage of Material

This Australian national standard was published in May 2012 by Standards Australia and is available for purchase from SAI Global[19] as a cost of 163.48 AUD[20] [May 2017]. It is Part 1 of a four-part series collectively identified as AS5388-2012 "Forensic Analysis" and introduced earlier in 3.4.2.1. It is specific to criminal justice. Part 1 has 48 pages, and its structure is as follows:

1. Scope
2. Referenced and related documents
3. Definition and abbreviations
4. Underpinning principles
5. Systematic approach to scene examination
6. Occupational health and safety-hazardous materials
7. Recording material in situ
8. Item collection
9. Item transport, storage, and security
10. Analysis and examination of items.

The standard specifies the requirements for conformance applicable to the activities in the title: recognition, recording, recovery, transport, and storage of evidential materials. As a standard that applies to the examination of crime scenes, it is discussed in greater detail in 6.6.2.

This standard does not include requirements for digital evidence. Among the normative references is ISO/IEC 17025 but not ISO/IEC 17020, perhaps reflecting the fact that organizations conducting crime scene examination are accredited to

[19] The commercial arm of Standards Australia.

[20] This and other prices for parts of AS5388 include local sales tax which may not be levied on overseas purchasers.

ISO/IEC 17025 in Australasia. It helpfully makes clear that "It is neither practical nor desirable to collect everything at a crime scene ....". It is a highly prescriptive standard. In terms of maintaining sample integrity and the forensic exploitation of the crime scene, the requirements of this standard are similar to others with comparable scope. It has a particular focus on the occupational health and safety of crime scene examiners and the general public. It includes consideration of environmental, biological, radiological, and chemical hazards. It details how a variety of samples are recovered, e.g., fingernail clippings and entomological samples. It includes a helpful glossary and list of abbreviations. These and other informative and helpful appendices included in the standard are listed below.

A. Definitions and abbreviations for AS5388 series standards
B. Powers of search and seizure
C. Specialist functions of possible assistance at the crime scene
D. Precautions to be taken when handling sharps
E. Crime scene notes
F. Guidelines for the use of forensic medical examination kit to collect biological samples for forensic analysis
G. Presumptive tests
H. Entomological Samples
I. Packaging guidelines

3.4.2.2.3 TWG CSI Crime Scene Investigation: A Guide for Law Enforcement

This document was published in 2000. Although written and approved by the US Technical Working Group on Crime Scene Investigation, it has the added authority of the US Department of Justice (DOJ) sponsorship.

The guide states that it is just "one method of promoting quality crime scene investigation" admitting others. The stated scope of the guide is as follows:

> *This guide is intended for use by law enforcement and other responders who have responsibility for protecting crime scenes, preserving physical evidence, and collecting and submitting the evidence for scientific examination.*

The guide is freely available, it has 48 pages, and the structure is as follows:

Section A: Arriving at the Scene: Initial Response/Prioritization of Efforts
Section B: Preliminary Documentation and Evaluation of the Scene
Section C: Processing the Scene
Section D: Completing and Recording the Crime Scene Investigation
Section E: Crime Scene Equipment

The guide focuses on the crime scene management activities of controlling, preserving, recording, and evidence recovery. It assumes that scientific examination does not take place at the crime scene. It makes no reference to ISO/IEC 17025 or ISO/IEC 17020, which is unsurprising given its age. It is therefore of limited utility compared with AS5388 and ILAC Guide 19:08/2014.

3.4.2.2.4 ASTM E1188-11 (2017) Standard Practice for Collection and Preservation of Information and Physical Items by a Technical Investigator

The structure of this and many other ASTM standards is as follows:

1. Scope
2. Referenced documents
3. Significance and use
4. Procedure
5. Key words

Reproduced with permission ©ASTM Intl, 100 Barr Harbor Drive, West Conshohocken, PA 19428

The standard comprises two pages and is available for purchase from ASTM for 41 USD [December 2017].

The standard documents guidelines for the collection and preservation of evidence for further analysis. The standard is not specific to the criminal justice system. It provides guidance on maintaining the integrity of evidence in terms of continuity and storage. The evidence types specified are documentary information, physical evidence, and photographic documentation. Its limited scope is reflected in its brevity.

Like all ASTM standards, it is produced by the relevant community for that community. Conformity assessment is by self-regulation.[21]

This and other ASTM standards are offered by the US accreditation body A2LA, introduced in 2.3.3, as guidance for crime scene and presumably will be added to the Organization of Scientific Area Committees (OSAC) registry in due course, perhaps after some revision.

3.4.2.3 Laboratory Examination and Analysis

3.4.2.3.1 AS5388.2 Forensic Analysis Part 2: Analysis and Examination of Material

This is the second standard in the AS5388 series published by Standards Australia in May 2012 and is available for purchase from SAI Global at a cost of 163.48 AUD [May 2017]. Part 2 has 48 pages, and its structure is as follows:

1. Scope
2. Referenced and related documents
3. Definitions and abbreviations
4. Underpinning principles and requirements
5. Acceptance of physical material received for examination
6. Item continuity
7. Occupational health and safety
8. Recording physical material received for examination

[21] However, as discussed in 4.3.2.2.3, the US Organization of Scientific Area Committees (OSAC) is populating a registry of standards for use by accreditation bodies. Some of those standards will be ASTM standards; in which case conformity assessment will be conducted by an accreditation body.

9. Presumptive and preliminary tests
10. Order of examination
11. Sampling
12. Analysis and examination of physical material
13. Identification of physical by instrumental analysis
14. Identification of physical material using comparative examination
15. Linking and effect to a particular item
16. Recording the results of observations, analyses, and comparisons
17. Interpreting and reporting of results

Appendices **(A)** Defintions and Abbreviations **(B)** Presumptive and Preliminary Tests **(C)** Sampling to obtain material suitable for analysis **(D)** Statistical Sampling **(E)** Examples of hypothesis testing **(F)** Parameters relevant to validation.

As the title implies, the standard documents the requirements for the examination and analysis of evidential materials. The normative documents referenced include ISO/IEC 17025, ISO/IEC Guide 98 Part 1 and ISO/IEC 21748:2010 "Guidance for the use of repeatability, reproducibility and trueness estimates in measurement uncertainty estimation."

As with Part 1, this standard is helpfully informative in the detailed exposition of the forensic science process. For example, it lists the questions that forensic science is required to address the "unknowns." It is a guide on how forensic science should be managed, practiced, and delivered and could be cut and pasted into a forensic science provider's documented standard methods and procedures.

The standard distinguishes between analytical and comparative techniques used in forensic science (12.1), which "share a common scientific methodology."

The standard sets criteria for method selection (13.2). However, no mention is made of meeting the needs of the customer required by ISO/IEC 17025:2017 (6.2.1.3). Customer/stakeholder input is required in selecting a method of appropriate selectivity and limit of detection (LOD). Ideally, the required method performance criteria should be first determined as discussed in 2.2.4.3.1 and later in 3.4.5.2. Issues associated with method selection are further discussed in Section 7 of this work.

The common confusion between sensitivity and LOD is evident in 13.4 of the standard. In analytical chemistry, which is the subject of this section of the standard, sensitivity is the gradient of the response curve; a more sensitive method will produce a higher signal in response to the amount of substance present than a less sensitive method. What is meant by "very sensitive" here is a lower LOD. While higher sensitivity meaning a lower LOD has entered common use, particularly in biological disciplines, it is incorrect.

The standard supports, to a degree, the principle of orthogonality or independence, which in simple terms means obtaining the same result by two independent methods as a condition for concluding that a particular substance is present (13.6). As the standard rightly states, one highly selective method might suffice. That is certainly the case with the high resolution and high mass accuracy mass spectrometric methods available today which offer sufficient selectivity to provide evidence of chemical identity to a very high degree of certainty. Such methods are discussed later in 3.4.5.2.

In this section of the standard, a further confusion arises, i.e., between selectivity and specificity. In analytical chemistry, a method is specific if no component of a sample other than the substance of interest contributes to the result or signal. There are no degrees of specificity, either a method is specific or it is not. Selectivity is the ability to discriminate between the substance of interest and other potentially interfering components of a sample and is measured by degree.

A practical example is detecting the presence of a psychoactive substance in a powder of mixed components using a method that combines separation and detection. The degree of selectivity is the extent to which the signal obtained is the result of the psychoactive substance alone without any contribution or interference from other components in the powder.

The IUPAC has determined that it is unlikely that any method is specific and discourages use of the term (Vessman et al., 2001).

It is noteworthy that selectivity and specificity are not recorded in Appendix A (definitions and abbreviations) of this standard.

3.4.2.3.2 ASTM E860-07 (2013)e1 Standard Practice for Examining and Preparing Items That Are or May Become Involved in Criminal or Civil Litigation

This standard has a very limited scope which might be summarized as the ensuring stakeholder needs are met when examining or testing evidential materials and documenting conformance with the standard.

3.4.2.4 Interpretation (Investigative and Evaluative Opinions) of Scientific Information

3.4.2.4.1 Introduction

Before introducing the standards, the dual role of the forensic scientist as an investigator and evaluator, introduced in 1.2.3, should be considered together with the three-stage model of the forensic science process shown in Fig. 1.2. During the investigative phase of the process, the inferential method of abduction is employed initially. Abduction is a type of logical inference which goes from observation/result/finding to an explanation, ideally trying to find the simplest and most likely explanation. Through abduction, the forensic scientist as investigator, offers a list of possible rational explanations which may be of assistance in progressing the investigative phase of the forensic science process.

A tribunal of fact may call a forensic scientist as an expert witness to help establish facts. To do that the forensic scientist will evaluate competing propositions favorable to the parties to the dispute using a likelihood ratio approach, introduced next in 3.4.2.4.2, to formulate an evaluative opinion of evidential weight.

An investigative opinion offered by a forensic scientist in the role of investigator meets the needs of the investigation, usually law enforcement, or police, and perhaps the prosecuting authority. An evaluative opinion offered by a forensic scientist in the role of evaluator meets the needs of the court or tribunal of fact.

3.4.2.4.2 The Association of Forensic Science Providers Standard (Association of Forensic Science Providers, 2009)

In 2009, the AFSP (Association of Forensic Science Providers) published "Standards for the formulation of evaluative forensic science expert opinion". This standard codifies the process of case assessment and interpretation (CAI) described in a number of papers authored by then employees of the Forensic Science Service which pioneered the approach to forensic science management and practice (Cook et al., 1998b; Evett et al., 2000). CAI is discussed later in 3.4.2.4.4.

The AFSP Standard comprises four pages and the structure is as follows:

1. Scope
2. Definitions
3. Guiding principles
4. Standards
5. Guidance notes
6. Glossary of terms
7. Examples

The scope is simply stated as follows:

> *Forensic Expert Opinion formulated in the Evaluative or Evidential mode across all scientific disciplines. It does not include investigative opinion or factual and technical reporting.*

Investigative and evaluative opinions are defined in Section 2 of the standard. A fuller definition of an evaluative opinion is documented and, given the importance of the concept, it is reproduced below.

> *An opinion of evidential weight (evaluation of a likelihood ratio), based upon case specific propositions and clear conditioning information (framework of circumstances) that is provided for use as evidence in court. An evaluative opinion is an opinion based upon the estimation of a likelihood ratio.*

The four foundational principles of evaluation are introduced: balance, logic, robustness, and transparency.

- Balance: consider at least two hypotheses/propositions
- Logic: consider the probability of the evidence given the proposition[22]
- Robustness: base opinion on sound science and valid data

[22] Considering the probability of the proposition given the evidence is called transposing the conditional, it is a logical fallacy exemplified by assuming that an animal is a cat given it has four legs is as likely as an animal has four legs given that it is a cat; for the mathematically literate $pX|Y \neq pY|X$. This logical fallacy is also known as the prosecutor's fallacy. The logic of conditional probability is very important in the evaluation of scientific evidence it is discussed more fully in 9.2.2.

- Transparency: demonstrate the basis for the opinion[23]

The requirement for independence and impartiality on the part of a forensic scientist acting as an expert witness is emphasized. In addition, as the role of the forensic scientist is to help the court reach a safe decision by a fair process to the best of his or her ability, the forensic scientist should report at "activity" level "wherever possible."

Activity level is a member of the hierarchy of propositions that might be considered by a forensic scientist in formulating an evaluative opinion (Cook et al., 1998a,b).

The hierarchy in ascending order of propositions is as follows:

- Subsource
- Source
- Activity
- Court

"Court" level is for the fact-finder. Using DNA profiling evidence as an example, given a "match" between a questioned and reference profile using low template techniques (techniques able to produce a profile from just a few cells), an evaluative opinion would be based on the following hypotheses:

H_p,[24] the source of the questioned profile is the person who provided the reference profile or

H_d, the source of the questioned profile is someone else.

If the cellular source of the DNA in the questioned profile was not known, then the propositions are subsource, if the cellular source was known, e.g., from sperm cells, then the propositions are at source level.

Activity level propositions might be:

H_p, the DNA was deposited through intimate contact between the defendant and the complainant or

H_d, the DNA was deposited in some other way.

The evidence is evaluated by assigning a likelihood ratio in accordance with the following relationship:

$$LR = \frac{pE|Hp}{pE|Hd}$$

where

pE - probability of the evidence, a "match"

$|H$ - given one hypothesis or the other

[23] This is compliant with the requirements set out in *Davie v Magistrates of Edinburgh* [1953] SC 34 discussed in Section 4.3.3.2.1 and various codes of practice such as Criminal Procedure Rules 19 and the Code of Conduct for Expert Witnesses discussed in 3.4.7.1.3.

[24] By convention the subscript "p" denotes a hypothesis favorable to the prosecution in a criminal case. Also by convention *Hp* is the numerator (above the line).

The main requirements for conformance are set out in §4. The glossary, guidance, and examples aid an understanding of the likelihood ratio approach to interpretation, which has been widely endorsed by the forensic science community (Berger et al., 2011).

Conformity could be assessed by including this standard within the documented QMS of an accredited forensic science provider.

This standard provides the basis for the ENFSI guidelines, discussed next in3.4.2.4.3, and the four principles were endorsed by the Statistics and Law Section of the Royal Statistical Society (RSS) in its comments to the US National Commission of Forensic Science regarding expression of "scientific certainty"[25] (Statistics and Law Section of the Royal Statistical Society n.d.).

3.4.2.4.3 ENFSI Guidelines for Evaluative Reporting in Forensic Science

The guide was published in 2015 and is based on the AFSP Standard. It is freely available for download. The document comprises 127 pages, and the structure is as follows:

1. Scope
2. Evaluative reporting
3. Standard framework
4. Guidance notes
5. Glossary
6. References
7. Examples (worked case examples)
    - DNA
    - Glass
    - Speaker recognition
    - Footwear marks 1 and 2
    - CCTV
    - GSR 1 and 2

Reproduced with permission ©ENFSI

The stated aim of the guide is to standardize and improve evaluative reporting among ENFSI members. The scope excludes intelligence, investigative, and technical reporting; only evaluative reporting is covered.

The guidelines document a detailed and comprehensive set of requirements for most disciplines which, together with "real-world" examples, greatly facilitate conformity assessment. It is also an excellent primer for gaining a practical understanding of the likelihood ratio approach to interpreting scientific evidence.

Some important points are made in the foreword of the guidelines and are worth quoting here.

[25] As stated in 1.2.1, science admits no certainty.

[L]ittle has been done to meet the challenge of ensuring that the reports [of forensic scientists] capture both the value and the limitations of the findings expressed in a manner understandable to a wide range of users including the police, lawyers and juries. In addition, Forensic Science as a recognized discipline, will not progress without a common language and without a shared understanding of what the findings mean. Without these, it will not progress and will be unable to assist judicial processes or law enforcement in addressing cross-border crime. ©ENFSI

The guidelines are quite prescriptive and refer to intelligence, investigative, and technical reporting as types distinct from evaluative reporting accepting that evaluative reporting often contains technical elements. The guidelines make clear that a likelihood ratio approach can be applied to all forensic disciplines. They also prescribe elements of the CAI model, discussed next in 3.4.2.4.4, for example, recommending case preassessment when circumstance permit and include a useful glossary.

As with most Level 3 standards, the level of detail and prescription renders conformance a challenge.

3.4.2.4.4 Royal Statistical Society (RSS) Practitioner Guides 1–4: Communication and Interpreting Statistical Evidence in the Administration of Criminal Justice: Guidance for Judges, Lawyers, Forensic Scientists, and Expert Witnesses

These guides are freely available for download from the website of the RSS. The stated aim of the guides is to improve the understanding and use of statistics in the administration of justice.

The Statistics and Law working group, which produced the guides, was initially formed in response to a number of court cases where the interpretation of statistics raised concerns. In 2002, the RSS wrote a letter to the British Lord Chancellor (Royal Statistical Society, 2015) setting out its concerns about the case of Sally Clark (R v Clark, 2003) and the miscalculation of the probability of two cases of sudden infant death syndrome in one family.[26]

The creation of the guides was also given impetus by the existence of the US Federal Judicial Center's Reference Manual of Scientific Evidence (Federal Judicial Centre & National Research Council, 2011), mentioned in the introduction to this section, and the lack of a similar document for UK jurisdictions covering statistical evidence and probabilistic reasoning.

The guides were prepared by the Statistics and the Law working group, now entitled the Statistics and the Law section, a multidisciplinary team of experts in law, statistics, and forensic science.

[26] The miscalculation was performed by an eminent pediatrician acting as an expert witness for the prosecution, Professor Sir Roy Meadow, who, in support of his theory Munchausen's Syndrome by Proxy (MSBP), derived "Meadow's Law"—"one cot death is a tragedy, two is suspicious and three is murder".

Although the guides are stated to be specific to the criminal justice system, the principles may be applied to the use of forensic science to resolve any legal dispute including issues of regulatory compliance.

The first three guides set out the fundamentals of probability and statistical evidence in criminal proceedings, the probative value of DNA evidence and the logic of forensic proof.

Part 1—Fundamentals of Probability and Statistical Evidence in Criminal Proceedings.

Authors—Colin Aitken, Paul Roberts, and Graham Jackson.

Published in November 2010.

Part 1 has 122 pages, and its structure is as follows:

1. Introduction
2. Probability and statistics in forensic contexts
3. Basic concepts of probabilistic inference and evidence
4. Interpreting probabilistic evidence—anticipating traps for the unwary
5. Summary and checklist

Appendices

- **A.** Glossary
- **B.** Technical elucidation and illustrations
- **C.** Select case law precedents and further illustrations
- **D.** Select bibliography

Reproduced with permission ©RSS

The stated scope of Part 1 is the application of probability and statistics in criminal proceedings. It introduces and explains basic terminology and concepts and identifies common errors in reasoning.

The guide is written as a continuous narrative, but each section may be considered separately for reference purposes. It is a reasonably exhaustive primer on statistics and probabilistic reasoning and as such is far from concise. It recognizes the continuing challenge of accurately communicating statistical evidence. Its verbosity is a barrier to conformity assessment.

Part 2—Assessing the probative value of DNA evidence.

Authors—Roberto Puch-Solis, Paul Roberts, Susan Pope, and Colin Aitken.

Published in March 2012.

Part 2 has 124 pages, and it is structured as follows:

1. DNA Evidence in Criminal Proceedings
2. The DNA Profile
3. DNA Profiles as Evidence in Criminal Proceedings
4. Assessing the Probative Value of Single Donor Profiles
5. Two Person ("Mixed") Questioned Profiles
6. Low Template DNA (LTDNA)
7. Presenting DNA Evidence in the Courtroom

Appendices

A. Bibliography

B. The UK DNA Database and Familial Searching

C. Y-STR Profiles

D. Mitochondrial DNA Profiles

E. Glossary

Reproduced with permission ©RSS

The scope of the guide is the probabilistic foundations of DNA profiling evidence and the evaluation of its probative value in criminal trials. In common with Part 1, it tends to be verbose but it is a reasonably exhaustive guide to its subject. In addition to guidance on the evaluation of DNA evidence, it includes a history of the evidence type and an introduction to the underlying science. The appendices are informative and helpful. Again, verbosity renders conformity assessment difficult.

Section 6.1 includes a very important point on the likelihood ratio approach to the evaluation of evidence in general, which is reproduced below with emphasis added.

> *Likelihood ratios are a strictly rational and mathematically validated mechanism for quantifying evidential weight or probative value, i.e.,* the strength *of evidential support for a particular proposition. They are employed by many forensic scientists in their casework. Although likelihood ratios also feature in Bayes' Theorem,* ***there is nothing inherently or distinctively 'Bayesian' about the use of likelihood ratios or the importance of considering the probability of evidence under competing propositions. It is simply a matter of elementary logic*** *that evidence compatible with guilt could also be compatible with innocence, and one cannot, therefore, assess its relevance or probative value without first considering how a particular item of evidence might bear on* both *sides of the argument, for and against. This inquiry is inescapably probabilistic.* ©*RSS*

Part 3—The Logic of Forensic Proof: Inferential Reasoning in Criminal Evidence and Forensic Science.

Authors Paul Roberts and Colin Aitken.

Published in May 2014.

Part 4 has 159 pages, and its structure is as follows:

1. The Inferential Logic of Judicial Evidence and Proof

2. Propositions and Logical Inferences

3. Neo-Wigmorean Analysis

4. Bayesian Networks

5. Summary—Appreciating the Logic of Forensic Proof

Bibliography

Reproduced with permission ©RSS

The scope of the guide is applying the logic of inferential reasoning in criminal proceedings. It introduces and explains the fundamentals of inferential reasoning and aims to be of practical use to equip the reader to cope with the forensic demands of inferential reasoning.

In common with the other parts, it is a wordy document even though the authors claim that it has

[B]een shorn of dispensable technicality and is necessarily introductory and truncated,

Given its introductory nature, is does provide a reasonably exhaustive guide to the application of inferential reasoning. It describes the three forms of inferential reasoning—abduction, induction and deduction—and introduces a graphical means of linking evidence, propositions, and conclusions and sets out the logical rigor of the approaches discussed.

The concepts introduced cannot be considered simple and the vocabulary and terminology used, while no doubt accurate, sometimes makes comprehension difficult.

Part 4—Case Assessment and Interpretation (CAI) of Expert Evidence.

Authors—Graham Jackson, Colin Aitken, and Paul Roberts.

Published in January 2015.

This final part of the guide has 140 pages and the following structure:

1. Introduction to Case Assessment and Interpretation (CAI)
2. Principles of CAI and the Role of the Forensic Expert
3. CAI Protocol
4. CAI in Forensic Case Work: Three Detailed illustrations
5. How to Read Forensic Reports and Interpret Expert Opinions

CAI Aide-memoire

Bibliography

Reproduced with permission ©RSS

The scope of Part 4 is the process of CAI: a strictly logical and probabilistic approach to addressing the facts in issue in judicial proceedings. It incorporates the likelihood ratio approach to the interpretation of scientific information and recognizes the principles of balance, logic, robustness, and transparency introduced earlier in 3.4.2.4.2.

Although stated as specific to criminal proceedings, the principles might apply more broadly. It is very practically focused, examines the process of investigation and evaluation, and recognizes the dual role of a forensic scientist as investigator and evaluator. It also introduces and explains the useful concept of the forensic scientist as a reducer of uncertainty in the judicial process.

The three types of inferential reasoning are again explained together with the difference between investigative and evaluative opinion, concepts introduced earlier in 3.4.2.4.2. The guide highlights the problems associated with categorical opinions of "yes," "no," or "inconclusive."

CAI was the basis of the AFSP Standard and in turn the ENFSI Guidelines discussed earlier in 3.4.2.4.2 and 3.4.2.4.3, respectively. In common with those standards, Part 4 of the guide offers a standard against which conformance with the norms of forensic science management, practice, and delivery might be assessed.

Given its application to the "nuts and bolts" of the forensic science process, it is worth quoting the advantages of employing CAI given in Part 4 and reproduced below:

- "[CAI] clarifies the role of forensic expertise in criminal investigations, highlighting a vital distinction between investigative advice and evaluative opinions;
- identifies the different forms of logical reasoning characteristic of expert assistance in its investigative and evaluative modes;
- provides an illuminating taxonomy of the formulations currently routinely employed in forensic practice to report scientific findings, covering a spectrum ranging from hard scientific facts to evaluative expert opinions;
- rests on a rigorous logical method for evaluating the results of forensic examinations probabilistically[27];
- explains how the form in which evaluative opinion is expressed maps onto a "hierarchy of issues," such that the probative value of the evidence may change according to the issue addressed; and
- enables discrete evaluations of particular scientific inquiries to be amalgamated into a single evaluative opinion, addressed to issues at activity level (the level which may, at least sometimes and in certain circumstances, provide greatest assistance to criminal investigators and fact-finders)." Reproduced with permission ©RSS

The original objective of CAI was

> *To enable decisions to be made which will deliver a value for money service meeting the needs of our direct customers [the police forces of England & Wales] and the Criminal Justice System.*
>
> **Cook et al. (1998a,b).**

According to the authors, Part 4 addresses principles of forensic CAI, with particular regard to how forensic scientists should approach the task of assessing what types of examination, analysis, or testing should be commissioned, and for what purposes. CAI enables practitioners to properly advise stakeholders, particularly law-enforcement agencies, as to how forensic inquiries might be conducted effectively and efficiently. It also considers how forensic science and other expert evidence is, or should be, presented and evaluated in criminal trials. CAI leads to the production and implementation of an investigative strategy that is logically, rationally, and scientifically defensible. Having set out the advantages, Part 4 gives a nuts and bolts description of the process of CAI.

Part 4 highlights some conformance challenges, e.g., the need for the CAI approach to be adopted for Streamlined Forensic Reporting introduced by prosecuting authorities in England and Wales and discussed in Section 7.

[27] This stage is documented and published as the APSP Standard (Association of Forensic Science Providers, 2009) and ENFSI Guidelines (ENFSI, 2015).

Commentators have considered the implementation of CAI ambitious and identified some issues, e.g., the increased role of the forensic scientists in the investigative step of the forensic science process and CAI's poor fit with the market created in England and Wales (Lawless, 2010). Prior to its announced closure in December 2010, CAI had not become standard practice within the Forensic Science Service. Indeed the trend in England and Wales toward reducing forensic science laboratories to little more than testing laboratories, and forensic scientists to technicians, both under the control and direction of the police (Gallop and Brown, 2014) was by then well established. Therefore, the main impact of the CAI model was in leading to the development and publishing of the AFSP Standard, which in turn resulted in the ENFSI Guideline for Evaluative Reporting in Forensic Science.

CAI, together with it "successors," constitutes a very important standards framework in forensic science, and compliance is a mark of good practice. Evaluative opinions arrived at by some other process are likely to be unreliable.

3.4.2.4.5 ASTM Standard Practice for Evaluation of Scientific or Technical Data E678-07 (Reapproved 2013)

This standard comprises just two pages and is available from ASTM at a cost of 41 USD [December 2017]. It is not specific to forensic science and given the reasonably exhaustive standards discussed above it is only mentioned here for completeness. It may, of course, provide a brief checklist to assess conformance.

3.4.2.5 Reporting

3.4.2.5.1 ENFSI Guidelines for Evaluative Reporting

The guidelines discussed earlier in 3.4.2.4.3 also include the requirements for reporting evaluative opinions.

3.4.2.5.2 ASTM E 620-11 Reporting Opinions of Scientific or Technical Experts

The edition current at the time of writing [Decembers 2017], was published in 2013. It comprises two pages and is available from ASTM at a cost of 41 USD [December 2017]. This standard sets out the required contents of an expert report on opinions. Other standards are equally applicable, and it is only mentioned here for completeness.

3.4.2.5.3 ASTM E1020-13e1 Standard Practice for Reporting Incidents That May Involve Criminal or Civil Litigation

This edition current at the time of writing [December 2017], was published in 2013. It comprises two pages and is available from ASTM for 41 USD [December 2017]. It documents the requirement for recording factual information in an incident report. In dealing with factual reporting, it is distinguished from E620. This standard might apply to that part of crime scene examination concerned with factual reporting for the purpose of incident reconstruction.

3.4.3 Standards Applying to the Competence of the Organization

3.4.3.1 Forensic Science Regulator's Codes of Practice and Conduct for Forensic Science Providers

The edition of this standard current at the time of writing [December 2017], was published in October 2017. It is freely available for download. It has 58 pages, and the structure is given below. The corresponding clauses/sections of ISO/IEC 17025:2005 are given in brackets. The Codes require revision to take account of ISO/IEC 17025:2017.

1. Introduction
2. Scope
3. Normative references
4. Terms and definitions
5. Management requirements
6. Business continuity
7. Independence, impartiality, and integrity
8. Confidentiality
9. Document control (ISO/IEC 17025:2005 ref. 4.3)
10. Review of requests, tenders, and contracts (ISO/IEC 17025:2005 ref. 4.4)
11. Subcontracting (ISO/IEC 17025:2005 ref. 4.5)
12. Packaging and general chemicals and materials (ISO/IEC 17025:2005 ref. 4.6)
13. Complaints (ISO/IEC 17025:2005 ref. 4.8)
14. Control of nonconforming testing (ISO/IEC 17025:2005 ref. 4.9)
15. Control of records (ISO/IEC 17025:2005 ref. 4.13)
16. Internal audits (ISO/IEC 17025:2005 ref. 4.14)
17. Technical requirements (ISO/IEC 17025:2005 ref. 5.2)
18. Competence
19. Accommodation and environmental conditions (ISO/IEC 17025:2005 ref. 5.3)
20. Test methods and method validation (ISO/IEC 17025:2005 ref. 5.4)
21. Control of data (ISO/IEC 17025:2005 ref.5.4.7)
22. Equipment (ISO/IEC 17025:2005 ref. 5.5)
23. Measurement traceability - intermediate checks
24. Handling of test items (ISO/IEC 17025:2005 ref. 5.8)
25. Assuring the quality of test results (ISO/IEC 17025:2005 ref. 5.9)
26. Reporting the results (ISO/IEC 17025:2005 ref. 5.10)
27. Bibliography
28. Abbreviations
29. Glossary

The Codes also include a Code of Conduct for forensic science practitioners, which is discussed later in 3.4.4 and in 4.3.1 and is reproduced as Appendix B.

Forensic science providers offering laboratory or crime scene-based services to the criminal justice system fall within the scope of this standard. It is, therefore, specific to criminal proceedings. The standard does not apply to accountancy, psychiatry, or forensic medicine. Although the standard strictly applies only in the jurisdiction of England and Wales, providers in the other jurisdictions of the United Kingdom have voluntarily agreed to be bound by standards set by the Regulator (Forensic Science Regulator n.d.).

The normative references are as follows with references in this work in brackets:

- ISO/IEC 17025:2005, General requirements for the competence of testing and calibration laboratories; (3.2.2)
- ILAC G19:08/2014, Modules in a Forensic Science Process; (3.3.2.2)
- ISO/IEC 17020:2012, General criteria for the operation of various types of bodies performing inspection; (3.2.3)
- ILAC-P15:06/2014, Application of ISO/IEC 17020:2012 for the Accreditation of Inspection Bodies (now superseded by ILAC-P15:07/2016 and discussed earlier in this Section); and
- UKAS-RG 201:2015, Accreditation of Bodies Carrying Out Scene of Crime Examination (Edition 2) (3.3.3).

The Codes are supplements to ISO/IEC 17025 and ISO/IEC 17020, and the Regulator requires them to be included in the documented QMS of accredited providers. Conformance assessment is therefore conducted by the accrediting body, UKAS.

The requirements of independence, impartiality, integrity, and confidentiality are stated and explained.

Validation is a major section of the Codes, and the requirements are set out in considerable detail, expanding on that included in the ISO Standards and ILAC Guides. The Codes restate the technical requirement that all methods and procedures used must be validated prior to "implementation" or use. Meeting the needs of the "end user" is emphasized, and how that might best be achieved is explained. The Codes include a requirement for a documented validation plan and a validation "library" of relevant documents. Conformance with the validation requirements set out in this code is significantly more resource demanding that in the ILAC Guides but ensure conformance with the requirements of ISO/IEC 17025 and forensic science stakeholders.

In offering guidance on evaluating uncertainty of measurement, as conformance with ISO/IEC 17025 requires, the code refers to Appendix N "Uncertainties for Test Results" of the UKAS M 3003 publication "The Expression of Uncertainty and Confidence in Measurement." The UKAS guide is discussed earlier in 3.3.3. The UKAS guide recognizes that testing laboratories may find estimating uncertainty of measurement more difficult than calibration laboratories and provides helpful guidance.

The Regulator's Codes address case assessment and requires an examination strategy to be prepared and documented but does not mention the CAI approach discussed earlier in 3.4.2.4.4.

The Regulator's Codes of Practice and Conduct are probably the most exhaustive statement of requirements for the management, practice, and delivery of forensic science that is fit-for-purpose. Forensic science providers in the jurisdictions of the United Kingdom must conform to this standard to gain and maintain accreditation to ISO/IEC 17025 and ISO/IEC 17020. Providers elsewhere would do well to conform.

3.4.3.2 National Commission on Forensic Science—National Code of Professional Responsibility for Forensic Science and Forensic Medicine Providers

In March 2016, the National Commission on Forensic Science adopted this standard and recommended that the US Attorney General require DOJ (Department of Justice) forensic science providers to conform to the code and "strongly urge all" other forensic science stakeholder to conform to or require conformance to this standard. In September of that year, the Attorney General implemented the Code within the DOJ.

Although aimed at forensic science providers, and properly introduced here, it is closely similar to the Forensic Science Regulators' Code of practice for individual practitioners discussed later in 3.4.4.1.

The code is brief and comprises just 16 points which are reproduced below and as Appendix C.

1. Accurately represent relevant education, training, experience, and areas of expertise
2. Be honest and truthful in all professional affairs including not representing the work of others as one's own
3. Foster and pursue professional competency through such activities as training, proficiency testing, certification, and presentation and publication of research findings
4. Commit to continuous learning in relevant forensic disciplines and stay abreast of new findings, equipment, and techniques
5. Utilize scientifically validated methods and new technologies, while guarding against the use of unproven methods in casework and the misapplication of generally accepted standards
6. Handle evidentiary materials to prevent tampering, adulteration, loss, or nonessential consumption of evidentiary materials
7. Participation in any case in which there is a conflict of interest shall be avoided
8. Conduct independent, impartial, and objective examinations that are fair, unbiased, and fit-for-purpose
9. Make and retain contemporaneous, clear, complete, and accurate records of all examinations, tests, measurements, and conclusions, in sufficient detail to allow meaningful review and assessment by an independent professional proficient in the discipline
10. Ensure interpretations, opinions, and conclusions are supported by sufficient data and minimize influences and biases for or against any party

11. Render interpretations, opinions, or conclusions only when within the practitioner's proficiency or expertise
12. Prepare reports and testify using clear and straightforward terminology, clearly distinguishing data from interpretations, opinions, and conclusions and disclosing known limitations that are necessary to understand the significance of the findings
13. Reports and other records shall not be altered and information shall not be withheld for strategic or tactical advantage
14. Document and, if appropriate, inform management or quality assurance personnel of nonconformities and breaches of law or professional standards
15. Once a report is issued and the adjudicative process has commenced, communicate fully when requested with the parties through their investigators, attorneys, and experts, except when instructed that a legal privilege, protective order or law prevents disclosure.
16. Appropriately inform affected recipients (either directly or through proper management channels) of all nonconformities or breaches of law or professional standards that adversely affect a previously issued report or testimony and make reasonable efforts to inform all relevant stakeholders, including affected professional and legal parties, victim(s) and defendant(s).

Reproduced with the permission of OSAC

In addition to being closely similar to the Regulator's Code for practitioners, it is also similar to the other codes discussed later in 3.4.4.

3.4.3.3 ANAB ISO/IEC 17025:2005—Forensic Science Testing Laboratories: Accreditation Requirements (AR 3028)

The standard is based on the ASCLD/LAB-International Supplemental Requirements for the Accreditation of Forensic Science Testing Laboratories published in 2011, which is still available for download.

It was first published prior to implementation of the ASCLD/LAB to ANAB transition process, which began on the 1st June 2017, the date on which the standard became effective, and ends at the end of December 2018. At the time of writing [December 2017], the current version was dated the 22nd of August 2017. The standard is freely available for download. It has 22 pages, and the structure is as follows:

1. Scope
2. References
3. Terms and definitions
4. Management requirements
5. Technical requirements

Reproduced with permission ©ANAB

The standard supplements the requirements of ISO/IEC 17025:2005 Sections 4 and 5 and applies to forensic science providers offering testing services.

The normative references are as follows:

- ILAC P8—ILAC MRA: Supplementary Requirements and Guidelines for the Use of Accreditation Symbols and for Claims of Accreditation Status by Accredited Laboratories and Inspection Bodies.
- ILAC P9—ILAC Policy for Participation in Proficiency Testing Activities.
- ILAC P10—ILAC Policy on the Traceability of Measurement Results.
- ILAC G19—Modules in a Forensic Science Process.
- ISO 9000:2015—Quality management systems—Fundamentals and vocabulary
- ISO/IEC 17000:2004—Conformity assessment—Vocabulary and general principles
- ISO/IEC 17025:2005—General requirements for the competence of testing and calibration laboratories
- Joint Committee for Guides in Metrology (JCGM), International vocabulary of metrology—Basic and general concepts and associated terms (VIM) (Sèvres, France: International Bureau of Weights and Measures [BIPM]-JCGM 200).
- US DOJ, Federal Bureau of Investigation (FBI), National DNA Index System (NDIS) Operational Procedures Manual.
- US Department of Justice (DOJ), Federal Bureau of Investigation (FBI), Quality Assurance Requirements for DNA Testing Laboratories.

The standard requires conformance with "Guiding Principles of Professional Responsibility for Crime Laboratories and Forensic Scientists" discussed later in 3.4.4.2.

The standard specifies minimum educational requirements for particular forensic scientific disciplines. It is noteworthy that for comparison disciplines that might be accredited to ISO/IEC 17020 no minimum qualification is specified.

The standard contains detailed requirements applying to proficiency tests or PTs (5.9.3). It specifies that "where available and appropriate" providers of PTs must be accredited to ISO/IEC 17043 by an accreditation body that is a signatory to the Asia Pacific Laboratory Accreditation Cooperation mutual recognition agreement or Inter-American Accreditation Cooperation[28] multilateral recognition arrangement and has the applicable PT(s) within the scope of its accreditation. ANAB accredited forensic science providers must conform to this standard.

3.4.4 Standards Applying to the Competence of the Individual Forensic Scientist

3.4.4.1 The Forensic Science Regulator's Code of Conduct for Forensic Science Practitioners

This Code is part of the Regulator's Codes of Practice and Conduct discussed earlier in 3.4.3.1. It lists 10 requirements recorded on a single page and is reproduced below and as

[28] APLAC and IAAC are both regional members of ILAC.

Appendix B. It is based on the CRFP code of conduct discussed in 4.3.1.2.1 and the UKFSLG code in 4.2.

"As a practitioner:

1. Your overriding duty is to the court and to the administration of justice.
2. Act with honesty, integrity, objectivity and impartiality, and declare at the earliest opportunity any personal, business and/or financial interest that could be perceived as a conflict of interest.
3. Provide expert advice and evidence only within the limits of your professional competence.
4. Take all reasonable steps to maintain and develop your professional competence, taking account of material research and developments within the relevant field.
5. Establish the integrity and continuity of items as they come into your possession and ensure these are maintained whilst in your possession.
6. Seek access to exhibits/productions/information that may have a significant impact on your findings.
7. Conduct casework using methods of demonstrable validity.
8. Be prepared to review any casework if any new information or developments are identified that would significantly impact on your findings.
9. Inform a suitable person within your organisation if you have good grounds for believing there is a situation that may result in a miscarriage of justice.
10. Preserve confidentiality unless the law obliges, a court/tribunal orders, or a customer explicitly authorises disclosure."

Reproduced with permission © Crown Copyright

By including this Code of Conduct within the Regulator's Codes and requiring the Codes to be incorporated into the documented QMS of accredited providers, conformity is assessed by the accrediting body, in this case, UKAS.

This is an example of the optimal separation between standards development/setting, conformity assessment and service provision, and the independence of those bodies.

3.4.4.2 ANAB Guiding Principles on Professional Responsibility for Crime Laboratories and Forensic Scientists

The edition of the standard current at the time of writing [Decembers 2017], came into effect in November 2016 and comprises four pages. It is freely available for download. The structure is as follows:

Preamble

Professionalism

Competency and Proficiency

Clear communications.

Reproduced with permission ©ANAB

Although the title suggests that it applies to organizations, it is in practice a code of conduct for individuals.

Conformance with this standard is a requirement of ANAB, which is included in the ANAB [supplemental] ISO/IEC 17025 accreditation requirements discussed earlier in 3.4.3.3.

This arrangement is less than optimal as the accrediting body and the standards developing/setting body are one and the same.

It is noteworthy that both the Regulator's Code and ANAB's guide require objectivity on the part of the individual forensic scientist. Objectivity is one of the hallmarks of scientific inquiry as discussed in Section 1, a lack or insufficiency of objectivity could be considered a nonconformance with either standard. The requirement for objectivity is discussed further in Section 7.

3.4.4.3 The Forensic Specialities Accreditation Board—Standards for Accrediting Forensic Speciality Certification Boards

The Forensic Specialities Accreditation Board (FSAB) is a private US company that accredits organizations or professional boards that in turn certify as competent individual forensic scientists in specific disciplines; the FSAB accredits the certifiers.

Until recently this body lay outside the recognized quality standards framework based on international standards. At the time of writing [December 2017], it is progressing towards conformance to ISO/IEC 17011, discussed earlier in 3.2.4. Once conformance to ISO/IEC 17011 is achieved, the FSAB will require the certifying bodies, now termed conformity assessment boards (CAB), to conform to ISO/IEC 17024, discussed earlier in 3.2.5, and be accredited to that standard by FSAB.CABs applying for initial accreditation after February 2018 must conform to ISO/IEC 17024, CABs reaccreditating after February 2018 should conform to that standard and from 2021 must. The certifying bodies that were accredited by the FSAB prior to this initiative are:

- American Board of Criminalistics;
- American Board of Forensic Toxicology;
- Board of Forensic Document Examiners;
- American Board of Forensic Document Examiners;
- American Board of Forensic Anthropology;
- Forensic Photography Certification Board;
- Latent Print Certification Board;
- Tenprint Fingerprint Certification Board;
- International Association of Arson Investigators;
- Certified Fire Investigator Board;
- Crime Scene Certification Board;
- Footwear Certification Board;
- Forensic Art Certification Board; and
- Bloodstain Pattern Examiner Certification Board.

This initiative of the FSAB represents a major and welcome development in the quality standards framework applicable to forensic science. As mentioned in 3.2.5 above and having been considered in 2008, as recorded in 4.3.1, the adoption of ISO/IEC 17024 has thus far been resisted by the forensic science industry. However, as explained in 3.2.5

and further discussed in 7.4.1 the current position where forensic science providers rely on organizational competence conforming to ISO/IEC 17025 as an assurance of staff competence lacks independence and is suboptimal.

While there is no doubt that conforming to ISO/IEC 17011 and then requiring CABs to gain accreditation to ISO/IEC 17024 is a challenging and lengthy task, if and when established it will provide a model that the rest of the industry can adopt.

3.4.4.4 The Codes of Conduct[29] of Professional Bodies

Four professional bodies are considered in alphabetical order. Prior to looking at each code in some detail the way in which professional bodies fit into a quality standards framework needs to be explored. Professional bodies generally exist to serve the interests of their members and protect the reputation of the profession. In addition, a public service ethos is often encouraged and expected. Most professional bodies have a code of conduct (however named) but not all assess and/or enforce conformance. Where a professional body does regulate its membership, it generally does so with the aim of protecting the reputation of the profession. In contrast, a regulatory body must act solely in the public interest. The primacy of member's interests and those of the profession makes professional bodies suboptimal regulators. Optimally, a regulatory body should regulate professional bodies, or at least professional activities, which would go some way to complying with the need to separate the roles of standards setting, conformance assessment, and service provision.

Accreditation to ISO/IEC 17025 gives primacy to meeting stakeholder needs, including those of a regulatory authority. A practical approach to incorporating the code of conduct of a professional body within a quality standards framework is to include the code in the documented QMS of the accredited forensic science provider. Once incorporated, conformance can be assessed by internal and external audit of the QMS.

3.4.4.4.1 The American Academy of Forensic Sciences—Code of Ethics and Conduct

All members (members and affiliates) of the Academy are bound by the code. It is placed within the bylaws of the Academy, being Article 2. The code is brief, being on one page, and general in coverage. It is reproduced as Appendix D. It might be summarized as follows:

1. Every member and affiliate of the Academy shall refrain from exercising professional or personal conduct adverse to the best interests and objectives of the Academy.

[29] As explained in the introduction/conventions, Code of Conduct includes Codes of Ethics, Behaviors, Practice, etc.

2. No member or affiliate of the Academy shall materially misrepresent his or her education, training, experience, area of expertise, or membership status within the Academy.
3. No member or affiliate of the Academy shall materially misrepresent data or scientific principles upon which his or her conclusion or professional opinion is based.
4. No member or affiliate of the Academy shall issue public statements that appear to represent the position of the Academy without first obtaining specific authority from the Board of Directors.

Reproduced with permission ©AAFS

These may be paraphrased as protecting the reputation of the Academy and requiring the member to be honest. The full version implies the requirement for maintaining competence but otherwise the code's requirements are a little vague in comparison to other codes of conduct.

The brevity and general nature of the code make it an insufficient guide to good practice in a specific set of circumstances. However, its brevity and general nature may be a consequence of the disparate membership of the Academy, which is open to all engaged in the "forensic enterprise," as reported in 2.2.4.5.1. The general nature of the code does offer flexibility in scope. There is no mechanism for conformity assessment. There is a complaints procedure. In making a complaint, there is no requirement to cite the part of the code breached. Complaints brought to the attention of the Board of Directors are passed to the Ethics Committee for investigation according to the procedures given at 6.4 "Ethics Committee Rules and Procedures" of the Academy's Policy and Procedure Manual (PPM). The Ethics Committee is a standing committee of the Academy, which reports and makes recommendations to the Board of Directors. The Board may ratify the decision of the Ethics Committee. Members found to have breached the Code can be sanctioned.

The American Academy of Forensic Sciences PPM is freely available for download. The structure of 6.4 is as follows:

1. Composition
2. Investigation initiating action
3. General provisions
4. Investigations
5. Hearings
6. Board procedures
7. Sanctions
8. Appeal to the membership
9. Effects of sanctions

Reproduced with permission ©AAFS

The outcomes for members who are found to have breached the code are censure, suspension, or expulsion. Corrective or preventative actions are not recognized outcomes.

3.4.4.4.2 Australia and New Zealand Forensic Science Society—Code of Professional Practice

The code came into effect in 2014 and comprises four pages. The Code of Practice for Registered Professional Engineers in Queensland, Australia, is referenced. The Australia and New Zealand Forensic Science Society (ANZFSS) code is reproduced as Appendix E.

All professional members of the ANZFSS are bound by the code. Its structure is as follows:

1. Obligations to society
2. Obligations to clients and employers
3. General professional obligations

Reproduced with permission ©ANZFSS

It is a little more detailed and tightly focused than the American Academy of Forensic Sciences code and includes requirements similar to those of the Forensic Science Regulator's Codes given earlier in 3.4.4.1. It includes the requirement for objectivity but, interestingly, does not specifically require impartiality or independence.

The code is referred to in the society's Rules of Association (11.1) which, like the code, is freely available for download. The Rules of Association were published in 2016 and include a procedure for taking disciplinary action against a member for breach of the Rules (17) but not specifically complaints regarding a breach of the code.

There is no mechanism for conformity assessment and no publicly documented procedure for processing complaints. The outcomes of disciplinary procedures against members are reprimand, suspension, or expulsion. Corrective or preventative actions are not recognized outcomes.

3.4.4.4.3 Code of Ethics of the California Association of Criminalists[30]

The Code of Ethics of the California Association of Criminalists dates from 1957 and is the most detailed, learned, and comprehensive of the extant codes applying to individual forensic scientists. One disadvantage of a detailed code is a lack of flexible scope. Circumstances may arise that lie outside the sope, and it may not be practicable to revise the code to bring those circumstances within scope.

The edition current at the time of writing [December 2017], was published in 2010. It is freely available and comprises five pages. The structure is as follows:

1. Ethics relating to scientific method
2. Ethics relating to opinions and conclusions
3. Ethical aspects of court presentation
4. Ethics relating to the general practice of criminalistics
5. Ethical responsibilities to the profession.

[30] The term criminalistics is mostly encountered in the United States. It can have a number of meanings including as a synonym for forensic science.

Reproduced with permission ©CAC

The code prescribes and proscribes competencies, behaviors, and practices. The code sets out the requirements that must be met by a forensic scientist both as a scientist and as an expert witness.

Conformity assessment and a complaints procedure are documented in "The Code of Ethics Enforcement of the California Association of Criminalists." The edition of the standard current at the time of writing [December 2017], was published in 2015 and comprises 11 pages. The structure of the enforcement procedure is as follows:

Statement of principles,

- The allegation and its investigation,
- Powers and procedures of enforcement by the Board,
- Procedures for appeal and hearing of appeal.

Reproduced with permission ©CAC

The procedure is very detailed and aims to meet the requirements of natural justice—a fair process and a safe decision. The stated duty and responsibility of the California Association of Criminalists is to "supervise, investigate and enforce its member's adherence to the code"; by this means conformity is monitored and assessed.

Complaints are first considered by the California Association of Criminalists president. Once it is established that the complaint has merit, the ethics committee investigates and makes a recommendation for consideration by the Board.

For members found to have breached the Code, the sanctions available are reprimand, suspension, or expulsion. Corrective or preventive actions are not recognized among the outcomes.

3.4.4.4.4 Chartered Society of Forensic Sciences—Code of Conduct

The edition of the code current at the tie of writing [December 2017], dates from 2015. The code itself is short, just one page. However, in contrast to other professional codes, it is part of a standards' framework. In addition to requiring members to act in the interests of the Society and the profession it mandates compliance with the Forensic Science Regulator's Code of Conduct, discussed earlier in 3.4.4.1, and the Criminal Procedure Rules (CrimPR) discussed later in 3.4.7.1.3.[31]

In common with other professional bodies, the Society relies on disciplinary regulations as a means of enforcement. However, it also has a separate complaints procedure. Complaints are first received by the Secretary of the Society who manages the processing of the complaint. Depending on the nature and seriousness of the complaint, it might be referred to the governing body of the society, the Council. The evidence is gathered

[31] It is of interest to note that these regulations apply only in the jurisdiction of England and Wales. The Society has an international membership. Members practicing in other jurisdictions must agree to comply with standards that do not apply in their jurisdiction.

by a Membership and Ethics Committee. If the complaint might result in disciplinary action, the Council appoints a disciplinary committee which considers the matter and makes a recommendation for consideration by the Council. The sanctions available are suspension or expulsion. Corrective or preventative actions are not recognized among the outcomes.

3.4.4.5 Occupational Standards—Assuring the Competence of the Individual

3.4.4.5.1 Australasian Forensic Field Sciences Accreditation Board

The Australasian Forensic Field Sciences Accreditation Board (AFFSAB) is managed by NIFS (National Institute of Standards) and ANZPAA (Australia New Zealand Police Advisory Agency). The AFFSAB certifies as competent fingerprint, firearms, and crime scene examiners, ensuring, through recertification, that examiners maintain competence. The Board reviews the performance of examiners who fail to comply with established occupational standards.

Although the term "accreditation" is used, the convention in this work, and in forensic science in general, is that organizations are accredited, and individuals are certified as competent.

The certification process is set out in a "Policy and Processes For Certification" document which. at the time of writing [December 2017], is under revision.

Certification is based on experience, qualifications, knowledge and management recommendation. Recertification is required every five years.

AFFSAB certification is odd within the Australasian forensic science quality standards framework. The concept of individual certification has been tried and rejected for most other disciplines (ANZFSS n.d.), partly on the grounds stated earlier, that ISO/IEC 17025 accredited forensic science providers are responsible for the competence of their employees. However, if seen as a standard for law enforcement agents administered and controlled by law enforcement agencies, the existence of the standard is better understood. It should be noted that this arrangement raises conflicts-of-interest issues, introduced earlier in 3.1 and discussed further in Section 7, and is not part of a quality standards framework based on ISO/IEC standards.

3.4.4.5.2 Skills for Justice and National Occupational Standards

In the United Kingdom, Skills for Justice (SFJ) has produced a series of National Occupational Standards (NOSs) for forensic scientists that provide a framework for staff training and competence assessment.

NOSs are statements of the standards of performance individuals must achieve when carrying out functions in the workplace, together with specifications of the underpinning knowledge and understanding. They are outcome based and set out the requirements for competent performance of individual forensic science practitioners.

Like all occupational standards, they can help accredited providers meet the requirements of ISO/IEC 17020 and ISO/IEC 17025 in terms of ensuring the competence of their technical or inspection staff.

The standards produced by SFJ can be used to prepare procedural standards to cover staff training and development.

The standards have the following simple structure:

1. Overview
2. Performance Criteria
3. Knowledge and understanding

Conformity assessment of accredited forensic science providers incorporating occupational standards within their QMS is by the accreditation body.

Providers wishing to avail themselves of the services provided by SFJ must become members. The cost of membership at the time of writing [April 2017] is a 3.5 GBP per employee with a minimum fee of 1,000 GBP.

However, the standards are freely available for download from the UK Standards website (UK Standards n.d.) and constitute a source of occupational standards that might be easily incorporated into the quality management system of a forensic science provider.

In terms of crime scene examination, the requirements set out in these standards are closely similar to those in ILAC G19:08/2014, discussed earlier in 3.3.2.

The development of occupational standards is charted in "Ensuring Competent Performance in Forensic Science" (Hadley and Fereday, 2008).

3.4.5 Level 3 Standards Applying to the Validation of Analytical Measurements

3.4.5.1 Valid Analytical Measurement (VAM) and the Six VAM Principles

In the late 1980s and early 1990s, traceability in analytical measurement relying on reference materials did not exist and at the time work being done by the CIPM (Comitè international des poids et measures—the highest authority on metrology) in developing a standards framework for analytical measurement was expected to take many years, if not decades, to complete (Gillespie and Upton, 2005).

The potential impact on commerce and society in general by the unreliability of analytical measurements due to poor practice prompted the VAM program within the United Kingdom. The program began in 1992 as an initiative of the then UK Department of Trade and Industry (DTI). The DTI's program on VAM was an integral part of the UK National Measurement System. The aim of the VAM program was to help analytical laboratories demonstrate the validity of their data and to facilitate mutual recognition of the results of analytical measurements.

The VAM program was a long-term commitment to improving the quality of analytical measurement within the United Kingdom and across Europe via EURACHEM.

The program addressed five main issues:

1. The use of validated methods,
2. The availability and use of certified reference materials,
3. The use of internal quality assurance procedures,
4. Inter-laboratory participation in proficiency testing schemes, and
5. Third party audits and assessments to ensure recognition of a laboratory's quality assurance protocol.

The aim of the VAM program was to raise awareness among analytical service providers of the importance of obtaining reliable results and, through the principles set out, how reliability could be achieved, i.e., to improve the quality of the analytical measurements in the United Kingdom. The work centered on three main areas of activity:

1. defining and disseminating good analytical practice which would enable laboratories to deliver reliable results every time,
2. developing the tools which would enable laboratories to implement good analytical practice, and
3. working with analysts in other countries to ensure comparability of analytical measurements across international boundaries.

Conformance was voluntary, and there were no conformity assessment mechanisms in place.

Good analytical practice is defined by the six VAM principles:

1. Analytical measurements should be made to satisfy an agreed requirement.
2. Analytical measurements should be made using methods and equipment which have been tested to ensure they are fit for purpose.
3. Staff making analytical measurements should be both qualified and competent to undertake the task.
4. There should be a regular independent assessment of the technical performance of a laboratory.
5. Analytical measurements made in one location should be consistent with those elsewhere.
6. Organizations making analytical measurements should have well defined quality control and quality assurance procedures.

Originally recorded by M Sargent and published in Analytical Proceedings including Analytical Communications, May 1995, Vol 201

The VAM initiative and program predate the introduction of ISO/IEC 17025 in 1999. The initiative was mainly one of outlining, informing, and encouraging good practice in making analytical measurements. The six principles provide an excellent and concise summary of the standards that must be met to ensure valid measurement that can be relied on in forensic science. Nonconformance with any of the principles casts doubt on the reliability of results and measurements and consequently scientific information.

3.4.5.2 EC 2002/657/EC

Of particular importance in forensic chemistry is European Commission decision 2002/657/EC implementing Council directive 96/23/EC concerning the performance of analytical methods and the interpretation of results. The standard is freely available from the European Union website.

Although having direct application to the monitoring of certain substances, and residues thereof, in live animals and animal products, forensic chemistry as a whole would benefit from compliance particularly in terms of the quality of evidence and harmonization.

The directive seeks to bring the concept of outcome-based high-level standards to forensic chemistry.

> *(6) As a result of advances in analytical chemistry since the adoption of Directive 96/23/EC the concept of routine methods and reference methods has been superseded by criteria approach, in which performance criteria and procedures for the validation of screening and confirmatory methods are established.*

The document is a detailed and scientifically rigorous approach to method selection and validation. It includes an extensive glossary of method performance criteria and covers most methods of separating the substance of interest from other components in the sample, in both the liquid and gas phase, and detection of the separated substance of interest by spectrometric and spectroscopic techniques. It uses frequentist[32] (classical) tests of significance for the interpretation of results.

Deciding stakeholder requirements by starting with the necessary method performance criteria is a more scientific approach than merely adapting existing in-house methods.

Of particular relevance in mass spectrometry is the introduction of identification points for results. The relationship between a range of classes of mass fragment and identification points earned is shown in Table 3.6, and examples of the number of identification points earned for a range of techniques and combinations thereof is shown in Table 3.7.

Some knowledge of mass spectrometric techniques is required to fully understand these tables. However, the important factor to note is that the number of points needed for identification is dependent on the target substance **but the minimum is three**. [Emphasis added]

The directive in general and the above tables, in particular, make clear the power of modern high mass accuracy and resolution instruments such as those incorporating an Orbitrap mass analyzer. In simple terms, such instruments produce results of chemical identity with a degree of certainty that exceeds all other methods or combination of methods provided the substance of interest is separable, to a degree, in the liquid phase from other components of the sample.

[32] There are two fundamental approaches to statistical inference: frequentist and Bayesian.

Table 3.6 The relationship between a range of classes of mass fragment and identification points earned based on Table 5 from 96/23/EC

Mass spectrometric technique	Identification points earned per ion
Low resolution mass spectrometry (LR-MS)	1.0
LR-MS^n precursor ion	1.0
LR-MS^n transition products	1.5
High Resolution MS	2.0
HR-MS^n precursor ion	2.0
HR-MS^n transition products	2.5

(1) Each ion may only be counted once.
(2) GC-MS using electron impact ionization is regarded as being a different technique to GC-MS using chemical ionization.
(3) Different analytes can be used to increase the number of identification points only if the derivatives employ different reaction chemistries.
(4) For substances in Group A of Annex 1 to Directive 96/23/EC, if one of the following techniques are used in the analytical procedure: HPLC coupled with full-scan diode array spectrophotometry (DAD); HPLC coupled with fluorescence detection; HPLC coupled to an immunogram; two-dimensional TLC coupled to spectrometric detection; a maximum of one identification point may be contributed, providing that the relevant criteria for these techniques are fulfilled.
(5) Transition products include both daughter[a] and granddaughter products.
[a]IUPAC recommends that anthropogenic terms should not be used.

Table 3.7 Examples of the number of identification points earned for a range of techniques and combinations thereof (n = an integer)

Techniques	Number of ions	Points
GC-MS (EI or CI)	N	n
GC-MS (EI and CI)	2 (EI) + 2 (CI)	4
GC-MS (EI or CI) 2 derivatives	2 (Derivative A) + 2 (Derivative B)	4
LC-MS	N	n
GC-MS-MS	1 precursor and 2 daughters	4
LC-MS-MS	1 precursor and 2 daughters	4
GC-MS-MS	2 precursor ions, each with 1 daughter	5
LC-MS-MS	2 precursor ions, each with 1 daughter	5
LC-MS-MS-MS	1 precursor, 1 daughter, and 2 granddaughters	5.5
HRMS	N	2 n
GC-MS and LC-MS	2 + 2	4
GC-MS and HRMS	2 + 1	4

CI, chemical ionization, another means of creating ions; *EI*, electron impact, a means of creating ions (electronically charged species) of the sample components; *GC*, gas chromatography, a means of separating the components of a sample in the gas phase; *HRMS*, high resolution mass spectrometry; *LC*, liquid chromatography, a means of separating the components of a sample in the liquid phase; *MS*, mass spectrometry, a means of detecting and identifying the components of a sample.

One weakness in the document is the inclusion of specificity rather than selectivity. As explained earlier in 3.4.2.3.1, IUPAC has recommended that the term "specificity" should be avoided as in logic no method is specific in the sense of a response to one substance to the exclusion of all others. A second less important weakness is the use of anthropogenic terms for product ions, i.e.,"daughter."

Conformance is mandated by EU law for laboratories providing the specified analytical services. However, where a forensic science provider is using spectrometric measurements, e.g., in toxicology, conformance would constitute good practice.

3.4.5.3 EURACHEM/CITAC Guide to Quality in Analytical Chemistry

The edition of the guide current at the time of writing [December 2017], was published in January 2017. It is freely available for download from the EURACHEM website.

The aim of the guide is to provide laboratories with guidance on best practice for the analytical operations they carry out. The guide covers both qualitative and quantitative analyses carried out on a routine or nonroutine basis. The normative references are

ISO/IEC 17025:2005 General requirements for the competence of testing and calibration laboratories

ISO/IEC 17000:2004 Conformity assessment—Vocabulary and general principles

ISO 9000:2015 Quality management system standards

JCGM 200:2012 International vocabulary of metrology (VIM)—Basic and general concepts and associated terms

The guide focuses on meeting the requirements of ISO/IEC 17025. However, it is also intended to help laboratories comply with the Principles of Good Laboratory Practice,[33] ISO 15189, ISO 9001, or laboratories not seeking accreditation or certification but wishing to establish a QMS. The authors anticipate that the guide will be of benefit to disciplines other than analytical chemistry.

The guide comprises 66 pages, and its structure is as follows:

1. Notes for the reader
2. Introduction
3. Definitions and terminology
4. Accreditation
5. Scope of accreditation
6. The analytical task
7. Specification of analytical requirement
8. Analytical strategy

[33] This is a standard published by the Organisation for Economic Cooperation and Development and applies to laboratories that conduct safety testing of a number of types of chemical products. It has no particular relevance in forensic science.

9. Nonroutine analysis
10. Personnel
11. Sampling, sample handling, and preparation
12. Environment
13. Equipment
14. Reagents and consumables
15. Metrological traceability
16. Measurement uncertainty
17. Methods/procedures for calibrations and tests
18. Method validation
19. Calibration
20. RMs
21. Quality control and proficiency testing
22. Computers and computer controlled systems
23. Laboratory audit and review

Appendix A—Quality audit: Areas of particular importance to a chemistry laboratory

Appendix B—Instrument calibration and performance checks

Bibliography

Reproduced by permission of Eurachem

Laboratory-based forensic science providers accredited to ISO/IEC 17025:2017 must conform to this guide. Conformity assessment will be by the accrediting body. Otherwise, conformance would be expected for any forensic science provider including analytical chemical methods as part of its service.

3.4.5.4 The Fitness for Purpose of Analytical Methods—A Laboratory Guide to Method Validation and Related Topics

The edition of the guide current at the time of writing [December 2017], was published by EURACHEM in 2014. It is freely available from the EURACHEM website.

It is noteworthy that the guide references the six VAM principles, discussed earlier in 3.4.5.1, and states that they are still relevant and consistent with ISO/IEC 17025. The main aim of the guide is to assist laboratories implement VAM Principle 2.

> *Analytical measurements should be made using methods and equipment which have been tested to ensure they are fit for purpose.*

The guide applies to all laboratories conducting analytical tests or measurements including forensic science providers.

The guide comprises 70 pages, and its structure is as follows:

1. Introduction
2. What is method validation?
3. Why is method validation necessary?

4. When should methods be validated or verified?
5. How should methods be validated?
6. Method performance characteristics
7. Using validated methods
8. Using validation data to design quality control
9. Documentation of validated method
10. Implications of validation data for calculating and reporting results

Annex A—Method documentation protocol
Annex B—Statistical basis of LOD calculations
Annex C—Analysis of variance (ANOVA)
Annex D—Notes on qualitative analysis
Bibliography
Reproduced by permission of Eurachem

ISO/IEC 17025, ILAC G19:2002, and ILAC G19:08/2014 all mandate the validation of methods used by forensic science providers. This document is a definitive guide to the validation of analytical chemical methods employed in forensic science.

3.4.6 Level 3 Standards Applying to Specific Disciplines

As might be expected, discipline-specific standards are numerous. Most are developed and documented by just three bodies: ENFSI in Europol member states, the Forensic Science Regulator in England and Wales, and OSAC in the United States. Standards Australia has also developed and published some discipline-specific standards.

What follows are mainly lists of these standards. The detail will be examined in Section 6.

3.4.6.1 ENFSI Best Practice Manuals and Forensic Guidelines

ENFSI documents discipline-specific standards as Best Practice Manuals (BPM), those extant at the time of writing [December 2017], are listed in Table 3.8, and Forensic Guidelines in Table 3.9.

Each standard is freely available for download from the ENFSI website. The main text usually occupies around 10 pages. The typical structure of a BPM is as follows:

1. Aims
2. Scope
3. Definition and terms
4. Resources
5. Methods
6. Validation and estimation of uncertainty of measurement
7. Proficiency testing
8. Handling items

Table 3.8 ENFSI discipline-specific standards—best practice manuals

#	Discipline	References	Issue and Date
1	Investigation of Fire Scenes	ENFSI-BPM-FEI-01	Version 01—November 2015
2	Examination of Handwriting	ENFSI-BPM-FHX-01	Version 01—November 2015
3	Recovery, Identification and Analysis of Explosives Traces	ENFSI-BPM-EXP-01	Version 01—November 2015
4	Application of Molecular Methods for the Forensic Examination on Non-Human Biological Traces	ENFSI-BPM-APS-01	Version 01—November 2015
5	DNA Pattern Recognition and Comparison	ENFSI-BPM-DNA-01	Version 01—November 2015
6	Fingerprint Examination	ENFSI-BPM—FIN—01	Version 01—November 2015
7	Microscopic Examination of Human and Animal Hair and Comparison	ENFSI-BPM-THG-03	Version 01—November 2015
8	Road Accident Reconstruction	ENFSI-BPM-RAA-01	Version 01—November 2015
9	Chemographic Methods in Gunshot Residue Analysis	ENFSI-BPM-FGR-01	Version 01—November 2015

Table 3.9 ENFSI discipline-specific standards—forensic guidelines

Title	References	Edition	Date
Guidelines on Sampling of Illicit Drugs for Quantitative Analysis[a]	DWG-GQS-002	Issue No.001	April 2014
ENFSI Guideline for Evaluative Reporting in Forensic Science[b]		Version 3.0	March 08 2015
Recommended Minimum Criteria for the Validation of Various Aspects of the DNA Profiling Process	ENFSI DNA WORKING GROUP	Issue No.001	November 2010
[DNA] Contamination prevention guidelines	ENFSI DNA WORKING GROUP	Issue No.001	November 2010
Education and Training Outline for Forensic Drug Practitioners	DWG-GDL-003	Issue No.003	October 26 2015

[a]This standard seems to have been withdrawn and replaced by the UNODC Guide published in 2009 (UNODC, 2009) and now bearing the ENFSI logo.
[b]This standard is discussed in 3.4.2.4.3

9. Initial assessment
10. Prioritization and sequence of examinations
11. Reconstruction of events
12. Evaluation and interpretation
13. Presentation of evidence
14. Health and Safety
15. References/Bibliography

Appendices

The structure of each guide varies but usually includes aims, scope, definitions and terms, and references.

3.4.6.2 Forensic Science Regulator's Discipline-Specific Standards

These are listed in Table 3.10. They are all freely available for download from the Regulator's website. The structure varies. All UK-based forensic science providers that are accredited have agreed to be bound by the Regulator's standards. Providers incorporate the relevant standards into their documented QMS, and conformity assessment is therefore conducted by the accreditating body.

3.4.6.3 Organization of Scientific Area Committees

As detailed in Section 2, the Organization of Scientific Area Committees (OSAC) was formed in 2014 through a memorandum of understanding between the National

Table 3.10 FSR discipline-specific standards

Subject	Published	Pages
Sexual assault referral centers and custodial facilities: DNA anti-contamination	2016-07-22	20
Crime Scene DNA: anti-contamination	2016-07-12	45
Laboratory DNA: anti-contamination	2015-12-31	47
Bloodstain pattern analysis: codes of practice	2015-12-14	23
Cognitive bias effects relevant to forensic science examinations	2015-10-30	96
Alcohol back calculation for road traffic investigations	2015-05-08	7
Fingerprint examination: terminology, definitions and acronyms	2015-03-24	27
Code of practice and conduct 2015: fingerprint comparison	2015-03-24	22
Forensic science providers: validation	2014-11-14	53
DNA analysis: codes of practice and conduct	2014-09-17	11
Allele frequency databases and reporting guidance for the DNA-17 profiling	2014-09-14	15
DNA contamination detection	2014-09-12	49
Interpreting DNA evidence	2012-12-06	27

Institute of Standards and Technology (NIST) and the Department of Justice (DOJ) for the purpose of developing documentary standards related to forensic science. NIST has the role of administrator for the OSAC and is responsible for developing a quality standards framework for forensic science in the United States in response to the 2009 NRC report (National Research Council, 2009).

Discipline-specific groups have been established as shown in Fig. 4.3. OSAC is charged with populating a register of approved standards and relies on each Scientific Area Committee (SAC) to identify and develop standards for inclusion in the registry. The process is graphically represented by Fig. 4.1.

As explained in 4.3.2, standards in the registry will be incorporated into the documented QMS of accredited providers of the particular discipline and conformity assessed by an accreditation body.

On January 11, 2016, the OSAC Forensic Science Standards Board voted to elevate ASTM Standard E2329-14 "Standard Practice for Identification of Seized Drugs" to the OSAC Registry of Approved Standards. The standard is used by forensic laboratories as a protocol for testing seized drug evidence to determine if drugs of abuse, such as cocaine or heroin, are present. This was the first standard posted to the registry.

However, the adoption of this standard and its inclusion in the registry has not been without controversy (National Institute of Standards, 2016) and identifies the risk of standards being included in the registry that lack the necessary scientific rigor called for by the NRC report (National Research Council, 2009).

With the exception of DNA, the OSAC will be looking first to ASTM for candidate standards. Those that might relate to the provision of forensic science are listed in Tables 3.11 and 3.12 for Document Examination. ASTM Standards are available for purchase from ASTM and usually cost 41 USD each [December 2017].

In the case of DNA, the Biology/DNA SAC has selected the Academy Standards Board, formed by the American Academy of Forensic Sciences early in 2016, as the Standards Development Organization to which documents developed within the SAC will be submitted. The standards, almost certainly, will be an adaptation or an adoption of the SWGDAM (Scientific Working Group on DNA Analysis Methods) standards listed in Table 3.13. The standards are freely available for download from the SWGDAM website.

3.4.6.4 AS5239-2011 "Examination of Ignitable Liquids in Fire Debris"

This standard was developed by Standards Australia to cover a perceived gap and as a pilot for the development for AS5388-2012 "Forensic analysis," discussed earlier in 3.4.2 (ANZPAA NIFS, 2016). This standard is of particular interest as it is among the first to recognize the potential influence of cognitive bias. It introduce the concepts of blinding and sequential unmasking by which an examining forensic scientist is protected from potentially biasing information, measures which have found support in the literature (Krane et al., 2008). AS5388 is discussed in detail in Section 6.

Table 3.11 ASTM discipline-specific standards

Designation	Title
E1386—15	Standard Practice for Separation of Ignitable Liquid Residues from Fire Debris Samples by Solvent Extraction
E1388—12	Standard Practice for Sampling of Headspace Vapors from Fire Debris Samples
E1412—16	Standard Practice for Separation of Ignitable Liquid Residues from Fire Debris Samples by Passive Headspace Concentration With Activated Charcoal
E1413—13	Standard Practice for Separation of Ignitable Liquid Residues from Fire Debris Samples by Dynamic Headspace Concentration
E1588—16a	Standard Practice for Gunshot Residue Analysis by Scanning Electron Microscopy/Energy Dispersive X-ray Spectrometry
E1610—14	Standard Guide for Forensic Paint Analysis and Comparison
E1618—14	Standard Test Method for Ignitable Liquid Residues in Extracts from Fire Debris Samples by Gas Chromatography-Mass Spectrometry
E1843—16	Standard Guide for Sexual Assault Investigation, Examination, and Evidence Collection
E1967—11a	Standard Test Method for the Automated Determination of Refractive Index of Glass Samples Using the Oil Immersion Method and a Phase Contrast Microscope
E1968—11	Standard Guide for Microcrystal Testing in the Forensic Analysis of Cocaine
E1969—11	Standard Guide for Microcrystal Testing in the Forensic Analysis of Methamphetamine and Amphetamine
E2057—10(2015)	Standard Specifications for Preparation of Laboratory Analysis Requests in Sexual Assault Investigations
E2123—16	Standard Practice for Transmittal of Evidence in Sexual Assault Investigation
E2124—15	Standard Practice for Specification for Equipment and Supplies in Sexual Assault Investigations
E2125—11	Standard Guide for Microcrystal Testing in the Forensic Analysis of Phencyclidine and Its Analogues
E2154—15a	Standard Practice for Separation and Concentration of Ignitable Liquid Residues from Fire Debris Samples by Passive Headspace Concentration with Solid Phase Microextraction (SPME)
E2224—10	Standard Guide for Forensic Analysis of Fibers by Infrared Spectroscopy
E2225—10	Standard Guide for Forensic Examination of Fabrics and Cordage
E2227—13	Standard Guide for Forensic Examination of Non-Reactive Dyes in Textile Fibers by Thin-Layer Chromatography
E2228—10	Standard Guide for Microscopic Examination of Textile Fibers
E2326—14	Standard Practice for Education and Training of Seized-Drug Analysts
E2327—15e1	Standard Practice for Quality Assurance of Laboratories Performing Seized-Drug Analysis
E2329—14	Standard Practice for Identification of Seized Drugs

Table 3.11 ASTM discipline-specific standards—cont'd

Designation	Title
E2330—12	Standard Test Method for Determination of Concentrations of Elements in Glass Samples Using Inductively Coupled Plasma Mass Spectrometry (ICP-MS) for Forensic Comparisons
E2451—13	Standard Practice for Preserving Ignitable Liquids and Ignitable Liquid Residue Extracts from Fire Debris Samples
E2548—16	Standard Guide for Sampling Seized Drugs for Qualitative and Quantitative Analysis
E2549—14	Standard Practice for Validation of Seized-Drug Analytical Methods
E2764—11	Standard Practice for Uncertainty Assessment in the Context of Seized-Drug Analysis
E2808—11	Standard Guide for Microspectrophotometry and Color Measurement in Forensic Paint Analysis
E2809—13	Standard Guide for Using Scanning Electron Microscopy/X-ray Spectrometry in Forensic Paint Examinations
E2881—13e1	Standard Test Method for Extraction and Derivatization of Vegetable Oils and Fats from Fire Debris and Liquid Samples with Analysis by Gas Chromatography-Mass Spectrometry
E2882—12	Standard Guide for Analysis of Clandestine Drug Laboratory Evidence
E2926—13	Standard Test Method for Forensic Comparison of Glass Using Micro X-ray Fluorescence (μ-XRF) Spectrometry
E2927—13	Standard Test Method for Determination of Trace Elements in Soda-Lime Glass Samples Using Laser Ablation Inductively Coupled Plasma Mass Spectrometry for Forensic Comparisons
E2937—13	Standard Guide for Using Infrared Spectroscopy in Forensic Paint Examinations
E2997—16	Standard Test Method for Analysis of Biodiesel Products by Gas Chromatography-Mass Spectrometry

The standard is available from SAI as a cost of 137.16 AUD [May 2017], it comprises 20 pages plus appendices, and its structure is as follows:

1. Scope
2. Referenced and related documents
3. Definitions and abbreviations
4. Sample storage
5. Reagents
6. Apparatus
7. Sample extraction
8. Instrument analysis
9. Data analysis
10. Classification
11. Examination results report

Table 3.12 ASTM standards relating to document examination

Designation	Title
E444—09	Standard Guide for Scope of Work of Forensic Document Examiners
E1658—08	Standard Terminology for Expressing Conclusions of Forensic Document Examiners
E2195—09	Standard Terminology Relating to the Examination of Questioned Documents
E2285—08	Standard Guide for Examination of Mechanical Checkwriter Impressions
E2286—08a	Standard Guide for Examination of Dry Seal Impressions
E2287—09	Standard Guide for Examination of Fracture Patterns and Paper Fiber Impressions on Single-Strike Film Ribbons and Typed Text
E2288—09	Standard Guide for Physical Match of Paper Cuts, Tears, and Perforations in Forensic Document Examinations
E2289—08	Standard Guide for Examination of Rubber Stamp Impressions
E2388—11	Standard Guide for Minimum Training Requirements for Forensic Document Examiners
E2494—08	Standard Guide for Examination of Typewritten Items
E2710—11e1	Standard Guide for Preservation of Charred Documents
E2711—11	Standard Guide for Preservation of Liquid Soaked Documents
E2765—11	Standard Practice for Use of Image Capture and Storage Technology in Forensic Document Examination

Appendices

A. Hydrocarbon classes encountered in ignitable liquid residues
B. Definitions and abbreviations
C. Desorption solvents
D. Ignitable liquid reference library
E. Typical gas chromatogram of "petrol"
F. Typical total ion chromatogram of "petrol"
G. Typical extracted ion profiles of "petrol"
H. Ignitable liquid classification by GC/MS
I. Characteristic ions in mass spectra of ignitable liquids

3.4.6.5 ISO 18385:2016 Minimizing the Risk of Human DNA Contamination in Products Used to Collect, Store, and Analyze Biological Material for Forensic Purposes—Requirements

This standard is included for completeness. Although it relates to the discipline of DNA analysis, it applies to organizations producing consumables and reagents used in DNA analysis. The standard specifies a requirement for manufacturers to minimize the risk

Table 3.13 SWGDAM standards

Subject	Approved	Pages
Interpretation Guidelines for Autosomal STR Typing by Forensic DNA Testing Laboratories	Jan 12 2017	90
Contamination Prevention and Detection Guidelines for Forensic DNA Laboratories	Jan 12 2017	29
Recommendations for the Efficient DNA Processing of Sexual Assault Evidence Kits	May 12 2016	34
Guidelines for the Validation of Probabilistic Genotyping Systems	Jun 15 2015	12
Guidelines for the Collection and Serological Examination of Biological Evidence	Jan 15 2015	19
Interpretation Guidelines for Y-Chromosome STR Typing	Jan 9 2014	20
Guidelines for Missing Persons Casework	Jan 9 2014	28
Training Guidelines	Jan 17 2013	30
Validation Guidelines for DNA Analysis Methods	Dec 5 2016	15
QAS[a] Clarification Document	May 6 2013	3
Interpretation Guidelines for Mitochondrial DNA Analysis by Forensic DNA Testing Laboratories	Jul 18 2013	23
Mitochondrial DNA Nomenclature Examples Document	May 5 2014	5
Quality Assurance Standards for DNA Databasing Laboratories	Sep 1 2011	29
The FBI Quality Assurance Standards Audit for DNA Databasing Laboratories	Sep 1 2011	99
Quality Assurance Standards for forensic DNA Testing Laboratories	Sep 1 2011	29
The FBI Quality Assurance Standards Audit for forensic DNA Testing Laboratories	Sep 1 2011	99

[a]Quality assurance standards.

of occurrence of detectable human nuclear DNA contamination in products used by the global forensic community. The standard is available for purchase from ISO at a cost of 118 CHF [December 2017].

3.4.7 Level 3 Standards Applying to the Legal Process

3.4.7.1 Common Law Jurisdictions

3.4.7.1.1 US Federal Rules of Evidence Rule 702—Testimony by Expert Witnesses [2011]

The rule is as follows:

> *A witness who is qualified as an expert by knowledge, skill, experience, training, or education may testify in the form of an opinion or otherwise if:*

(a) the expert's scientific, technical, or other specialized knowledge will help the trier of fact to understand the evidence or to determine a fact in issue;
(b) the testimony is based on sufficient facts or data;
(c) the testimony is the product of reliable principles and methods; and
(d) the expert has reliably applied the principles and methods to the facts of the case.

This rule governs the admissibility of all expert evidence, not just scientific evidence. Under this rule the judge acts as a gatekeeper for expert evidence. In the case of science, the so-called Daubert criteria apply (Daubert v. Merrel Dow Pharamceuticals, 1993);

1. Whether the theory or technique employed by the expert is generally accepted in the scientific community;
2. Whether it has been subjected to peer review and publication;
3. Whether it can be and has been tested;
4. Whether the known or potential rate of error is acceptable; and
5. Whether the research was conducted independent of the particular litigation or dependent on an intention to provide the proposed testimony?

The issue of admissibility and judicial gatekeeping is explored in 4.3.3.1.

It is important to note that individual States are not necessarily bound by Federal rules or precedents.

3.4.7.1.2 Australian Commonwealth Consolidated Acts: Evidence Act 1995—Section 79

The legislation draws to some extent on US Federal Rule 702, which was first introduced in 1975. However, the rule on the admissibility of expert testimony appears to be governed by common law requirements that the testimony is based on specialized knowledge outside the common knowledge of the fact-finder, and the facts supporting the testimony should also be admissible. Section 79 of the act is as follows:

> *Exception: opinions based on specialised knowledge*
>
> *(1) If a person has specialised knowledge based on the person's training, study or experience, the opinion rule does not apply to evidence of an opinion of that person that is wholly or substantially based on that knowledge.*

3.4.7.1.3 Australian Federal Court Rules

These are mostly practice directions. The structure of Part 23 of the 2011 rules relating to expert evidence is as follows:

Division 23.1	Court experts
Division 23.01	Appointment of Court expert
Division 23.02	Court expert's report
Division 23.03	Court expert's report—use at trial
Division 23.04	Other expert's reports on the question
Division 23.2	Parties' expert witnesses and expert reports
Division 23.11	Calling expert evidence at trial
Division 23.12	Provision of guidelines to an expert
Division 23.13	Contents of an expert report
Division 23.14	Application for expert report
Division 23.15	Evidence of experts

The required contents of an expert report set out in 23.13 are as follows:

"(1) An expert report must:

(a) be signed by the expert who prepared the report; and
(b) contain an acknowledgement at the beginning of the report that the expert has read, understood and complied with the Practice Note; and
(c) contain particulars of the training, study or experience by which the expert has acquired specialised knowledge; and
(d) identify the questions that the expert was asked to address; and
(e) set out separately each of the factual findings or assumptions on which the expert's opinion is based; and
(f) set out separately from the factual findings or assumptions each of the expert's opinions; and
(g) set out the reasons for each of the expert's opinions; and
(ga) contain an acknowledgement that the expert's opinions are based wholly or substantially on the specialised knowledge mentioned in paragraph (c); and
(h) comply with the Practice Note.

(2) Any subsequent expert report of the same expert on the same question need not contain the information in paragraphs (1) (b) and (c)."

Federal Court (Criminal Proceedings) Rules 2016 Part 6—Expert evidence requirements are as follows:

> ***Rule 6.01*** *provides that a party to criminal proceedings who retains an expert, or who proposes to call an expert at trial, must give the expert a copy of any practice note dealing with guidelines for expert witnesses. Practice notes are available on the Court's website.*
>
> ***Rule 6.02*** *sets out what must be contained in an expert's report. Among other things, the report must contain an acknowledgement that the expert has read, understood and complied with any practice note dealing with guidelines for expert witnesses.*
>
> ***Rule 6.03*** *provides that a party may only call an expert to give evidence at a trial if the party has delivered a copy of an expert report that complies with Rule 6.02 to all other parties. The copy reports must be delivered at least 21 days before the trial date, unless the Court sets a different time limit.*

A better understanding of the Australian rules regarding expert testimony can be gained by consulting the Australian Law Reform Commission Report 102 (Australian Law Reform Commission n.d.).

3.4.7.1.4 England and Wales Forensic Science Regulator: Legal Guidance

The common law rules on expert testimony also apply in the jurisdictions of the United Kingdom. The Regulator has helpfully collected all the relevant rules together in this guidance document. The full title is "Guidance on the obligations placed on expert witnesses in the criminal justice system in England and Wales." It is freely available for download. It is specific to criminal justice in the jurisdiction of England and Wales but has wider utility, particularly in other common law jurisdictions. The edition current at the time of writing [December 2017], is Issue 5 FSR-I-400 published on the second of August 2017 and it comprises 165 pages. The structure of the guide is as follows:

1. Executive summary
2. Introduction
3. Modification
4. Key judicial guidance
5. The role of the expert witness
6. Duty of disclosure and preservation
7. Admissibility of expert testimony
8. Form of written expert evidence: Mandatory requirements
9. Coroners courts system
10. Guidance on particular evidence types
11. Guidance on particular issues
12. Secondary sources of guidance or professional obligation
13. Guidelines
14. Acknowledgments
15. Review

16. Reference
17. Abbreviations
18. Table of authorities

Reproduced with permission © Crown Copyright

It is clear that the guide aims to be exhaustive. It catalogs the requirements of the criminal justice system in England and Wales as they apply to forensic scientists giving expert testimony but it has far greater utility. The guide is a rich resource for all stakeholders in the forensic science process.

It is noteworthy that the requirement for objectivity is stated in Section 1.4.3 of the guide and again in Section 5.5, which seems at odds with the provision of opinion evidence supported by experience alone described in 8.6.4. The requirement for objectivity and the apparent reliance on subjective opinion is considered further in 7.2.2.1.

The guide makes reference to Part 19 of the Criminal Procedure Rules (CrimPR) and includes the requirements for conformance in this guide. CrimPR is the mandatory requirement referred to in Section 8 of the guide. Part 19 of CrimPR is freely available from the website of the Crown Prosecution Service. The relevant sections of Part 19 are reproduced in Appendix F and in 4.3.3.2.2. They set out the expert's duty to the England and Wales criminal justice system and to the court.

The implication from the requirements of this guide is that the use of nonaccredited and nonvalidated methods must be disclosed in experts' reports.

3.4.7.1.5 New Zealand Code of Conduct for Expert Witnesses (High Court Rules 2016 Schedule 4)

This code applies to civil proceedings but practitioners acting in criminal matters often voluntarily abide by the code. The judiciary prefer conformance. It is freely available from the NZ government website.

The code is a concise statement of requirements and is reproduced in full below and in Appendix I.

"Duty to the court

1. An expert witness has an overriding duty to assist the court impartially on relevant matters within the expert's area of expertise.
2. An expert witness is not an advocate for the party who engages the witness.

Evidence of expert witness

3. In any evidence given by an expert witness, the expert witness must—
   (a) acknowledge that the expert witness has read this code of conduct and agrees to comply with it:
   (b) state the expert witness' qualifications as an expert:
   (c) state the issues the evidence of the expert witness addresses and that the evidence is within the expert's area of expertise:
   (d) state the facts and assumptions on which the opinions of the expert witness are based:

(e) state the reasons for the opinions given by the expert witness:
(f) specify any literature or other material used or relied on in support of the opinions expressed by the expert witness:
(g) describe any examinations, tests, or other investigations on which the expert witness has relied and identify, and give details of the qualifications of, any person who carried them out.

4. If an expert witness believes that his or her evidence or any part of it may be incomplete or inaccurate without some qualification, that qualification must be stated in his or her evidence.

5. If an expert witness believes that his or her opinion is not a concluded opinion because of insufficient research or data or for any other reason, this must be stated in his or her evidence.

Duty to confer

6. An expert witness must comply with any direction of the court to—
(a) confer with another expert witness:
(b) try to reach agreement with the other expert witness on matters within the field of expertise of the expert witnesses
(c) prepare and sign a joint witness statement stating the matters on which the expert witnesses agree and the matters on which they do not agree, including the reasons for their disagreement.

7. In conferring with another expert witness, the expert witness must exercise independent and professional judgment, and must not act on the instructions or directions of any person to withhold or avoid agreement."

3.4.7.1.6 Expert Evidence in Canada

Legal standards applying to forensic science offered as expert evidence in Canada are based on case law. The most important being *R v Mohan* (R v Mohan, 1994) regarding the admissibility of expert evidence which depends on the following criteria:

- relevance;
- necessity in assisting the fact-finder;
- the absence of any exclusionary rule; and
- adequately qualified expert.

In *Mohan,* the Supreme Court of Canada held that a novel scientific theory or technique is subject to special scrutiny and must satisfy a basic threshold of reliability.

> *Expert evidence which advances a novel scientific theory or technique is* ***subjected to special scrutiny to determine whether it meets a basic threshold of reliability*** *and whether it is essential in the sense that the trier of fact will be unable to come to a satisfactory conclusion without the assistance of the expert. The closer the evidence approaches an opinion on an ultimate issue, the stricter the application of this principle. [Emphasis added].*

In a further refinement, the Supreme Court in *R v J.(J-L)* (R v J.L.J, 2000) determined that a trial judge could evaluate the reliability of novel science or techniques on the basis of the US Daubert criteria discussed earlier in 3.4.7.1.1.

In *White Burgess* (White Burgess Langille Inman v Abbott, 2015), the Supreme Court stated that expert witnesses have a duty to the court to give fair, objective, and nonpartisan opinion evidence. They must be aware of this duty and willing and able to carry it out.

Three concepts underlie the various formulations of the duty of an expert:

- Impartiality—the opinion must be impartial in that it reflects an objective assessment of the questions at hand.
- Independence—it must be independent in that it is the product of the expert's independent judgement, uninfluenced by the identity of the party retaining him or her or the outcome of the litigation.
- Absence of bias—it must be unbiased in the sense that it does not unfairly favour one party's position over another. The expert's opinion should not change regardless of which party retained him or her.

However, the Supreme Court recognized that these concepts must be applied to the realities of adversarial litigation. Experts are generally retained, instructed, and paid by one of the adversaries. According to the court, "these facts alone do not undermine the expert's independence, impartiality and freedom of bias."

As discussed in 4.3.4 and Section 7, preventing bias requires procedures to be in place and a documented record of conformance.

3.4.7.2 Civil Law Jurisdictions

The law as it relates to expert witnesses in civil law jurisdictions is varied and at times complex. Because the system is inquisitorial, there is an assumption that expert witnesses are neutral. Expert witnesses tend not to be cross-examined or have their testimony challenged. The main requirement is competence, which is usually measured by qualifications and experience. As made clear in Section 1.3.4, qualifications and experience are incomplete measures of competence, particularly for forensic scientists where complying with scientific norms alone is insufficient to demonstrate competence.

In common with all other jurisdictions, miscarriages of justice have occurred as a result of insufficiently competent experts giving unreliable evidence.

Perhaps the most developed standards applying to expert testimony are those of the Netherlands.

3.4.7.2.1 The Netherlands (Dutch) Code of Criminal Procedure

The Expert Witness in Criminal Cases Act, which became law on January 1, 2010, has brought about many changes in current Dutch criminal procedure. One of the more substantial changes concerns the creation of a national public register of expert witnesses

(Nederlands Register Gerechtelijk Deskundigen; the NRGD) based on section 51k of the Dutch Code of Criminal Procedure (CCP).

At the end of 2010, the register was opened for the registration of DNA-experts, Handwriting experts, and Forensic Behavioral experts. The register now includes nine fields of expertise [December 2017].

In the Dutch CCP, the starting point of the legal framework relating to experts in criminal cases was the framework for experts in preliminary judicial investigations. That framework was preserved in slightly altered form in 2010. But the examining judge now also has the option of initiating research by experts outside the ambit of preliminary judicial investigations. The CCP permits the examining judge to appoint one or more experts at the request of the suspect or on demand of the public prosecutor. These experts do not have to be registered (Nijboer et al., 2011). In the event of the appointment of an expert who is not included in the register the reasons why he is considered to be an expert have to be given.

The public prosecutor, however, may only appoint an expert who is listed in the register of experts. The defendant can ask the prosecutor for an additional examination or give directions regarding the examination to be carried out. The defendant may call on the examining judge if the prosecutor refuses to act accordingly.

The new section 51j(4) of the CCP offers the examining judge the opportunity of deciding, prior to the trial hearing, that an expert examination carried out on the instructions of the defense should be considered equivalent (in terms of state funding) to an expert examination at the request of the public prosecutor or the judge.

The legal basis for the register of experts can be found in a new title in the CCP that is devoted entirely to experts. The explanatory memorandum clearly explains the aims of the register of experts. By compiling a register of experts, the public prosecutor and defense counsel are given the opportunity to appoint expert witnesses who meet generally approved standards such as educational qualifications.

The law also requires that the expert provides an opinion "that his knowledge teaches him". The expert has to provide an explanation as to how he or she arrived at the conclusion reported. Furthermore, the expert has to mention which method was used, explain why the method is reliable and the extent of competence in applying the method.

As with all civil law jurisdictions, the court is not restricted to the evidence presented by parties to the case, e.g., the expert evidence of the defense and prosecution.

3.4.7.2.2 Belgium Sections 43 and 44 of the Code of Civil Procedure

In Belgium, the public prosecutor and the examining judge have substantial discretion as to which expert is appointed. The suspect, however, has no substantial input during criminal investigations where it concerns a potential expert examination. Only in the preliminary judicial investigation will the suspect and the victim (as a civil party) have the right to ask the investigating judge to appoint and instruct an expert.

There are no legal standards relating to court-appointed experts in Belgium. The sole provision that allowed courts to draft lists of experts was recently abolished. Now there are only unofficial lists. Moreover, some authors state that experts appointed by the judge or public prosecutor are paid a pittance. That could present a risk in situations in which wealthy suspects use highly qualified expert witnesses. The present situation has been criticized by many authors.

3.4.7.2.3 Germany Strafprozeßordnung StPO; Code of Criminal Procedure Section 73 and 74

In Germany, the law states that the court in principle has to choose an expert from the *öffentlich bestellte Sachverständigen*, experts "accredited" by a public-law body at state level, the *Kammern*. The *Kammern* maintain a register of such experts, whom it has appointed, so that finding a suitable (accredited) expert in a specific area need not be problematic for the court. The court may, however, if circumstances dictate, depart from the principle that it has to choose from the pool of accredited experts registered with the *Kammern*. In practice that happens very frequently. The public prosecutor may also retain experts in the preliminary judicial investigation. At the trial hearing, the defendant may request that an expert witness be allowed to present evidence. Such a request cannot be dismissed if the expert witness that the defendant wishes to call is evidently more knowledgeable than the expert retained by the court. The defendant may also challenge an expert on a number of grounds defined in law.

Anyone who considers themselves to be an expert in a given field may have their ability tested. Before an expert can be accredited by a *Kammer*, a selection procedure must apply. This procedure primarily covers the ability to draft reports and tests whether the candidate has an above-average level of expertise. Accreditation is typically for 5 years. Accredited experts are subject to regular screening by the *Kammer* for which they are registered. As long as they meet the criteria, their accreditation can be extended. The individual *Kammern* have detailed the criteria (i.e., special expertise and personal suitability) in their own Expert Regulation (*Sachverständigenordnung*). The most frequently applied criteria are an above-average level of expertise in a specific field, the skills to draw up an expert report, and the requirements of impartiality and independence.

Not all expertise, however, is to be found among accredited experts; the German Federal Criminal Office (*Bundeskriminalamt*) and the various state criminal offices have a high level of expertise in specific fields, such as DNA analysis and forensic science in support of criminal justice.

In Germany, expert registrations are not linked to criminal procedure. Authorities that play a part in criminal proceedings have no role in the registration of experts.

3.4.7.2.4 Expert Evidence in France (Code de Procédure Penale)

In France, rules regarding experts are enshrined in legislation regarding the preliminary judicial investigation.

The investigating judge is the key figure in the preliminary judicial investigation. It is up to the judge to determine whether the appointment of an expert is required. The experts carry out their examination under the examining judge's aegis. Experts require the examining judge's permission for specific investigative acts. The judge also determines when the expert examination is closed. Adversarial argument in this phase is guaranteed. The parties have a 10-day period to supplement or amend the questions drafted by the examining judge. In addition, they may (save in exceptional conditions such as expedited proceedings) demand that an additional expert be appointed. During the investigation, parties may exercise some control on the course of events through the examining judge. Once the expert report is presented, the examining judge must convene the parties and their counsel to advise them of the conclusions. The examining judge may initially ask the expert to draft a preliminary report, giving the parties the opportunity of responding to the preliminary report. Where necessary, the expert can be called to explain aspects of the report in greater detail. Another option is an examination of the draft report by a party's expert witness. The expert can then draft the final report. Challenging the expert reports is thus largely a part of the preliminary judicial investigations rather than of the trial itself. This prevents time being wasted with a discussion of the subject matter, most of which would be beyond the average lay member of the Cour d'Assises.

There is a register of experts held at the Court of Cassation; in addition, each Court of Appeal has a register of experts. An expert may, in principle, be registered with the Court for a probationary period of 2 years. After this period, each expert is assessed on the basis of experience and knowledge of legal matters by the General Assembly of Magistrates. The expert is then formally registered for a term of 5 years on the basis of a complete application form and the substantiated opinion of a panel of 17 judges and experts. For formal inclusion in the register of the Court of Cassation, experts must have been registered with a Court of Appeal for an unbroken period of at least 3 years. Inclusion in the register of the Court of Cassation is for a term of 7 years. Certain standards have to be met by registered experts; these standards focus primarily on ability, independence, impartiality, and mentality. For experts, registration is often essential; in principle only registered experts can be appointed by the courts. Only in very specific cases is there a possibility of a nonregistered expert being appointed.

3.5 LEVEL 4 STANDARD—METHODS AND PROCEDURES

Standard methods and procedures are the procedural standards setting out how the standards discussed above are given effect. They will constitute a large part of the documented QMS of the forensic science provider accredited by an accreditating body.

3.6 CONCLUDING REMARKS

This section has demonstrated that the quality standards framework applying to the management, practice, and delivery of forensic science is complex, and conformance is demanding and challenging such that the risk of nonconformance is high. Conformance to the standards introduced in this section constitutes good practice; nonconformance may call into question the reliability of scientific information.

Stakeholders should be aware that accreditation does not guarantee conformance with a standard. Assessment of conformity by an independent fourth Party may reveal nonconformances that the accreditation body is not aware of.

A typical quality standards framework is as follows. The forensic science provider should be accredited to either ISO/IEC 17025 or ISO/IEC 17020 as interpreted by ILAC Guide 19:2002 for laboratory-based providers and the UKAS Guide RG201 for crime scene-based providers. The provider should conform to the standard to which it is accredited. Forensic scientists employed by an accredited provider are "certified" as technically competent by their employer. It should be noted that this process is not independent. As explained in this section, it is the methods used by a provider that define the scope of accreditation. Scientific information offered by a forensic scientist must lie within that scope. If not, the method used must be fully validated with documentary evidence of that validation. When offering expert evidence, the forensic scientist must disclose the use of methods that lie outside the scope of accreditation. Scientific information produced using a method that lies outside scope and has not been fully validated cannot be considered reliable.

Full validation of methods incorporating measurement should include an interlaboratory comparison exercise provided by a supplier compliant with ISO/IEC 17043. Traceability should be assured by the use of RMs produced in conformance to ISO/IEC 17034, and the expression of the uncertainty associated with the measurement should conform to ISO/IEC Guide 98. If any of these elements are absent, then the quality of the measurement result will be reduced. The result obtained will be less reliable than it otherwise might be and stakeholders, particularly fact-finders, must be made aware of this.

In terms of the evaluation of scientific evidence, the AFSP Standard (Association of Forensic Science Providers, 2009) and ENFSI Guidelines (ENFSI, 2015) should be complied with. CAI (Cook et al., 1998a,b) offers an overall model of good forensic practice incorporating a likelihood ratio approach to evaluation.

When assessing the fitness-for-purpose of the quality standards framework, it should be born in mind that, ideally, standards development/setting, conformity assessment, and service provision/operation should be undertaken by separate and independent bodies. Any overlap in these roles risks a conflict of interests.

Forensic scientists acting as expert witnesses must be aware of their duties and responsibilities and conform to the standards required. A good example of those requirements is the code of conduct published by the Forensic Science Regulator and discussed earlier in 3.4.4.1.

As has been made clear in this Section and in Section 4, judicial authorities and fact-finders are not competent to distinguish between reliable and unreliable scientific evidence unaided (Shaw, 2011) (The Law Commission, 2011). Therefore, it remains the ethical responsibility of forensic scientists and forensic science providers to ensure that scientific evidence is fit-for-purpose and, if not fully so, to disclose that fact to the relevant stakeholder, particularly the fact-finder and judicial authority.

The general trend in quality management is toward reducing complexity and increasing flexibility as demonstrated by ISO 9001:2015, whereas quality management in forensic science appears to be moving in the opposite direction with the increased risk of nonconformance.

As demonstrated, the standards landscape is very crowded. Having a variety of standards (however named) for essentially the same process is hard to justify and cannot be in the best interests of justice or law enforcement. In addition, the plethora of standards risks variances in practice and although quality is improved by conformance, the existence of different standards (and different approaches to conformance) contradicts the very notion, and the aim, of standardization.

REFERENCES

AFFSAB, January 23, 2013. Policy and Processes for Accreditation – Fingerprint and Firearm Examiners and Crime Scene Investigators. Australasian Forensic Field Sciences Accreditation Board.

Alexander, K.L., April 27, 2015. Crime. Washington Post. https://www.washingtonpost.com/local/crime/national-accreditation-board-suspends-all-dna-testing-at-district-lab/2015/04/26/2da43d9a-ec24-11e4-a55f-38924fca94f9_story.html?utm_term=.4f5efd753400.

ANAB, n.d. Anab Guidance on ISO/IEC 17020 Accreditation for Forensic Inspection Agencies. https://anab.qualtraxcloud.com/ShowDocument.aspx?ID=1204.

ANZFSS, n.d. Membership. Australian and New Zealand Forensic Science Society. http://anzfss.org/membership/.

ANZPAA NIFS, May 18, 2016. Deconvoluting Forensic Standards. ANZPAA NIFS.

ANZPAA NIFS, July 2017a. AFFSAB future dircections. In: ANZPAA NIFS NEWS Vol. 18 Issue 2. ANZPAA NIFS, Melbourne.

ANZPAA NIFS, 2017b. Publications. ANZPAA. http://www.anzpaa.org.au/forensic-science/our-work/products/publications.

Association of Forensic Science Providers, 2009. Standards for the formulation of evaluative forensic science expert opinion. Science and Justice 49, 161–164.

Australia New Zealand Policing Advisory Agency (ANZPAA), n.d. Specialist Advisory Groups Criteria for SAG Meetings.pdf. ANZPAA. http://www.anzpaa.org.au/nifs/resources/sags.

Australian Law Reform Commission, n.d. 9. The Opinion Rule and Its Exceptions. ALRC. http://www.alrc.gov.au/publications/9.%20The%20Opinion%20Rule%20and%20its%20Exceptions/opinions-based-specialised-knowledge.

Berger, C.E.H., Buckleton, J., Champod, C., Evett, I.W., Jackson, G., 2011. Response to Faigman et al. Science and Justice 215.

BIPM, 1980. JCGM100. ISO. http://www.iso.org/sites/JCGM/GUM/JCGM100/C045315e-html/C045315e_FILES/MAIN_C045315e/AA_e.html.

Codes of Practice and Conduct, February 2016. Codes of Practice and Conduct. https://www.gov.uk/government/uploads/system/uploads/attachment_data/file/499850/2016_2_11_-_The_Codes_of_Practice_and_Conduct_-_Issue_3.pdf.

Cook, R., Evett, I.W., Jackson, G., Jones, P.J., Lambert, J.A., 1998a. A hierarchy of propositions: deciding which level to address in casework. Science and Justice 231–239.

Cook, R., Evett, I.W., Jackson, G., Jones, P.J., Lambert, J.A., 1998b. A model for case assessement and interpretation. Science and Justice 38 (3), 151–156.

Crown Prosecution Service, February 2015. Guidance of Expert Evidence – Crown Prosecution Service. CPS. http://www.cps.gov.uk/legal/assets/uploads/files/expert_evidence_first_edition_2014.pdf.

Daubert v. Merrel Dow Pharmaceuticals, 509 (U.S.), 1993.

Evaluation of measurements data - Guide to the expression of uncertainty in measurement JCGM 100:2008

ENFSI, 2015. ENFSI Guideline for Evalauative Reporting in Forensic Science. Guide. ENFSI, Wiesbaden.

Evett, I.W., Jackson, G., Lambert, J.A., McCrossan, S., 2000. The impact of the principles of evidence interpretation on the structure and content of statements. Science and Justice 233–239.

Federal Judicial Centre & National Research Council, 2011. Reference Manual on Scientific Evidence. National Academies Press, Washington DC.

Forensic Science Regulator, n.d. https://www.gov.uk/government/organisations/forensic-science-regulator/about.

Gallop, A., Brown, J., 2014. The market future for forensic science services in England & Wales. Policing 1–11.

Gillespie, A., Upton, S., 2005. Marketing valid analytical measurement. In: Bievre, P.De, Gunzer, H. (Eds.), Validation in Chemical Measurement. Springer, Berlin, pp. 143–147.

Hadley, K., Fereday, M.J., 2008. Ensuring Competent Performance in Forensic Practice: Recovery, Analysis, Interpretation, and Reporting. CRC Press, Boca Raton.

House of Commons Science and Technology Committee, 2011. The Forensic Science Service: Seventh Report of Session 2010–12. Parliamentary Committee Report. The Stationary Office, London.

ISO, 15 September 2015. Quality Management Systems – Fundamentals and Vocabulary. In: ISO 9000: 2015(E). ISO, Geneva.

ISO, 2015. Qulaity Management Principles. Guide. In: ISO 9001:2015(E). ISO, Geneva.

ISO, n.d. ISO/TC 272 Forensic Sciences. http://www.iso.org/iso/home/standards_development/list_of_iso_technical_committees/iso_technical_committee.htm?commid=4395817.

ISO/IEC, May 2016. Principles and Rules for the Structure and Drafting of ISO and IEC Documents. In: ISO/IEC Directive Part 2. ISO/IEC, Geneva.

JCGM, July 2009. Common Documents. BIPM. http://www.bipm.org/utils/common/documents/jcgm/JCGM_104_2009_E.pdf.

Krane, et al., 2008. Sequential Unmasking: A Means of Minimizing Observer Effects in Forensic DNA Interpretation. Journal of Forensic Sciences 1006–1007.

Lawless, C., 2010. A Curious Reconstruction? The Shaping of 'marketized' Forensic Science. Discussion Paper No. 63. The London School of Economics and Political Science, London.

Magnusson, B., Örnemark, U., 2014. Eurachem Guide: The Fitness for Purpose of Analytical Methods – A Laboratory Guide to Method Validation and Related Topics. Eurachem.

NATA, July 2013. Gap Analysis of AS 5388 and NATA Accrediation in the Field of Forensic Science. NATA. https://www.nata.com.au/nata/phocadownload/publications/Guidance_information/checklist-worksheets-site-notification-forms/AS5388-Gap-Analysis.pdf.

National Institute of Forensic Science, n.d. Criteria for SAG Meetings. http://www.anzpaa.org.au/nifs/resources/sags.

National Institute of Standards, March 17, 2016. NIST Statement on ASTM Standard E2329-14. http://www.nist.gov/forensics/nist-statement-on-astm-e2329-14.cfm.

National Research Council, 2009. Strengthening Forensic Science in the United States: A Path Forward. Committee Report. The National Academies Press, Washington D.C.

Nijboer, J.A., Keulen, B.F., Elzinga, H.K., Kwakman, N.J.M., 2011. Expert Registers in Criminal Cases. Governance in Criminal Proceedings. RUG. http://www.rug.nl/rechten/congressen/archief/2011/governancemeetslaw/workingpapers/papernijboerkeulen.pdf.
R v Clark, 2003. Crim 1020 (EWCA).
R v J.L.J, 2000. SCC 51 (The Supreme Court of Canada).
R v Mohan, 1994. 2 SCR 9 (The Supreme Court of Canada).
R v T, 2010. Crim 2439 (EWCA).
Robertson, J., 2013. Australian forensic science reaches new standards! Editorial. Australian Journal of Forensic Sciences 345–346.
Robertson, J., Kent, K., Wilson-Wilde, L., 2014. The development of a core forensic standards framework for Australia. Forensic Science Policy & Management: International Journal 59–67.
Royal Statistical Society, February 13, 2015. News. Statslife. http://www.rss.org.uk/Images/PDF/influencing-change/rss-use-statistical-evidence-court-cases-2002.pdf.
Schecter, M., March 25, 2011. ASCLD Lab and Forensic Laboratory Accredition. Scribd. https://www.scribd.com/document/83354323/Marvin-Schecter-ASCLD-Lab-and-Forensic-Laboratory-Accreditation#.
Scientific Working Group on DNA Analysis Methods (SWGDAM), July 17, 2014. ByLaws of the Scientific Working Group on DNA Analysis Methods (SWGDAM). http://www.swgdam.org/#!bylaws/galleryPage.
Shaw, K., 2011. Expert evidence reliability: time to grasp the nettle. The Journal of Criminal Law 368–379.
Skills for Justice, 2017. Forensic Science. http://www.sfjuk.com/sectors/forensic-science/.
Skills for Justice, n.d. Skills for Justice Forensic Science. Skills for Justice Web Site. http://www.sfjuk.com/sectors/forensic-science/.
Statistics and Law Section of the Royal Statistical Society, n.d. NCFS Recommendations regarding the use of the term 'Reasonable Scientific Certainty'. rss. http://www.rss.org.uk/Images/PDF/influencing-change/2016/ncfs-scientific-certainty-rss-stats-and-the-law-section-comment.pdf.
The Detail, December 18, 2011. Justice and Crime. thedetail. http://www.thedetail.tv/articles/the-trials-of-fsni.
The Law Commission, 2011. Expert Evidence in Criminal Proceedings in England and Wales. London.
UNODC, Guidelines on Representative Drug Sampling, 2009. United Nations New York.
UK Standards, n.d. NOS Forensic. http://www.ukstandards.org.uk/Pages/results.aspx?u=http%3A%2F%2Fwww%2Eukstandards%2Eorg%2Euk&k=Forensic.
Vessman, J., Stefan, R.I., van Staden, J.F., Danzer, K., Lindner, W., Burns, D.T., Fajgelj, A., Müller, H., July 2001. Projects. Old IUPAC. http://old.iupac.org/projects/posters01/vessman01.pdf.
White Burgess Langille Inman v Abbott, 2015. SCC 23 (The Supreme Court of Canada).

SECTION 4

Historical Perspective: Significant Events/Steps in the Development of Quality Management in Forensic Science

4.1 INTRODUCTION

As defined by the International Organization for Standardization (ISO) in ISO 9000: 2015 3.6.2, quality is the degree to which a set of inherent characteristics of an object fulfills requirements; the object being forensic science. In this section, the inherent characteristics are catalogued from an historical perspective. Knowing when and how a particular characteristic, for example, understanding the duties and responsibilities of an expert witness, became a requirement to demonstrate competence provides a deeper understanding of quality management in forensic science. This and other characteristics catalogued in this work distinguish forensic science and demonstrate that a forensic scientist requires competencies and behaviors beyond those of a scientist.

In most jurisdictions today, there is a quality standards framework in place, including institutions, which assures the quality of forensic science and the reliability of the scientific information provided. The journey from nonexistent or rudimentary quality control and quality assurance measures to current quality standards frameworks was not straightforward and had many twists and turns that result in a tangled narrative. There may be other approaches to framing the historical development of quality management. However, in this work, the major events that led to the need for improvements in the quality of forensic science, set out in 4.2—4.4, are taken as a starting point and the resulting paths followed. The paths are interrelated and intersect at various points, eventually arriving at the quality standards frameworks now in place. Drawing these various strands together and presenting a coherent summary is the aim of this section.

The quality and reliability of the scientific evidence placed before courts of law and other tribunals of fact have significantly improved in the last three decades. However, progress is often marked by an initial rush to rely on partially validated techniques, producing evidence presented by insufficiently competent practitioners, which is superficially strong but of questionable reliability contributing to unsafe outcomes. There

Quality Management in Forensic Science
ISBN 978-0-12-805416-1, https://doi.org/10.1016/B978-0-12-805416-1.00004-9

then follows a period of scientific and judicial review and a stepwise improvement in the quality of the scientific evidence, such that it becomes fit-for-purpose. This pattern is demonstrated in the forensic exploitation of the DNA molecule, which is discussed in 4.4.

The responsive nature of forensic science, in terms of quality, is perhaps its greatest weakness. The weakness is contributed to by the fact that the majority of forensic science is commissioned and paid for, directly or indirectly, by law enforcement and prosecuting agencies. Therefore, it is perhaps unsurprising that forensic science in support of criminal justice, certainly in the first instance, is made fit for the purpose of securing convictions thereby meeting customer needs.

The proposition that forensic science has advanced through its quality failures is well supported and discussed in detail in this Section. However, failures must be balanced by the success of DNA profiling. DNA profiling, via the innocence project (Innocence Project n.d.), has helped overturn the convictions of many individuals secured with less scientific and poorer quality evidence.

The need for a quality standards framework providing regulation and oversight of forensic science developed in response to three issues:

- miscarriages of justice,
- the poor performance/competence from the point of view of both science and law, and
- the discriminating power of DNA evidence.

4.1.1 Miscarriages of Justice

The genesis of the quality management systems now employed by most forensic science providers can be traced to a series of miscarriages of justice that occurred in the jurisdiction of England and Wales (E&W) in the mid-1970s and were uncovered or admitted in the early 1990s. These cases are listed in Table 4.1.

At this point, it is important to mention again the innocence project (Innocence Project n.d.) that has uncovered numerous miscarriages of justice and led to the

Table 4.1 Miscarriages of Justice in England & Wales

Case	Charge	Convicted	Acquitted
Birmingham 6	Murder	1975	1991
Guildford 4	Murder	1975	1989
McGuire 7	Possessing Nitroglycerine	1974	1991
Judith Ward	Murder	1974	1992

exoneration of many of those convicted wrongly. Its impact on the development of quality management is in exposing poor-quality science in certain forensic disciplines.

Concerns about poor-quality science are recorded and addressed in the 2009 United States (US) National Research Council (NRC) report (National Research Council, 2009), which continues to have a major impact on the development of quality management in forensic science and is discussed in some detail in 4.3.2.

4.1.1.1 Performance/Competence

One of the first steps toward the introduction of quality management in forensic science was taken by the American Society of Crime Laboratory Directors (ASCLD). As recorded in 4.3.1, the members began to establish voluntary quality and management standards from about 1974 in response to "varied" results obtained from members participating in interlaboratory proficiency tests.

In addition to its 2009 report, other reports by the NRC on various aspects of forensic science highlighted poor, or at least, questionable, scientific practice in a number of forensic scientific disciplines and made recommendations for improvement. These other NRC reports are discussed in 4.3.2.2.

The law has also responded to suboptimal practice and measures have been introduced in most jurisdictions with the aim of improving the quality of scientific evidence placed before tribunals. These measures, identified in 4.3.3, have, to some extent or other, been incorporated into quality management systems.

The impact of cognitive bias on the quality and reliability of scientific evidence has slowly become recognized. As recorded in 4.3.4, bias-avoidance measures are being developed and incorporated into quality management systems.

4.1.1.2 DNA

The forensic exploitation of the DNA molecule as an evidence type and its discriminating power led to powerful challenges when introduced initially. These challenges resulted in the early adoption of quality standards specifically for DNA evidence. The impact of DNA evidence on the development of quality management is discussed in 4.4.

Each of these issues is now explored in some detail.

4.2 MISCARRIAGES OF JUSTICE

4.2.1 Government Response

Unreliable scientific evidence and poor forensic practice have contributed to miscarriages of justice in many jurisdictions. These events have led to improvements in the quality of forensic science. One example is the wrongful conviction of Lindy and Michael

Chamberlain in Australia's Northern Territory in 1982. Their wrongful conviction was the subject of a Royal Commission of Inquiry (Morling, 1987), which in turn led to the establishment of the Australasian National Institute of Forensic Science (NIFS) in 1991 and the national laboratory accreditation program in 1994.

However, it is in the United Kingdom (UK) jurisdiction of E&W that miscarriages of justice, contributed to by unreliable scientific evidence and poor forensic practice, had the greatest impact on the development of quality management in forensic science. These events are the main focus of this subsection. It was the response to those miscarriages of justice by UK institutions that began the process that led to the adoption of the quality management systems in place today. The chronology of the main UK events is set out in Table 4.2.

Concerns about the safety of the convictions of many imprisoned for terrorist-related offenses in which explosives evidence was adduced at trial grew over the years (Mullins, 1986). These cases are listed in Table 4.1. Court of Appeal judge Sir John May was commissioned by the UK government to inquire into some of those convictions. He was appointed in 1989 following the quashing of the Guildford 4 convictions and the related case of the McGuire 7. His inquiries then lead to the establishment of a Royal Commission on Criminal Justice in 1991. The Commission headed by Viscount Runciman reported (Royal Commission on Criminal Justice, 1993) in 1993 to a mixed response (Young and Sanders, 1994; Bridges, 1994; Runciman, 1994). It was a rapid response to a political crisis of confidence in the criminal justice system, and the Commission was a means of restoring that confidence as was the message regarding the small scale of the problem. The Commission was announced on the day that the Birmingham 6 were acquitted at their second appeal. It would be fair to say that there was also a crisis of public confidence in forensic science and the finding of Sir John May (May 1990) that forensic scientists had deliberately given misleading evidence and perverted the course of justice brought the reputation of forensic science in E&W to its lowest ebb.

Separately, and in parallel to the Commission, the UK House of Lords Select Committee on Science and Technology initiated its own inquiry out of concern for the quality of scientific evidence, and the increasing role science was expected to play in law enforcement. The Select Committee focused on the laboratory, leaving the courtroom to the Commission. The terms of reference of the House of Lords inquiry were simply;

> *[T]o examine the scientific quality of public and commercial forensic science services in the UK.*

In the foreword to its report, published in April 1993 (House of Lords Select Committee on Science and Technology, 1993), the Select Committee stated that

> *It seems to us highly desirable to try to identify the apparent shortcomings in the quality of forensic science, to seek their causes, and to propose remedies and safeguards which would ensure that further errors would not occur, thereby materially assisting in the judicial process and the confidence of the public in it.*

Table 4.2 Events in the Development of Quality Management in England & Wales

Year	Event	Details	Quality Outcome
1989–91	Miscarriages of justice	Convictions quashed	Major quality failures revealed
1989–91	May Enquiry	Review of explosives related convictions	Major quality failures revealed
1999–93	Royal Commission	On criminal justice	FSAC proposed and code of practice
1993	House of Lord's Select Committee on Science and Technology	Report on forensic science	Advisory board and register proposed
1993	UKFSLG response		Code of conduct adopted and collaborative exercises/proficiency tests introduced
1996	ISO 9001 and M10	Quality standards	Providers certified to ISO 9001 and accredited to M10
1996	Caddy Report	Quality failures identified	Inspectorate recommended
1999	CRFP	Established	Register of competent forensic scientists complying with a Code of Conduct
1999	ISO/IEC 17025	International standard for laboratory based providers first published	Providers accredited
2002	ILAC G19	Guidance on the application of ISO/IEC 17025 to forensic science laboratories	
2005	House of Commons Select Committee on Science and Technology	Report 'Forensic Science on Trial'	FSAC and regulator proposed
2007	Rawley and Caddy Report	Quality failures identified in the case of Damilola Taylor	Assistants to be registered as competent. Powers, duties and responsibilities of the Regulator
2008	Caddy, Taylor and Linacre Report	Validity of low template DNA methods reviewed	Need for minimum national standards
2008	FSAC and FSR	Operational	
2009	AFSP Standard	Standard for evaluative opinions	

Continued

Table 4.2 Events in the Development of Quality Management in England & Wales—cont'd

Year	Event	Details	Quality Outcome
2011	Law Commission Report	Admissibility of expert evidence	The need for a reliability test for expert evidence
2012	Criminal Procedure Rules Part 33 (now 19)	Expert evidence	Expert's duty to the court and content of an expert report specified
2014	Criminal Practice Direction Part 33A (now 19A)	Expert evidence	Admissibility and reliability of expert evidence, relevance, need for, and competence of the expert

AFSP, Association of Forensic Science Providers; *CRFP*, Council for the Registration of Forensic Practitioners; *FSAC*, Forensic Science Advisory Council; *FSR*, Forensic Science Regulator; *ILAC*, International Laboratory Accreditation Cooperation; *UKFSLG*, United Kingdom Forensic Science Liaison Group.

In its report, the Select Committee made the first call for an Advisory Board and a register for forensic scientists. Conclusion 8 of that report recommended;

> *[A] system of individual registration of all forensic scientists. Scientists should be registered according to speciality, and at one of two levels … Registration should depend on qualifications, experience, references and a casebook; it should be subject to review and withdrawal. It should be administered by the Government, with the help of a small Board, and delegated to the appropriate professional body wherever possible*

One chapter of the Royal Commission report published in July 1993 was devoted to forensic science and another to expert evidence. The report contained hundreds of recommendations (352), 50 of which related in some degree to the practice and delivery of forensic science.

The UK government's response to the Commission's recommendations came in two stages; an interim response in 1994 and a final response in 1996.

The main outcome was the establishment of the Criminal Cases Review Commission to consider suspected miscarriages of justice and, where appropriate, refer cases to the Court of Appeal.

Lack of disclosure was identified as a major contributor to what were eventually deemed to be miscarriages of justice. Disclosure, particularly of used and unused prosecution evidence, was given statutory force.

In terms of quality, the Commission's recommendations echoed the call by the House of Lords Select Committee for an Advisory Board. It recommended the establishment of a Forensic Science Advisory Council (FSAC) to report to the Home Secretary (UK minister of internal security) on the performance, achievements, and efficiencies of forensic science laboratories. It was proposed that the FSAC would oversee the development of formal accreditation through the then National Measurement Accreditation Service (NAMAS—the predecessor of UKAS the UK Accreditation

Service). The FSAC would also oversee progress in the development of a code of practice for forensic scientists. The "accreditation" of individual forensic scientists was rejected, as was the need for a register of competent experts. The status of the employer was considered to be a reliable indicator of competence.

It was not until 2008 that the UK government established the FSAC, and then only in support of the Forensic Science Regulator, a post created at the same time, see 4.3.1.2.2.

4.2.2 The Providers' Response—Quality Standards

The immediate response by UK forensic science providers to these miscarriages of justice and taking account of the recommendations of the Royal Commission on Criminal Justice and the Select Committee was twofold; adopting quality standards and establishing a liaison group to identify, develop, establish, and maintain good forensic practice. The overall aim of the providers was to improve performance and restore confidence in forensic science.

At that time, in the reports that were issued in 1993, none of the major stakeholders; the courts, police, or prosecuting authorities, required forensic science to comply with quality standards. Adopting quality management as a remedy and a safeguard was an initiative of the providers alone. Even at the time of writing [December 2017], compliance is not yet mandated in E&W although it is recognized by many stakeholders that conformance to quality standards is essential.

By the end of 1996 all the major forensic science providers in the UK were certified to the quality management standard ISO 9001 (or its then British equivalent BS 5750), and accredited by NAMAS to the standard M10 "General criteria of competence for calibration and testing laboratories," which in turn conformed to ISO/IEC Guide 25 "General requirements for the competence of calibration and testing laboratories." As recorded in 4.5, in 1999 the separate standards covering management and technical competence were combined in ISO/IEC 17025:1999 "General requirements for the competence of testing and calibration laboratories". Forensic science providers in E&W were among the first to gain accreditation to the then new standard, ISO/IEC 17025:1999.

It should be recalled from Section 3 that ISO/IEC 17025 is not a standard specifically for forensic science laboratories. It was not until the International Laboratory Accreditation Cooperation (ILAC) Guide 19, "Guidelines for Forensic Science Laboratories" was published in 2002 that forensic science laboratories (and accreditation bodies) had a clear understanding of how the management, practice, and delivery of forensic science might conform to ISO/IEC 17025.

Today, in 2017 most, if not all, of the major forensic science providers in the developed world are accredited to ISO/IEC 17025.

4.2.3 The Providers' Response—Liaison

The second response to the miscarriages of justice, the Royal Commission, and the Select Committee was by the UK Forensic Science Liaison Group (UKFSLG). UKFSLG is now the Association of Forensic Science Providers (www.afsp.org.uk).

UKFSLG was the first group borne of the need to improve the quality of forensic science that looked to international quality standards as a means meeting that need. UKFSLG was formed with the following aims:

- To liaise and exchange information appropriate at that level on matters concerning forensic science,
- To maintain cooperation and liaison between UK laboratories on scientific and technical matters, research, and training,
- To seek to establish UK standards in forensic science, and
- To liaise with other organizations as necessary to promote forensic science in the UK and overseas (Gough, 1997).

One of the first UKFSLG outcomes was a Code of Practice for forensic practitioners, reproduced as Appendix H. Some UKFSLG members incorporated the Code into their quality management system. Compliance with the Code therefore became subject to independent oversight and was enforceable.

Another outcome was establishing a Collaborative Exercises Group to provide proficiency tests conforming to ISO/IEC Guide 43 "Proficiency testing by interlaboratory comparisons, as a means of monitoring and improving performance".

That UKFSLG Code of Practice was later adopted by the Council for the Registration of Forensic Practitioners (CRFP), discussed later in 4.3.1.2.1, and it was used as a basis of the Forensic Science Regulator's Code discussed in 3.4.4.1 and reproduced as Appendix B.

The UKFSLG identified and shared good practice and in due course all members gained accreditation to the standard ISO/IEC 17025.

4.3 PERFORMANCE

4.3.1 Assuring Competence

4.3.1.1 Evidence of Poor Practice/Performance

As defined by ISO 9000:2015(E) 3.10.4, competence is the ability to apply knowledge and skills to achieve intended results. In addition, the objects of quality management include the assurance of competent organizations and individuals. In the history of forensic science, there have been many examples of insufficient competence; three are detailed below with the outcomes.

Members of ASCLD began to establish voluntary quality and management standards from about 1974. The initiative was in response to the results of a national proficiency testing program conducted by the Forensic Science Foundation. Some of the results obtained were a major cause for concern (Peterson et al., 1978). However, that event led initially to the creation of a standards development and conformance assessment body, ASCLD/Laboratory Accreditation Board (ASCLD/LAB), rather than accrediting member laboratories to the international standard ISO/IEC 17025. It was not until 2008 that ASCLD/LAB was recognised as operating in conformance to ISO/IEC 17011 "Conformity assessment—General requirements for accreditation bodies accrediting conformity assessment bodies" and was thus assessed as competent to accredit ASCLD/LAB members to ISO/IEC 17025 (ASCLD, 2016).

In 1996 Professor Brian Caddy, the then Director of the Forensic Unit at the University of Strathclyde, Scotland, issued a report on contamination at the UK Forensic Explosives Laboratory (B. Caddy, 1996). Professor Caddy found a systemic weakness in the laboratory's quality assurance procedures and made recommendations for improvements.

His report included a personal recommendation for the establishment of an Inspectorate of Forensic Sciences. He envisaged an individual with the legal right to enter and assess any operational forensic science laboratory, initiate inquiries into alleged miscarriages of justice, identify solutions, and implement them. The proposed inspectorate would liaise with accrediting bodies. He also envisaged a register of both organizations and individuals with registration fees supporting the Inspectorate.

Professor Caddy offered the alternative of a professional body to monitor and govern the forensic science "profession". The body would require a code of conduct and ethics, together with a means of enabling members to demonstrate competence.

The UK Government's immediate response to Professor Caddy's report was to consider the establishment of a Forensic Science Inspectorate. It noted that the Royal Commission on Criminal Justice did not see the need for statutory regulation, but proposed instead the establishment of an FSAC with a range of functions similar to those of the proposed Inspectorate.

Published in 1997 the US Office of the Inspector General's report into the Federal Bureau of Investigation (FBI) (Office of the Inspector General, 1997) stated,

> *In response to allegations of wrongdoing and improper practices within certain sections (mainly the Explosives Unit) of the Federal Bureau of Investigation (FBI) Laboratory the Department of Justice Office of the Inspector General (OIG) conducted an investigation. The subsequent report issued in April of 1997 found scientifically flawed testimony, inaccurate testimony, testimony beyond the competence of examiners, improper preparation of laboratory reports, insufficient documentation of test results, scientifically flawed reports, inadequate record management and retention, and failures of management to resolve serious and credible allegations of incompetence.*

From today's quality management perspective, this catalog of quality failures is hard to comprehend but it reflects, to some extent, the poor standards of practice commonly in place at the time.

Again, from today's perspective, the report's recommendations seem obvious. They include:

- seeking accreditation of the laboratory by ASCLD/LAB;
- requiring examiners in the explosives unit to have scientific backgrounds in chemistry, metallurgy, or engineering;
- mandating that each examiner prepare and sign a separate report instead of a composite report without attribution to individual examiners;
- establishing a review process for analytical reports by unit chiefs;
- preparing adequate case files to support reports;
- monitoring court testimony to preclude examiners from testifying to matters beyond their expertise or in ways that are unprofessional; and
- developing written protocols for scientific procedures.

In short, the report called for a fit-for-purpose, independently accredited, quality management system.

It is important to note that the monitoring of court performance of forensic scientists is an issue still to be satisfactorily resolved.

These three events support the contention that quality failures mark the starting point and provided the impetus for the development of the quality management systems employed in forensic science today.

4.3.1.2 Responses

4.3.1.2.1 A United Kingdom Register

The idea of a register of competent forensic scientists came to fruition in 1999 when the UK CRFP was incorporated in August of that year. The CRFP was created with the full support of the major stakeholders; parliament, government, forensic scientists, lawyers, and the judiciary. Its governance was broadly based with representation by all stakeholders and, most importantly, the customer community.

Several factors contributed to the creation of the CRFP, the main ones, discussed earlier, being:

- The poor performance and insufficient competence of forensic scientists that contributed to the miscarriages of justice listed in Table 4.1,
- The House of Lords Select Committee on Science and Technology report on forensic science that recommended the establishment of an Advisory Board and a register for forensic scientists to be administered by the Government with the help of a small Board (House of Lords Select Committee, 1993), and
- The report by Professor Brian Caddy on contamination at the Forensic Explosives Laboratory suggested the creation of a register of competent practitioners (Caddy, 1996).

Pressure for a register of competent forensic scientists also arose from concerns about the provision of forensic science by individuals employed by organizations lacking an appropriate, or any, quality management system, e.g., university-based experts.

The CRFP differed from other "certification" schemes for individuals in a number of positive ways. It was a strictly a regulatory body and not a professional body. Registration included assessment of competence based on the independent review of current casework, not just qualifications, training, and experience. The competencies, to be demonstrated were as follows: (and are also reproduced as Appendix G).

1. Knowing the hypothesis or question to be tested
2. Establishing that items submitted were suitable for the requirements of the case
3. Confirming that the correct type of examination has been selected
4. Confirming that the examination was carried out competently
5. Recording, summarizing, and collating the results of the examination
6. Interpreting the results in accordance with established scientific principles
7. Considering alternative hypotheses
8. Preparing a report based on the findings
9. Presenting oral evidence to court and at case conferences
10. Ensuring that all documentation is fit for purpose

The responsibility for gaining and maintaining these competencies rested with the individual and not the organization. Registrants were also required to comply with a code of conduct (based on the UKFSLG code see Section 4.2.3 and Appendix H). Registration was only open to practitioners; managers, teachers, researchers, and others with no portfolio of current casework were ineligible. The CRFP also had effective conformance assessment and enforcement, or fitness-to-practice, procedures.

For various reasons, not all within its control, the CRFP never met its self-financing objective. The UK government withdrew financial support and the CRFP ceased trading in March 2009. Thus, it would appear that the CRFP has little relevance. However, its birth, life, and death are closely linked to the development of quality management in forensic science, and the independent assessment of individual competence is still considered as part of the quality standards framework in some jurisdictions, particularly in the United States, given the initiative by the Forensic Specialties Accreditation Board (FSAB) discussed in 3.4.4.3, and in the Netherlands as discussed in 4.3.1.2.3. Consideration of its life cycle provides useful insights.

In November 1996 a group of key stakeholders, including the main forensic science providers in the UK, met to consider setting up a professional body for forensic science. The outcome of that meeting was the creation of a working group lead by the then chair of the House of Lords Select Committee on Science and Technology, Lord Dainton.

The remit given to the group was,

> *[T]o examine whether a system of self regulation could be devised which would ensure and safeguard standards of professional competence and integrity for forensic scientists.*

The group's report (Forensic Science Working Group, 1997) was delivered in November 1997. Its recommendation was not the creation of a professional body for forensic science but a "well structured registration system." The report included a "road map" for the creation of a register that would;

- be self-financed,
- be affordable,
- assure the competence and integrity of those registered,
- cover all those involved in the forensic science process from crime scene to court, and
- be nonstatutory.

The UK government's response to this report was broadly positive, to the extent of welcoming the proposal to set up a registration body for forensic scientists and being supportive of initiatives by the then president-elect of the House of Lords Select Committee on Science and Technology, Lord Dainton.

In its development, a distinction between a professional body and one managing a register became an issue that is relevant to the development of quality management. In the report of the Forensic Science Working Group (Forensic Science Working Group, 1997), led by Lord Lewis, to the Forensic Science Steering Group, led by Dr Janet Thompson, then Chief Executive of the Forensic Science Service, the distinction was explored and the conclusion drawn as follows:

A professional body:

- sets standards of admission to include levels of competence,
- maintains standards of integrity through codes of practice, conduct, and ethics,
- has disciplinary measures to maintain standards and objectives, and
- functions as a learned society.

A professional body is governed by its members and serves their needs while including an ethos of public service having regard to the public interest. A profession is self-regulating.

A regulatory body serves the needs of the customer or stakeholder community. The government of a regulatory body must, therefore, include representatives of that community to be seen to be independent of the profession it regulates.

The CRFP focused on the competence of the individual and used the powerful instrument of casework peer review to assess performance. By this means the quality management system of the employing organization also came into consideration. As highlighted in 1.3.4, qualifications and experience are not always accurate measures of competence.

At the time it ceased trading in 2009, the CRFP registered as competent, and had in place fitness-to-practice procedures for; crime scene examiners, fingerprint examiners, small forensic science providers, sole practitioners, and university-based practitioners.

With the closure of the CRFP, small organizations and sole practitioners that could not make a business case for bearing the considerable cost of accreditation to the international standards ISO/IEC 17025 or ISO/IEC 17020 lost their only means of independently demonstrating competence. This gap still exists at the time of writing [December 2017].

Registered crime scene examiners also lost regulatory cover and, at the time of writing [December 2017], will not regain it until October 2020 (Forensic Science Regulator, 2014). Registered fingerprint examiners are expected to gain regulatory cover in October 2018.

The challenges in regulating small providers, sole, and university-based forensic practitioners using standards aimed at organizations are significant and might, at least in part, explain an absence of regulation.

There seems to be no clear reason for the delay in accrediting crime scene examination. Accreditation for crime scene examination in the UK has been available since 2011. At the time of writing [December 2017], the only organization accredited by UKAS is a private company. The major provider of crime scene examination is the police. The target for accreditation for organizations providing crime scene examination is 2020. It is generally recognized that mistakes made at the crime scene are often irreparable and regarded as having a severe negative impact on the quality of scientific evidence, e.g., inculpatory/exculpatory evidence might not be collected. There is a resultant risk to the criminal justice system.

One of the arguments advanced at the time the CRFP closed was that the management at laboratories accredited to ISO/IEC 17025 was responsible for ensuring the competence of their staff, which is the case, obviating the need for the external regulation of individuals. Therefore, CRFP registration was redundant. However, accreditation to ISO/IEC 17025 does not constitute an independent, third party, assessment of individual competence and the standard places no responsibility on the individual forensic scientists to gain or maintain competence. There remains a place for such assessment within a quality standards framework which the FSAB initiative, described earlier in 4.3.1.2 and in 3.4.4.3, seems destined to occupy.

With the closure of the CRFP, the concept of the independent "certification" of individual forensic scientists was abandoned by the UK government, and it seems unlikely that this gap in the quality standards framework will be closed in the UK. However, developments in the US, see 3.4.4.3 and 4.3.2.2.3, and the Netherlands, see 4.3.1.2.3, and the debate around a forensic science "profession" (J. Robertson, 2014) will keep the issue on the agenda.

The essential question is, does independently assessing the competence of individuals improve the quality of forensic evidence? There is evidence that it does, e.g., R v T (2010). In that judgment the E&W appellate court found that a trained forensic scientist employed by an accredited forensic science provider lacked essential competencies. The finding also called into question the competence of the organization.

4.3.1.2.2 A Forensic Science Regulator in England and Wales and a Forensic Science Advisory Council

In March 2005 the House of Commons Select Committee of the UK parliament published its report entitled "Forensic Science on Trial" (House of Commons Science and Technology Committee, 2005). This report was mainly prompted by the government's plan to "privatize" the Forensic Science Service, which was, at that time, an executive agency of the Home Office (the UK police and internal security ministry). In anticipation of further commercialization of the market in forensic science, the report recorded the Home Office model for the regulation of the market being created:

> *a single quality assurance regulator … accrediting suppliers who wish to provide services to the police and, by arrangement, other entities within the CJS [criminal justice system].*

According to this model,

> *[A]ccreditation would be granted at the corporate level but the accreditation process would be based on appropriate quality standards applying to:*

- The corporate body;
- The products and services provided; and
- The individuals responsible for the service".

This aligns with the main quality requirements for an accredited organization:

- a competent organization,
- competent individuals, and
- valid methods and procedures.

The Home Office model foreshadowed the quality standards framework currently in place in E&W, oversight by the Forensic Science Regulator supported by an FSAC and accreditation of forensic science providers to either ISO/IEC 17025 or ISO/IEC 17020. It should be noted that the committee was clearly of the view that the recommended FSAC, and not an individual, would exercise the role of market overseer and regulator.

"Forensic Science on Trial" discussed the issue of the quality of forensic science education which, although important, is beyond the scope of this work save to say that the issues of meeting the needs of the CJS and employers and employer recognition of courses are always current.

The report also drew attention to criticisms and concerns about the CRFP along the lines of who assess the competence of the CRFP?

> *The CRFP must itself be subject to regular independent auditing of the assessment processes used to grant accreditation and renewal of accreditation, as well as the disciplinary procedures. It is essential that the CRFP is, and is seen to be, transparent, accountable and independent. It must also be seen to exercise its duty of care by vigorous and appropriate actions in respect of malpractice allegations about registrants.*

Accreditation of the CRFP to the standard ISO/IEC 17024 "General requirements for bodies operating certification of person" would have met that requirement, but that was rejected by the CRFP in 2008.

The Select Committee report also discussed the prosecutor's fallacy, explained in 3.4.2.4 and discussed in Section 7, and the need for clearer and more accurate presentation of statistical evidence in relation to DNA profiling. At the time of writing [December 2017], communicating statistical evidence remains an unresolved issue and is mentioned in Section 7.

The main recommendation regarding quality was the creation of an FSAC.

[W]ith responsibility for taking an overview of forensic science, from education and training through to R&D and its use in court. We recommend the establishment of a Forensic Science Advisory Council to serve as a regulator for the developing market in forensic service and as an independent source of advice. The Forensic Science Advisory Council could also oversee cross-cutting inspections of the entire chain of processes by which forensic science is employed in the criminal justice system. We also highlight the need for proper independent oversight, with ethical and lay input, of the National DNA Database.

The committee also recommended that the FSAC exercise a "gatekeeping" role.

The absence of an agreed protocol for the validation of scientific techniques prior to their being admitted in court is entirely unsatisfactory. Judges are not well-placed to determine scientific validity without input from scientists. We recommend that one of the first tasks of the Forensic Science Advisory Council be to develop a 'gatekeeping' test for expert evidence. This should be done in partnership with judges, scientists and other key players in the criminal justice system, and should build on the US Daubert test.

The gatekeeping role remains an issue in forensic science at the time of writing [December 2017] and is further discussed in 4.3.3.1 and mentioned in Section 7. The "US Daubert test" is discussed in 4.3.3.1.2.

Accreditation to ISO/IEC 17025 and 17020 requires scientific techniques, or methods, falling within the scope of accreditation to be validated, see 1.4.2. Where techniques are novel or rarely used, they will necessarily fall outside the scope. However, the forensic science community is now sufficiently mature to know that all methods, whether or not they fall within the scope of accreditation, must be validated before evidence based on those methods is presented. This is required by ILAC Guide 19:2002 and G19-08/2014. The essential validation study can be a powerful tool in gatekeeping.

In response to the Select Committee's report and taking particular account of the creation of a market in forensic science, the UK government established the role of the Forensic Science Regulator in July 2007. The role was required to ensure a level playing field for all providers and that quality standards were maintained in the face of the growing market and increased competition. At the time of writing [December 2017], this role is unique as is a market in forensic science provision.

From a presentation given by the Regulator shortly after his appointment in July 2008 his vision was:

To achieve:

- comprehensive standards framework
- provider,
- practitioner and
- method (product or service)
- level playing field for all suppliers and practitioners
- quality standards maintained in the face of the changing market and increased competition.

The Regulator has produced many helpful guidance documents, in particular, the various codes of practice and conduct, and played a significant role in assuring the reliability of scientific evidence. However, the vision expressed in 2008 has yet (in December 2017) to be realized. Some providers and practitioners lie outside the current quality standards framework, some providers are not accredited thereby holding a competitive advantage over those that are and putting the CJS at risk, and quality failures continue to occur (Burn, 2017).

One of the Regulator's first achievements was to bring about the closure of the CRFP which he considered surplus to requirements (Forensic Science Regulator, 2009). He (as the post holder was at the time) also commissioned the review of low template DNA (see 4.4.4). In the past, such reviews would have been commissioned directly by a government minister as in the case of the review of contamination at the Forensic Explosives Laboratory (B. Caddy, 1996) and the performance review of the Forensic Science Service in the case of Damilola Taylor (Rawley and Caddy, 2007).

The Regulator has conducted reviews of a number of quality failures and made recommendations for remedial action. He also gave evidence to the Scottish Fingerprint Inquiry (Campbell, 2011).

Although not directly relevant to the development of quality management the novel role of a judicial advisor, *or amicus curiae,* is of interest. The Regulator has advised the E&W Court of Appeal. In *Reed* (R v Reed, Reed and Garmson, 2009):

> *He [the Regulator] also made clear that he did not consider validation a necessary pre-condition for the admission of scientific evidence, provided the obligations under Rule 33.3(1) [now rule 19, see Section 4.3.3.2.2] of the Criminal Procedure Rules were followed.*

This position seems at odds with the current position of the Regulator as set out in Section 20 of the codes, that validation is essential (Forensic Science Regulator, 2016). It is also contrary to the technical requirements of ISO/IEC 17025.

However, the justices expressed the view that:

With the establishment of the Forensic Science Advisory Council and the Forensic Science Regulator, there may be very much more assistance available to the court, as there was in this case on appeal for us, to help it in its assessment of whether the evidence is sufficiently reliable for it to be admitted, but the ultimate decision remains that of the court on the principles we have set out.

The Regulator also played a part in Broughton (R v Broughton, 2010).

[T]here is now a considerable body of opinion from respected independent scientists and the Forensic Science Regulator that LTDNA [low template DNA] techniques, including those used to generate the profiles relied upon by the Crown in this case, are well understood, have been properly validated and are accepted to be capable of generating reliable and valuable evidence

This role of the Regulator assisting appellate court judges with their gatekeeping role of assessing the admissibility of scientific evidence is novel, of significant utility and may expand.

4.3.1.2.3 Netherlands Register of Court-Appointed Experts

In common with other jurisdictions, the Netherlands experienced a number of miscarriages of justice to which expert evidence was thought to have contributed. In the late 2000s there was an "unprecedented" number, and the Dutch government decided to reform the regulation of experts and expert evidence in criminal procedures (Nijboer et al., 2011).

Although all forensic science laboratories in the Netherlands are accredited to ISO/IEC 17025, independent assessment of the competence of the individual is considered an important element in the Dutch quality standards framework (van Asten et al., 2015). This is in contrast to the UK, which, as discussed in 4.3.1.2., has rejected such assessment and relies on ISO/IEC 17025 with some supplementals.

In 2010 the Experts in Criminal Cases Act came into effect and, as a response, the Netherlands Register of Court Experts (Nederlands Register Gerechtelijk Dekundigen or NRGD) was established. The NRGD is located within the Ministry of Justice. The NRGD is the first register for court experts with a legal basis. Registrants are required to comply with a code of conduct. The NRGD is managed by an independent Board of Court Experts. The aim of the Experts in Criminal Cases Act is twofold. On the one hand it is intended to strengthen the position of the defense. The Act explicitly grants a suspect the right to request an additional investigation or counter inquiry. On the other hand, the Act signifies a tightening up of the quality, reliability, and competence of court experts (NRGD n.d.).

At the time of writing [Decembers 2017], there are registrants in the disciplines of:

- DNA analysts and interpretation,
- Handwriting,

- Weapons and ammunition,
- Forensic psychiatry and psychology,
- Toxicology, and
- Drugs analysis and interpretation.

Apart from psychiatry and psychology, numbers are low (van Asten et al., 2015).

It is fair to say that registration is not without its critics, and the register will be reviewed by the Ministry of Justice after some years of operation (Nijboer et al., 2011).

4.3.1.2.4 Other Jurisdictions and Territories

No jurisdiction other than E&W has a Forensic Science Regulator, and unless a market in forensic science is introduced elsewhere that situation is unlikely to change.

As discussed in 3.4.7.2.3, Germany does have a register of experts, but this is not relevant to the criminal justice system where expertise is drawn from either the Bundeskriminalamt or BKA, the German federal forensic science provider, or the Landeskriminalamt or LKA, state providers.

As discussed in 3.4.7.2.4, France also maintains a register of experts. The register is held by the Court of Cassation; in addition, each Court of Appeal has a register of experts. In principle only registered experts can be appointed by the courts and this principle is rarely challenged.

With the above exceptions, no other jurisdictions maintain a register of competent forensic scientists. It should be borne in mind that in all jurisdictions it is the judge, or the person holding judicial authority, that ultimately decides who qualifies as an expert.

In Australasia, competence is assessed and maintained by accreditation to ISO/IEC 17025. The providers are supported by NIFS. As mentioned in 4.2, NIFS was created in response to miscarriages of justice in Australia.

In the US, measures assuring the competence of organization and individuals, as well as the validity of methods, have come in large number after the publication of the 2009 NRC report (National Research Council, 2009). This will be the subject of discussion in the next section on the impact of science on performance.

4.3.2 The Impact of Science on Performance

4.3.2.1 Discipline-Specific Working Groups

Among other things, the quality of forensic science is dependent on the quality of the underlying science, the validity of the methods that apply that science, the accuracy of the results obtained, the rational and logical interpretation of those results in the context of the case, and the competence to communicate scientific evidence for the benefit of justice.

Quality control and assurance in the laboratory were covered in Section 1. Compliance with laboratory quality standards will significantly enhance the confidence that can be placed in a result. This subsection focuses on how the quality of the underlying science affects validation, interpretation, and communication; factors that reflect the competence of both the organization and the individual.

Many national and multinational institutions have contributed to the scientific development of forensic science. One of the main contributors to ensuring the soundness of the underlying science is discipline-specific working groups. Such working groups can also ensure that scientific and technological advances are exploited and validated for forensic use. In addition, they also identify and promote good practice. In effect they are standards development bodies and can also be conformance assessment bodies.

In the US, the Federal Bureau of Investigation (FBI) established its first Technical Working Group (TWG) on DNA Analysis Methods (TWGDAM) in 1988 and other discipline-specific TWGs from the early 1990s onward. In time, the FBI renamed their TWGs as Scientific Working Groups (SWG); TWGDAM became SWGDAM. Other US law enforcement agencies, such as the Bureau of Alcohol Tobacco and Firearms (ATF) and Drug Enforcement Administration (DEA), also sponsored discipline-specific working groups. In 1988 the Senior Managers of Australian and New Zealand Forensic Science Laboratories (SMANZL) created its first Specialist Advisory Groups (SAG). A decade later the European Network of Forensic Science Institutes (ENFSI) created its first Expert Working Groups (EWG).

As discussed later in 4.4, SWGDAM played a significant role in the development of quality standards for DNA evidence in the US. SWGDAM guidelines were adopted as a national standard.

As explained in 4.3.2.2.3 below, the creation of the US National Commission on Forensic Science (NCFS) in 2014 led to the replacement of all but SWGDAM and one other SWG by subcommittees of Scientific Area Committees, which are now part of the Organization of Scientific Area Committees (OSAC).

To these discipline-specific working groups, the AFSP should be added, which had similar aims and published its own standard for the formulation of evaluative opinions (Association of Forensic Science Providers, 2009). That standard was later adopted and adapted by ENFSI and published as a guide for all ENFSI member institutes (ENFSI, 2015).

The principle aim of these various groups is to maintain and improve the quality of forensic science in their discipline. These groups had a number of weaknesses that are set out in 4.3.2.2.3. Those weaknesses included being essentially groups established and maintained by forensic science providers with little engagement with other stakeholders in the justice system. In addition, combining the role of provider, standards development and conformance assessment risks a conflict-of-interests and is therefore suboptimal.

The one external and independent group that has affected the science of forensic science perhaps greater than any other is the US National Research Council (NRC) of the National Academies, which is discussed next.

4.3.2.2 Reports of the United States National Research Council

The NRC was established by the National Academy of Sciences to associate the broad community of science and technology with the Academy's purposes of furthering knowledge and advising the US federal government. The NRC has become the principal operating agency of both the National Academy of Sciences and the National Academy of Engineering in providing services to the government, the public, and the scientific and engineering communities.

In addition to the Academies of Sciences and Engineering, the National Academies also include the Institute of Medicine. The National Academies role is as advisers to the nation on science, engineering, and medicine (The National Academies n.d.).

The NRC has, from time to time, considered issues in forensic science and offered recommendations. Of the NRC reports on forensic science, the 2009 report (National Research Council, 2009) had, and continues to have, the greatest impact on the quality of forensic science, particularly in the US. The relevant reports of the NRC are discussed next.

4.3.2.2.1 DNA[1] (National Research Council, 1992; National Research Council, 1996)

In response to numerous questions and doubts about the then new DNA fingerprinting technology[2], the NRC formed a committee in 1989 to study the issues. In 1992 the NRC issued its report (National Research Council, 1992), which was intended to end the debate on the admissibility of evidence based on DNA fingerprinting, as it was then called.

Unfortunately, the report itself became the target of criticism from scientists and lawyers on both sides of the admissibility argument and a second committee was set up toward the end of 1994.

By the time the second report was published in 1996 (National Research Council, 1996), old technology was being replaced; STR/PCR[3] was overtaking VTNR/RFLP, as a result the relevance of the report was weakened. However, this latest report did call for quality standards to be complied with and for laboratories to be accredited (recommendation 3.1). It also recommended that laboratories should participate regularly in proficiency tests and the results made available for court proceedings (recommendation 3.2). The 1996 report was educational and informative.

Making the results of proficiency tests available for court use is not yet common practice and may not be for the foreseeable future. However, the recent

[1] The forensic exploitation of the DNA molecule had a major impact on quality management, which is considered in 4.4 below.

[2] Which was based on variable number tandem repeats (VNTR) and restriction fragment length polymorphism (RFLP).

[3] the profiling of short tandem repeats (STR) with polymerase chain reaction (PCR) amplification.

recommendation regarding transparency of quality management system documents by the now defunct US NCFS (National Commission on Forensic Science, 2016) may hasten change.

It should be noted in passing that the NRC was not supportive of a Bayesian approach to the evaluation of evidence believing that it required fact finders to estimate prior probabilities and that US courts would be unwilling to expect fact finders to do so. Bayesian reasoning is further discussed in Section 7.

4.3.2.2.2 Bullet Lead (National Research Council, 2004)

The next report concerned the compositional analysis of bullet lead (CABL). The basic idea being to compare the chemical composition of bullet lead found at a crime scene with that of ammunition associated with a suspect.

This forensic technique had been used since the 1960s to provide evidence of association in thousands of criminal cases until a retired FBI examiner began questioning the procedure. The FBI consequently asked the National Academy of Sciences to review the technique. The resultant NRC report, published in 2004, undermined the reliability of CABL. The report found that the available data did not support any expert claim that a crime bullet came from a particular box of ammunition. In the wake of the NRC report, several State courts excluded CABL evidence, finding that, because the evidence was based on erroneous scientific foundations, CABL no longer satisfied the requirements of *Frye* (see 4.3.3.1.2) for the admissibility of scientific expert testimony (Clemons v State, 2006).

The NRC recommended that the FBI should use a different statistical analysis for the technique and that, given variations in bullet manufacturing processes, expert witnesses should make clear the very limited conclusions that CABL results can support. The report also recommended that the FBI take additional measures to ensure the validity of CABL results, which include improving documentation, publishing details, and improving on training and oversight.

The NRC found that compositionally similar bullets may be present in different boxes of ammunition and compositionally different bullets may be present in the same box of ammunition, confounding the evidence type.

On the September the 1st 2005 the FBI, in the light of the NRC findings and court rulings, ceased to conduct bullet lead examination arguing that the cost outweighed the benefit but highlighting:

> *One factor significantly influenced the Laboratory's decision to no longer conduct the examination of bullet lead: neither scientists nor bullet manufacturers are able to definitively attest to the significance of an association made between bullets in the course of a bullet lead examination.*
>
> ***Federal Bureau of Investigation (2005)***

The evidential value of bullet lead analysis was poor and the evidence type potentially misleading. Controversially, the FBI stood by the results of earlier work.

4.3.2.2.3 Strengthening Forensic Science (National Research Council, 2009)

The NRC of the US National Academies, 2009, report recorded the message sent by the forensic science community,

> *The forensic science system, encompassing both research and practice, has serious problems that can only be addressed by a national commitment to overhaul the current structure that supports the forensic science community in this country. This can only be done with effective leadership at the highest levels of both federal and state governments, pursuant to national standards, and with a significant infusion of federal funds.*

The report has had, and continues to have, a worldwide impact on forensic science research, practice, management and delivery, and, consequently, quality management. In the US, the report led directly to the creation in 2014 of the NCFS discussed later.

The NRC report was commissioned by the US Congress to identify the needs of the forensic science community and conduct a detailed assessment of forensic science research, practice, management and delivery, identifying needs, strengths and weakness and make recommendations accordingly.

In response to its congressional charge, the NRC formed an independent Forensic Science Committee that included members of the forensic science community, members of the legal community, and a "diverse" group of scientists. The committee began its work in 2006.

The report was critical of the quality of forensic science and recognized the need to standardize practices in the US. It contained 13 recommendations. The main recommendation was the creation of a National Institute of Forensic Science (NIFS not to be confused with the Australasian NIFS) to establish and enforce good practice for individual practitioners and forensic science providers. The establishment of NIFS in the US was seen as the key to implementing most of the other recommendations. Recommendation 3 is worth quoting in full as it has the greatest relevance to quality management:

> *Recommendation 3:*
>
> *Research is needed to address issues of accuracy, reliability, and validity in the forensic science disciplines. The National Institute of Forensic Science (NIFS) should competitively fund peer-reviewed research in the following areas:*
>
> *(a) Studies establishing the scientific bases demonstrating the validity of forensic methods.*
> *(b) The development and establishment of quantifiable measures of the reliability and accuracy of forensic analyses. Studies of the reliability and accuracy of forensic techniques should reflect actual practice on realistic case scenarios, averaged across a representative sample of forensic scientists and laboratories. Studies also should establish the limits of reliability and accuracy that analytic methods can be expected to achieve as the conditions of forensic evidence vary. The research by which measures of reliability and accuracy are determined should be peer reviewed and published in respected scientific journals.*

(c) The development of quantifiable measures of uncertainty[4] in the conclusions of forensic analyses.
(d) Automated techniques capable of enhancing forensic technologies."

The recommendation to create a NIFS was not the only one with major impact potential. Recommendation 4: that Congress via NIFS should facilitate the removal of all public forensic laboratories and facilities from the administrative control of law enforcement agencies or prosecutors' offices; if implemented, would result in a sea change in the management and delivery of forensic science in the US. This recommendation is assessed in Section 7[4].

The responses to those 13 recommendations are detailed in a paper by John Butler of the US National Institute of Standards and Technology (NIST) (Butler, 2015). The quotes that follow are taken from that paper.

As an initial response, the White House Office of Science and Technology Policy coordinated the establishment of the Subcommittee on Forensic Science under the National Science and Technology Council to "identify challenges and opportunities for addressing the NRC report recommendations."

In the absence of significant progress toward the establishment of the National Institute of Forensic Science recommended in the NRC report as the means of implementing most of the other recommendations, NIST and the Department of Justice (DOJ) created the National Commission on Forensic Science (NCFS).

The NCFS was chartered in 2013 and launched in February 2014 together with the Organization of Scientific Area Committees (OSAC). The NCFS was focused on policy and OSAC on quality. OSAC is discussed in detail in Section 2.

The NCFS was a 2-year renewable federal advisory committee to the DOJ that provided policy recommendations to the Attorney General. It comprised academics, judges, lawyers and laboratory managers.Its latest charter expired in April 2017 and was not renewed.

According to that charter the objectives and scope of activities for the NCFS included providing:

[R]ecommendations and advice to the DOJ concerning national methods and strategies for:

- strengthening the validity and reliability of the forensic sciences (including medico-legal death investigation);
- enhancing quality assurance and quality control in forensic science laboratories and units;

[4] At the time of writing [March 2017] there is little or no evidence of progress on measurement uncertainty.

- identifying and recommending scientific guidance and protocols for evidence seizure, testing, analysis, and reporting by forensic science laboratories and units; and
- identifying and assessing other needs of the forensic science communities to strengthen their disciplines and meet increasing demands generated by the criminal and civil justice systems at all levels of government.

OSAC is charged with improving the quality of forensic science in the US (Organization of Scientific Area Committees (OSAC) for 2016). It is to "help identify and develop technically sound, consensus-based documentary standards and guidelines to improve the practice of forensic science in a coordinated manner."

The NIST administered OSAC, overseen by a Forensic Science Standards Board (FSSB), is to provide leadership in developing discipline-specific standards of practice. AS discussed in 2.7, OSAC is working with the Standards Developing Organizations such as ASTM International in building a registry of discipline-specific quality standards. Ultimately standards and guidelines that populate an OSAC registry will enable accreditation bodies to assess the conformance of forensic science providers to the discipline-specific standards. The process is graphically represented in Fig 4.1.

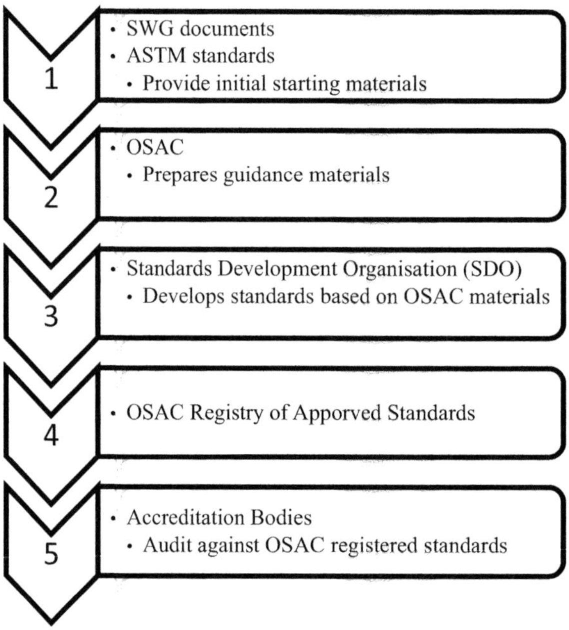

Figure 4.1 OSAC standards development and registry.

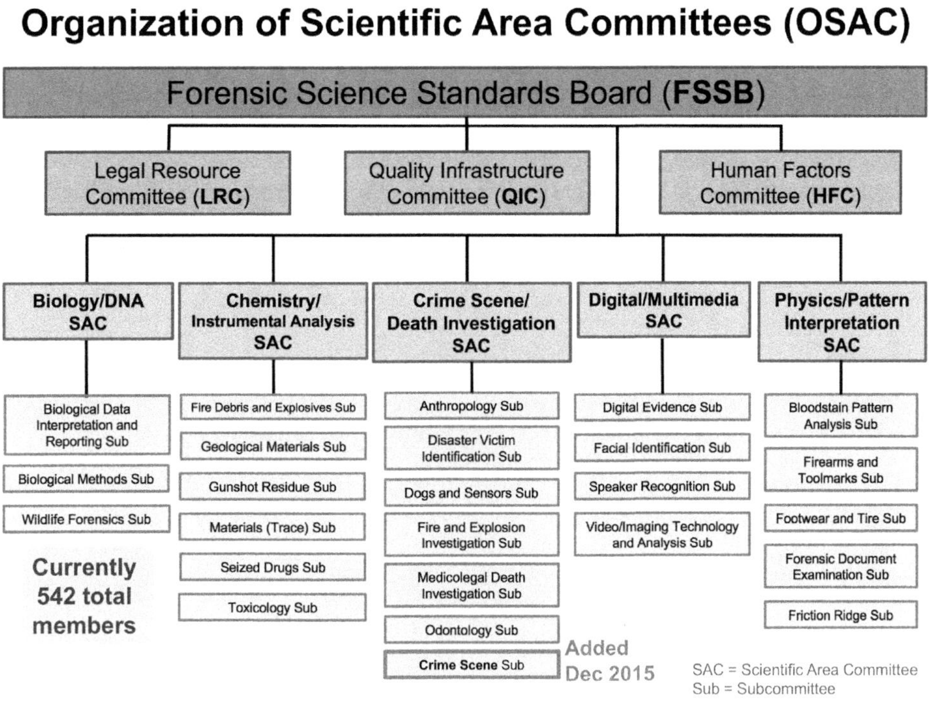

Figure 4.2 OSAC organization.

OSAC consists of 33 operating units, a FSSB, 3 resource committees, 5 scientific area committees (SACs), and 24 subcommittees that focus on discipline-specific needs. The organization of the OSAC is graphically represented in Figs. 4.2 and 4.3.

The discipline-specific SACs that will identify and develop the standards have replaced all but two[5] of the SWGs and TWGs. The working groups operated independently and without consistent procedures. They were criticized by the co-Chair of the NRC's Forensic Science Committee, Judge Harry Edwards. He questioned their value giving the following reasons:

- SWG committees meet irregularly and have no clear or regular sources of funding;
- there are no clear standards in place to determine who gains membership on SWG committees;
- neither SWGs nor their recommendations are mandated by any federal or state law or regulation;
- SWG recommendations are not enforceable;

[5] The DNA SWG SWGDAM and the digital evidence SWG SWGDE will continue to be funded by the DOJ for the time being. Others, previously supported by the DOJ, had their funding cut in April 2014.

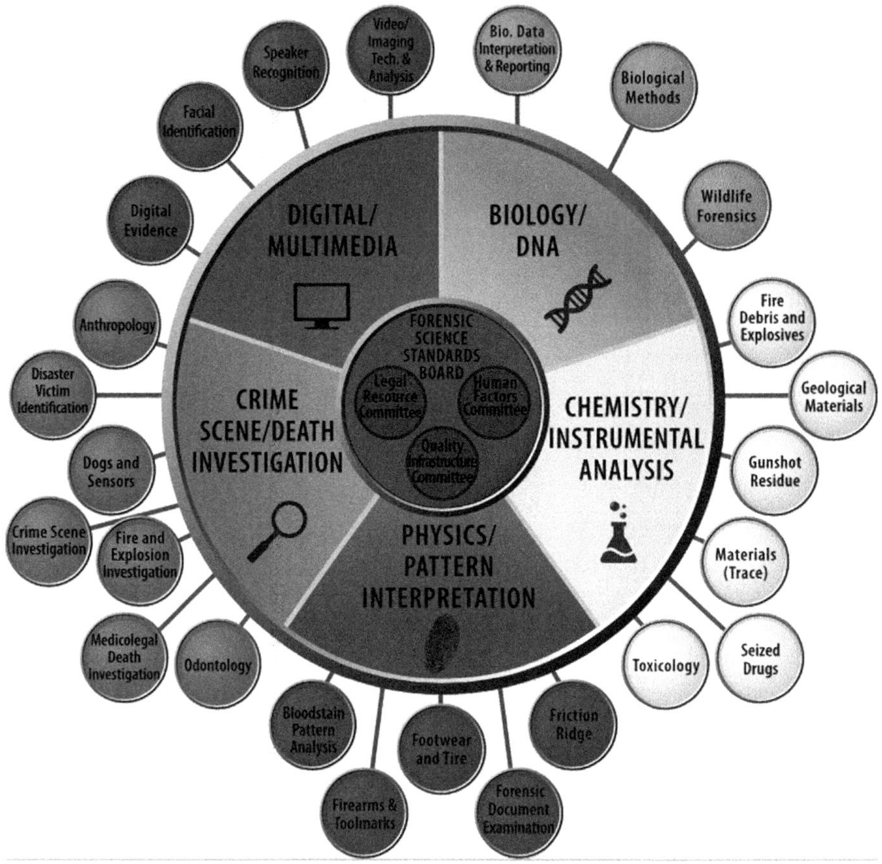

Figure 4.3 Scientific area committeess.

- a number of SWG guidelines are too general and vague to be of any great practical use;
- SWG committees have no way of knowing whether state or local agencies even endorse the standards;
- complaints are not filed when a practitioner violates an SWG standard; and
- SWG committees do not attempt to measure the impact of their standards by formal study or survey (Edwards, 2010)

Judge Edwards summarized his concerns as follows:

In other words, there is nothing to indicate that the standards are routinely followed and enforced in a way to ensure best practices in the forensic science community

Replacing the working groups removed those bodies responsible, at least in part, for the poor practice identified in the NRC report.

It should be noted in passing that the concerns regarding conformity assessment and enforcement might also apply to ENFSI EWGs and SMANZL SAGs.

In November 2015, the NCFS issued a series of draft standards including a 16-point Code of Professional Responsibility for Forensic Science Providers (Docket No.DOJ-LA-2015-0009-0002) (NCFS, 2017a,b) with the recommendation that compliance should be mandatory for DOJ agencies[6] and expected for others. The NCFS code is similar in many respects to the codes of the Forensic Science Regulator (Forensic Science Regulator, 2016). The code is discussed in 3.4.3.2 and reproduced as Appendix C.

Also, among this set of outputs or work products, was a recommendation that forensic science providers should place their quality management system documents in the public domain (Docket No.DOJ-LA-2015-0009-0003) again, with a mechanism to enforce compliance by DOJ agencies. This was put into effect by the US Attorney General on September 6, 2016 (Office of the Attorney General, 2017).

These, and other work products, have been adopted by the NCFS and many have been implemented by the Attorney General.

A further adopted work product of particular significance is a recommendation for "Universal Accreditation" that echoes the recommendation made in the NRC report (NCFS, 2017a,b). If accepted and implemented this would require all forensic science providers to be accredited to the relevant international standard. Compliance would be enforced by the Attorney General by denial of instruction. The work product recognizes the challenges in implementation and sets out a strategy. Interestingly, providers engaged in defense review are not defined as forensic science providers for the purpose of Universal Accreditation and therefore lie outside its scope. This differs from the position in E&W where the intention is for such providers to be included within the scope of a statutory requirement for accreditation (Forensic Science Regulator, 2013), although statutory accreditation in the UK may be some way off (N. Blackwood, 2016).

All the work products adopted by the NCFS are listed on the DOJ Website (The United States Department of Justice, 2017). Those adopted so far, if implemented, will constitute a robust and wide-ranging quality standards framework with effective conformity assessment and enforcement mechanisms. Incorporating OSAC registered standards into the quality management system of accredited forensic science providers will be the most effective means of assessing and enforcing conformance.

As reported earlier, the NCFS charter expired on April 23, 2017, and was not renewed. In addition, NIST is now assessing performance and looking to improve OSAC and create OSAC 2.0. A request for information seeking input on potential

[6] The FBI (Federal Bureau of Investigation), DEA (Drug Enforcement Administration), and the ATFE (Bureau of Alcohol, Tobacco, Firearms and Explosives).

changes was issued on August 30, 2017. It is to be hoped that progress toward the quality standards framework specified by the NCFS and OSAC will not be slowed or stalled.

4.3.3 The Impact of Law on the Development of Quality Management with Regard to Performance

4.3.3.1 The Admissibility and Reliability of Scientific Evidence

4.3.3.1.1 Admissibility and Reliability in England and Wales

The Law Commission of E&W is a statutory independent body created by the Law Commissions Act 1965 to keep the law under review and to recommend reform where it is needed. The aim of the Commission is to ensure that the law is fair, modern, simple, and cost-effective.

On March 21, 2011, the Commission published Report Number 325 "Expert Evidence in Criminal Proceedings in England and Wales" (The Law Commission, 2011).

The continuing admission of unreliable expert evidence leading to serious miscarriages of justice prompted a study that led to the report.

An important finding was that:

> *Too much expert opinion evidence is admitted without adequate scrutiny because no clear test is being applied to determine whether the evidence is sufficiently reliable to be admitted*

In that report, the Commission proposed that expert evidence should be admissible in criminal proceedings only if certain tests were met [emphasis added]:

- the court must be satisfied that it would provide information which is likely to be **outside a judge or jury's experience and knowledge**, and which would give them the help they need in arriving at their conclusions;
- the **witness must be qualified** to give the evidence;
- the evidence is not made inadmissible as a result of clause 3 (**impartiality**);
- In addition, expert opinion evidence is admissible in criminal proceedings only if it is **sufficiently reliable** to be admitted (see clause 4).

The first three bullet points are not new but the fourth is and introduces a reliability test.

The decision on reliability would be for the trial judge alone and expert opinion evidence would be deemed sufficiently reliable if:

(a) the opinion is soundly based, and
(b) the strength of the opinion is warranted having regard to the grounds on which it is based.

According to the Law Commission report, certain matters could, in particular, provide a reason for determining that expert opinion evidence is not sufficiently reliable:

1. the opinion is based on a hypothesis which has not been subjected to sufficient scrutiny (including, where appropriate, experimental or other testing), or which has failed to stand up to scrutiny;
2. the opinion is based on an unjustifiable assumption;
3. the opinion is based on flawed data;
4. the opinion relies on an examination, technique, method or process which was not properly carried out or applied, or was not appropriate for use in the particular case;
5. the opinion relies on an inference or conclusion which has not been properly reached.

Furthermore, the Law Commission recommended that when assessing the reliability of expert opinion evidence, the court must have regard to "relevance"; which should be widely defined.

The Law Commission produced a draft Bill based on its report. However, the UK Government declined to enact the draft Bill due to a lack of certainty as to whether the additional costs incurred would be offset by savings. Instead, the government invited the Criminal Procedure Rule Committee to consider amendments to the Criminal Procedure Rules (CrimPR) to introduce, as far as possible, the spirit of the Law Commission's recommendations. The consequent amendments to CrimPR Part 33 (now CrimPR Part 19) and the new Practice Direction (CrimPD) 33A (now CrimPD 19A) were considered to be a means of implementing the Commission's recommendations (Stockdale and Jackson, 2016).

Therefore, the outcome of the Law Commission Report No. 325 published in 2011 is in effect the Criminal Procedure Rules Part 19, already reproduced as Appendix F and the Criminal Practice Directions Part 19A reproduced with part B as Appendix J.

Interestingly, the Report, at page 83, is critical of the so-called Daubert test (Daubert v. Merrel Dow Pharmaceuticals, 1993) for admissibility, or more precisely reliability, in the US. The trial judge is given wide discretion in determining evidential reliability even though she or he is unlikely to possess the competence to evaluate reliability. Daubert is discussed in the next section.

At the time of writing [December 2017] the Criminal Procedure Rules Part 19 "Expert Evidence" is the latest statement of the duties and responsibilities of expert witnesses in E&W and is an excellent statement of good practice.

4.3.3.1.2 Admissibility and Reliability in the United States of America

In the US, case law has resulted in trial judges being given the role of gatekeeper for scientific evidence.

***Frye v. United States*, 293 F. 1013 (D.C. Cir. 1923)** The "Frye standard", "Frye test," or "general acceptance test" is a procedure to determine the admissibility of scientific evidence. It provides that expert opinion based on a scientific technique is admissible only where the technique is generally accepted as reliable in the relevant scientific community.

This standard comes from *Frye v. United States*, 293 F. 1013 (D.C. Cir. 1923), a case in which the admissibility of polygraph tests as evidence was an issue. The Court held that expert testimony must be based on scientific methods that are sufficiently established and accepted. The court wrote:

> *Just when a scientific principle or discovery crosses the line between the experimental and demonstrable stages is difficult to define. Somewhere in this twilight zone the evidential force of the principle must be recognized, and while the courts will go a long way in admitting experimental testimony deduced from a well-recognized scientific principle or discovery, the thing from which the deduction is made must be sufficiently established to have gained general acceptance in the particular field in which it belongs.*

***Daubert v. Merrell Dow Pharmaceuticals*, 509 U.S. 579 (1993)** In this case, the US Supreme Court determined the standard for admitting expert testimony in federal courts. The Court held that the enactment of the Federal Rules of Evidence implicitly overturned the Frye standard; the standard that the Court articulated is referred to as the Daubert Standard.

The case involved scientific evidence based on methods that had not yet gained acceptance within the general scientific community.

This decision is considered of great importance in the US and has had an impact in other jurisdictions, e.g., it is referred to in the Law Commission report 325 discussed previously and the judicial gatekeeping role remains an issue in forensic science (Wójcikiewicz, 2013; Mathias, 2010).

The US Supreme Court required judges to assume the role of gatekeepers for scientific evidence. The justices made four observations that courts could consider in making the gatekeeping assessment:

- if the theory in question had been empirically tested;
- if the theory had been subject to peer review and published (this echoes *Preece* discussed in 4.3.3.2.1);
- if known or potential error rates were present; and
- the Court advised that the old "general acceptance" criteria of the Frye test could be considered.

In *Daubert*, seven members of the Court agreed on the following guidelines for admitting scientific expert testimony [emphasis added]:

- **Judge is gatekeeper**: Under the Federal Rule of Evidence 702 regarding the admissibility of expert testimony, the task of "gatekeeping", or assuring that scientific expert testimony truly proceeds from "scientific knowledge", rests on the trial judge.

- **Relevance and reliability**: This requires the trial judge to ensure that the expert's testimony is "relevant to the task at hand" and that it rests "on a reliable foundation". Daubert v. Merrell Dow Pharms., Inc., 509 US 579, 584–587. Concerns about expert testimony cannot be simply referred to the jury as a question of weight. Furthermore, the admissibility of expert testimony is governed by Rule 104(a), not Rule 104(b); thus, the Judge must find it more likely than not that the expert's methods are reliable and reliably applied to the facts at hand.
- **Scientific knowledge = scientific method/methodology**: A conclusion will qualify as scientific knowledge if the proponent can demonstrate that it is the product of sound "scientific methodology" derived from the **scientific method**
- **Illustrative Factors**: The Court defined "scientific methodology" as the process of formulating hypotheses and then conducting experiments to prove or falsify the hypothesis, and provided a set of illustrative factors (i.e., not a "test") in determining whether these criteria are met:
  - Whether the theory or technique employed by the expert is generally accepted in the scientific community;
  - Whether it has been subjected to peer review and publication;
  - Whether it can be and has been tested;
  - Whether the known or potential rate of error is acceptable; and
  - Whether the research was conducted independent of the particular litigation or dependent on an intention to provide the proposed testimony.

Two subsequent decisions of the court that further articulated *Daubert* constitute what is now termed the Daubert Trilogy and these are discussed next.

***General Electric Co. v Joiner*, 522 U.S. 136 (1997)** The Supreme Court ruled that it was not an abuse of discretion by judges to exclude the testimony that is not meeting the Daubert criteria. The court held that a district court judge may exclude expert testimony when there are gaps between the evidence relied on by an expert and his conclusion and that an abuse-of-discretion standard of review is the proper standard for appellate courts to use in reviewing a trial court's decision of whether it should admit expert testimony.

***Kumho Tire Co. v. Carmichael*, 526 U.S. 137 (1999)** The court held that the gatekeeping function described in *Daubert* applied to all expert testimony including that which is nonscientific proffered under Federal Rule of Evidence 702.

In 2000, the Federal Rule of Evidence 702 was amended in an attempt to codify and structure elements embodied in the "*Daubert* trilogy." The rule then read as follows:

If scientific, technical, or other specialized knowledge will assist the trier of fact to understand the evidence or to determine a fact in issue, a witness qualified as an expert by knowledge, skill, experience, training, or education, may testify thereto in the form of an opinion or otherwise, if (1) the testimony is based upon sufficient facts or data, (2) the testimony is the product of reliable principles and methods, and (3) the witness has applied the principles and methods reliably to the facts of the case.

(As amended Apr. 17, 2000, eff. Dec. 1, 2000.)

In 2011, Rule 702 was again amended to make the language clearer. The rule now reads:

A witness who is qualified as an expert by knowledge, skill, experience, training, or education may testify in the form of an opinion or otherwise if:

1. *The expert's scientific, technical, or other specialized knowledge will help the trier of fact to understand the evidence or to determine a fact in issue;*
2. *The testimony is based on sufficient facts or data;*
3. *The testimony is the product of reliable principles and methods; and*
4. *The expert has reliably applied the principles and methods to the facts of the case.*

(As amended Apr. 17, 2000, eff. Dec. 1, 2000; Apr. 26, 2011, eff. Dec. 1, 2011).

For a more up-to-date summary of the gatekeeping role of US judges see the case of *Morgan* (US v Morgan, 2014).

As an aid to exercising the gatekeeping role, a Reference Manual on Scientific Evidence has been prepared by Federal Judicial Centre aided by the NRC and, among others, the US National Academies. It is now in its third edition and is available for US justices (Federal Judicial Centre & National Research Council, 2011). The publication is an excellent guide for all forensic science stakeholders.

Melendez-Dais v Massachusetts, 129 S.Ct 2009 This was a case involving a drug conviction. At trial, the prosecutor introduced written certificates prepared by state laboratory analysts confirming that material seized by police and connected to the defendant was cocaine of a certain quantity. The analysts were not called to testify. The defendant claimed that the admission of the laboratory reports violated his Sixth Amendment right to confront the analysts who prepared the certificates. The Supreme Court ruled that, because the laboratory reports were testimonial statements against the defendant, the defendant was entitled to confront the persons giving this testimony at trial.

During the arguments before the Supreme Court, the State had urged that laboratory analysts should not be made to testify because forensic science evidence is the product "of neutral, scientific testing." The Court rejected this claim. The court first noted that serious deficiencies had been found in the forensic evidence used in criminal trials and concluded that this category of evidence was not uniquely reliable. The court then pointed out, by way of example, that:

> *The affidavits submitted by the [forensic] analysts [in the* Melendez-Diaz *case] contained only the bare-bones statement that '[T]he substance was found to contain: Cocaine.' At the time of trial, [the defendant] did not know what tests the analysts performed, whether those tests were routine, and whether interpreting their results required the exercise of judgment or the use of skills that the analysts may not have possessed.*

The Supreme Court decided that analyst reports are inadmissible as evidence against the accused unless the defendant is afforded an opportunity to cross-examine the analyst preparing the report.

> *Preparing reports with the sole purpose of establishing facts necessary to prove the defendant's guilt at trial, created at law enforcement's request, is precisely the kind of practice the Sixth Amendment was intended to prohibit.*
>
> ***Edwards (2010)***

In addition to protecting the rights of the defendant, this judgment supports the requirement that expert reports provide more than the "bare bones" and is in line with the E&W Criminal Procedure Rules discussed earlier in 4.3.3.1.1. "Bare bones" reporting is related to the controversial practice of streamlined forensic reporting now used in England & Wales and discussed in Section 7.

4.3.3.2 The Duties and Responsibilities of a Forensic Scientist Acting as an Expert Witness

4.3.3.2.1 Case Law

There is a significant body of case law concerning the duties and responsibilities of a forensic scientist acting and an expert witness. What follows is focused on those cases that have had a major impact on forensic science practice and relate to the quality of forensic science in general rather than to particular evidence types that are covered in Section 6. In common law jurisdictions, there are perhaps no more important cases than *Davie* and the *Ikarian Reefer*.

***Davie v Magistrates of Edinburgh* [1953] SC 34** It was argued by the appellant that the court is bound to accept uncontested scientific evidence. The Scottish Court of Session (an appellate court) rejected this, saying that an expert witness, however skilled or eminent, can give no more than evidence. The expert cannot usurp the functions of the fact finder [jury or judge], any more than a technical assessor can substitute his or her advice for the judgment of the court.

According to Lord President Cooper of the Scottish Court of Session, the duty of an expert witness [emphasis added],

> *is to furnish the Judge or jury with the necessary scientific criteria for testing the accuracy of their conclusions, so as to* ***enable the Judge or jury to form their own independent judgment*** *by the application of these criteria to the facts proved in evidence.*

The emphasis has been added to draw attention to the fact that in common law the basis for the expert's opinion is as important than the opinion itself; this might be considered a means of assuring transparency. Transparency is a requirement of Criminal Procedure Rules Part 19 referred to earlier in 4.3.3.1.1, the AFSP Standard (Association of Forensic Science Providers, 2009), is a requirement of good scientific practice, and might be considered to be one of the inherent characteristics (see 1.3.1) of reliable scientific evidence.

Furthermore, the expert must not usurp the role of the fact finder [emphasis added]:

> *The scientific opinion evidence, if intelligible, convincing and tested, becomes a factor (and often an important factor) for consideration along with the whole other evidence in the case, but the decision is for the Judge or jury. In particular* ***the bare ipse dixit of a scientist, however eminent, upon the issue in controversy, will normally carry little weight****, for it cannot be tested by cross-examination nor independently appraised, and the parties have invoked the decision of a judicial tribunal and not an oracular pronouncement by an expert.*

Ikarian Reefer**[1993] 2 Lloyds Rep 68** In this case Mr. Justice Cresswell said that he believed that a misunderstanding on the part of certain of the expert witnesses in the case as to their duties and responsibilities contributed to the length of the court proceedings. It was for these reasons that in the course of his judgment he set out the following duties and responsibilities of an expert witness.

> *Expert evidence should be the independent product of the expert uninfluenced as to form or content by the exigencies of litigation.*
>
> *An expert witness should provide independent assistance to the court by way of objective, unbiased opinion in relation to matters within his expertise.*
>
> *An expert witness should state the facts or assumption upon which his opinion is based. He should not omit to consider material facts which could detract from his concluded opinion.*
>
> *An expert witness should make it clear when a particular question or issue falls outside his expertise.*
>
> *If an expert's opinion is not properly researched because he considers that insufficient data is available, then this must be stated with an indication that the opinion is no more than a provisional. In cases where an expert witness who has prepared a report could not assert that the report contained the truth, the whole truth and nothing but the truth without some qualification, that qualification should be stated in the report.*
>
> *If, after exchange of reports, an expert witness changes his view on a material matter having read the other side's expert's report or for any other reason, such change of view should be communicated (through legal representatives) to the other side without delay and when appropriate to the Court.*

Preece v H.M.Advocate **[1981] Crim.L.R. 783** At trial in Edinburgh in 1972, the principal evidence against the defendant had been scientific evidence of blood and seminal stains, hairs, fibers, grass seeds, and other material said to link him to the murder victim. The scientific evidence was given mainly by Dr. Alan Clift. The accused Preece was convicted of murder. After Preece had been in prison for more than 7 years, questions were raised as to the quality of the scientific evidence and the scientific detachment of Dr. Clift. The case was referred back to the Scottish High Court on the allegations that Dr. Clift had withheld evidence he should have given about the victim's blood group, had failed to disclose that stains he had tested were not isolated seminal stains but mixed seminal and vaginal stains, and, as a result, had reached unwarrantable conclusions.

The High Court, having heard afresh the evidence of Dr. Clift along with the evidence of six eminent forensic scientists on the limited serological aspects of the case found it established:

1. that at the trial Dr. Clift had omitted the blood grouping and secretor status of the victim from his written report and failed to mention in evidence although he knew her to be Group A and probably a secretor;
2. that he had unwarrantably professed to be able to distinguish from mixed seminal and vaginal staining that the grouping of the male contributor was a Group A secretor; and
3. that there was no scientific support for Dr. Clift's claim that he could distinguish in the mixed staining the blood group substances derived from the male because these gave a stronger reaction than would have been characteristic of such substances emanating from the female[7], and Dr. Clift's evidence fell short of the standards of accuracy and objectivity required of an expert witness.

The court held that had the jury heard the new evidence they must have found Dr. Clift to be discredited as a scientific witness and that accordingly the whole of the scientific evidence he gave would have been regarded as unreliable, and the appeal must be allowed, and the conviction quashed.

Although this judgment was not without its critics, who felt that Dr. Clift had been unfairly treated (Moles et al., 1981), it did emphasize the duty of an expert witness to disclose any limitation to his or her evidence.

One outcome of this judgment was the need for the basis of scientific evidence to have been subject to peer review and published prior to use in casework. This requirement is echoed in *Daubert, discussed earlier in 4.3.3.1.2.*

[7] If Dr. Clift's method for distinguishing blood groups had been published in a peer reviewed scientific journal, then that would have constituted scientific support.

***R v Doheny and Adams* [1997] 1 Cr App R 369, CA.** This case was a landmark in the presentation of DNA evidence and in that respect discussed in Section 6. However, in terms of the duties and responsibilities of an expert witness, it repeated the injunction that the expert must not usurp the role of the jury.

> *When the scientist gives evidence it is important that he should not overstep the line which separates his province from that of the jury.*

4.3.3.2.2 Procedural Rules

2015 Criminal Procedure Rules Part 19 (Expert Evidence) (CrimPR) These rules are a synthesis of the common law and are, perhaps, the most comprehensive statement of the duties and responsibilities of the expert witness to the court and are of practical value to all forensic scientists; Section 19.2 reproduced below covers the duties.

> *19.2.*
>
> *(1) An expert must help the court to achieve the overriding objective*[8]*—*
>
> *(a) by giving opinion which is—*
>
> *(i) objective and unbiased; and*
>
> *(ii) within the expert's area or areas of expertise; and*
>
> *(b) by actively assisting the court in fulfilling its duty of case management under rule 3.2, in particular by—*
>
> *(i) complying with directions made by the court, and*
>
> *(ii) at once informing the court of any significant failure (by the expert or another) to take any step required by such a direction.*
>
> *(2) This duty overrides any obligation to the person from whom the expert receives instructions or by whom the expert is paid.*
>
> *(3) This duty includes obligations—*
>
> *(a) to define the expert's area or areas of expertise—*
>
> *(i) in the expert's report, and*
>
> *(ii) when giving evidence in person;*
>
> *(b) when giving evidence in person, to draw the court's attention to any question to which the answer would be outside the expert's area or areas of expertise; and*
>
> *(c) to inform all parties and the court if the expert's opinion changes from that contained in a report served as evidence or given in a statement.*

[8] The overriding objective(s) essentially being a fair trial and a safe verdict.

Equally importantly, in 19.4 the document sets out the requirement for the contents of an expert's report, which is reproduced below:

19.4

[A]n expert's report must—

(a) give details of the expert's qualifications, relevant experience and accreditation;

(b) give details of any literature or other information which the expert has relied on in making the report;

(c) contain a statement setting out the substance of all facts given to the expert which are material to the opinions expressed in the report, or upon which those opinions are based;

(d) make clear which of the facts stated in the report are within the expert's own knowledge;

(e) say who carried out any examination, measurement, test or experiment which the expert has used for the report and—

(i) give the qualifications, relevant experience and accreditation of that person,

(ii) say whether or not the examination, measurement, test or experiment was carried out under the expert's supervision, and

(iii) summarise the findings on which the expert relies;

(f) where there is a range of opinion on the matters dealt with in the report —

(i) summarise the range of opinion, and

(ii) give reasons for the expert's own opinion;

(g) if the expert is not able to give an opinion without qualification, state the qualification;

(h) include such information as the court may need to decide whether the expert's opinion is sufficiently reliable to be admissible as evidence;

(i) contain a summary of the conclusions reached;

(j) contain a statement that the expert understands an expert's duty to the court, and has complied and will continue to comply with that duty; and

(k) contain the same declaration of truth as a witness statement.

This is both a statement of good practice and a checklist to ensure that the forensic scientist's report includes all the necessary information to be of assistance to the court. Although applying only in E&W, it constitutes good practice and compliance should be expected in all jurisdictions. CrimPR 19 is reproduced as Appendix F.

In New Zealand there is a Code of Conduct for expert witnesses contained in Schedule 4 of the High Court Rules 2016. Compliance is mandated in the civil area and expected in the criminal area. The code echoes many of the requirements set out above, but it is more concise and less prescriptive than CrimPR 19 of E&W. The code is as follows:

Duty to the court

1 *An expert witness has an overriding duty to assist the court impartially on relevant matters within the expert's area of expertise.*

2 *An expert witness is not an advocate for the party who engages the witness.*

Evidence of expert witness

3 *In any evidence given by an expert witness, the expert witness must—*
   a. *acknowledge that the expert witness has read this code of conduct and agrees to comply with it:*
   b. *state the expert witness' qualifications as an expert:*
   c. *state the issues the evidence of the expert witness addresses and that the evidence is within the expert's area of expertise:*
   d. *state the facts and assumptions on which the opinions of the expert witness are based:*
   e. *state the reasons for the opinions given by the expert witness:*
   f. *specify any literature or other material used or relied on in support of the opinions expressed by the expert witness:*
   g. *describe any examinations, tests, or other investigations on which the expert witness has relied and identify, and give details of the qualifications of, any person who carried them out.*

4 *If an expert witness believes that his or her evidence or any part of it may be incomplete or inaccurate without some qualification, that qualification must be stated in his or her evidence.*

5 *If an expert witness believes that his or her opinion is not a concluded opinion because of insufficient research or data or for any other reason, this must be stated in his or her evidence.*

Duty to confer

6 *An expert witness must comply with any direction of the court to—*
   a. *confer with another expert witness:*
   b. *try to reach agreement with the other expert witness on matters within the field of expertise of the expert witnesses:*
   c. *prepare and sign a joint witness statement stating the matters on which the expert witnesses agree and the matters on which they do not agree, including the reasons for their disagreement.*

7 *In conferring with another expert witness, the expert witness must exercise independent and professional judgment, and must not act on the instructions or directions of any person to withhold or avoid agreement."*

For convenience, The New Zealand Code is reproduced as Appendix I.

4.3.4 Psychology and Performance

Second only to mathematics, or more precisely statistics, the external discipline to have had a major impact on the quality of forensic science is psychology. Cognitive bias, or observer effects, impact directly on performance.

As discussed in Section 1, the potential influence of cognitive bias has been recognized since at least the 17th century (Bacon 1620). However, our modern understanding of the influence of cognitive bias on human decision-making arrived with the work of Amos Tversky and Daniel Kahneman (1974). More forensically applied works include the seminal article by Michael Risinger et al. (2002), which charts the recognition, understanding, and effects of cognitive bias and its impact, both potential and actual, on the quality and reliability of scientific evidence. This 2002 review together with the work of others, particularly Itiel Dror et al. (Dror et al., 2005; Dror and Charlton, 2006), mark the beginning of a process whereby the forensic science community, initially blind to the existence and potential influence of cognitive bias, came first to recognize its existence and then devise strategies to limit its impact.

Michael Risinger and his colleagues propose a strategy that aims to go some way to remove, or at least limit, the effects of cognitive bias (Risinger et al., 2002). The main elements in the strategy were shielding the examining forensic scientist from domain-irrelevant information and appointing a coordinating forensic scientist who would also act as a single point of contact between the commissioning authority (e.g., police investigators) and the forensic science provider. The coordinating scientist would decide, in conjunction with the commissioning authority, the examinations required; optimally using the Case Assessment and Interpretation approach advocated by the then Forensic Science Service (Cook et al., 1998) and later formalized by the Association of Forensic Science Providers (2009), as discussed in 3.4.2.4. The coordinating scientist would control the sharing of information between forensic scientists filtering out domain-irrelevant information[9].

In 2015 the Forensic Science Regulator issued a guidance document on recognizing and managing the effects of cognitive bias FSR-G-217 (Forensic Science Regulator, 2015).

> *It aims to show readers how to recognize cognitive bias and therefore help to safeguard against biasing effects, through adherence to good practice.*

The Regulator has recorded the factors contributing to the risk of cognitive bias, which are listed in Table 4.3.

The guidance warns that,

[9] Research is required to measure the impact of this additional layer on the quality of scientific evidence.

Table 4.3 Cognitive Bias—Summary of Conditions Affecting the Risk of Cognitive Bias

Risk Source	Low Risk	High Risk
Result quality	Results are clear and unambiguous.	Results are complex, of poor quality and there is an increased reliance on subjective opinion.
Interpretation approach	There is a methodical approach with defined standards built on principles that have been tested and validated.	The approach is unresearched, ad hoc and personal to the practitioner.
Practitioner competence	Practitioners are well trained, experienced and continuously meet acceptable standards of competence.	The practitioners are inexperienced, unmonitored and left to adopt their own approach.
Checking	Full independent reinterpretation.	Checking is conducted collaboratively, or not conducted at all.

If the whole case file is handed over to an analyst with all the extraneous detail, then even if there is no perceptible bias there is the perception that it could have occurred and may be open to challenge in court.

It is noteworthy that the Regulator also supports and proposes a coordinating scientist referred to as a "leading practitioner." Other authorities refer to a "case manager" (Krane et al., 2008).

Therefore, a degree of consensus has emerged that an important element in bias-avoidance is the role of a coordinating forensic scientist who has full knowledge of the case, is the main point of contact with the commissioning stakeholder, directs the work, and protects examining forensic scientists from potentially biasing information while making sure they have sufficient information at the appropriate juncture to complete their task. If the coordinating scientist also undertook the role of non-testifying expert, as described in Section 7, then the examining forensic scientists would be better able to discharge his or her duties and responsibilities without exposure to the ethical dilemmas mentioned in Section 7.

The Regulator's guidance document adopts the strategies of Risinger, specified 13 years earlier, and details practical steps to mitigate bias through so-called "de-biasing" procedures with a documented record of compliance.

In E&W, at least, the coordinating scientist role is increasingly undertaken by the commissioning authority, i.e., the police (Gallop and Brown, 2014), which may amplify the effects of bias and reduce the quality and reliability of scientific evidence.

Given the role of the police in the forensic science market in E&W compliance with the Regulator's guide may be an uphill struggle. It is also far from clear that certain bias-avoidance strategies such as linear sequential unmasking will be effective in every case (Langenburg, 2016); more research is needed.

FSR-G-217 draws on a significant body of high-quality research and scholarship and it is extensive in scope. Compliance will be a significant challenge with changes in attitude, culture, and process required. The response of forensic science providers, accreditating bodies, and the rest of the stakeholder community will need to be monitored closely. The effect of noncompliance is now well known.

Despite the scholarship and research on cognitive bias and the inclusion of management strategies in regulatory frameworks, the latest ILAC Guidance document, ILAC G19:04/2014 Modules in a Forensic Science Process, is silent on bias-avoidance measures which is of concern as the guide particularly focuses on crime scene activities where biased processes, e.g., sample selection (Doyle and Doyle, 2012), may adversely affect the entire forensic process rendering scientific evidence unreliable.

It should be noted that ISO/IEC 17025 4.1 and ISO/IEC 17020 at 4.1.4 require accredited forensic science providers to identify and manage risks to impartiality. That includes demonstrating that staff are free from influences that might affect their technical judgment. Such influences will now include biasing pressures. The undue influence requirement might be more of a challenge to comply with now that the potential impact of cognitive bias is universally recognized. The risk of undue influence must be identified and managed, particularly in the commercial market in forensic scene in E&W where the police are the paymasters and may effectively exercise the role of coordinating scientist.

Indeed, the process within a forensic science laboratory outlined at 5.4 of the FSR-G-217, which is close to ideal, is very far from the practice where, for example, a piece of cloth cut from garment is sent to a forensic science provider for a specified test and the test result alone is reported to the (police) customer. Although this does indeed protect the forensic scientist from bias; sample recovery, sample selection, method selection, and interpretation/evaluation are all undertaken by the police customer, as such they fall within operational parameters excluded from the regulatory framework of either the Regulator or ISO/IEC 17025 and are exposed to all the biases of a prosecuting authority. In addition, the Recommended Good Practice (FSR-G-217 5.6) in the example given seems impossible to affect.

ISO/IEC 17020 is even stricter than ISO/IEC 17025 on controlling biasing factors that might affect the judgment of crime scene examiners and influence their results.

As reported earlier in 4.3.2.2.3, in 2014 the US OSAC for Forensic Science was established and included a Human Factors Committee (HFC).

The HFC is to provide guidance on the influence of systems design on human performance, on ways to minimize the effects of cognitive bias and on ways to remove errors from complex tasks. According to its terms of reference (Organization of Scientific Area Committees (OSAC) for 2016), this committee is responsible for:

- Working with relevant SACs and Subcommittees on discipline-specific human factors issues (e.g., determining domain-irrelevant information).
- Providing feedback and recommendations on human factors issues to be addressed in the development of draft standards and guidelines.
- Producing internal guidance documents that will support OSAC standards and guidelines development work.
- Providing guidance on the influence of system design on human performance, ways to minimize cognitive and confirmation bias, and mitigate errors in complex tasks.
- Preparing human factor impact statements for draft standards submitted for review, if appropriate, such as subjectivity in decision-making, error magnets, cognitive load, error identification, and mitigation.
- Provide feedback on the development of forensic science laboratory case notes and report templates, as appropriate

These aims and objectives are to some extent met and delivered in the Regulator's guide, FSR-G-217.

The inclusion of antibiasing measures in the quality management systems of accredited providers will ensure compliance, reducing the risk of bias influencing scientific outputs.

4.4 THE FORENSIC EXPLOITATION OF DNA AND ITS DEVELOPMENT AS AN EVIDENCE TYPE

4.4.1 Early Development

The growing impact of science on the development of quality management systems can be best charted by exploring the exploitation of the DNA molecule for the purpose of linking a suspect to or excluding a suspect from a crime scene. Such exploitation and the development of DNA methods of analysis provide a proxy for the progress of forensic science in general.

As with science, DNA evidence has evolved since its first use in 1986. At its initial introduction, and at each step of its evolution, the evidence type has had to overcome many challenges arising from its high discriminatory power and consequent evidential value. The major evolutionary steps are:

1. 1986 introduction
2. 1994 change in technology—profiling of short tandem repeats (STR)
3. 1995 introduction of databases
4. 1999 increased "sensitivity"—low template DNA
5. 1999 deconvolution of mixed profiles

There has also been a steady increase in the number of loci profiled, currently 17 in Europe and 20 in the US for autosomal or standard profiling.

The development of DNA as an evidence type has had a major influence on the development of quality management, on both the management and, to a greater extent, technical requirements: quality control, quality assurance, validation, and interpretation.

Current DNA profiling is rightly considered as meeting the "gold standard" of scientific evidence (National Research Council, 2009; Lynch, 2003). However, the early use of DNA evidence was problematic. It serves as an example of a novel technique rushed into use before adequate quality standards are in place. Trial judges in the late 1980s admitted what was later found to be unreliable scientific evidence on the grounds that DNA "Fingerprinting" methods were generally accepted in the scientific community and that false positives were virtually impossible (Lander, 1989).

In 1989 Eric Lander[10] (a then molecular biologist who served as an expert witness in early DNA Fingerprinting cases) wrote:

> *At present forensic science is virtually unregulated—with the paradoxical result that clinical laboratories must meet higher standards to diagnose strep throat than forensic labs must meet to put a defendant on death row.*
>
> ***Lander (1989)***

The first use of DNA analysis in a criminal investigation occurred in 1986. The investigation used DNA fingerprinting, as it was then called, to link semen stain samples, collected from two rapes/murders that had occurred 3 years apart in 1983 and 1986, in a small village in Leicestershire, UK. The probability of the match occurring by chance was calculated to be 5.8×10^{-8} (a very small number). This result not only linked the two crimes and helped secure the conviction of the perpetrator, but also excluded an innocent man implicated in the murders and led to the first mass screening project undertaken for DNA fingerprinting in the world.

The first DNA-based conviction in the US occurred shortly afterward in 1987. A Florida court convicted a man of rape after DNA analysis matched his DNA from a blood sample with that of semen traces found in a rape victim. The first state high court to rule in favor of admitting DNA evidence was West Virginia in 1989.

The initial novelty of DNA evidence and its high discriminatory power prompted very close scrutiny and a requirement that DNA evidence must be of sufficient quality to be relied upon.

4.4.2 Legal Challenges

In the first few years after its introduction, DNA evidence met little challenge. *People of New York v. Castro* 545 N.Y.S.2d 985 (Sup. Ct. 1989) was a murder case, now commonly regarded as the first serious challenge to the admissibility and reliability of DNA evidence.

[10] A founder of the Broad Institute of Harvard and MIT and as of September 2016 cochair of the President's Council of Advisors on Science and Technology (PCAST).

At the pretrial hearing in the New York Supreme Court, DNA evidence from a bloodstain on the defendant's watch was in question. The court determined that DNA identification theory, practice, and techniques were generally accepted among the scientific community and that pretrial hearings were required to determine whether the testing laboratory's method was compliant with scientific standards and produced reliable results for jury consideration.

The court recognized the difficulty of applying the *Frye* test to complex evidence and advanced a three-part refinement of the *Frye* test. A court should address the following questions in ruling on the admissibility of DNA fingerprinting:

Prong 1. Is there a theory that is generally accepted in the scientific community, which supports the conclusion that DNA forensic testing can produce reliable results?

Prong 2. Are there techniques or experiments that currently exist that are capable of producing reliable results in DNA identification and that are generally accepted in the scientific community?

Prong 3. Did the testing laboratory perform the accepted scientific techniques in analyzing the forensic samples in this particular case?

These questions might be translated into generic requirements for sound science, valid methods, and documented compliance.

In this case, DNA Fingerprinting was found to satisfy Prongs 1 and 2 but not 3 (Patton, 1990).

Stephen Patton, then of the Harvard Law School, drew attention to the weakness of the *Frye* test. He argued that although requiring "general acceptance" the *Frye* decision gives no guidance on what should be accepted and how detailed the inquiry should be.

> *The result in* Castro *was a sweeping acceptance in principle of a handful of procedures vaguely described as 'DNA forensic identification tests.' The court's broad holding neglected much of the detail in the test. Scientific evidence should be examined in greater detail and accepted in specific, not general terms. Furthermore, the results of the court's admissibility analysis should be reported more precisely. To analyse evidence in more detail, a general framework for review is needed.*
>
> ***Patton (1990)***

Patton was critical of the "shallowness" of this *Frye* hearing and thought that the justices had relied on the generality rather than the technique actually used in this case. The decision could not extend to other similar techniques due to the variation in procedures used.

Science, by its nature, is always advancing and providers demand the flexibility to use different methods. Therefore, variation will always be an issue. At the time of writing [March 2017] a debate continues over which of the different approaches to resolving mixed DNA profiles might give the most reliable answer (Carracedo et al., 2012). In accordance with the requirements of quality standards, methods should be fully validated prior to use. Variation or lack of harmony is discussed in Section 7.

Returning to *Castro*, the testing laboratory's procedures were called into question and expert testimony revealed that it had failed to use generally accepted, reliable techniques that could prove the blood on the watch was that of the victim; it had failed "Prong 3." Interestingly, the court did allow the DNA tests that ruled out the blood as that of Castro; upholding the DNA tests for exclusion but not inclusion because the process for determining a match is more complex than ruling out a match[11].

The development of DNA as an evidence type reinforces the importance of quality management in delivering reliable scientific evidence. In *State v. Schwartz*, 447 N.W.2d 422, 428 (Minn. 1989) the court ruled DNA evidence inadmissible on the grounds of noncompliance with quality standards.

> *While we agree with the trial court that forensic DNA typing has gained general acceptance in the scientific community, we hold that admissibility of specific test results in a particular case hinges on the laboratory's compliance with appropriate standards and controls, and the availability of their testing data and results. We answer the certified question accordingly. Because the laboratory in this case did not comport with these guidelines, the test results lack foundational adequacy and, without more, are thus inadmissible.*

Although accurate and reproducible, the original method of analysis, DNA "fingerprinting" based on restriction length fragment polymorphism, required the use of a large amount of high-quality DNA, which is not always recovered during forensic investigations.

Two advances occurred during the late 1980s and early 1990s that formed the basis of DNA analysis techniques as they are recognized today: the move to a new DNA marker, the micro satellite or STR for nuclear DNA and an alternative method for DNA visualization; PCR amplification with fluorescent labeling. These advances increased the "sensitivity" of DNA such that profiles could be obtained from small amounts of degraded DNA, which are often encountered in forensic casework.

This new technology initially faced legal challenges. However, by 2001 a number of US courts held that evidence obtained using the new technology was reliable and that it should no longer be subject to judicial scrutiny.

People v Hill, 107 Cal. Rptr. 2d 110, 89 Cal. App. 4th 48, 59–60 (Calif. 2001)
Lemour v State, 802 So. 2d 402 (Fla. Dist. Ct. App. 2001)
State v Butterfield, 27 P.3d 1133, 1144 (Utah, 2001)

4.4.3 The Development of Quality Standards for DNA evidence

The quality standards relating DNA evidence in the US predates the advent of ISO/IEC 17025 in 1999.

[11] Adopting different standards for inculpatory an exculpatory evidence is an issue worth exploring.

Prior to the release of the Guidelines for a Quality Assurance Program for DNA Analysis in 1989 by TWGDAM, no well-defined guidelines or quality standards existed to enable forensic DNA laboratories to document and comply with a quality management system. TWGDAM, a group of private and public-sector experts sponsored by the FBI, also worked with the NIST to develop model reference materials that US laboratories could use to assess the reliability of their equipment and the validity of DNA testing methods. TWGDAM, renamed SWGDAM (Specialist Working Group) in 1999, issued revisions to its initial guidelines in 1991, 1995, and 2004 (Calandro et al., 2005).

The TWGDAM/SWGDAM guidelines contain sections that apply both to the laboratories conducting DNA testing and to manufacturers of DNA analysis kits, instrumentation, and software.

The introduction of the FBI's Combined DNA Index System (CODIS) forensic DNA database, mandated by the federal DNA Identification Act of 1994, formalized the FBI's authority to establish a National DNA Index System (NDIS) for law enforcement purposes and prompted further challenges to validation and reliability.

The passing of the DNA Identification Act in 1994 gave the quality assurance of DNA evidence a statutory basis. This was a major step in the development of quality management. The Act effectively made TWGDAM, now SWGDAM, a standards development and setting body. In 1995 the US DNA Advisory Board (DAB), under the direction of the FBI, began its 5-year project to create a set of federal quality standards for forensic laboratories performing DNA analysis. The DAB standards relied on the work of TWGDAM.

Two sets of standards were created:

1. The Quality Assurance Standards for Forensic DNA Testing Laboratories (Forensic Standards) became effective in October 1998 to govern the activities of DNA laboratories that analyze crime scene evidence.
2. The Quality Assurance Standards for Convicted Offender DNA Databasing Laboratories (Offender Standards) became effective in April 1999 to govern the activities of DNA laboratories that analyze samples from convicted offenders.

The DAB standards, drawing heavily on ISO standards, included the following sections: organization and management, personnel, facilities, evidence control, validation, analytical procedures, equipment calibration and maintenance, reports, review, proficiency testing, corrective action, audits, safety, and use of subcontractor laboratories (Calandro et al., 2005).

In 2000 the DAB was disbanded passing responsibility for standards setting (back) to SWGDAM.

SWGDAM, through its quality assurance committee, recommends revisions to the FBI's quality assurance standards for DNA analysis. Adherence to these quality standards is required by US Federal Law as a condition of a laboratory's participation in NDIS. It is the role of the FBI to assess conformance to these standards by other laboratories.

The partnership between the providers and the commercial sector, which produce the necessary consumables, analysis kits, instruments, and software, driven by the size of the market and the power of DNA evidence ensured a marked degree of harmonization in quality standards unmatched to this day [December 2017] by any other evidence type.

Responsibility for complying with the standards set by SWGDAM rested with the technology suppliers and therefore validation was also their responsibility. This generated the need for "verification," checking that an externally validated (sometimes termed "developmental validation") method produces reliable results in the laboratory of the forensic science provider (sometimes termed "internal validation").

In passing, it should be noted that, although it is right and proper for forensic science providers (e.g., the FBI) to help set quality standards, it is far from optimal that the same provider acts as a conformance assessment body. Furthermore, given the criticisms leveled at the SWGs by Judge Edwards, cochair of the NRC Committee identifying the needs of the forensic science community (Edwards, 2010) and Recommendation 4 of the NRC report (National Research Council, 2009), a call for the removal of all public forensic laboratories and facilities from the administrative control of law enforcement agencies or prosecutors' offices, the role of the FBI and, to a lesser extent, SWGDAM in conformance assessment is at least questionable in that the process may lack the necessary degree of independence. The FBI's roles as forensic science provider, part of a standard setting body, conformance assessment body, and law enforcement agency may be conflicted.

In the UK, the National DNA Database was established in 1995 and claimed to be the first in the world. At that time, it was populated and managed by the Forensic Science Service, which was then accredited to the NAMAS standard M10 and certified to the quality management standard ISO 9001. Conformance to the necessary quality standards was assessed by an independent body.

It is now a common policy that only providers accredited to ISO/IEC 17025 for DNA analysis and approved by a relevant authority may populate national DNA databases.

4.4.4 Low Template DNA

Low Template DNA (LTDNA) is the generic name for a number of approaches to obtaining DNA evidence from quantities of DNA usually too small to produce a complete profile.

In 1999 the Forensic Science Service (FSS), a then UK government—owned commercial company, had started using a low template technique it had developed called

Low Copy Number (LCN) DNA. Initially, it would seem, for intelligence rather than evidential purposes.

In 2007 the evolution to generating STR profiles from low templates hit a major obstacle. The validity of the FSS method was questioned at the trial of a person charged with a number or terrorist-related offenses including the 1998 Omagh bombing in which 29 people were killed. Chain-of-custody procedures and records, which predated the introduction of LCN DNA, were found to be not fit-for-purpose such that the possibility of contamination and/or tampering robbed the LCN DNA evidence of any weight that it might have had and contributed to the acquittal of the accused. The prosecution had failed to establish the integrity of the LCN DNA evidence. In addition, the validity of the LCN DNA technique was questioned by the trial judge. Although that formed no part of the judgment, the use of LCN DNA was temporarily suspended while a review was conducted by the prosecuting authority of E&W, the Crown Prosecution Service (CPS). The essential quality question was, had the LCN DNA technique been fully validated prior to use as required by ILAC G19 2002 5.4.5.1? The court, on the evidence before it, decided the answer was "no" (R v Hoey, 2007) and the FSS was forced to defend their technique.

On the face of it at least, it seemed that LCN DNA was another example of a technique being rushed into service before being fully validated.

After a review by the CPS, the suspension was lifted on the January 14, 2008. The CPS issued its own guidance on LCN DNA (Crown Prosecution Service n.d.) asserting that the LCN DNA method was validated.

A review of LCN DNA was also commissioned by the Forensic Science Regulator. The remit was to examine the science rather than the validity of the methods used to apply the science. Accordingly, the review focused mainly on the science and found that it was sound. The review concluded that, with the proviso that certain caveats in relation to the interpretation of the results were noted, LCN DNA was fit for evidential use.

These interpretational caveats included recognition that the following information would not be known:

- the source of the DNA (cell type),
- the time at which it transferred, and
- the manner of transfer mechanism.

Not knowing the cellular source of the DNA profile obtained prompted the need for a new member of the hierarchy of propositions in the likelihood ratio (LR) approach to evaluation, discussed in 3.4.2.4.2: the subsource level with the propositions; the DNA came from person X, or the DNA came from another person.

Although the review found the underlying science sound, it did identify some quality issues, many of which echoed those recorded in the *Hoey* judgment, and called for the development of a set of standards as detailed in recommendation 19 of the review report.

> *National minimum technical standards for extraction, quantification/dilution and interpretation criteria need to be agreed by all forensic science providers. These standards should also be agreed by the Forensic Regulator's Forensic Science Advisory Council. The Forensic Science Regulator needs to coordinate all the information already available that is associated with extraction etc. techniques and by agreement with all stakeholders establish appropriate standards*
>
> **Caddy et al. (2008)**

Establishing the performance parameters of methods compliant with the standards once developed would require a validation study. In addition, the call for validation studies in the Promega recommendations, discussed below (Word, 2010), together suggest that, although the science was considered to be sound, the validity of the methods applying the science remained in question.

As detailed later, this review was far from the final word in the use of sensitive DNA profiling techniques collectively termed as LTDNA.

In defense of their method, the FSS argued prior use and that LCN was just an extension of the current technique SGM+[12] by running the PCR cycle more than 28 times and obtaining profiles from as few as 5–10 cells, the quantitative limit being in the range of 100–200 pg[13]. The view among many of the relevant scientific community at the time [2008/9] was that SGM + had been fully validated. The extra sensitivity of the LCN technique required suitable contamination-avoidance procedures to be in place and a detailed chain-of-custody record to be maintained as evidence against contamination and tampering. Provided these measures were in place the results could be considered reliable.

In time LCN became just one of a number of approaches developed by commercial forensic science providers to obtaining DNA profiles from small quantities of DNA.

The variety of approaches resulted in concerns about the quality of LTDNA evidence. A degree of consensus emerged in 2010 with LTDNA taking on a broader meaning. LTDNA now generally refers to any situation in which:

1. the amount of DNA available for amplification is limited due to small sample size or other factors (e.g., DNA degradation, PCR inhibition), and
2. interpreting the resulting DNA profile may require more considerations than interpreting single-source or mixed DNA profiles generated using higher amounts of DNA due to the potential for incomplete DNA profiles.

Word (2010).

As a result of the reviews referred to above, rulings by judicial authorities (R v Reed, Reed and Garmson, 2009; The People of the State of New York v Hemant Megnath, 2010; R v Broughton, 2010) and debate among academics and practitioners (Schneiders et al., 2011), it is reasonable to conclude that by 2011 LTDNA was generally accepted

[12] Second Generation Plus, a DNA profiling system introduced in 1998 profiling 10 loci + sex.

[13] a picogram, abbreviation pg, is 10^{-12} (a million millionth) of a gram.

within a significant part of the relevant scientific community and deemed admissible by most tribunals.

In 2010 (R v Broughton, 2010) the E&W Court of Appeal concluded that:

[T]he science of LTDNA is sufficiently well established to pass the ordinary tests of reliability and relevance and it would be wrong wholly to deprive the justice system of the benefits to be gained from the new techniques and advances which it embodies, in cases where there is clear evidence ... that the profiles are sufficiently reliable

However, the scientific community has yet to reach complete consensus, dissenting voices remain (Budowle and van Daal, 2011), and one US court has ruled LTDNA evidence inadmissible (People v Hector Espino, 2009). Of the publicly funded forensic science laboratories in the US, only the New York City Office of the Chief Medical Examiner conducts LTDNA employing only the quantitative condition of no less than 100 pg (10^{-12} of a gram) and increasing the number of PCR cycles from 28 to 31[14]. The US FBI does not conduct LTDNA analysis considering the results unreliable (US v Morgan, 2014).

The issues arising from the use of highly sensitive DNA techniques, where STR profiles can be obtained from just a few cells or some unspecified cellular materials, continue to this day. The deconvolution of mixed profiles invariably obtained using low template techniques is being achieved by use of complex mathematics. As this is beyond the understanding of fact finders (lay or judicial) the scientific community should reach consensus before use. There are different approaches to mixture interpretation each producing different answers based on the same data and a new area of controversy has opened up regarding validation (PCAST, 2016), which at the time of writing [December 2017] is approaching resolution.

In an attempt to promote consensus and ensure that LTDNA evidence is reliable Promega, a commercial supplier of DNA profiling technology, usefully defines LTDNA and lists the requirement for ensuring the quality of LTDNA evidence (Word, 2010):

Recommendations for the laboratory are:

1. *conduct comprehensive validation studies of all techniques used in the laboratory, with particular focus on sensitivity, mixture and non-probative-sample studies, to develop stochastic thresholds and interpretation policies that accurately reflect the data obtained and the limitations of the test system;*
2. *develop Standard Operating Procedures (SOP) very closely aligned with the procedures used in the validation studies;*
3. *report what can be defended scientifically using report wording and statistical calculations that accurately reflect the data obtained without bias;*

[14] In September 2016 OCME announced it was adopting new technologies to replace its LTDNA methods which would include STRmix, proprietary probabilistic genotyping software (Kupferschmid, 2016).

4. *make SOP, validation studies and electronic data (where printed profiles are inadequate for profile quality assessment) available in discovery;*
5. *provide ample training to analysts regarding validation studies, procedures and policies, and interpretation of DNA profiles with limitations prior to beginning DNA casework; and*
6. *use caution to not "overinterpret" the data by recognizing that some samples may have insufficient data to definitively include or exclude an individual as a possible contributor, resulting in an "inconclusive" statement.*

The introduction of LTDNA as an evidence type has highlighted the issues of validation, evidence integrity, and admissibility and emphasized the need for effective communication.

The advent of the probabilistic genotyping software used to interpret mixed profiles makes communicating the complex scientific evidence to fact finders a key competency and a significant challenge for the forensic scientist. Although increased complexity should, where possible, be resisted there seems little prospect of that occurring in the foreseeable future. The limiting factor may be that scientific evidence becomes so complex that its comprehension is beyond the capability of any one expert and cannot be made intelligible to the fact finder. In such a case the evidence may cease to be fit-for-purpose.

4.4.5 Mathematics and Logic in the Development of DNA Quality Standards

This section briefly outlines the role DNA evidence has played in establishing evaluative standards, which can be applied to other evidence types.

To interpret and evaluate DNA evidence, which is in essence frequency based and probabilistically expressed, forensic science needed to rely on mathematics and logic and in doing so has developed tools that may be applied to other evidence types. DNA from the outset has relied on random match probabilities (RMP), the probability that a person other than the suspect and randomly selected from a relevant population will share the profile obtained. This later developed into the so-called LR approach; the RMP is the denominator of the LR. The LR approach to the evaluation of scientific evidence and its impact on quality management is discussed in detail in Section 7.

Despite the misgivings of the judiciary in E&W as expressed in Doheny and Adams (1996) and R v T (2010) and resistance in the US and Australia, the LR approach to the evaluation of scientific evidence has been robustly defended by the forensic scientific community (Berger et al., 2011) and forms the basis of documented standards for evaluative evidence (Association of Forensic Science Providers, 2009; ENFSI, 2015).

Bernard Robertson and Tony Vignaux have made a helpful contribution to this debate (Robertson and Vignaux, 1995; Robertson and Vigneaux, 1993). They emphasize that,

> *Bayesian reasoning*[15] *is simply a formalization of generally applicable logic, and properly handled, should not pose undue problems for courts.*

Other authoritative authors support the use of the LR approach.

4.4.6 Final Remarks on DNA

This section has charted the historical development of DNA and has demonstrated that DNA evidence stands as a reasonable proxy for all other scientific evidence types, in terms of quality management. The history maps out the quality management requirements for all other evidence types in establishing reliability and to gain consensus within the scientific community and acceptance by the legal community. It highlights the need for validation and evaluative standards and has clarified issues concerning the admissibility of scientific evidence.

The history has also highlighted the tendency of forensic scientists, perhaps encouraged by certain stakeholders, to press new techniques into service before the process of validation is complete and consensus, or wide acceptance, has been reached.

Despite the inclination to premature use, close cooperation between stakeholders has resulted in the evolution of accepted standards for quality management in DNA laboratories and, as a consequence, the establishment of forensic DNA technology as an investigative tool that yields reliable information.

Compliance with these standards is a mandatory requirement for providers wishing to populate national DNA databases (Calandro et al., 2005).

As technologies are constantly evolving and new products become available, the necessity to validate and implement new procedures becomes ongoing and opens up new lines of challenge and the need for scrutiny. As the technology continues to advance, judicial and legislative reviews together with responsive quality management should continue to ensure that DNA analysis serves justice (Calandro et al., 2005).

The utility and power of DNA evidence to help convict the guilty and acquit the innocent meant that it had to be of unquestionable reliability and, from a shaky start and in the face of continuing challenges, that it has become. DNA evidence has been supported by legislative and judicial reviews and quality standards development since 1986. It

[15] Of which the LR is a part, see Section 3.4.2.4.2.

must be emphasized that careful scrutiny and challenge is the reason DNA evidence has developed into the robust and powerful investigative and evidential tool used today in the justice systems.

The advent of DNA evidence also resulted in an influx of scientists (and mathematicians) not infected by the culture that led to miscarriages of justice and poorly performing forensic science laboratories and scientists discussed earlier in 4.1. (Jonakait, 1991).

With adequate quality management in place, DNA evidence really is the "gold" standard and has impacted beneficially on every other evidence type and against which every other evidence type should now be measured.

4.5 THE DEVELOPMENT OF QUALITY STANDARDS

4.5.1 The Early History of Quality Standards

The origin of the quality standards in place today can be traced to the Second World War and the need for ammunition and armaments to comply with specified standards to ensure their reliability.

Postwar Japan is credited with a major advance in quality management under the influence of the Americans Joseph Juran and W. Edwards Deming.

The formation and growth of what became the European Union also played a part in the development of quality standards. The single European market required the free movement of goods, services, capital, and people - the four freedoms of the European Union. Ensuring that goods and services complied with common standards became essential to the successful operation of the single market. The consequence for forensic science was the 2005 Prüm Treaty on cross-border cooperation in combating crime discussed later in 4.5.6.2.

In 1970 The International Organization for Standardization (ISO) formed a Certification Committee (CERTICO) to establish a process to increase confidence that products were being manufactured in conformance to standards.

1979 was a busy year in which ISO Technical Committee 176 on Quality Management and Quality Assurance was established. In the UK, BS 5750 was published as a series of quality assurance standards. Z299, similar to BS 5750, was published in Canada. In the US the quality management system standard ANSI-ASQC Z1.15 was published.

In 1983 CERTICO published ISO/IEC Guide 40, "General Requirements for the Acceptance of Certification Bodies." The guide specified how to assess an organization engaged in product certification and was a precursor to guidance that would be used in quality management.

ISO recognized that conformity assessment dealt with more than product certification and in 1985 replaced CERTICO with the Conformity Assessment Committee (CASCO), which remains in place.

In 1986 ISO/CASCO published ISO/IEC Guide 48 "Guidelines for Third-Party Assessment and Registration of a Supplier's Quality System." The guidelines set out how assessment bodies that evaluate organizations' quality systems should operate.

BS 5750 was revised in 1987 to adopt verbatim the ISO 9000 series, and the ISO standards were adopted as the ANSI-ASQ[16] Q90 series standards in the US and as the EN[17] 29000 series by CEN and CENELEC[18], the European committees for standardization.

4.5.2 ISO 9000 Quality Management

The ISO 9000 series of quality standards for implementing and maintaining a quality management system is now internationally accepted and can be used as a criterion for third-party quality assessment.

Since its first publication in 1987, ISO 9001, which specifies the requirements for meeting the standard, has been reviewed and revised several times. The current edition, ISO 9001:2015, is the fifth and, as detailed in 3.2.1, it represents a significant change in structure and core terms. It is less prescriptive, focusing more on performance and risk management. In addition, it is designed to integrate more easily with other standards.

4.5.3 ISO/IEC Guide 25

Before the introduction of ISO/IEC 17025 in 1999, there was no internationally accepted standard for laboratories that demonstrated both management and technical competence and could provide a globally accepted basis for accreditation.

ISO/IEC Guide 25 "General requirements for the competence of calibration and testing laboratories" was a document drawn up by ISO/CASCO in response to a request by ILAC at a meeting held in Auckland, New Zealand, in October 1988.

The guide had been used since 1990 as a generic criteria document for the competence of testing and calibration laboratories. The declared purpose the guide was to establish the principle that "third party certification systems [for laboratories] should, to the extent possible, be based on internationally agreed standards and procedures." ISO guides are intended to be used for the preparation of national standards. By this means, a high degree of compatibility between standards prepared in different countries might be achieved "so as

[16] ANSI—American National Standards Institute, ASQ—American Society for Quality now merged as ANSI-ASQ National Accreditation Board (ANAB).

[17] EN—European Norm or standard.

[18] CEN—European Committee for Standardization, CENLEC the European Committee for Electrotechnical Standardization.

to facilitate bilateral and multilateral agreements." National and regional standards based on ISO/IEC Guide 25 would, therefore, be closely similar.

Among the standards based on ISO/IEC Guide 25 were EN 45001:1989 "General criteria for the operation of testing laboratories" and, in the UK, NAMAS standard M10 "General criteria of competence for calibration and testing laboratories." To demonstrate technical competence some continental European forensic science laboratories gained accreditation to EN 45001:1989, e.g., the Netherlands Forensic Institute in 1994 (van Asten et al., 2015) and the National Bureau of Investigation, Finland, in 1996 (Sippola and Saukko, 2015). In the UK, forensic science laboratories were accredited to M10. Although conformance was assessed against national standards, there was a considerable degree of uniformity between the requirements expressed in these various standards due to their conformance to ISO/IEC Guide 25.

To demonstrate managerial competence, and thus complete the quality management system, some UK forensic science laboratories[19] were accredited to the NAMAS standard M10 for technical activities and certified to ISO 9001, and its predecessor BS 5750, for their management system.

ISO/IEC Guide 25 stipulated that laboratories meeting the requirements of the guide also complied with the requirements of the ISO 9000 series of quality management standards when acting as suppliers producing calibration and test results. A number of ISO 9000 Certification Bodies started auditing laboratories against ISO 9000 standards and issued compliance certificates to that effect. This created confusion in the minds of testing and calibration laboratories customers whether a laboratory conforming to ISO 9000 can also be considered to be technically competent. ISO/IEC Guide 25 was silent on this. The question was clearly answered in the new standard ISO/IEC 17025:1999.

4.5.4 ISO/IEC 17025 Calibration and Testing Laboratories

ISO/IEC 17025 began life as a revision of ISO/IEC Guide 25:1990. During the revision process, it was decided to convert the guide into a standard against which conformances might be assesed, so providing a global basis for accreditation.

ISO/CASCO also decided that there should be as much compatibility as possible between ISO/IEC 17025 and ISO 9001, which was also under revision at the same time. The objective appears to have been to closely align the management requirements of ISO/IEC 17025 with ISO 9001 remembering that ISO/IEC 17025 includes both management and technical requirements. To be clear, the quality management system of an ISO/IEC 17025 accredited laboratory closely conforms to ISO 9001.

ISO/IEC 17025 was first published in 1999 and came into effective use after its adoption as a national standard, although the UK accreditation service, at the time NAMAS,

[19] The Forensic Science Service and the Forensic Explosives Laboratory were certainly two.

accredited against ISO/IEC 17025 in 1998 at that stage a draft international standard or DIS. The revised version of ISO 9001 was accepted in 2000.

As published, ISO/IEC 17025:1999 and ISO 9001:2000 were not as well aligned as intended and that remains so today [December 2017]. ISO 9001:2000 placed great emphasis on continual improvement in quality management. Although this was included in ISO/IEC 17025:1999, its importance as a part of the standard was not strongly emphasized. ISO policy is to review standards every 5 years. ISO/IEC 17025:1999 was reviewed accordingly and revised to more closely align with ISO 9001:2000. The major change was the introduction of an explicit requirement for continual improvement of the management system particularly with regard to communication with the customer and greater emphasis on the responsibilities of top management. ISO/IEC 17025:2005 was adopted as an ISO standard in May of 2005.

The main differences between the 1999 and 2005 editions are summarized as follows:

- Insistence on a demonstrated commitment to continually improve the quality management system and identify mechanisms for achieving this.
- Greater emphasis on the need to communicate with customers and, especially, to actively solicit feedback on service quality and ensure the resulting information is used as the basis for action to improve the management system.
- Greater emphasis on the need to use information from quality control data to evaluate the performance of the quality system and to identify opportunities for improvement.

The 2017 edition of ISO/IEC 17025 differs significantly from the 2005 edition, as discussed in Section 3, it is similar in structure to ISO/IEC 17020:2012 and takes account of ISO 9001:2015.

According to ISO, the main changes compared to the previous edition are as follows:

- the risk-based thinking applied in this edition has enabled some reduction in prescriptive requirements and their replacement by performance-based requirements;
- there is greater flexibility than in the previous edition in the requirements for processes, procedures, documented information, and organizational responsibilities.

4.5.5 ISO/IEC 17020 and ILAC Guide 19 08/2014

The inspection standard was originally developed by the European standardization organizations CEN/CENELEC as EN 45004 and published in March 1995. It was taken over by ISO/CASCO without changes as ISO/IEC 17020 and published in 1998.

As reported in Section 3, in 2006 ENFSI and the European Co-operation for Accreditation (EA) jointly selected ISO/IEC 17020:1998 "Conformity assessment — requirement for the operation of various types of bodies performing inspection" as the appropriate standard for crime scene examination. As with ISO/IEC 17025, an interpretive guidance document was required for forensic science. A guide was prepared jointly by ENFSI and EA and published in 2008 as EA-5/03 "Guidance for the implementation of ISO/IEC17020 in the field of crime scene activity".

In 2008 an ISO/CASCO Working Group revised the existing standard. The revised standard ISO/IEC 17020:2012 was published in March 2012.

Although ISO/IEC 17025 clearly applies to measurements and ISO/IEC 17020 to inspections, see 3.2.3, a perceived degree of overlap prompted the preparation of a single guide to cover the area of overlap. In 2014 ILAC published Guide 19:08/2014 "Modules in a Forensic Science Process." The guide is longer than either ISO/IEC 17020 or ISO/IEC 17025 and contains much prescriptive detail.

As reported in Section 3, accrediting bodies in the US and UK have offered accreditation to ISO/IEC 17020 for crime scene examination since 2011. Thus far there has been little take-up. According to the Forensic Science Regulator, Police managed crime scene examination units in the UK have until 2020 to obtain accreditation and that target might not be met. As reported in 3.2.3 crime scene examination units in Australasia are accredited to ISO/IEC 17025 and have no plan to change, particularly with Australian Standard 5388:2012 "Forensic Analysis," being developed into an ISO standard as discussed in Section 3. In addition, accrediting bodies make it clear that, in most circumstances, either international standard is fit for forensic purposes.

Therefore, apart from reporting the fact that a standard for crime scene examination is available with guidance, not much more can be written. Regarding the take up of ISO/IEC 17020, it is a matter of wait and see. Issues associated with the ISO/IEC 17020 conformance are discussed in 3.2.3.

4.5.6 Mandatory Accreditation to ISO/IEC 17025/17020

As recorded in this section, the vast majority of forensic science providers in the developed world have been accredited voluntarily since the early years of this century and so the potential impact of mandatory accreditation on the quality standards framework is quite limited, except, of course, as applied to crime scene examination.

The initiative does seem to be "closing the stable door after the horse has bolted." The exception being the accreditation to ISO/IEC 17025 of providers that populate national DNA databases. Accreditation is mandated in many jurisdictions for such providers and has been since the introduction of the standard in 1999.

However, the trend toward universal mandatory accreditation continues, and so there is merit in examining its history.

4.5.6.1 United States

As a result of the work of the NCFS, the position regarding mandatory accreditation in the US has recently become clearer (NCFS n.d.). In the past, the term "accreditation" was often used without specifying the standard or the accreditation body. To be clear, under discussion here is accreditation of forensic science providers to ISO/IEC 17020 and/or ISO/IEC 17025 required by the state or jurisdiction.

In 2003 the Texas Legislature passed a law requiring all laboratories and other entities conducting forensic analysis of physical evidence, whether public or private, to be "accredited" by the Texas Department of Public Safety (DPS) for the entity's analysis of evidence or testimony to be admissible in a criminal proceeding. On the 1st of September of that year, the DPS Laboratory Accreditation Program was created.

Since then, several other States have instituted similar laws, including Oklahoma in 2005, New York 2006, and Missouri in 2012. ASCLD/LAB was often the accepted accreditation body for both state-mandated accreditation and voluntary accreditation (Hueske and Wayland, 2011).

For a forensic science provider to be accredited by the Texas DPS, it was first to be accredited by an accrediting body recognized by the DPS. Therefore, the DPS, and more recently the Texas Forensic Science Commission and other State Commissions are not accrediting bodies according to the norms of quality management.

The only accrediting bodies initially listed by the DPS were Forensic Quality Services (FQS) and ASCLD/LAB. At that time only FQS accredited to ISO/IEC 17025, ASCLD/LAB did not.

ASCLD/LAB did not start accrediting to ISO/IEC 17025 until 2008 (ASCLD, 2016) the expectation being that it would not be until 2015 that all ASCLD/LAB "accredited" laboratories were accredited to ISO/IEC 17025 (Grubb, 2010). The status of ASCLD/LAB "accreditation" prior to 2008 is unclear.

ASCLD/LAB had a number of systemic weakness as an accrediting body. Representatives of the laboratories accredited by ASCLD/LAB formed the governing body[20], the Delegate Assembly (ASCLD, 2016). The organization also developed and set standards and assessed conformance: ASCLD/LAB was conflicted.

There were other aspects of the business of ASCLD/LAB highlighted in a critical memo (Schecter, 2011), which raised other conflict-of-interest issues.

In that lengthy memo to the New York State Commission on Forensic Science, its author, an attorney and commission member named Marvin E. Schechter, was highly critical of ASCLD/LAB. He claimed that the organization allows:

[20] The Delegate Assembly elects a Board of Directors, which direct managers who run the "accreditation" program.

a culture of tolerance for errors stemming from a highly forgiving corrections system, some times of major and/or lesser magnitudes, but many of which either violate ASCLD/LAB's ethics guidelines and/or standards. Laboratory inspections are always on notice to a laboratory rather than by surprise, and instead of inspectors picking the case files for review, this is done by lab technicians.

In addition to being a member of the NY Commission, Schechter was a member of the committee that produced the 2009 NRC report (National Research Council, 2009). That report also criticized the lack of strong national standards for laboratory management and administration. His 2011 memo went on to characterize ASCLD/LAB as an organization more interested in protecting its members' interests than in promoting accountability. If so, then it was not fit to support mandatory accreditation.

Schecter's position was challenged by ASCLD/LAB, unfortunately, using ad hominem arguments. Nevertheless, there is no doubt that the 2016 "merge" into ANAB[21] (ANAB, 2016) should resolve any conflict-of-interest issues and go some way to improving the independence of accrediting bodies in the US, support mandatory accreditation, and strengthen forensic science generally.

The organizations currently accrediting forensic science providers to ISO/IEC 17025 and ISO/IEC 17020 in the US are ANAB and A2LA (American Association for Laboratory Accreditation).

4.5.6.2 Europe/European Union

On the November 30, 2009, European Council, Justice and Home Affairs decision (Council Framework Decision, 2009/905/JHA) mandated ISO/IEC 17025 accreditation for DNA analysis and fingerprint development requiring members states to implement this decision by November 30, 2013, for DNA profiling and November 30, 2015 for fingerprint development. This was part of a process to ensure that the same standards applied within the EU to facilitate cross-border cooperation in the investigation of crime and terrorism and ensure evidence generated in one European jurisdiction would be admissible in another.

The decision has its origins in the Prüm Treaty signed by seven member states in 2005. Prüm allows the sharing information across borders to investigate crime and terrorism. The EU's Prüm Decisions allow automatic searches of DNA profiles, fingerprints, and vehicle license plates stored on one EU country's computer databases with every other country's databases, and sharing of information between police forces when there is a match.

[21] ANSI-ASQ National Accreditation Board.

4.5.6.3 England & Wales

As recorded earlier in 4.2.2, all the major providers of forensic science in the UK and Ireland voluntarily achieved accreditation to ISO/IEC 17025 in 1999 or soon afterward.

Since the creation of the Office of the Forensic Science Regulator in 2008, the Regulator has adopted policies and acted to assure the quality of forensic science. Statutory powers for the Regulator to mandate accreditation have been under consideration since 2011. An objective of mandatory accreditation was to create a "level playing field" between police and private sector providers in the forensic science market that exists in E&W. At the time of writing [December 2017] there is broad agreement that the Regulator should be given statutory powers, the final hurdle being the "lack of an appropriate legislative vehicle" (Blackwood, 2016). A timetable for legislation has yet to be announced by the UK government and the Brexit decision may well delay legislation for some years (BBC, 2017).

4.6 CONCLUDING REMARKS

This section has chronicled the development of quality management in forensic science beginning with miscarriages of justice in the 1970s, followed by the response in the early 1990s. Currently [December 2017] there is a maturing standards framework that includes international quality standards, increasingly competent accrediting bodies, guidelines, and national institutions, such as NIST/OSAC, NIFS, and FSAC/FSR, all playing a part in ensuring that forensic science is of sufficient quality to meet the needs of its stakeholders, particularly law enforcement and justice.

The impact of administrative, judicial, and scientific reviews on the development of quality management has been recognized, as has the role of DNA as an evidence type.

The contribution of statistics, particularly in relation to the evaluation of scientific evidence and the deconvolution of complex DNA mixtures, has been mentioned. As have the quality issues raised as science advances and attempts to offer more evidential value from less material. This section has made clear the vital need for a robust quality management system to assure the reliability of scientific evidence as science and technology progress.

The risk of cognitive bias has been recognized and is now being managed. From an initial position of denial, avoidance strategies have been developed and are now being incorporated into quality management systems. The Forensic Science Regulator in E&W has issued guidance and the HFC of OSAC has been established in the US. A common suggestion for managing cognitive bias is the appointment of a "coordinating scientist" engaging directly with the commissioning agents and shielding the examining scientist from unnecessary and potentially biasing information. Combining this role with that of a nontestifying expert could also help protect forensic scientists from ethical dilemmas as discussed in Section 7.

The merge of ASCLD/LAB into ANAB and the model adopted by OSAC for standards development and accreditation conform to the principle that service provision, standards development, and conformity assessment should be delivered independently of each other. Indeed, the general trend in forensic science is toward a greater separation of roles, independence, and transparency.

Whether the removal of the administration of forensic science providers from law enforcement, as recommended by the NRC, ever becomes a reality seems unlikely at present, particularly given the recent history of the Washington DC Consolidated Forensic Laboratory (Hsu, 2016). The potential impact of the NRC recommendation is assessed in Section 7 together with the episode affecting the DC laboratory in 5.6.

This section has clearly demonstrated that a forensic scientist requires competencies beyond those of a scientist, particularly in exercising the role of an expert witness. The independent assessment of individual competence remains an issue, with some jurisdictions including it in their quality standards framework, whereas others rely solely on ISO/IEC 17025/17020 accreditation.

Quality failures continue to occur and, given human nature, always will. However, with a mature and extensive quality standards framework in place, the risk is significantly reduced and the consequent impact on justice limited. In addition, effective quality management will result in corrective and preventative actions which will reduce the risk of future quality failures.

In summary, the quality standards framework in most of the developed world has reached a degree of maturity that, for the most part, ensures that laboratory-based forensic science is fit-for-purpose. Crime scene activities and the presentation of scientific evidence remain as areas in need of improvement. However, these regulatory gaps are recognized and the means of closing them is available.

In terms of the future; widening, implementing and embedding the current quality standards frameworks will continue. Recurrent quality failures indicate that there is still progress to be made. The requirement for mandatory accreditation is likely to strengthen. The independent assessment of and personal responsibility for individual competence will remain an issue for the foreseeable future, particularly if there is ever going to be forensic science profession. These issues will be explored further in Section 7.

REFERENCES

ANAB, April 22, 2016. Latest News. ANAB. http://anab.org/news/latest-news/anab-and-ascldlab-merge-operations/.

ASCLD, November 2016. History. ASCLD. http://www.ascld-lab.org/history/.

Association of Forensic Science Providers, 2009. "Standards for the formulation of evaluative forensic science expert opinion. Science and Justice 49, 161–164.

Bacon, F., 1620. Novum Organum.

BBC, March 20, 2017. UK Politics. BBC. http://www.bbc.com/news/uk-politics-39322297.

Berger, C.E.H., Buckleton, J., Champod, C., W Evett, I., Jackson, G., 2011. Response to Faigman et al. Science & Justice 215.

Blackwood, N., April 19, 2016a. Science and Technology Committee. UK Parliament. https://www.parliament.uk/documents/commons-committees/science-technology/Correspondence/160419-penning-forensic-science-regulator-15-16.pdf.

Bridges, L., 1994. Normalizing injustice: the royal commission on criminal justice. Journal of Law and Society 20–38.

Budowle, B., van Daal, A., 2011. Reply to comments by Buckleton and Gill on "Low copy number typing has yet to achieve 'general acceptance'". In: Budowle, B., et al. (Eds.), 2009. Forensic Sci. Int.: Genet. Suppl. Series 2, 551–552. FSI: Genetics, pp. 1–5.

Burn, C., March 3, 2017. News. The Yorkshire Post. http://www.yorkshirepost.co.uk/news/exclusive-200-criminal-cases-in-yorkshire-in-miscarriage-of-justice-probe-1-8418341.

Butler, J.M., 2015. U.S. initiatives to strengthen forensic science & international standards in forensic DNA. Forensic Science International: Genetics 4–20.

Caddy, B., 1996. Assessment and Implications of Centrifuge Contamination in the Trace Explosive Section of the Forensic Explosives Laboratory in Fort Halstead. Home Office Cm 3491. The Stationery Office Limited, London.

Caddy, B., Taylor, G.R., Linacre, A.M.T., 2008. A Review of the Science of Low Template DNA Analysis. Review. Forensic Science Regulator, Birmingham.

Calandro, L.M., Cornier, K., Reeder, D., June 1, 2005a. Evolution of DNA Evidence for Crime Solving – A Judicial and Legislative History. Forensic Magazine. http://www.forensicmag.com/article/2005/01/evolution-dna-evidence-crime-solving-judicial-and-legislative-history.

Campbell, A., 2011. The Fingerprint Inquiry Scotland. Public Inquiry. APS Group Scotland, Edinburgh.

Carracedo, A., Scheider, P.M., Butler, J., Prinz, M., 2012. Focus Issue—Analysis and Biostatistical Interpretation of Complex and Low Template DNA Samples. FSI Genetics, pp. 677–678.

Clemons v State. 389 (Court of Appeals of Maryland, October 3, 2006.

Cook, R., Evett, I.W., Jackson, G., Jones, P.J., Lambert, J.A., 1998. A model for case assessement and interpretation. Science & Justice 38 (3), 151–156.

Crown Prosecution Service. Low Copy Number DNA testing in the Criminal Justice System. The Crown Prosecution Service. https://www.cps.gov.uk/publications/prosecution/lcn_testing.html.

Daubert V. Merrel Dow Pharamceuticals. 509 (US), 1993.

Doyle, S., Doyle, D., 2012. The AFSP Standard—a lesson for law enforcement agencies. Science & Justice 17–19.

Dror, I.E., Charlton, D., 2006. Why experts make errors. Journal of Forensic Identification 600–616.

Dror, I.E., Peron, A.E., Hind, S.L., Charlton, D., 2005. When emotions get the better of us: the effects of contextual top-down processing on matching fingerprints. Applied Cognitive Psychology 799–809.

Edwards, H.T., 2010. "The National Academy of Sciences Report on Forensic Sciences: What it Means for the Bench and Bar." the Role of the Court in an Age of Developing Science & Technology. Superior Court of the District of Columbia, Washington, D.C., pp. 1–17

ENFSI, 2015. ENFSI Guideline for Evaluative Reporting in Forensic Science. Guide. ENFSI, Wiesbaden.

Federal Bureau of Investigation, September 1, 2005. National Press Release. The FBI. https://archives.fbi.gov/archives/news/pressrel/press-releases/fbi-laboratory-announces-discontinuation-of-bullet-lead-examinations.

Federal Judicial Centre National Research Council, 2011. Reference Manual on Scientific Evidence. National Academies Press, Washington D.C.
Forensic Science Regulator, 2009. A Review of the Options for the Accreditation of Forensic Practitioners. Consultation Paper. Office of the Forensic Science Regulator, London.
Forensic Science Regulator, November 2013. Consultations. UK Government. https://www.gov.uk/government/uploads/system/uploads/attachment_data/file/256614/New_statutory_powers_for_the_forensic_science_regulator.pdf.
Forensic Science Regulator, July 25, 2014. Publications. UK Government. https://www.gov.uk/government/publications/forensic-science-regulator-newsletter-number-24.
Forensic Science Regulator, October 30 , 2015. Cognitive Bias Effects Relevant to Forensic Science Examinations. FSR-g-217. Forensic Science Regulator, Birmingham.
Forensic Science Regulator, February 2016. Codes of Practice and Conduct. https://www.gov.uk/government/uploads/system/uploads/attachment_data/file/499850/2016_2_11_-_The_Codes_of_Practice_and_Conduct_-_Issue_3.pdf.
Forensic Science Working Group. Report, 1997. The Royal Society of Chemistry, London.
Gallop, A., Brown, J., 2014. The market future for forensic science services in England & Wales. Policing 1−11.
Gough, T.A., 1997. Quality Assurance in Forensic Science: The UK Situation. Accreditation and Quality Assurance, pp. 216−223.
Grubb, M., 2010. ASCLDLAB. Attonrney General California. http://ag.ca.gov/meetings/tf/pdf/ASCLDLAB_%20NAS.pdf.
House of Commons Science and Technology Committee, 2005. Forensic Science on Trial.
House of Lords Select Committee, 1993. Report on Forensic Science, 5th Report.
House of Lords Select Committee on Science and Technology, 1993. Forensic Science. Session 1992−1993 6th Report. The Stationery Office, London.
Hsu, S.S., March 2 , 2016. D.C. Crime Lab Restarts DNA Testing on Limited Basis After Shutdown Cast Doubts Over Analysis. The Washington Post.
Hueske, E.E., Wayland, J., 2011. State mandated accreditation of Texas crime laboratories: a look back and a look to the future. Forensic Science Policy & Management: International Journal 135−140.
Innocence Project. http://www.innocenceproject.org/.
Jonakait, R.N., 1991. Forensic science: the need for regulation. Harvard Journal of Law and Technology 109−191.
Krane, D.E., et al., 2008. Sequential unmasking: a means of minimizing observer effects in forensic DNA interpretation. Journal of Forensic Science 1006−1007.
Kupferschmid, T.D., September 19, 2016. OCME. http://www.identacode.org/916_OCME_Implementing_New_Technologies_Final_to_customers.pdf.
Lander, E.S., 1989. DNA fingerprints on trial. Nature 501−505.
Langenburg, G., 2016. Addressing Potential Observer Effects in Forensic Science: A Perspective from a Forensic Scientist Who Uses Linear Sequential Unmasking Techniques. In: ANZFSS 23rd International Symposium on the Forenscic Sciences. Auckland.
Lynch, M., 2003. God's Signature: DNA Profiling, the New Gold Standard in Forensic Science. Endeavour, p. 93.
Mathias, D., 2010. Observations on LCN DNA Analysis. http://www.oocities.org/veneziophile/Lcndna.pdf.
May, J., 1990. Interim Report on the Maguire Case. Inquiry. HMSO, London.
Moles, R.N., Sangha, B., Brownlie, A.R., June 19, 1981. Networked Knowledge − Law Report. Networked Knowledge. http://netk.net.au/UK/Preece.asp.
Morling, T.R., 1987. Royal Commission of Inquiry into Chamberlain Convictions. Royal Commission Report. Government Printer, Canberra.
Mullins, C., 1986. "Error of Judgement: The Truth about the Birmingham Bombers". Pub Chatto and Windus, London.
National Commission on Forensic Science, March 22, 2016. Work Products Adopted by the Commission. National Commission on Forensic Science. https://www.justice.gov/ncfs/file/839706/download.

National Research Council, 1992. DNA Technology in Forensic Science. National Academy Press, Washington D.C.
National Research Council, 1996. The Evaluation of Forensic DNA Evidence. National Academy Press, Washington D.C.
National Research Council, 2004. Forensic Analysis Weighing Bullet Lead Evidence. The National Academies Press, Washington D.C.
National Research Council, 2009. Strengthening Forensic Science in the United States: A Path Forward. The National Academies Press, Washington D.C.
NCFS. Universal Accreditation. US Department of Justice. https://www.justice.gov/ncfs/file/624026/download.
NCFS, February 1, 2017a. Work Products. The United States Department of Justice. https://www.justice.gov/ncfs/file/839711/download.
NCFS, February 1, 2017b. Work Products. United States Department of Justice. https://www.justice.gov/ncfs/file/477851/download.
Nijboer, J.A., Keulen, B.F., Elzinga, H.K., Kwakman, N.J.M., 2011. Expert Registers in Criminal Cases. Governance in Criminal Proceedings. RUG. http://www.rug.nl/rechten/congressen/archief/2011/governancemeetslaw/workingpapers/papernijboerkeulen.pdf.
NRGD. About the NRGD. https://english.nrgd.nl/about-the-nrgd/.
Office of the Attorney General, web page: DOJ Responses to NCFS Recommendations, Web Site: US DOJ Archives, Year: 2017, accessed Dec 15 2017 https://www.justice.gov/opa/file/891366/download
Office of the Inspector General, April 1997. Table of Contents. oig.justice.gov. https://oig.justice.gov/special/9704a/index.htm.
Organization for Scientific Area Committees (OSAC) for, January 28, 2016. OSAC HFC Terms of Reference. NIST. https://www.nist.gov/sites/default/files/documents/forensics/osac/OSAC-Terms-of-Reference-HFC-. v-1-3.pdf.
Patton, S.M., 1990. DNA Fingerprinting: The Castro Case. Harvard Journal of Law & Technology, pp. 223–240.
People v Hector Espino. NA076620 (Los Angeles County Superior Court, March 18, 2009).
Peterson, J.L., Fabricant, E.L., Field, K.S., Thornton, J.I., 1978. Laboratory Proficiency Testing Research Program. Research Report. National Institute of Law Enforcement and Criminal Justice, Washington D.C.
Rawley, A., Caddy, B., 2007. Damilola Taylor: An Independent Review of Forensic Examination of Evidence by the Forensic Science Service. Case Review. The Home Office, London.
R v Broughton. Crim 549 (EWCA, 2010).
R v Doheny, Adams. Crim 728 (EWCA, 1996).
R v Hoey. 49 (NICC, 2007).
R V Reed, Reed and Garmson. Crim 2698 (E&W Court of Appeal, 21 December 2009).
R v T. Crim 2439 (EWCA, 2010).
Risinger, M.D., Saks, M.J., Thompson, W.C., Rosenthal, R., 2002. The Daubert/Khumo Implications of Observer Effects in Forensic Science: Hidden Problems of Expecatation and Suggestion. California Law Review, pp. 1–56.
Roberts, P., 2016. LTDNA Evidence on Trial. Frontiers in Genetics, pp. 1–13.
Robertson, J., 2014. Forensic science professions: key issues and future directions. In: Encyclopedia of Criminology and Criminal Justice. Springer, New York, pp. 1820–1829.
Robertson, B., Vignaux, G.A., 1995. Interpreting Evidence: Evaluating Forensic Science in the Court Room. John Wiley and Sons Ltd., Chichester.
Robertson, B., Vigneaux, G.A., 1993. Probability—the logic of the law. Oxford Journal of Legal Studies 457–478.
Royal Commission on Criminal Justice, 1993. https://www.gov.uk/government/uploads/system/uploads/attachment_data/file/271971/2263.pdf.
Runciman, W.G., 1994. Some Afterthoughts on the Royal Commission on Criminal Justice in England and Wales. London Review of Books, pp. 7–11.

Schecter, M., March 25 , 2011. ASCLD Lab and Forensic Laboratory Accredition. Scribd. https://www.scribd.com/document/83354323/Marvin-Schecter-ASCLD-Lab-and-Forensic-Laboratory-Accreditation#.

Schneiders, P.M., Butler, J.M., Carracedo, A., 2011. Publications and letters related to the forensic genetic analysis of low amounts. Forensic Science International: Genetics 1—15.

Sippola, E., Saukko, P., 2015. History and Currnet status of forensic science and medicine in Finland. In: Ubelaker, D.H. (Ed.), The Global Practice of Forensic Science, vol. 99. John Woley & Sons Ltd, Chichester.

Stockdale, M., Jackson, A., 2016. Expert evidence in criminal proceedings current challenges and opportunities. Journal of Criminal Law 344—363.

The Law Commission, 2011. Expert Evidence in Criminal Proceedings in England and Wales." London.

The National Academies. About us. http://www.nationalacademies.org/brochure/index.html.

The People of the State of New York v Hemant Megnath, February 8 , 2010. 20037 (The Supreme Court, Queens County.

The United States Department of Justice, February 1, 2017. Nationa Commission on Forensic Science Work Products. https://www.justice.gov/ncfs/work-products-adopted-commission.

Tversky, A., Kahneman, D., 1974. Judgement under uncertainty: Heuristics and biases. Science 1124—1131.

US v Morgan, October 2 , 2014. No 12-CR-223 VM (United States District Court, S.D. New York.

van Asten, A., Neuteboom, W., Sijtze, W., Zeno, G., 2015. The Netherlands. In: Ubelaker, D.H. (Ed.), The Global Practice of Forensic Science, vol. 223. John Wiley & Sons Ltd., Chichester.

Wójcikiewicz, J., 2013. Judges' attitude towards scientific evidence. Revija za kriminalistiko in kriminologijo 249—255.

Word, C., 2010. What is LCN?—definitions and challenges. Promega Corporation. https://at.promega.com/~/pdf/resources/profiles-in-dna/2010/what-is-lcn-definitions-and-challenges/.

Young, R., Sanders, A., 1994. The royal commission on criminal justice: a confidence trick? Oxford Journal of Legal Studies 435—448.

SECTION 5

Current Practice: The Practical Application of Quality Management

5.1 INTRODUCTION

This section aims to accurately describe in some detail how quality management in forensic science currently [December 2017] operates in practice.

The application of Level 1 standards to the management, practice, and delivery of forensic science, introduced in Section 3, is explored in more detail. The structure and some detail of a documented QMS (quality management system) are presented, together with a structure for methods and procedures. The route to accreditation is described. Flexible scope accreditation, as a means of addressing the issue of novel evidential materials or circumstances, is introduced and its limits discussed. Finally an example of the impact of quality failures is described.

It should be noted that ISO provides an online browsing platform for all its standards, which offers sight of the first few sections in full and the complete structure.

5.2 THE PRACTICAL APPLICATION OF ISO/IEC 17025 AND 17020

The structure of both ISO/IEC 17025 and ISO/IEC 17020 is mandated by ISO's Committee on Conformity Assessment (ISO/CASCO) and is as follows:

- General requirements
  - impartiality, independence, and confidentiality;
- Structural requirements
  - legal matters, organizational structure, and top management;
- Resource requirements
  - personnel, facilities, equipment, systems, and support services;
- Process requirements
  - methods and procedures;
- Management requirements

Again, as mandated by ISO/CASCO, there are two options available to fulfill the management requirements, Option A and B.

Option A is specified in the standards and requires the laboratory to address the requirements of:

- Management system documentation,
- Control of management system documents,

ISBN 978-0-12-805416-1, https://doi.org/10.1016/B978-0-12-805416-1.00005-0

- Control of records,
- Actions to address risks and opportunities,
- Improvement,
- Corrective action,
- Internal audits,[1] and
- Management reviews.

Alternatively, **Option B** allows a laboratory that has established and maintains a management system conforming to ISO 9001 (which is capable of supporting and demonstrating the consistent fulfillment of the general, structural, resource, and process requirements) to be recognized as fulfilling the intent of the management system requirements as outlined in Option A.

However, ABs (accreditation bodies) may expect organizations taking Option B to be certified to ISO 9001 by a certification body accredited by an AB, which is signatory to the International Accreditation Forum Multilateral Recognition Agreement (MLA) or to a regional MLA for the certification of management systems. In that case it might be more cost-effective to take Option A.

5.2.1 ISO/IEC 17025:2017

This International Standard was introduced in 3.2.2. As reported there, the standard is available for purchase from ISO at a cost of 138CHF [December 2017] and has 30 pages (36 including the Annexes). The structure of the standard, which is shared with ISO/IEC 17020, complies with the latest ISO/CASCO requirements and is as follows:

1. Scope
2. Normative references
3. Terms and definitions
4. General requirements
5. Structural requirements
6. Resource requirements
7. Process requirements
8. Management requirements

   Annexes

   A. Metrological traceability

   B. Management system

   Bibliography

[1] Audits are a systematic, independent and documented process for obtaining evidence and evaluating it objectively to determine the extent to which the audit criteria are fulfilled (ISO 9000:2015 3.13.1). Internal audits are also termed first party audits.

ISO/IEC 17025:2017 specifies the general requirements for the competence, impartiality, and consistent operation of forensic science providers as defined in the standard. Conformance demonstrates that the provider operates competently, i.e., in accordance with the principles of ISO 9001 introduced in 3.2.1, and generates valid results that can be relied on by stakeholders, particularly law enforcement and justice.

It covers testing performed using standard methods,[2] nonstandard methods, and laboratory-developed methods. It is noteworthy that the 2017 edition does not define the term "standard method" but a note to Section 6.2.1.5 implies that such methods are

> *... published either in international, regional or national standards, or by reputable technical organizations, or in relevant scientific texts or journals, or as specified by the manufacturer of the equipment [employed]. ©ISO/IEC 2017 — All rights reserved*

The standard is for use by providers in developing their management system for quality, administrative, and technical operations. Customers, regulatory authorities, and ABs may also use it in confirming or recognizing the competence of forensic science providers.

Accreditation to ISO/IEC, 17025 not only provides authoritative assurance of the technical competence of a provider to undertake specified tests but also addresses particular aspects relevant to forensic science such as continuity of evidence, management of case files, and storage of exhibits. Accreditation determines the competence of staff, the validity and suitability of methods, the appropriateness of equipment and facilities, and the ongoing assurance and confidence in outcomes through internal quality control.

The normative references are

- JCGM 200:2012 "International vocabulary of metrology—Basic and general concepts and associated terms," introduced in Section 3.2.2.1 [ISO/IEC Guide 98], and
- ISO/IEC 17000 "Conformity assessment—Vocabulary and general principles."

The need for impartiality and confidentiality is stated in Section 4. According to the standard the term "impartiality" has a broad meaning. Impartiality is defined in Section 3.1 of the standard as the "presence of objectivity" and the notes further explain

> *Objectivity means that conflicts of interest do not exist or are resolved so as not to adversely influence subsequent activities of the inspection body.*

and

> *Other terms that are useful in conveying the element of impartiality are: independence, freedom from conflict of interests, freedom from bias, lack of prejudice, neutrality, fairness, open-mindedness, even-handedness, detachment, [and] balance. ©ISO/IEC 2017 — All rights reserved*

[2] As explained earlier, "standard methods" might be taken to mean those published either in international, regional or national standards, or by reputable technical organizations, or in relevant scientific texts or journals, or as specified by the manufacturer of the equipment used, see 7.2.1.5 of ISO/IEC 17025:2017.

The impartiality requirement in the latest edition of the standard is novel. Meeting the requirement for impartiality (in its many forms), as noted in 3.2.2, may be a challenge for some providers, particularly those that are actually part of a law enforcement agency.

As explained in 3.2.3 and later in 5.2.2, the inspection standard ISO/IEC 17020 additionally includes the requirement for independence. ISO/IEC 17020 includes minimum requirements for independence based on the relationship between the provider and stakeholder commissioning the inspection, ISO/IEC 17025 includes no such provision.

One aim of the impartiality requirement is to ensure that all personnel are free from undue influence and pressures that could adversely impact on the quality of the forensic science provided.

Section 5 of the standard sets out the structural requirements for the forensic science provider. These requirements include the following:

- the provider is an entity that is legally responsible for its activities,
- top management is identified and is responsible for all activities,
- stakeholder needs are met,
- activities that lie within the scope of accreditation are defined and documented and accreditation for those that fall outside not claimed,
- the organizational structure is defined, and
- a quality manager (however named) with the necessary resources and authorities is appointed.

The standard does not identify the post of quality manager, but the duties and responsibilities specified in Section 5.6 might be best undertaken by someone with such a title.

Section 6 specifies resource requirements, personnel, facilities and environmental conditions, equipment, metrological traceability, and externally provided product and service. The importance of competent personnel is recognized in the detail. Staff must act impartially, be supervised, and be competent. The need for a competent practitioner is one of the three top-level requirements together with a competent organization and valid methods. The organization is required to determine competence criteria, have in place a means of evaluation, and a means of ensuring that personnel possess and retain the required competencies. Management must authorize personnel to perform specific tasks, for example, to operate specific types of instruments, to issue test reports, to interpret specific test results, and to train or supervise others. The authorization date must be recorded.

Documented procedures and records are required for determining competency requirements personnel selection, training, authorizing, and monitoring.

Resource requirements also include those related to the following:

- Laboratory facilities and environmental conditions
  - Environmental conditions must not adversely affect the quality of test results. This means, for example, that equipment should operate within the manufacturer's specifications for humidity and temperature.
  - Environmental conditions must be controlled, monitored, and recorded. Particular attention must be paid to maintaining the integrity of evidential items. Conditions include biological sterility, dust, electromagnetic disturbances, radiation, humidity, electrical supply, temperature, sound, and vibration levels.
  - Tests must be stopped when the environmental conditions are outside specified ranges.
  - Areas with incompatible activities must be separated.
  - Access to work areas must be controlled.
- Equipment

  The term equipment is broadly defined by the standard and includes measuring instruments, software, measurement standards, reference materials, reference data, reagents, and consumables that can influence the result.

  Key points are
  - Equipment should conform to specifications relevant to the tests. This means that equipment specifications should first be defined so that when conforming to defined specifications the equipment is suitable to perform the tests.
  - Equipment and its software should be identified and documented.
  - Equipment should be calibrated and/or checked to establish that it meets the laboratory's specification requirements.
  - Records of equipment and its software should be maintained and updated if necessary. This includes version numbers of firmware and software. It also includes calibration and test protocols.
  - Calibration status should be indicated on the instrument along with the last and the next calibration dates.
- metrological traceability.

  The forensic science provider must establish and maintain metrological traceability. Traceability is a prerequisite for comparability of test and calibration results. Traceability of standards to SI units[3] may be achieved through an unbroken link of calibration comparisons between the laboratory standard, secondary standard, and primary or national standard. However, traceability to SI units is not always

[3] International System of units based on the meter, kilogram, second, ampere, kelvin, candela, and mole.

possible in forensic science. Therefore, a provider can demonstrate metrological traceability to an appropriate reference such as:

- certified values of reference materials provided by an accredited producer,[4] or
- results of reference measurement procedures, specified methods, or consensus standards.

- externally provided products and services.

This requires forensic science providers to assure the quality of products and services supplied externally and on which the provider will rely in delivering products and services. Requiring external providers to conform to the relevant ISO standard would satisfy this requirement.

Section 7 is the largest in the standard. It details the requirements for conducting the conformity assessment activity, which, in this work, is the forensic science process, or parts thereof. This section includes most of the technical requirements such as method validation and estimating uncertainty. The process and requirements are graphically represented in Fig. 5.1.

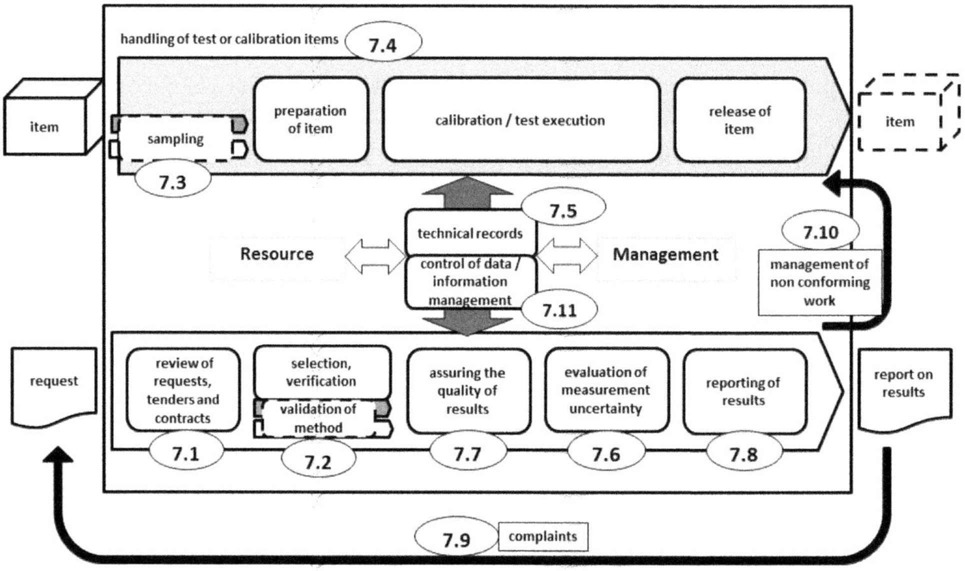

Figure 5.1 The conformity assessment process according to ISO/IEC 17025:2017 Section 7—process requirements. *(Reproduced with permission of ISO).*

[4] accredited to ISO/IEC 17034 "General requirements for the competence of reference material producers," discussed in 3.2.2.2.

Method validation is a key component of the technical requirements of ISO/IEC 17025 and one of the three top-level requirements for conformance together with a competent organization and competent personnel.

ISO defines validation as follows:

> *[The] confirmation through the provision of objective evidence that the requirements for a specific intended use or application have been fulfilled.*[5] *©ISO/IEC 2015 — All rights reserved*

In the context of forensic science, a valid method is one that meets stakeholder needs, particularly those of law enforcement and justice, and has been objectively demonstrated to do so.

As noted in 3.2.2, validation is always a balance between costs, risks, and technical possibilities. A highly accurate result may not be required by the customer. Law enforcement agencies are often satisfied with a categorical result[6]: "yes," "no," or "inconclusive."

According to Section 6.2.2, nonstandard methods, laboratory-developed methods, and standard methods used outside their intended scope (modified standard methods) must be validated. The provider must conduct a method validation study and record the procedure used and the results obtained. The provider must also document a statement that the method is fit for its intended purpose.

Standard methods and others not requiring validation must be verified by ensuring that the required performance can be achieved. Verification is defined by ISO as:

> *[The] confirmation through the provisions of objective evidence that the specified requirements have been fulfilled.*[7] *©ISO/IEC 2015 — All rights reserved*

For a standard analytical method, verification would require the provider to check that method performance characteristics, such as limit of detection, precision, accuracy, etc. can be achieved.

The full structure of Section 7 is as follows:

7.1 Review of requests, tenders, and contracts
7.2 Selection, verification, and validation of methods
7.3 Sampling
7.4 Handling of test or calibration items
7.5 Technical records
7.6 Evaluation of measurement uncertainty
7.7 Assuring the quality of results
7.8 Reporting of results

[5] ISO 9001:2015 "Quality management systems—Fundamentals and vocabulary" 3.8.13.
[6] The weakness of this form of reporting is explained in Section 7.
[7] ISO 9001:2015 "Quality Management systems—Fundamentals and vocabulary" 3.8.12.

7.9 Complaints
7.10 Management of nonconforming work
7.11 Control of data—Information management

Documented procedures and records are required for most subsections.

Section 8 specifies the management system requirements. It offers two options, conformance with the remainder of this section, Option A.

8.2 Management system documentation
8.3 Control of management system documents
8.4 Control of records
8.5 Actions to address risks and opportunities
8.6 Improvement
8.7 Corrective action
8.8 Internal audits
8.9 Management reviews

Section 8.5 on risks and opportunities is novel and follows the risk-based thinking approach required by ISO 9001:2015 and discussed in Section 3.2.1. This section requires the laboratory to plan and implement actions to address risks and opportunities.

Option B is conformance with the principles of the quality management standard ISO 9001, introduced in Section 3.2.1.

Forensic science providers certified to ISO 9001:2015 can rely on conformance to that standard to meet the requirements specified in this section, which is Option B. However, as mentioned earlier in Section 5.2, the AB may require certification to ISO 9001: 2015 as evidence of conformance, in which case Option A would be more cost-effective.

5.2.1.1 ISO/IEC 17025 Guidance Documents

As reported in Section 3.2.2 ISO/IEC 17025:2017 was published in November 2017. There will now be a 3-year implementation period during which accredited forensic science providers will need to transition to conformance to the new edition. Once the new edition is implemented, the guidance documents introduced and discussed in Section 3.3 will no longer apply and therefore no further discussion is warranted. This section will need to wait for the next edition of that work.

5.2.2 ISO/IEC 17020:2012 "Conformity Assessment—Requirements for the Operation of Various Types of Bodies Performing Inspection"

This International Standard was introduced in 3.2.3. In forensic science, this standard applies to and assures the competence of organizations providing crime scene examination, their employees, and the validity of their methods. It is also considered suitable for application to feature-comparison disciplines, such as marks and impressions. Therefore, it is the second most important standard in forensic science after ISO/IEC 17025 and its practical application is discussed in some detail here.

According to ISO, ISO/IEC 17020:2012 specifies the requirements for the competence of bodies performing inspection and for the impartiality and consistency of their inspection activities. It applies to inspection bodies of type A, B, or C, as defined in the standard and it applies to any stage of inspection. The various types of inspection body are described below.

A broad definition[8] of inspection is to examine closely, to test an individual activity against established standards for that activity, and/or to make a comparison. Inspection involves observation, examination, comparison of materials or items. Inspection might also involve measurement and tasting. The process includes examination of an object and determination of its conformity with specific requirements on the basis of professional judgment. Using fingerprints as an example, an unknown print is compared against a suspect's print and then a judgment is made as to whether the two items are similar or not. The reliance on judgment rather than measurement is a distinguishing feature of ISO/IEC 17020. As crime scene examination and feature-comparisons are essentially inspection activities, ISO/IEC 17020 is the appropriate standard.

As reported in 3.2.3, the standard has 18 pages and is available for purchase from ISO at a cost of 88CHF [December 2017]. The structure of the standard complies with the latest ISO/CASCO requirements and is the same as that of ISO/IEC 17025.

1. Scope
2. Normative references
3. Terms and definitions
4. General requirements
5. Structural requirements
6. Resource requirements
7. Process requirements
8. Management System Requirements

Annex A (normative)—Independence requirements for inspection bodies
Annex B (informative)—Optional elements of inspection reports and certificates
Bibliography

The normative reference is
ISO/IEC 17000 "Conformity assessment—Vocabulary and general principles"

[8] Inspection is defined by ISO as [the] determination of conformity to specified requirements (ISO 9000: 2015 3.11.7).

Section 4 specifies the general requirements of impartiality and confidentiality in common with ISO/IEC 17025; however, ISO/IEC 17020 additionally requires independence.

Impartiality is defined in Section 3.8 of the standard and has the same meaning as that in ISO/IEC 17025 above.

In simple terms, an inspection body and the inspector employed must be demonstrably and unequivocally free of undue influence when conducting an inspection and reporting results.

ISO/IEC 17020 specifies minimum requirements for independence depending on the conditions under which the forensic science provider performs the inspection. These are classified as type A, B, or C, which essentially categorizes the degree of relationship between the inspection body and the commissioning agency or organization:

- Type A is a fully independent third-party inspection body.
- Type B is an inspection body that provides first- or second-party inspections or both, but it is a separate and identifiable part of the commissioning organization with a clear separation of the duties, responsibilities, and management of inspection personnel from others performing different functions within the same organization.
- Type C is an inspection body that provides first- or second-party inspections or both, but it does not form a separate and identifiable part of the commissioning organization.

Type C inspection bodies are the least independent and require special measures to assure independence and impartiality. As reported in 3.3.3.1, the UK Accreditation Service, UKAS, has placed crime scene examination bodies under the direct control of police in this category. Where crime scene examination bodies are under operational control of law enforcement agencies, extra safeguards are needed to demonstrate independence and impartiality. The necessary degree of independence can be achieved by ensuring adequate segregation of responsibilities and accountabilities between inspection and other activities within the organization. The standard requires a documented record of conformance.

In common with ISO/IEC 17025, Section 5 specifies the structural requirements. These are similar to those of ISO/IEC 17025 setting out the legal, management, and organizational requirements. However, safeguarding impartiality is emphasized in ISO/IEC 17020, Section 5.2.1. Section 5.2.4 of the standard requires an inspection body that is part of a legal entity performing other activities to clearly define the relationship between inspection and noninspection activities. The requirement for a compliance officer is also specified and termed a "Technical Manager." The importance of this role is emphasized by the additional requirement to have named deputies to act in the absence of the technical manager, 5.2.6.

Section 6 specifies resource requirements: personnel, facilities and equipment, and subcontracting. As with ISO/IEC 17025 competent personnel is an essential requirement.

Documented procedures for selecting, training, authorizing, and monitoring personnel (6.1.5) are required.

The resource requirements also include those related to facilities and equipment. Equipment maintenance procedures must be documented (6.2.5) as must procedures for dealing with defective equipment (6.2.14).

Subcontracting or outsourcing is permitted and may be required where demand exceeds the inspection body's capacity or resources. The accredited forensic science provider is required to ensure and be able to demonstrate that the subcontractor is competent and conforms to the necessary standards.

As explained in the introduction, 3.2.3, the standard recognizes that inspection activities can overlap with testing and calibration activities. As the ILAC (International Laboratory Accreditation Cooperation) Guide P15:07/2016 makes clear in 6.2.7, where metrological traceability is required and testing is performed ISO/IEC 17025 is the applicable standard. As discussed later in 5.4, ABs can add ISO/IEC 17025 accreditation of such activities as an extension to scope.

As with ISO/IEC 17025, Section 7 deals with the activity itself; the process of inspection, in this work crime scene examination and feature-comparisons.

The process requirements fall under the following headings:

7.1 Inspection methods and procedures
7.2 Handling inspection items and samples
7.3 Inspection records
7.4 Inspection reports and certificates
7.5 Complaints and appeals
7.6 Complaints and appeals process

Documented instructions on planning, sampling, and inspection are required, if needed (7.1.2).

In ISO/IEC 17025 the requirement for method validation formed a major part of this section; in contrast ISO/IEC 17020 is silent. As mentioned above and explained in 3.3.2.2, any testing or measurement carried out by an inspector would need to be accredited to ISO/IEC 17025 as an extension to scope.

Subsection 7.1 covers inspection methods that are defined in the requirements against which the inspection is to be performed. The requirements can have a number of sources: regulations and contracts, those decided by the inspection body or required by the commissioning stakeholder. In contrast to ISO/IEC 17025 the text helpfully defines "standard" and "nonstandard" methods.

A standard inspection method is one that has been published, for example, in international, regional or national standards, or by reputable technical organizations or by co-operation of several inspection bodies or in relevant scientific text or journals. This means that methods developed by any other means, including by the inspection body itself or by the client, are considered to be non-standard methods. ©ISO/IEC 2012 — All rights reserved

If nonstandard inspection methods are used, the standard requires the method to be "appropriate and fully documented." Method validation and verification are not specified requirements.

Feature-comparison disciplines rely on method validation, which is discussed more fully in Section 6.3, and this requirement is specified in the ISO/IEC 17020 guidance/requirements documents issued by ABs, e.g., the UKAS (UKAS, 2015) and ANSI-ASQ National Accreditation Board (ANAB, 2017).

Standard inspection methods for crime scene examination are documented in the following publications:

- Crime Scene Investigation—A Guide for Law Enforcement (National Forensic Science Technology Centre, 2013)
- Managing Scenes—College of Policing Authorised Professional Practice, Section 9 (College of Policing, 2014)
- AS 5388.1:2012 Forensic Analysis Part 1 Recognition recording, recovery, transport and storage of material

Section 8 specifies the management system requirements. In common with ISO/IEC 17025 it offers two options, A and B. As ISO/IEC 17020:2012 predates ISO 9001:2015, the structure of section 8 differs slightly from that of ISO/IEC 17025:2017 as risk-based thinking is not made explicit. However, it would be wise for forensic science providers accredited, or preparing for accreditation, to this standard to plan and implement actions to address risks and opportunities.

The structure of this section is as follows:

8.2 Management system documentation
8.3 Control of documents
8.4 Control of records
8.5 Management review
8.6 Internal audits
8.7 Corrective action
8.8 Preventative actions

Forensic inspection bodies certified to ISO 9001:2015 can rely on conformance to that standard to meet the requirements specified in this section, which is Option B. However, as mentioned earlier in 5.2, the AB may require certification to ISO 9001: 2015 as evidence of conformance, in which case Option A would be more cost-effective.

5.3 THE ELEMENTS OF A QUALITY MANAGEMENT SYSTEM (QMS) CONFORMING TO ISO/IEC 17025/20

The QMS is documented. As explained in 3.2.1, ISO 9001:2015 is the quality management standard, the structure of which conforms to the High Level Structure (HLS) consistent with Annex SL to the ISO Directives, Part 1, and that structure is:

1. Scope
2. Normative references
3. Terms and definitions
4. Context of the organization
5. Leadership
6. Planning
7. Support
8. Operation
9. Performance evaluation
10. Improvement

The standard applies the following quality management principles:

- customer focus,
- leadership,
- engagement of people,
- process approach,
- improvement,
- evidence-based decision-making, and
- relationship management.

The standard adopts a process approach to QMS development, implementation, and improvement based on the Plan, Do, Check, Act cycle:

- **Plan**: establish the objectives of the QMS and its processes, and the resources needed to deliver results in accordance with stakeholder needs and the organization's policies, and identify and address risks and opportunities;
- **Do**: implement what was planned;
- **Check**: monitor and (where applicable) measure processes and the resulting products and services against policies, objectives, requirements and planned activities, and report the results; and
- **Act**: take actions to improve performance, as necessary.

As mentioned above, the International Standards ISO/IEC 17025 and 17020 allow forensic science providers the option of conforming to ISO 9001, Option B, or conforming to Section 8 of those standards. Either option fulfills the management system requirements of the International Standards ISO/IEC 17025 and ISO/IEC 17020.

Forensic science providers that conform to ISO/IEC 17025 and 17020 are deemed by ISO to generally operate in accordance with the principles of ISO 9001. Although ISO offers the option to be certified to ISO 9001, or merely operate in conformance to that standard, most accredited forensic science providers rely solely on conformance to ISO/IEC 17025 and/or 17020 to demonstrate the effectiveness of their QMS. In essence it demonstrates conference to ISO 9001.

Unfortunately the International Standards ISO 9001, ISO/IEC 17025, and 17020 are not completely harmonized. The lack of harmonization and the availability of differing options for conformance may result in organizations operating to different standards. Such an outcome would not be consistent with the aim of standardization. The lack of complete harmonization is the result of the life cycle and development of each standard. The latest edition of ISO 9001 postdates the latest edition of ISO/IEC 17020 and therefore ISO/IEC 17020:2012 does not reflect ISO 9001:2015. ISO/IEC 17025:2017 postdates ISO 9001:2015 and so risked-based thinking, which is fundamental to ISO 9001:2015, is incorporated in ISO/IEC 17025:2017 in the need to address risks and opportunities.

For forensic science providers that are yet to gain accreditation, or need to transition, to ISO/IEC 17025:2017, using the HLS of ISO 9001:2015 and the quality management principles (see 3.2.1) in constructing and documenting the QMS would be a straightforward task and result in a more valuable and robust system.

The structure of the QMS therefore will depend on the option chosen. Whether Option A or B is exercised, the International Standards ISO/IEC 17025 and 17020 permit organizations to choose their own format and style of collating and presenting policy and information, e.g., records, in documents. Collating that information in one document, formerly called a "quality manual," is no longer a requirement but is still an option and maybe the best one.

As gleaned from the International Standards, the essential information that needs to be documented is as follows:

- The scope of the QMS, which includes the organization's external environment, culture, values, performance and stakeholders;
- Quality policy, and quality objectives, which must align with the context and strategic direction of the organization;
- The control and maintenance of documented information—records, procedures, and processes; additional records should be retained;
- A plan to identify and respond to risks that might influence the organization's performance, i.e., its ability to provide conforming products and services and meet stakeholder needs;
- A plan to identify and respond to opportunities that might improve the organization's performance;
- An internal audit plan to periodically check the effectiveness of the QMS and conformance to the International Standard; and

- A plan for periodic management reviews to ensure the continuing suitability, adequacy, effectiveness of the QMS, and its alignment with the strategic direction of the organization.

The entire requirements for the documentation of the QMS are set out in the relevant standard. To conform to an International Standard a forensic science provider must document what it does, justify it, and do what it documents.

5.3.1 Operational Technical Methods and Procedures—Structure

As explained earlier in 5.2, ISO considers a standard method to be one that has been published either in international, regional, or national standards, or by reputable technical organizations, or in relevant scientific texts or journals, or as specified by the manufacturer of the equipment employed.

Confusingly, forensic science providers, particularly those that are laboratory based, sometimes use the term "standard method" to describe their operational methods and procedures.

In this work the term "standard operating procedure" (SOP) is used for a technical method or procedure that has been validated or verified as fit-for-purpose by the forensic science provider and falls within the scope of accreditation. SOPs are the documented and controlled methods and procedures that meet the Process requirements of Section 7 of both ISO/IEC 17025 (7.2) and ISO/IEC 17020 (7.1) and are the Level 4 Standards introduced in 3.5. The International Standards require forensic science providers to have documented methods and procedures for all activities within the scope of accreditation. Although the structure of methods and procedures will vary according to the activity, those that describe an analytical test conducted by an ISO/IEC 17025 accredited provider might be structured as follows:

1. Scope and field of application
2. References
3. Essential knowledge
4. Health and safety
5. Summary of the process to include principle and performance characteristics
6. Materials
7. Apparatus/instrument—description and operation
8. Apparatus/instrument preparation—to check performance parameters are as required
9. Sample preparation to include positive and negative controls
10. Analytical procedure to include instrument calibration
11. Calculation of results
12. Interpretation of results

Steps 1–5 and 12 would apply equally to an ISO/IEC 17020 accredited forensic inspection method. Crime scene examination would also require documented procedures for:

- scene control and preservation,
- control of records,
- the recovery of evidence,
- contamination avoidance, and
- maintaining evidence integrity.

Where justified, and with adequate safeguards in place, relevant parties should be able to inspect the documented methods and procedures employed by practitioners to check conformance with the International Standard.

It is of relevance to note that the US Attorney General adopted an National Commission on Forensic Sciences recommendation that Department of Justice agencies, such as the FBI (Federal Bureau of Investigation), should place its QMS in the public domain taking account of security and privacy issues (Office of the Attorney General, 2016).

Some US forensic science providers have already placed SOPs in the public domain, e.g., the Department of Forensic Science in Washington DC (District of Columbia, Department of Forensic Science, 2017).

It should be recalled that forensic science providers are accredited for methods that lie within the scope of accreditation. Deviations are permitted but the revised method must at least be verified and the deviation disclosed to relevant stakeholders. ISO/IEC 17025: 2017 at 7.2.1.3 additionally requires deviations to be documented, technically justified, and authorized. When methods outside the scope of accreditation are used that fact should be disclosed.

Where a method has been accredited for the detection of a particular class of evidential material and it is anticipated that new members of that class may be encountered at some time then flexible scope accreditation, discussed later in Section 5.5, is an option to consider which avoids operating outside the scope of accreditation.

5.4 OBTAINING AND MAINTAINING ACCREDITATION

Accreditation is the formal recognition that an organization is competent to perform specific processes, activities, or tasks (which are detailed in a scope of accreditation) in a reliable, credible, and accurate manner. The technical definition of accreditation is given in ISO/IEC 17000:2004 "Conformity assessment—Vocabulary and general principles."

The provision of accreditation must:

- be objective, transparent, and effective;
- use assessors (and subcontractors) that are reliable, ethical, and competent in both the accreditation processes and the relevant technical fields.

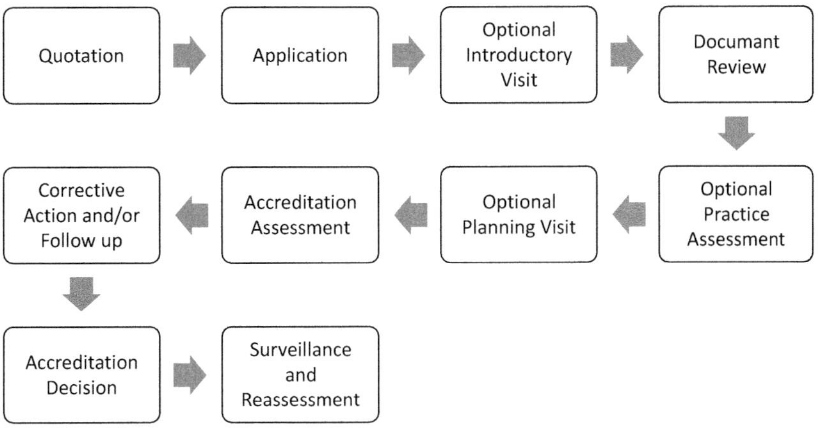

Figure 5.2 ANAB steps to accreditation. *(Reproduced with permission.*

Accreditation delivers confidence in certificates and conformity statements—the outputs. It underpins the quality of results by ensuring their traceability, comparability, validity, and commutability.

ABs differ in the route they offer to accreditation, for example that adopted by ANAB is shown in Fig. 5.2. However, the essential steps are:

- preparation,
- application,
- preassessment (optional),
- assessment, and
- accreditation.

5.4.1 Preapplication Preparation

The first step is to decide if accreditation is necessary. Obtaining accreditation is a burdensome process that cannot be undertaken lightly and will require the allocation of significant resources. However, the trend is toward mandatory accreditation and therefore there may come a time when providers will have no choice other than to become accredited.

Once the decision to obtain accreditation has been made, a project manager for the process of gaining accreditation should be appointed and resources allocated.

It would also be wise, at an early juncture, to appoint a competent quality manager who could also act as the project manager. Having an individual who understands quality management and has experience of the accreditation process will be a major asset. In addition, maintaining accreditation will require a quality manager.

The next step is to decide which standard is most appropriate. For most activities involving tests that rely, to some extent of analytical chemistry, ISO/IEC 17025 is the most appropriate. For crime scene examination and feature-comparison disciplines, ISO/IEC 17020 is likely to be the appropriate standard.

Some providers may undertake activities that are properly accredited to both standards. In which case the majority of activities should be accredited to one standard and the remainder accredited to the other as an extension to scope.

As discussed in Section 6, Australasian providers are accredited to ISO/IEC 17025 for all activities with AS 5388 as a supplement for NATA (National Association of Testing Authorities, Australia) accredited providers.

The relevant ILAC application and interpretation guidance documents, which are discussed in 3.3, should be obtained and studied. Some ABs such as NATA and ANAB issue their own guidance documents, which can also aid application and interpretation. These are freely available for download and are of benefit irrespective of the actual AB selected.

A copy of the relevant standard should be purchased and studied. Using the guidance documents, the preliminary scope of accreditation should be decided. The organization's QMS is then documented in accordance with the standard. A gap analysis to identify areas that need addressing is a useful exercise in achieving this aim. In simple terms the task is to document what you do and do what you document. Once the QMS is documented an audit should be conducted to check conformance with the International Standard.

In preparing documentation, the need to avoid over documentation should be born in mind. As discussed in 1.3.10, the larger and more complex the QMS the more costly it will be to maintain and the greater the risk of nonconformance. International Standards are quite clear on what needs to be documented. The documentation required is specified in the International Standards, Section 8 in ISO/IEC 17025/20 and 7.5 in ISO 9001:2015 making use of the structure introduced in 3.2.1. Do not document anything that is not specified in the standard.

When documenting, avoid unnecessary detail. This can be achieved, in part, by assuming that operators are competent when documenting methods and procedures. In the case of a competent analytical chemist the procedure for restoring optimal performance to a gas chromatographic separation system need to include nothing beyond one or more of baking, shortening, or replacing the column and/or changing the injection port liner.

A major preparatory step is the selection of an AB. Many are prepared to accredit organizations beyond national borders, and in some territories/regions there is more than one. One important issue is the availability of competent technical assessors. Organizations seeking accreditation should ensure that technical assessors are available and competent before entering into a contract with an AB. In addition, accreditation is a costly process and if a choice is available cost could be a factor in selection.

The AB selected should be a signatory of an ILAC MRA (Mutual Recognition Agreement/Arrangement) as discussed in 3.2.4.

5.4.2 Application

This usually involves completing a form, providing information, and paying an application fee that is usually nonrefundable. The AB will also require proof of legal status and proof that a licensed copy of the appropriate standard has been purchased. The AB will need to see the quality management documentation required by the International Standard and determined by the applicant as being necessary for the effectiveness of its QMS. Those requirements are set out in Section 8 of ISO/IEC 17025/20 and in the structure of ISO 9001. As discussed earlier in 5.2, the choice lies with the provider.

If the AB considers the applicant ready, then a quotation is prepared, and if accepted by the applicant a contract entered into. Alternatively the application may be rejected.

Once a contract is in place the AB will appoint an assessment manager and a member of staff to act as a guide and point of contact through the process.

Candidate technical assessors with the expertise to cover the scope of application will be considered in consultation with the applicant and suitable assessors appointed.

The assessment manager will guide the organization through the process and agree timescales for key milestones.

5.4.3 Preassessment Visit (Optional)

A preassessment is an informal visit to determine how ready the organization is for accreditation and hopefully confirm that it is. A preassessment visit is optional and will incur additional costs, but it can be a valuable step in the process that may avoid delays in gaining accreditation.

ABs usually recommend a preassessment visit by the assessment manager and possibly a technical assessor. The visit addresses the scope of accreditation requested and normally involves a number of days of effort.

If a preassessment visit is decided on then the AB will provide a quotation for the work involved and a report on the findings of the preassessment following the visit.

5.4.4 Conformity Assessment

Once the applicant is ready, having addressed any issues raised during the preassessment visit, formal assessment takes place.

This is conducted by a lead assessor (often the assessment manager) supported, as necessary, by technical assessors with the expertise to cover the scope of accreditation. The length of the visit will depend on the scope requested. The AB will provide a quotation for the work involved.

The assessment visit will typically involve the following:

- an opening meeting to agree the arrangements,
- a detailed review of documented information (records and procedures),

- interviews with staff and managers,
- witnessing key activities,
- a full vertical and horizontal audit, and
- a debrief of the visit to discuss findings.

The AB will provide a full report during or immediately following the assessment visit. This report will detail any findings or improvement actions identified against accreditation requirements. The applicant may challenge the findings and the need for improvements actions.

Should any actions be required, the AB will set an agreed time limit within which the actions must be cleared to its satisfaction. The time limit can vary, but it is often around 3 months.

5.4.5 Accreditation

Once actions are satisfactorily cleared, the assessment manager will submit a recommendation to some higher, ideally independent, authority for a decision. The role of the decision-maker is to check that the process conforms to ISO/IEC 17011.

Following ratification of the decision to grant accreditation, a certificate of accreditation is issued. The schedule defining the scope is made publicly available on the website of the AB.

Once accreditation is granted, continuing conformance is assessed and maintained by a program of internal audits, an annual external audit, and reaccreditation, usually after a period of 4 years.

The AB should aim to audit the entire QMS over the accreditation cycle. However, external audits are often risk-based and therefore parts of the QMS may not be subjected to external audit over the cycle, risking undetected nonconformances.

5.4.6 Disclosure of Documented Information

Conformance with any of the International Standards requires a commitment to continual improvement, which aims to improve performance. Actions to address risks and opportunities for improvement will be raised at every audit. Some of these may be corrective or result in preventative controls. Most will be minor nonconformances.

Whether or not minor nonconformances should be disclosed or be disclosable is a matter of debate. The purpose of quality audit is to improve performance. If the results of audit were disclosable then that may adversely affect the process. Internal auditors might be reluctant to raise nonconformances if that risk adversely affects the reputation of the organization. In addition, the organization itself might develop a defensive culture. The ethos of continual improvement is best served by rigorous internal audit and a completely open relationship with the AB. The voluntary disclosure of external audit results may be a reasonable way forward.

There can be little doubt that accreditation represents a major advance in assuring the quality of forensic science provided. However, as exemplified by the episode described later in 5.6, accreditation is not an absolute guarantee of quality. In addition, ABs make clear that accreditation is based on the information made available to and assessed by the AB. The implication being that there may be information of which the AB is unaware that might demonstrate nonconformance to the extent that accreditation is not warranted. Such an episode is described in 5.6. Therefore, where there are reasonable grounds to suspect nonconformance, relevant stakeholders should have access to the documented QMS, particularly SOPs.

5.4.7 Sanctions

Major nonconformances may result in sanctions applied by the AB. Sanctions available are: suspension of accreditation, withdrawal, or a reduction in scope. Suspension is usually the result of the organization not conforming to part of the standard. Withdrawal usually follows suspension where the suspended organization has failed to satisfactorily address the nonconformances that led to suspension. The organization should cease the activities that are the subject of sanction. Organizations under sanction will be listed as such on the AB's website.

The purpose of sanctions is to restore conformity by improving performance. Organizations under sanction and wishing to regain accreditation are usually given around 30 days to document a plan and submit it to the AB. The plan must identify corrective actions, explain how they are to be implemented, and provide a time scale for completion. The organization under sanction may need to conduct a root cause analysis to identify the primary source of the nonconformance. A typical root cause is a lack of training in a particular area.

5.5 FLEXIBLE SCOPE ACCREDITATION

Flexible scope accreditation can allow a forensic science provider to undertake certain tests, and to report the results as accredited, even though the test may not be explicitly stated on its accreditation schedule but is performed within boundaries defined by flexible scope accreditation.

An example of the need for flexible scope is the use of an accredited method to detect a previously unencountered or novel illicit substance but falling within a particular class, such as an amphetamine type stimulant or alkaloid.

Flexible scope accreditation mostly applies to analytical tests and forensic science providers accredited to ISO/IEC 17025.[9] However, it can apply to any activity within an

[9] ANAB states that it offers flexible scope for forensic inspection bodies accredited to ISO/IEC 17020.

existing scope. Guidance is provided by ILAC in the form of Guide 18:04/2010, currently [December 2017] under revision, which refers to ISO/IEC 17025:2005. Guidance is also available from EA as EA-2/15 M:2008.

Through flexible scope the forensic science provider has the recognized flexibility, to modify methods, validate the changes, and apply them without having to ask the AB for extensions to the scope. Such modifications to methodology must not incorporate new measurement principles not previously covered in the scope of accreditation.

Conformance to flexible scope accreditation is particularly demanding in terms satisfying the requirements for competence, both organizational and individual, and technical validity.

Not all ABs offer flexible scope accreditation. It is not a requirement mandated by ILAC as part of the MRA. Those that do offer flexible scope can vary in the interpretation of flexible scope and its implementation. Therefore, even though there may be a need, flexible scope accreditation may not be available. However, with ABs now accrediting forensic science providers in most jurisdictions and with more than one AB in some, forensic science providers that might wish to acquire such accreditation have some choice.

Flexible scope accreditation places more of the responsibility onto the provider itself to demonstrate competence, validity, and consistency of operation. The competence to apply knowledge, skills, and experience must be defined as the focus moves from what is accredited to what the provider is capable of and competent to do.

UKAS lists the circumstances in which flexible scope might apply:

- the inclusion of new or amended tests in accordance with a generic method;
- the modification of existing methods to broaden their applicability (e.g., to deal with new materials tested or properties measured, etc.); and
- the inclusion of newly revised or technically equivalent standard methods that are already covered by accreditation.

Examples of the variations that might be permitted are:

- matrix or sample type,
- sample preparation,
- reagents,
- equipment, provided the same measurement principles apply, and
- method, with the same proviso.

The limits of flexible scope must be clearly defined. The provider must demonstrate to the AB that it has the knowledge, experience, and competence to work within the full range of its flexible scope, as well as possessing suitable laboratory environments and equipment.

The limits should be set with respect to the range of:

- the materials/products tested;
- type of test (e.g., chemical, physical, mechanical, etc.);

- properties measured;
- measurement; and
- equipment/techniques used.

Variations that would not be permitted include:

- the underlying methodology (extraction, analysis, detection),
- in major classification/scientific discipline,
- the use of equipment/kits outside of manufacturers' specifications, and
- moving from manual to automated even if underlying methodology is the same.

A forensic science provider that wishes to apply for a flexible scope must be accredited to demonstrate competence in the general area. It must demonstrate that it has a management system in place that can control its proposed approach while continuing to comply with the requirements of the International Standard.

The provider must make clear to stakeholders which activities are covered by flexible scope. Indeed, an accredited provider must always disclose activities that fall outside the scope of any claimed accreditation.

5.6 A QUALITY FAILURE

After due process the Washington DC Department of Forensic Sciences (DFS) Laboratory had its accreditation partially suspended by its AB, ANAB, in April 2015.

The episode is illustrative of the following points that:

- accreditation is no absolute guarantee of quality,
- ABs are as capable of quality failures as any other organization, and
- in certain circumstances, conformity assessment by a fourth party is justified.

The activity in question was the interpretation of mixed DNA profiles, which remains a controversial issue as discussed in Section 7. In 2010, the Specialist Working Group on DNA Analysis Methods issued new interpretation guidelines, which importantly required practitioners to evaluate the questioned profile prior to comparison with the known profile and introduced thresholds above which signals were considered to be "true" and below which signals were ignored. These changes had a significant effect on reported results. In October 2013 the DFS gained accreditation for the interpretation of mixed profiles, it seems, based on pre-2010 standards. The DFS then failed to adopt the new guidelines hence the suspension.

From 2013 until accreditation was suspended, no issue that warranted suspension of accreditation was identified by the AB. As stated earlier, audits should be risk-based; activities where a nonconforming product might have a significant impact should be prioritized. An accredited activity in a controversial area capable of producing highly probative evidence should be considered high risk.

Concerns were raised by stakeholders, which finally resulted in an unscheduled audit by ANAB. The audit report is available (ANAB, 2015). The corrective actions identified included:

- revision of the complaints procedure,
- revalidation of methods,
- new interpretation guidelines, and
- retraining of personnel.

Overall the DFS was found not to conform to either the FBI Quality Assurance Standard,[10] introduced in 3.4.6.3, discussed in 4.4.3 and Section 6, or ISO/IEC 17025 for the activity in question.

The major evidence that calls into question the competence of ANAB is the 18 months or so during which quality auditors from ANAB and internal auditors at the DFS missed nonconformances of such magnitude as to warrant suspension of accreditation.

The advances in DNA profiling and the failure to take account of those developments certainly contributed to the suspension of accreditation. Quality management in forensic science must be responsive to change as science continuously advances.

REFERENCES

ANAB, June 1, 2017. "AR 3055." ISO/IEC 17020:2012-Forensic Inspection Bodies – Accreditation Requirements. ANSI-ASQ National Accreditation Board, Milwaukee.

ANAB, April 24, 2015. Surveillance and Remote Surveillance Audit – DC Department of Forensic Sciences. DFS, DC. https://dfs.dc.gov/sites/default/files/dc/sites/dfs/page_content/attachments/ANAB%20Report%20Final%202015.pdf.

College of Policing, January 28, 2014. Managing Investigations: College of Policing. College of Policing Authorised Professional Practice. https://www.app.college.police.uk/app-content/investigations/managing-investigations/#managing-scenes.

National Forensic Science Technology Centre, 2013. Crime Scene Investigation – A Guide for Law Enforcement. Guidance. NFSTC, Largo.

Office of the Attorney General, September 6, 2016. "Recommendations of the National Commission on Forensic Science; Announcement for NCFS Meeting Eleven." Memorandum for Heads of Department Components. Department of Justice, Washington DC.

UKAS, August 2015. "RG 201 Edition 2." Accreditation of Bodies Carrying Out Scene of Crime Examination. United Kingdom Accreditation Service, Feltham.

[10] In the United States not all forensic science providers which undertake DNA profiling are accredited to the FBI QAS standard. Only those that populate the National DNA database are required to be so. If, as seems the case, the DFS had not adopted the 2010 SWGDAM Guidelines for the interpretation of mixed DNA profiles then it could not have been accredited to the FBI QAS standard.

SECTION 6

Discipline-Specific Quality Management

6.1 INTRODUCTION

In this section Level 3 standards that constitute the quality standards framework for particular disciplines are examined. This section follows on from 3.4.6.

In this section a distinction is made between fields and disciplines. The reason for this distinction is exemplified by the field of document examination, which includes the disciplines of handwriting comparison and the chemical analysis of inks. These disciplines require very different skills and bodies of knowledge. Evidence of competence in one discipline is not evidence of competence in the other. A discipline is defined by a common set of competencies.

Before focusing on individual disciplines, some general characteristics of forensic science as a method of enquiry are highlighted.

As introduced in 1.2.2, among the processes at work in forensic science are identification, quantification, and classification[1]. These processes include two types of test: analytical and functional. These test types were also introduced in 1.2.2 and further developed in 3.3.2.2. Analytical tests identify and quantify, whereas functional tests compare and classify. Disciplines that mainly rely on functional tests are feature-comparison disciplines and, as such, can be separated from the others that mainly rely on analytical tests. As stated in 1.2.2 analytical tests are more appropriately accredited to the standard ISO/IEC 17025 and functional tests, which are an inspection activity, to ISO/IEC 17020[2].

In functional testing, questioned material is examined and compared to known or reference material. As discussed later in 6.3.1, the order of examination and comparison affects the reliability of the result, and early exposure to the reference material introduces the risk of cognitive bias. The purpose of the comparison is generally to determine the degree of resemblance between the questioned and the reference material and consider whether or not they originate from a common source; i.e. classification. Comparisons may also be made between two or more items to determine whether one item is the source of the other, or whether an observed effect arose in a particular way.

[1] These processes will contribute, in some measure, to every forensic science output. However, in each discipline one will take precedence.

[2] As reported in ##, accreditation bodies will accredit forensic inspection bodies undertaking analytical testing to the relevant parts of ISO/IEC 17025 as an extension ion to the scope of ISO/IEC 17020.

Quality Management in Forensic Science
ISBN 978-0-12-805416-1, https://doi.org/10.1016/B978-0-12-805416-1.00006-2

Feature-comparison disciplines can be further classified according to whether or not test results obtained and conclusions drawn are supported by analytical instrumentation. Those that rely on analytical instrumentation include:

- DNA profiling using capillary electrophoresis,
- measuring the refractive index (RI) and density of glass, and
- chemical profiling of drugs.

Those feature-comparison disciplines that are not supported by analytical instrumentation include:

- fingerprints,
- handwriting,
- toolmarks,
- hair, and
- physical fit.

From the point of view of quality management, DNA-based evidence is in a class of its own. As discussed at length in 4.4, DNA has set standards for all other fields and disciplines. Therefore, quality management in relation to DNA evidence will be considered first.

As stated above, DNA profiling is essentially a feature-comparison discipline. Comparison between questioned and reference profiles, or types, is at the heart of the discipline and conclusions drawn rely on, to some extent, professional judgment. However, it is also one of the most scientifically based disciplines as the comparison is based on analytical test results to a degree which sets it apart from other feature-comparison disciplines. In addition, results are expressed probabilistically, often as a likelihood ratio. The likelihood ratio approach to the evaluation of evidence is a means of presenting evidence that is widely endorsed as reported in 3.4.2.4.

To emphasize the relationship between DNA and other feature-comparison disciplines, those other disciplines are consider next, followed by; the extensive discipline of forensic chemistry, other applications of biology, and finally crime scene examination. The structure of this section is therefore as follows:

- DNA
- Other feature-comparison disciplines
- Forensic Chemistry
- Forensic Biology
- Scene examination

Although the quality of forensic science should be the same everywhere, quality standards frameworks are, to some extent, jurisdiction/region specific. This variation is another factor that works against standardization and harmonization within forensic science and thwarts attempts to shape forensic science as a body of knowledge and method of enquiry in its own right.

The regions considered here are, in alphabetical order:

- Australasia
- Europe
- United Kingdom/England and Wales (E&W)
- United States of America (US)

The quality standards framework that applies to disciplines in these regions will serve as a proxy for other regions.

As part of this introduction, the quality standards framework for each region will be introduced followed by a discussion of specific disciplines. Where warranted, the standards framework for the region is listed in a table.

6.1.1 Discipline-Specific Quality Management in Australasia

As explained in 2.6, the main forensic science providers in both Australia and New Zealand are part of ANZFEC (Australia and New Zealand Forensic Executive Committee). ANZFEC funds and oversees the National Institute of Forensic Science (NIFS), which exercises standards development roles, among others. NIFS is a directorate of ANZPAA (Australia and New Zealand Policing Advisory Agency) and as such NIFS is answerable to the ANZPAA board. In this arrangement forensic science provision in Australia and New Zealand (NZ) may be considered coherent, certainly from the perspective of law enforcement. A further common feature is that Australasian forensic science providers accredit feature-comparison activities to the standard ISO/IEC 17025 and have specifically rejected ISO/IEC 17020 (ANZPAA NIFS, 2016).

What distinguishes forensic science provision in Australia and NZ is that Australian providers are accredited by NATA (National Association of Testing Authorities) and in NZ the main provider, ESR (Institute of Environmental Science and Research), is accredited by the US accrediting body ANAB (ANSI-ASQ National Accreditation Board).

As both accredit to the standard ISO/IEC 17025, there should be no substantive difference. However, there is in fact a major difference. As discussed in 3.4.3.3, ANAB publishes supplementary Accreditation Requirements for forensic science providers. ESR must conform to these supplementary requirements. In addition, for specific disciplines, standards approved by the US OSAC (Organization of Scientific Area Committees) discussed in 2.7 or the earlier Scientific Working Groups might apply. In contrast, Standards Australia (SA), mentioned in 2.2.4.2.5, has published the standard AS5388:2012 "Forensic Analysis," introduced in 3.4.2. NATA has agreed to assess conformance of providers to this standard as an extension to scope of ISO/IEC 17025. Providers must also be accredited to ISO/IEC 17025 (or ISO/IEC 17020) as this Level 3 standard does not include the competence of the organization or individual within its scope.

As discussed in 3.4.2.1, AS5388 is a detailed standard applying to the forensic science process, from crime scene to court. It is intended to be a "core" standard from which discipline-specific standards might be developed. However, the scope of this standard already includes feature-comparison disciplines and most are referred to in the text. Furthermore, in this work AS5388 is considered a Level 3 standard, see 3.4. AS5388 therefore provides the Australian standards framework for many of the disciplines discussed in this section.

It should be noted that AS5388 is the basis for the development by ISO Technical Committee 272 of ISO standard 21043−1 to 5. This development is discussed in Section 7.

Another distinguishing feature of the quality standards landscape in Australia is that individuals engaged in fingerprint, firearms/tool mark examination and crime scene examination are "accredited" or, in this work, certified as competent by the Australasian[3] Forensic Field Science Accreditation Board (AFFSAB), as discussed in 2.3 and 3.4.4.5.1. At the time of writing [December 2017] the requirements for certification were under revision. The requirements are documented in 'Policy and Processes For Certification'.

Although AS5388, like ISO/IEC 17025, is a standard to which organizations are accredited and the AFFSAB standard applies to individuals, there is an overlap between these standards, which, presumably, will be resolved as AS5388 is developed into an ISO standard and the AFFSAB standard is revised.

Therefore, the quality standards framework in Australia comprises accreditation by NATA to ISO/IEC 17025, and AS5388 when requested, for all forensic scientific disciplines, and the certification of individuals by AFFSAB for crime scene, fingerprints, and firearm examination.

Australian forensic science providers accredited to ISO/IEC 17025 must rely on AS5388:2012 "Forensic Analysis" to provide the framework for all feature-comparison disciplines.

At the time of writing [December 2017] the NZ forensic science provider ESR is accredited to the standard ISO/IEC 17025 by the US body ANAB. Therefore, ESR must meet all but the jurisdictionally specific requirements of ANAB that are specified in the documents listed in the US Standards' Framework Table for each discipline, e.g., Table 6.6 for DNA, together with ANAB's supplemental Accreditation Requirements, recorded in 3.4.3.3.

6.1.2 Disciplined Specific Quality Management in Europe Table 6.1

Discipline-specific standards are developed by Working Groups and published by ENFSI (European Network of Forensic Science Institutes).

[3] Despite the name the standard only applies in Australia.

Table 6.1 General Standards Framework: Europe

Title	Body	Year	Ref
Guideline for evaluative reporting in forensic science	ENFSI	2015	
Guidance on the conduct of proficiency tests and collaborative exercises within ENFSI	ENFSI	2014	QCC-PT-001
Guidelines for the Single Laboratory Validation of Instrumental and Human Based Methods in Forensic Science	ENFSI	2013	QCC-VAL-002
Guidance for the management of computers and software in laboratories with reference to ISO/IEC 17025:2005[a]	EUROLAB	2006	TR 2/2006

ENFSI—European Network of Forensic Science Institutes.
[a]This applies to an earlier edition of ISO/IEC 17025.

6.1.3 Discipline Specific Quality Management in the UK/E&W Table 6.2

At the time of writing [December 2017], and for the foreseeable future, the quality standards framework in the UK/E&W is provided by the Forensic Science Regulator's general Codes of Practice and Conduct with appendices for some of the higher impact disciplines and guidance documents. The main requirement of the codes being conformance to ISO/IEC 17025 for laboratory-based activities involving analtytical testing or ISO/IEC 17020 for crime scene activities involving inspection, as appropriate.

It should be noted that the United Kingdom is in fact three separate jurisdictions; E&W, Scotland, and Northern Ireland. Part of the Regulator's standards framework applies only in E&W.

As reported in 2.4.4, forensic science providers in Scotland and Northern Ireland have voluntarily agreed to be bound by the Regulator's Codes in so far as they apply to the jurisdiction in which the provider operates.

As an aid the UK standards framework applying to forensic science providers is set out in Table 6.2 with those that are accepted by providers throughout the United Kingdom in bold and those applying only in E&W in the lighter text. When appropriate, forensic science providers are incorporating the Regulator's standards into their own documented QM system.

6.1.4 United States

As reported in 2.7, OSAC is populating a register of discipline-specific standards. These standards are adopted by the OSAC from the SWGs (Specialist Working Groups) and

Table 6.2 Discipline Specific Quality Management in England and Wales (E&W) and the United Kingdom (UK) General Standards Framework

Title	Body	Year	Ref
Legal Obligations	FSR	2017	FSR-I-400
Codes of Practice and Conduct for Forensic Science Providers and Practitioners in the Criminal Justice System	FSR	2016	
Cognitive bias effects relevant to forensic science examinations	FSR	2015	FSI-G-217
Criminal Procedure Rules Part 19	Ministry of Justice	2015	
Validation	FSR	2014	FSI-G-201
Criminal Practice Directions: Amendment No. 2	Judiciary E&W	2014	EWCA Crim 1596
Guide Booklet for Experts	ACPO/CPS	2010	
The Criminal Procedure and Investigations Act 1996 as amended by the Criminal Justice Act 2003	UK Parliament	2003	

ACPO—Association of Chief Police Officers [of E&W]; *CPS*—Crown Prosecution Service [of E&W]; *E&W*—England & Wales; *FSR*—Forensic Science Regulator.

ASTM International. Standards selected are submitted to standards development organizations (SDOs) for development. The main SDO, which was established for this purpose, is the American Academy of Forensic Science (AAFS) Standards Board (ASB). If OSAC approves the standard it is listed in a registry of approved standards.

OSAC maintains a catalog of relevant external discipline-specific standards it recognizes but has not yet [December 2017] been approved. The catalog is a useful source of information for many discipline-specific standards. It is available as an excel spreadsheet (NIST 2017a). Many of the standards discussed in here are listed in the OSAC catalog.

As will become clear, many standards developed by US SWGs find application in other regions; either alone, in support of or in conjunction with the standards of that region. The replacement of the SWGs with SACs (Scientific Area Committees) and their subcommittees, graphically depicted in Fig. 2.2, and the process of populating the OSAC registry mean that the overall US quality standards framework is in a state of development at the time of writing [December 2017]. It may be that standards that currently apply, such as those published by SWGs and ASTM International, will be significantly revised before they are registered by OSAC. In any event, it will be some time, maybe years, before the current quality standards framework has been revised and the register populated. In the meantime the current SWG and ASTM Intrenational standards apply with the risk that they may not be fit-for-purpose.

6.2 DNA

Given its importance in the development of quality management in forensic science, this evidence type has been extensively covered in 4.4. The quality standards framework will be detailed here.

It should be recognized that DNA evidence can be obtained from the following sources:

- the cell nucleus (nDNA), as autosomal profiles,
- the Y chromosome only (Y-STR)—the male line of inheritance; and
- the mitochondria of cells (mitochondrial DNA, mtDNA), as sequences—linking child and mother.

In Y-STR profiling, DNA from the male Y chromosome alone is profiled and therefore the discriminating power of this techniques is far less than when profiles are obtained from multiple chromosomes. DNA evidence is reported probabilistically and often evaluated using a likelihood ratio approach, discussed in 3.4.2.4. Typical Y-STR likelihood ratios are often of the order of 10^2 (hundreds). In contrast profiling DNA from multiple chromosomes yields likelihood ratios much greater than 10^6 (millions).

Y-STR profiling is employed when the sample is expected to contain both male and female DNA, and the male DNA is expected to be a minor component.

In a cell there are numerous mitochondria but only one nucleus. Therefore, mtDNA potentially offers more starting or template DNA than nuclear DNA. However, mitochondrial DNA is only passed from mother to child, whereas in nuclear DNA profiles of both parents are represented.

The detail of DNA profiling is highly technical. The general process is given in Fig. 6.1. The actual process will depend on the kit/technology employed and the source of the DNA profiled.

Because of the sensitivity of methods there is high risk of contamination. Robust measures must be in place to reduce, if not eliminate, this risk.

It is fair to say that at the time of writing [December 2017] a standards framework applying to the deconvolution of mixed DNA profiles using a process known as probabilistic genotyping, introduced in 4.4.4, is not yet mature.

6.2.1 Australasia Table 6.3

As explained in 6.1, laboratory-based forensic science providers in Australia accredited to ISO/IEC 17025 additionally rely on one comprehensive standard that applies to all the major disciplines including DNA typing, AS5388. However, there is an additional standard relevant to DNA typing and that is AS5483—2006 "Minimizing the risk of

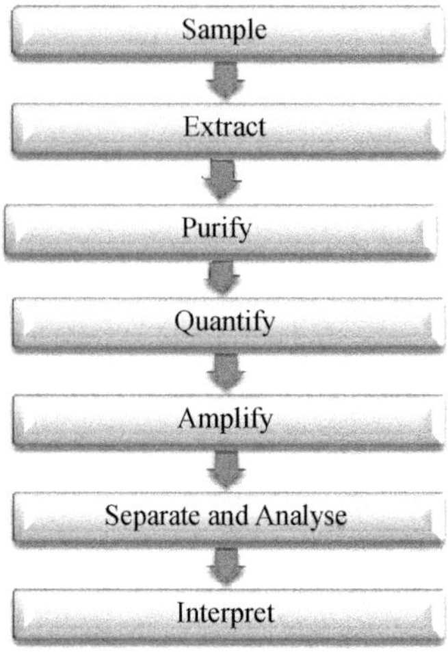

Figure 6.1 Typical DNA Sample Processing (Actual process will be kit/technology dependent).

Table 6.3 Australasian Standards Framework: DNA

Title	Body	Year	Ref
Minimizing the risk of human DNA contamination in products used to collect, store and analyze biological material for forensic purposes—Requirements	ISO	2016	ISO 18385
Minimizing the risk of contamination in products used to collect and analyse biological for forensic DNA purposes	AS	–	AS5483

contamination in products used to collect and analyze biological materials for forensic DNA purposes." This standard is now an ISO standard. Both are listed in Table 6.3.

The quality standards framework applying to data included in the various state and NDNADs (national DNA databases) in Australasia is unclear. It seems there are no requirements beyond accreditation to ISO/IEC 17025.

It should be noted that although part of ANZFEC, discussed in 2.6, ESR, the NZ, provider is accredited by ANAB and therefore it must meet all but the jurisdictionally specific requirements of ANAB, which are specified in the documents listed in Table 6.6 US. In addition ANAB's supplementary Accreditation Requirements will apply.

6.2.2 Europe Table 6.4

The European standards framework for DNA profiling includes requirements set by the Council of the European Union in its decision 2008/616/JHA, which aims to ensure the comparability of DNA data and facilitate the cross-border comparison of profiles. Among the requirements is conformance to ISO/IEC 17025. The effect of this Council decision is that all providers must be accredited to ISO/IEC 17025 for producing DNA data that are to be loaded onto a national database. Most of the other standards have been prepared by the ENFSI DNA Expert Working Group and are published by ENFSI.

6.2.3 UK/E&W Table 6.5

The standards published by the Forensic Science Regulator and which apply to UK forensic science providers are listed in Table 6.5.

In addition, only providers accredited to ISO/IEC 17025 by UKAS (UK Accreditation Service) are authorized by the NDNAD Strategy Board to load DNA data onto the NDNAD. The Strategy Board also authorizes DNA test kits for use.

Table 6.4 European Standards' Framework: DNA

Title	Body	Year	Reference
DNA-database management. Review and Recommendations	ENFSI	2016	DNA Working Group
Best Practice Manual for DNA Pattern Recognition and Comparison	ENFSI	2015	ENFSI-BPM-DNA-01
Concept Training Document	ENFSI	2010	DNA Working Group
Contamination prevention guidelines	ENFSI	2010	DNA Working Group
Recommended Minimum Criteria for the Validation of Various Aspects of the DNA Profiling Process	ENFSI	2010	DNA Working Group 001
Contamination prevention guidelines	ENFSI	2010	DNA Working Group 001
Stepping up of cross-border cooperation—exchange of DNA data	EU Council	2008	2008/616/JHA
Recommendations on the interpretation of mixtures	FSI	2006	160(2–3)90-101
Method of Software Validation	NORDTEST	2003	NT TR 535

ENFSI—European Network of Forensic Science Institutes; *EU* Council—Council of the European Union; *FSI*—Forensic Science International; *NORDTEST*—A Nordic standards development body.

Table 6.5 UK Standards' Framework: DNA

Title	Body	Year	Reference
Crime scene DNA: anticontamination guidance	FSR	2016	FSR-G-206
Legal Obligations (Section 10)	FSR	2016	FSR-I-400
Laboratory DNA: anticontamination guidance	FSR	2015	FSR-G-208
Allele frequency databases and reporting guidance for the DNA-17 profiling	FSR	2014	FSR-G-213
DNA analysis: codes of practice and conduct	FSR	2014	FSR-C-108
DNA contamination detection	FSR	2014	FSR-P-302
Interpreting DNA evidence	FSR	2012	FSR-G-202

FSR—Forensic Science Regulator.

6.2.4 US Table 6.6

At the time of writing [December 2017], the Scientific Working Group on DNA Analysis Methods (SWGDAM) is in effect the SDO for the discipline both in the United States and worldwide. It monitors developments in the field and recommends revision to the FBI's Quality Assurance Standards for DNA Analysis to which all contributors to the US NDNAD must be accredited. Conformance is a statutory requirement of the Federal DNA Identification Act. SWGDAM also publishes its own guidelines, which should be conformed to by forensic science providers wishing to demonstrate competence in DNA typing. The principle group within SWGDAM for drafting revisions is the Quality Assurance Committee.

As reported earlier in 6.1 and in 2.2.4.2.2, the AAFS has established its own SDO, the AAFS Standards Board. This body has recently [December 2017] published a draft standard developed by the Biology/DNA Interpretation and Reporting subcommittee of OSAC. The draft is entitled "Standards for Validation Studies of DNA Mixtures, and Development and Verification of a Laboratory's Mixture Interpretation Protocol."

6.3 FEATURE-COMPARISON DISCIPLINES

6.3.1 Introduction

There are a wide range of evidence types that fall to this category. The list of the major ones is given earlier in 6.1. A more complete list is given below. The list should also include DNA, but this is dealt with separately in 6.2 above.

- Bite marks
- Bloodstain Patterns

Table 6.6 US Standards Framework: DNA

Title	Body	Year	Reference
Standards for Validation Studies of DNA Mixtures, and Development and Verification of a Laboratory's Mixture Interpretation Protocol (in draft)	ASB	2017	ASB 020
ISO/IEC 17025:2005 Forensic Science Testing Laboratories Accreditation Requirements[a]	ANAB	2017	AR 3028
ISO/IEC 17020:2012 Forensic Inspection Bodies Accreditation Requirements	ANAB	2017	AR 3055
Interpretation Guidelines for Autosomal STR Typing by Forensic DNA Testing Laboratories	SWGDAM	2017	–
Validation Guidelines for DNA Analysis Methods	SWGDAM	2016	–
Guidelines for STR Enhanced Detection Methods	SWGDAM	2014	–
Quality Assurance Standards for Forensic DNA Testing Laboratories	FBI	2011	–
An Update: The Evaluation of Forensic DNA Evidence.	NRC	1996	–

ANAB—ANSI-ASQ National Accreditation Board; *ASB*—American Academy of Forensic Sciences (AAFS) Standards Board; *FBI*—Federal Bureau of Investigation; *NRC*—National Research Council of the US National Academy of Sciences; *SWGDAM*—Scientific Working Group on DNA Analysis Methods.
[a]This document is based on the earlier edition of ISO/IEC 17025 and will require significant revision to take account of ISO 17025:2018.

- Fabrics
- Fibers
- Fingerprints
- Firearms and ammunition—spent and unspent
- Foot wear
- Glass
- Hair
- Handwriting
- Inks/Paints
- Papers
- Plant material
- Soil

- Tire marks
- Toolmarks

Not all feature-comparison evidence types will be considered. Those that are will stand as proxies for those omitted.

Feature-comparison is essentially an inspection activity, for the most part, relying on functional testing. As explained in 3.2.3, such disciplines should be accredited to ISO/IEC 17020.

The generic comparison procedure complying with good practice will include the following steps:

1. Characterization of the questioned material and assessment of suitability
2. Characterization of the reference material
3. Comparison
4. Conclusion
5. Blind verification with conflict resolution if needed
6. Probabilistic/Evaluative reporting

The aim of comparison being classification involving the stepwise reduction in the size of the class to which the questioned material belongs. This process resulting in either exclusion from the class to which the reference material belongs or inclusion, the degree of resemblance being such that the questioned material belongs to the same class as the reference material and, ideally, the size of that class is one. In which case, the conclusion can be drawn that the questioned and reference material are from the same source.

6.3.1.1 Individualization

As stated in 1.2.2, individualization, i.e., attributing the source of the questioned material to that of the reference material excluding all others, is a rejected concept in forensic science. Feature-comparison should rely on the frequency of occurrence of features, and conclusions should be expressed probabilistically. Unfortunately, at the time of writing [December 2017] that is not generally the case in the practice of these disciplines and the reluctance to accept a probabilistic approach, and the attachment to individualization continues (Jayaprakash, 2013; Biedermann and Taroni, 2013; Cole, 2014). Therefore, this remains a problem area in the practice of forensic science and one in which those with regulatory authority could take a lead. The latest annex to the Codes of Practice and Conduct of the Forensic Science Regulator on fingerprint examination, listed in Table 6.8, is silent on this issue and in effect supports categorical reporting, e.g., match/no match/inconclusive and individualization.

A probabilistic approach to the evaluation of feature-comparison evidence requires a body of relevant research. In simple terms, the distinctive features of the material in question need to be established and the frequency of their occurrence in the relevant population need to be determined. Knowing, or having an estimate of, the frequency of occurrence of distinguishing features allows the degree of resemblance between questioned and reference materials to be evaluated probabilistically. The lack of this foundational research is a major weakness of feature-comparison disciplines, apart that is from DNA typing, and was identified in the 2009 NRC Report (NRC, 2009). The call for foundational research was repeated in the recent PCAST (President's Council of Advisors on Science and Technology) report (PCAST, 2016). In addition to strengthening the evidence type as a whole, such research would allow evidential weight to be attached to what are now inconclusive results and enable probabilities to be reported in the place of possibilities. It seems that, certainly in the case of fingerprints, OSAC recognizes the need and the fact that with such research the discipline will become less subjective and more scientific (OSAC, 2015). The lack of foundational research is the result of examiners from the earliest days of the discipline believing that categorical opinions sufficed and that with relevant training and experience a comparison between the questioned and reference materials could result in an accurate classification, in some cases with 100% certainty.

6.3.1.2 Categorical Opinions

Categorical opinions will be discussed further in Section 7, but at this juncture it is important to draw attention to the relevant issues. Categorical opinions, e.g., match/no match/ inconclusive, rely on consideration of the likelihood of a common source given the degree of resemblance observed between the questioned and reference material. This is not in accord with logic or good practice, which demands the consideration of the likelihood of the degree of resemblance observed, given a common source and comparing that to the likelihood of the degree of resemblance observed, given different source. As explained in 3.4.2.4 this is the likelihood ratio and expressed mathematically as:

$$LR = \frac{pE|Hp}{pE|Hd}$$

There are databases for some of the evidence types considered in this section. A list is maintained by NIST, the US National Institute of Standards and Technology (NIST 2017b). The population of these databases might be considered to constitute foundational research. However, the quality of the data populating the databases is uncertain and most are intended to be used as investigational tools, e.g., to narrow searches and identify candidates for further examination, rather than for evaluating evidence.

6.3.1.3 Cognitive Bias

When conducting subjective comparisons between questioned and reference, or known, materials the questioned material should be examined and characterized before observing the reference material. To do otherwise risks cognitive bias. This order is part of what is termed "sequential unmasking" in the literature where it finds academic support (Krane et al., 2008; Dror et al., 2015). However, in many feature-comparison disciplines, the documented procedure and/or the practice is to conduct steps 1–3 simultaneously or start with step 2, characterization of the reference material, with the risk of cognitive bias. Therefore, the best assurance of the quality of the reported result is a blind review by an equally competent examiner untainted by domain-irrelevant information and unaware of the original result. Ideally, the verifying examiner should not even know the identity of the original examiner lest peer pressure biases the verification. However, such an arrangement may be impracticable.

6.3.1.4 Subgroups

Classifying feature-comparison disciplines into subgroups is difficult. One distinguishing feature is the degree to which inspection and professional judgment are relied on. Handwriting comparisons rely largely on inspection and professional judgment with ISO/IEC 17020 as the appropriate standard. In contrast paint comparison relies on instrumental methods of analysis and the statistical analysis of data, and less on professional judgment for the purpose of source attribution with ISO/IEC 17025 as the appropriate standard.

As discussed earlier and in 1.2.2, the concept of individualization has been rejected in forensic science. When offering an opinion as to source, the opinion should be given probabilistically; likelihood of a "match" given the degree of resemblance observed; and not categorically.

This leads to the major distinction between DNA and the other feature-comparison disciplines; DNA evidence is presented probabilistically, and with the rejection of "individualization", this has driven progress toward the probabilistic delivery of evidence in the other feature-comparison disciplines.

In all the text that follows, the quality standards framework that applies to each discipline will be described by tabulating the components and, where they occur, highlighting departures from what is generally considered to be good practice as outlined above.

Feature-comparison disciplines not relying on analytical instrumentation will be discussed first, followed by bloodstain pattern analysis (BPA). Feature-comparison disciplines relying on analytical instrument such as paint and glass are discussed in 6.4.2.

6.3.2 Feature-Comparison Disciplines Not Relying on Analytical Instrumentation

6.3.2.1 Introduction

In these disciplines the examiner is the instrument, the tests are functional and the most apporriate standard ISO/IEC 17020. As with all disciplines, a test result is obtained by an individual following a test method. The quality of the test result, as always, is dependent on the competence of the organization, the competence of the individual, and the validity of the method. With methods that produce a quantitative result the quality of the test result is given by the measurement uncertainty, introduced in 1.4.6, which gives the range in which the true result is believed to lie. For qualitative results, such as those provided by feature-comparison disciplines not relying on analytical instrumentation, what might be a measure of quality? There has been much debate about error rates, in particular prompted by the recent PCAST report (PCAST, 2016). It would seem that the knowledge that when a fingerprint examiner declares a "match" and there is an *x*% chance that the result is false would help the fact finder evaluate the fingerprint evidence. The argument against this approach is threefold. Proficiency test (PT) results for individual examiners are not a proper basis for a measure of quality. For forensic science providers accredited to either ISO/IEC 17025 or 17020, poor performance of an individual calls into question the competence of the organization, which must ensure that personnel have the necessary competence. Where the method/instrument is separated from the examiner, it would be true that all PTs truly measured are the competence of the organization in terms of staff selection, training, and development. Secondly, it is the validation study determining the performance of the method, which provides a measure of quality not the performance of the individual. The difficulty is that in feature-comparison disciplines not relying on instrumentation the examiner is the instrument, and so aggregated PT results for many competent examiners in different organizations and across time may have a role in determining quality. Thirdly, and most importantly, error rates as a measure of quality has been rejected by most if not all forensic scientists (Morrison et al., 2017). The most rational and logical means of expressing the quality of a result is to report a likelihood ratio. This approach is mentioned earlier and discussed in 3.4.2.4 and again in Section 7. In this approach the frequency of occurrence of certain features is acquired through research, and the examiner reports a likelihood ratio, in terms of the degree of resemblance observed is *x* times more likely if the question and reference materials have the same source rather than some other explanation for the resemblance observed.

6.3.2.2 Fingerprint Examination[4]

The development of fingerprint examination has suffered from being a discipline mainly practiced by skilled examiners rather than scientists. The discipline was developed in a law enforcement environment and, even today, it is conducted mostly by law enforcement agents or within a law enforcement environment. The results are highly subjective and based on a common-sense approach. The claim to individualization, i.e., identification to the exclusion of all others (Champod, 2015), which, at one time, seemed to have been rejected by examiners has not according to Simon Cole (Cole, 2014). The discipline lacks scientific rigor. There are as yet no data to support probabilistic conclusions. In addition, there is no agreed standard as to the degree of resemblance between questioned and

[4] The examination of fingerprints is also called friction ridge examination and dactyloscopy. In this work these terms are synonymous.

reference prints required for a "match". However, the ease of acquisition and the potential probative power of this evidence type has enabled practitioners and the standards applied to gloss over these foundational issues.

An additional weakness is that, in practice, the first step is often to compare the questioned print with those held on a database, and this is achieved using pattern recognition software. So, the process can begin with the examiner considering a positive result obtained using an automated fingerprint identification system with the unavoidable risk of cognitive bias.

The ease of acquisition and potential probative power of fingerprint comparisons as an evidence type have resulted in a particular focus on this evidence type by academics, mathematicians, and logically rigorous scientists. These factors, and various miscarriages of justice, also explain the extensive standards framework that now applies to this evidence type.

Regarding the procedure, fingerprint examiners rely on three levels of detail in characterizing prints:

Level 1 detail: overall pattern and aggregate ridge flow

Level 2 detail: individual ridge paths and ridge characteristics

Level 3 detail: individual ridge unit shapes and pores

Effective bias avoidance measures must be in place. Good practice requires the full characterization of the questioned material and recording features of significance before examining the reference material. The examination should be verified[5] by a competent examiner blinded to the result obtained and ideally the identity of the first examiner.

Unfortunately, at the time of writing [December 2017], the standard operating procedure (SOP) analysis, comparison, evaluation, and verification usually abbreviated as ACE-V does not incorporate all those measures. It should be noted that although documented sequentially the sequence is rarely followed in practice (Forensic Science Regultor, 2017), at least not in the United Kingdom.

There are regional variations in the ACE-V process. In the United Kingdom the Forensic Science Regulator does not require the questioned materials to be characterized before examining the reference material, nor is there a requirement for blind verification. In Europe ENFSI recognizes the different types of verification listed below but recommends blind verification and a documented conflict resolution policy:

- Blind—using ACE but blind to the original result,
- Open—using ACE and knowing the original result, and
- Critical Finding check—reviews the work of the first examiner using ACE.

ENFSI requires characterization of the questioned material prior to comparison with reference materials.

[5] In this context, "verification" means repeating the examination.

In the United States, SWGFAST (Scientific Working Group on Friction Ridge Analysis, Study and Technology) requires questioned materials to be characterized and documented prior to comparison with the reference material. There is no requirement for blind verification.

Regarding reporting, fingerprint results are mostly reported as categorical opinions, e.g., "match," "no match," or "inconclusive," with the consequent weakness discussed earlier and in Section 7. However, the recently created OSAC Friction Ridge Subcommittee has recognized the need for further research on the process of fingerprint examination in an effort to increase the objectivity of the evidence type and move to probabilistic reporting (NIST 2017c). Increasing objectivity will improve the overall reliability of the evidence type, and probabilistic reporting will increase its value by attaching evidential weight to otherwise inconclusive examinations.

6.3.2.2.1 Australasia

In Australia, there is no publically available description of ACE-V or an alternative SOP. In Australia fingerprint examiners are certified as competent by the AFFSAB and organizations by NATA, which assesses conformance to ISO/IEC 17025 and AS5388 where appropriate. Although using the term "accreditation" as applied to individuals is appropriate, in this work the convention followed is that organizations are accredited and individuals are certified.

As discussed in 2.3 the AFFSAB also regulates other forensic inspection activities (firearms/toolmarks and crime scene examination). The AFFSAB is managed by the NIFS, which is introduced in 2.6.

At the time of writing [December 2017] the documented requirements for obtaining and maintaining certification, contained in 'Policy and Processes For Certification', were under revision.

6.3.2.2.2 Europe Table 6.7

As with DNA, the European standards framework for fingerprints includes requirements set by the Council of the European Union in its decision 2008/616/JHA, which aims to ensure the comparability of fingerprint data (images) and facilitate cross-border cooperation.

6.3.2.2.3 UK Table 6.8

In the United Kingdom, fingerprint examination is accredited to ISO/IEC 17025, or at least that is the assumption in the Regulator's Codes. This is at odds with the emerging consensus that fingerprint examination, in common with all feature-comparison techniques, is an inspection activity mainly relying on comparison and professional judgment, and therefore more appropriately accredited to ISO/IEC 17020. However, it is clear that accreditation bodies are willing to accredit this activity to ISO/IEC 17025.

Table 6.7 European Standards' Framework: Fingerprints

Title	Body	Year	Ref
Best Practice Manual for Fingerprint Examination[a]	ENFSI	2015	ENFSI-BPM–FIN–01
Fingermark Visualisation Manual	HOCAST	2014	ISBN 9718782462347
Standard for the Documentation of Analysis, Comparison, Evaluation, and Verification (ACE-V) (Latent)	SWGFAST	2009	#8
Stepping up of cross-border cooperation—exchange of dactyloscopic[b] data	EU Council	2008	2008/616/JHA

EU Council—Council of the European Union; *HOCAST*—Home Office[c] Centre for Applied Science and Technology; *OSAC*—Organization of Scientific Area Committees; *SWGFAST*—Scientific Working Group of Friction Ridge Analysis, Study and Technology, now the OSAC Friction Ridge Subcommittee (FRS).

[a]In this document mandatory requirements are indicated by the word "must" rather than "shall". It includes brief SOPs and glossary.

[b]Fingerprint images.

[c]The Home Office is the UK police ministry.

Table 6.8 UK Standards' Framework: Fingerprints

Title	Body	Year	Ref
Code of practice and conduct—fingerprint comparison[a]	FSR	2017	FSR-C-128
Codes of Practice and Conduct—Fingerprint visualisation and imaging	FSR	2017	FSR-C-127
Legal Obligations (Section 10)	FSR	2016	FSR-I-400
Fingerprint Examination—Terminology, Definitions and Acronyms	FSR	2015	FSR-I-402

[a]This standard requires conformance to ISO/IEC 17025 and not ISO/IEC 17020. As discussed in 7.3.1, fingerprint examination is an inspection activity and therefore more appropriately accredited to ISO/IEC 17020.

Standards applying to the capture and sharing of biometric fingerprint data are absent and are not referenced in the standards listed.

6.3.2.2.4 US Table 6.9

The standards framework relates as much to the capture and exchange of biometric data gleaned from fingerprints as to the practice of fingerprint examination. Both types of standards are listed in the table for completeness. The extent of the framework is a reflection of the forensic utility of fingerprints and the long history of use. The direct relationship between forensic utility and the extent of the standards framework is further supported by the limited framework for hair comparison resulting from the declining forensic utility of that evidence type which is discussed later in 6.3.2.4.

Table 6.9 US Standards' Framework: Fingerprints

Title	Body	Year	Ref
Information Technology—Biometric Data Interchange Format—Part 2: Finger Minutiae Data	ISO	2011	ISO/IEC 19794-2
Information Technology—Biometric Data Interchange Format—Part 4: Finger Image Data	ISO	2011	ISO/IEC 19794-4
Information Technology—Biometrics—Tenprint Capture Using Biometric Application Programming Interface (BioAPI)	ISO	2009	ISO/IEC 29141
American National Standard for Information Systems—Data Format for the Interchange of Fingerprint, Facial & Other Biometric Information—Part II	ANSI/NIST	2008	ANSI/NIST-ITL 1-2008
American National Standard for Information Systems—Data Format for the Interchange of Fingerprint, Facial & Other Biometric Information—Part I	ANSI/NIST	2007	ANSI/NIST-ITL 1-2007
Information Technology—Biometric Data Interchange Format—Part 3: Finger Spectral Data	ISO	2006	ISO/IEC 19794-3
Extended Feature Set Profile Specification	NIJ/NIST		NIST SP 1134
Markup Instructions for Extended Friction Ridge Features	NIJ/NIST		NIST SP 1151
Latent Interoperability Transmission Specification	NIJ/NIST		NIST SP 1152
Writing Guidelines for Requests for Proposals for Automated Fingerprint Identification Systems	NIJ/NIST		NIST SP 1155
Writing Guidelines to Develop a Memorandum of Understanding for Interoperable Automated Fingerprint Identification Systems	NIJ/NIST		NIST SP 1156
Guideline for the Articulation of the Decision-Making Process for the Individualization in Friction Ridge Examination (Latent/Tenprint)	SWGFAST		
Individualization/Identification Position Statement (Latent/Tenprint)	SWGFAST		

Continued

Table 6.9 US Standards' Framework: Fingerprints—cont'd

Title	Body	Year	Ref
Latent to Latent Examinations (Latent) Position Statement	SWGFAST		
Limited Examination Considerations for Latent Print Sections (Latent) Position Statement	SWGFAST		
Position Statement on the Role of AFIS Ranks and Scores and the ACE-V Process	SWGFAST		
Recommendations for Competency Testing of Noncertified Latent Print Examiners (Latent) Position Statement	SWGFAST		
Recommendations for Research	SWGFAST		
Standard for a Quality Assurance Program in Friction Ridge Examinations (Latent/Tenprint)	SWGFAST		
Standard for Consultation (Latent/Tenprint)	SWGFAST		
Standard for Friction Ridge Automation Training (Latent/Tenprint)	SWGFAST		
Standard for Friction Ridge Comparison Proficiency Testing Program (Latent/Tenprint)	SWGFAST		
Standard for Friction Ridge Impression Digital Imaging (Latent/Tenprint)	SWGFAST		
Standard for Reporting Friction Ridge Examinations (Latent/Tenprint)	SWGFAST		
Standard for Simultaneous Impression Examination (Latent)	SWGFAST		
Standard for the Application of Blind Verification of Friction Ridge Examinations (Latent/Tenprint)	SWGFAST		
Standard for the Definition and Measurement of Rates of Errors and Inappropriate Decisions in Friction Ridge Examination (Latent/Tenprint)	SWGFAST		
Standard for the Documentation of Analysis, Comparison, Evaluation and Verification (ACE-V) (Latent)	SWGFAST		

Table 6.9 US Standards' Framework: Fingerprints—cont'd

Title	Body	Year	Ref
Standard for the Documentation of Analysis, Comparison, Evaluation and Verification (ACE-V) in Tenprint Operations (Tenprint)	SWGFAST		
Standard for the Review of Testimony of Friction Ridge Examiners (Latent/Tenprint)	SWGFAST		
Standard for the Technical Review of Friction Ridge Examinations (Latent/Tenprint)	SWGFAST		
Standard for the Validation and Performance Review of Friction Ridge Impression Development and Examination Techniques (Latent/Tenprint)	SWGFAST		
Standard Terminology of Friction Ridge Examination (Latent/Tenprint)	SWGFAST		
Standards for Examining Friction Ridge Impressions and Resulting Conclusions (Latent/Tenprint)	SWGFAST		
Standards for Examining Friction Ridge Impressions and Resulting Conclusions (Latent/Tenprint)—Section 5.3.2.3 ONLY	SWGFAST		
Standards for Minimum Qualifications and Training to Competency for Friction Ridge Examiner Trainees (Latent/Tenprint)	SWGFAST		
Uniform Automated Fingerprint Identification System (AFIS) Feature Symbols Position Statement (Latent/Tenprint)	SWGFAST		

SWGFAST—Scientific Working Group on Friction Ridge Analysis, Study and Technology.

It should be noted that SWGFAST operations came to a close in 2014 with the transfer of all documents to the OSAC Friction Ridge Subcommittee of the Physics/Pattern Recognition SAC.

Existing SWGFAST standards and guidelines remain in effect until new OSAC documents are published. With the exception of SWGDAM this statement is true for all SWGs.

6.3.2.3 Handwriting

Document examiners (those who conduct handwriting comparisons) usually report categorically[6], in common with most other feature-comparison disciplines but with a greater number of categories than the "match/no match/inconclusive" of other disciplines. The terms used appear probabilistic but there are no objective data in support and no numerical equivalent can be given.

The categories representing different amounts of subjective belief as to authorship are given below; the questioned and reference material is:

+4 of common authorship (author of the reference material wrote the questioned material)
+3 high (strong) probability of common authorship
+2 probably of common authorship
+1 indications of (evidence to suggest)
0 inconclusive
−1 indications of no common authorship
−2 probably
−3 high probability
−4 not of common authorship (author of the reference material did not write the questioned material)

The numbers have been added to emphasize the fact that this is a nine-point scale with four positive and four negative opinions with an inconclusive category.

Most standards warn that an opinion of "common authorship" does not equate to certainty and should not be taken as such by fact finders. This is in contrast to fingerprint examination where individualization is claimed and "matches" supporting opinions of absolute certainty.

As mentioned, despite the terms used there are, as yet, no data to support probabilistic conclusions that can be reached in handwriting comparisons. In addition, there is no agreed standard as to the degree of resemblance between questioned and reference materials required to determine common authorship. However, with the digital technology and computing power available today it may be possible to populate databases with handwriting features. Some progress in this direction has already been made.

The Forensic Information System for Handwriting, which is a database maintained by the US Secret Service, enables document examiners to scan and digitize text writings such as threatening notes. By a series of plotted arithmetic and geometric values, searches are made on images in the database, producing a list of probable matches.

Closed databases also exist, such as the "Frequency Occurrence of Handwriting and Hand-Printing Characteristics" database. This particular database exists in the form of

[6] As discussed later in the section, a probabilistic approach is available.

two Microsoft Access Spreadsheets, one for cursive writing and the other for printed writing. The spreadsheets are in the possession of Tom Vastrick, Ellen Schuetzner, Heather Burske, Mark Johnson, and Michele Boulanger.

In Australia researchers at La Trobe University have published what amounts to a standard for handwriting examination, which, according to ANZPAA NIFS, has been adopted by all Australasian providers (Bird and Found, 2016). The standard includes the evaluation of evidence using a likelihood ratio approach, discussed in 3.4.2.4, which is probabilistic and fundamentally different from the categorical opinions usually offered and described earlier. As reported earlier in 6.3.1.2, categorical opinions consider the likelihood of common authorship given the degree of resemblance observed where logic and good practice demand the consideration of the likelihood of the degree of resemblance observed given common authorship and given different authorship, termed in this work the likelihood ratio approach to the evaluation of evidence.

6.3.2.3.1 Australasia

In Australia, the examination and comparisons of handwriting lies within the scope of AS5388 adopted by laboratory-based providers accredited to ISO/IEC 17025.

In addition the Modular Method, pioneered at the University of La Trobe and referred to earlier in this section (Bird and Found, 2016), is available. In this approach there is no requirement to characterize the questioned material before examining the reference material. In addition, blind verification or review is not among the provisions. Thus, the approach does not conform to good practice.

The NZ Police are accredited to ISO/IEC 17025 by ANAB. ANAB's supplementary Accreditation Requirements will apply, as may the US standards listed in Table 6.10.

6.3.2.3.2 Europe

The only published standard is the BPM (Best Practice Manual) for the Forensic Examination of Handwriting ENFSI-BPM-FHX-01 2015. A high-level description of the BPM procedure is depicted in Fig. 6.2. Generally there is no requirement to fully characterize questioned material before comparison with reference material. One of the early steps is an assessment of both the questioned and reference writing for suitability. Reviews are open. Critical findings must be checked, but verification is not required unless the checker disagrees with the examiner.

The document lacks sufficient procedural detail. This permits variation in method and interpretation, which is far from a standardized approach and may be the result of the lack of a harmonized approach to handwriting examination and comparison among ENFSI members.

Examiner competence is acquired through training and experience and assessed by proficiency tests and casework review. This is the case for most, if not all, feature comparison examiners.

6.3.2.3.3 UK/E&W

The Forensic Science Regulator has yet to publish an appendix to the Codes of Practice and Conduct, and at the time of writing [December 2017], there are publicly available plans to do so.

The potential for cognitive bias is recognized in the Guidance on Cognitive Bias Effects listed in Table 6.2.

6.3.2.3.4 US Table 6.10

The Scientific Association of Forensic Examiners procedure requires characterization of the questioned material before examining the reference material.

Table 6.10 US Standards' Framework: Handwriting

Title	Body	Year	Ref
Reporting Opinions Standard for Handwriting Examination	SAFE	2016	2016–12
Guide for Examination of Handwritten and Hand-Printed Materials	SAFE	2016	—
Guide for Taking Request Writing	SAFE	2016	—
Guide for Writing a Forensic Handwriting Examination Report	SAFE	2016	—
Scope of Work of Forensic Document Examiners	SAFE	2016	—
Standard Terminology for Expressing Conclusions of Forensic Document Examiners (withdrawn[a] 2017, no replacement)	ASTM	—	E1658-08
Standard Terminology Relating to the Examination Questioned Documents	ASTM	—	E2195-09
Standard Guide for Examination of Handwritten Items (withdrawn 2016, no replacement)	ASTM	—	E2290-07
Standard Guide for Examination of Altered Documents (withdrawn 2013, no replacement)	ASTM	—	E2331-04
Standard Guide for Minimum Training Requirements for Forensic Document Examiners	ASTM	—	E2388-11

SAFE—Scientific Association of Forensic Examiners.
[a]Withdrawn in January 2017 in accordance with Section 10.6.3 of the Regulations Governing ASTM Technical Committees, which requires that standards shall be updated by the end of the eighth year since the last approval date.

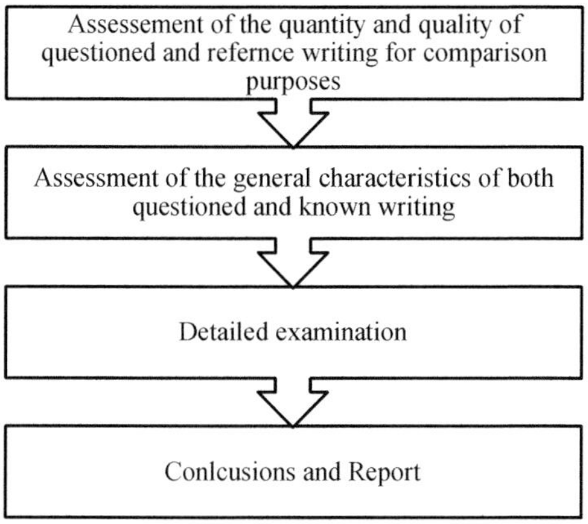

Figure 6.2 European Network of Forensic Science Institutes handwriting examination procedure.

SWG standards remain in force until replaced by standards approved by OSAC and placed on the OSAC register.

The reason given by ASTM International for withdrawal of some of the standards listed is that the standards have not been updated in the specified time. ASTM International sates that withdrawal is in accordance with Section 10.6.3 of the Regulations Governing ASTM Technical Committees, which requires standards to be updated by the end of the eighth year since the last approval date.

6.3.2.4 Toolmarks (Includes Firearms/Ammunition) Comparison Microscopy

A toolmark examination is a comparative study to determine whether or not a striated or impressed mark was produced by a particular tool. The underlying mechanism for the origination of toolmarks is that when a harder object (the tool) comes in contact with a softer object (work piece), the harder object will impart its marks or features on the softer object. In the case of the marks imparted to ammunition, the gun is considered a tool. Hence, the discipline of toolmark comparison is often included within the field of firearms examination.

6.3.2.4.1 Australasia

In Australia the examination and comparisons of toolmarks lies within the scope of AS5388 adopted by laboratory-based providers accredited to ISO/IEC 17025.

Examiners who conduct tool mark comparisons that lie within the field of firearms examination may be certified as competent by the AFFSAB according the requirements to be set out in the revised "Policy and Processes For Certification" which, as mentioned earlier and discussed in 3.4.4.5.1, is currently [December 2017] under revision.

The certification of crime scene examiners by the AFFSAB is refereed to later in 6.6.

As mentioned earlier, despite its name the AFFSAB does not operate in NZ (New Zealand). There are no NZ standards publically available.

6.3.2.4.2 Europe

ENFSI has published no BPM or other guidance. There are no standards publically available.

6.3.2.4.3 UK/E&W

The Forensic Science Regulator has yet to publish an appendix to the Codes of Practice and Conduct and, at the time of writing [2017], has no plans to do so.

The potential for cognitive bias is recognized in the Guidance on Cognitive Bias Effects listed in Table 6.2.

6.3.2.4.4 US Table 6.11

The SWGGUN (Scientific Working Group for Firearms and Toolmarks) standards tabulated are available in the ATFE (Association of Firearms and Toolmark Examiners) Admissibility Resource Kit (ATFE, 2017).

As with other SWGs, in 2013 the federal government withdrew funding and its functions were incorporated into the OSAC FA/TM (Firearm and Toolmarks) subcommittee of the Physics/Pattern Interpretation SAC. The standards listed in Table 6.11 are from the OSAC FA/TM webpage. Links to all the standards listed in Table 6.11 can be found on the OSAC FA/TM webpage.

SWGGUN standards remain in force until replaced by standards approved and placed on the OSAC register.

According to the AFTE:

> *The examination process used in Toolmark Identification is similar to those used in the other comparative disciplines in forensic science. This process begins with a study of the most general characteristics (class) of items to be compared, progressing through (subclass) to the analysis and comparison to the most specific characteristics (individual).*

There is no requirement to characterize the questioned material first. Toolmarks can be deemed unsuitable for examination. Comparisons between questioned and reference material are made side-by-side. The ATFE "Range of Conclusions" are "identification" that seems to be the equivalent of "consistent with" allowing the mark to be consistent with having been made with other tools, so, some way short of identification in the sense of individualization. However, this position appears to be contradicted in "The foundations of Firearm and Toolmark Identification" document, which claims that an opinion of "common source" is possible. The other two categories in the range are "inconclusive" and "elimination."

6.3.2.5 Hair

The comparison of hair is a highly specialized and detailed discipline and, as the FBI stresses, is not a part-time activity (FBI and Oien, 2009). Hair comparison is handicapped by the fact that different people can share the same microscopic characteristics and hairs

Table 6.11 US Standards' Framework: Toolmarks

Title	Body	Year	Ref
Code of Ethics	SWGGUN	2013	–
Guidelines for the Documentation of the Examination of Tools and Toolmarks	SWGGUN	2013	–
Guidelines for the Documentation of the Examination of Ammunition and Ammunition Components	SWGGUN	2013	–
The Foundations of Firearms and Toolmark Identification	SWGGUN	2013	–
Guidelines for the Documentation of Firearm Examinations	SWGGUN	2012	–
Guidelines: Criteria for Identification	SWGGUN	2012	–
Recommended Guidelines for Developing a Training Manual	SWGGUN	2012	–
Code of Ethics	AFTE	2009	–
Quality Assurance Guidelines	SWGGUN	2009	–
Transition from ASCLD/LAB Legacy to ISO/IEC 17025	SWGGUN	2009	–
Guidelines for the Standardization of Comparison Documentation	SWGGUN	2008	–
Minimum Qualifications for Experienced Firearm and Toolmark Examiners	SWGGUN	2006	–
Minimum Qualifications for Firearm and Toolmark Examiner Trainees	SWGGUN	2006	–
Conclusion Scales	SWGGUN	–	–
Elimination Factors Related FA/TM[a] Examinations	SWGGUN	–	–
Glossary	SWGGUN	–	–
Systemic Requirements for the Forensic Firearms and Toolmark Laboratory	SWGGUN	–	–

SWGGUN—Scientific Working Group for Firearms and Toolmarks. In 2013 SWGGUN was replaced by the OSAC Firearms and Toolmarks Subcommittee. The AFTE (Association of Firearm and Toolmark Examiners) has documented some standards, e.g., a glossary and a "range of conclusions"; neither are publicly available.
[a]Firearm/Toolmark.

from the same source can vary to the extent of being declared from different sources. Richard Saferstein has concluded:

> *The course of events is clear: microscopic hair comparison must be regarded by police and courts as presumptive in nature, and all positive microscopic hair comparisons must be confirmed by DNA determinations.*
>
> ***Saferstein (2015a)***

With the advent of being able to obtain both mitochondrial and nuclear DNA evidence from hair (Ottens et al., 2013) together with the heavy investment of resources necessary to establish and maintain a capability, hair comparison is in decline.

The limited standards framework for hair comparisons may be a symptom of, or even a contributor to, the poor reputation for quality this evidence type has recently gained as evidenced by the FBI's acknowledgement of overstating the strength of evidence prior to 2000 (Hsu, 2015), the recent PCAST report (PCAST, 2016), and the recent addendum (PCAST, 2017). The discipline may not survive.

6.3.2.5.1 Australasia

Hair comparison lies within the scope of AS5388 for laboratories accredited to ISO/IEC 17025.

In NZ, ESR is accredited to ISO/IEC 17025 for the physical determination and comparison of hair using comparative microscopy.

6.3.2.5.2 Europe

The Textile and Hair Group has published a BPM entitled "The Microscopic Examination and Comparison of Human and Animal Hair," ENFSI-BPM-THG-03 Nov 2015. It is based on US SWGMAT (SWG for Materials Analysis) standards. Significant features are listed in the document.

6.3.2.5.3 UK/E&W

The Forensic Science Regulator has yet to publish an appendix to the Codes of Practice and Conduct and, at the time of writing [December 2017], there are no published plans to do so.

The potential for cognitive bias in this discipline is recognized in the Guidance on Cognitive Bias Effects listed in Table 6.2.

6.3.2.5.4 US Table 6.12

The listed document entitled "Forensic Hair Comparison: Background Information for Interpretation" makes clear the weaknesses of this evidence type. It also mandates conformance to the SWGMAT guidelines, also listed.

SWGMAT standards remain in force until replaced by standards approved and placed on the OSAC register.

6.3.3 Bloodstain Pattern Analysis (BPA)

In BPA, examinations are carried out to determine whether or not an observed effect could have arisen in a particular way. Functional testing may involve experimental simulations under controlled conditions being compared with patterns observed at the scene. Therefore, BPA is a comparison technique.

In contrast to those feature-comparison disciplines discussed in 6.3.2, BPA requires the use of instrumentation and the making of measurements. It involves the classification, identification, and/or interpretation and evaluation of bloodstain patterns at scenes and in

Table 6.12 US Standards' Framework: Hair

Title	Body	Year	Ref
Forensic Hair Comparison: Background Information for Interpretation	FBI	2009	FSC 2009 11.2
Forensic Human Hair Examination Guidelines	SWGMAT	2005	–
Forensic Human Hair Training Guidelines	SWGMAT	–	–

FBI—US Federal Bureau of Investigation; *FSC*—Forensic Science Communications, published by the FBI; *SWGMAT*—Scientific Working Group for Materials Analysis.

the laboratory. The aim is to determine the sequence of events that resulted in the pattern observed.

The discipline relies on observation, measurement, trigonometry, and some understanding of the laws of physics. BPA is often aided by computer modeling and simulation in determining what happened and when at the scene of violent crimes. Types of information provided include: direction, angle, location, and movement. BPA is therefore an inspection activity aided by instrumentation. The overall activity is most appropriately accredited to ISO/IEC 17020 with the supporting measurement activities accredited to ISO/IEC 17025 as an extension to scope.

6.3.3.1 Australasia

In Australia, BPA lies within the scope of AS5388 for laboratories accredited to ISO/IEC 17025.

In NZ, ESR provides a service accredited to ISO/IEC 17025 by ANAB. Therefore, ANAB supplementary Accreditation Requirements, introduced and detailed in 3.4.2.3, apply and also, presumably, the US SWGSTAIN (SWG in Bloodstain Pattern Analysis) standards framework specified below and listed in Table 6.14 (US).

6.3.3.2 Europe

There are no documented BPA-specific standards publically available. However, given European participation in SWGSTAIN the standards of that organization may apply. They are listed in Table 6.14.

6.3.3.3 E&W/UK Table 6.13

The Regulator's annex to the Codes of Practice and Conduct appendix for BPA relies to a certain extent on SWGSTAIN standards.

In common with all of the Regulator's standards, the annex is intended to be incorporated into the provider's quality management system from the date of publication.

Table 6.13 Standards Framework: BPA

Title	Body	Year	Ref
Codes of practice and Conduct: Bloodstain Pattern Analysis	FSR	2015	FSR-C-102
Bibliography	SWGSTAIN	2012	–
Recommended terminology	SWGSTAIN	2009	–
Guidelines for the Minimum Educational and Training Requirements for Bloodstain Pattern Analysts	SWGSTAIN	2008	–

SWGSTAIN—US Scientific Working Group on Bloodstain Pattern Analysis (BPA).

6.3.3.4 US Table 6.14

SWGSTAIN comprised BPA experts from North America, Australia, NZ, and Europe. SWGSTAIN served as a professional forum in which practitioners in BPA and related fields discussed and evaluated methods, techniques, protocols, quality assurance, education, and research. In common with most other SWGs the work of this group has been transferred to OSAC. Responsibility for standards now rests with the BPA subcommittee of the Physics/Pattern Interpretation SAC. The SWGSTAIN standards remain in effect until the OSAC registers applicable standards.

6.4 FORENSIC CHEMISTRY

6.4.1 Introduction

This is a very broad field. Many disciplines including, for example, DNA profiling and fingerprint visualization rely on the science of chemistry. It includes some comparison disciplines such as chemical profiling, which rely heavily on analytical chemistry and mathematics to make the comparisons and consider the question of source. However, the major application of forensic chemistry is in the identification and quantitation of illicit substances mainly drugs. The term drug refers to illicit psychoactive substances.

6.4.2 Comparison/Classification

6.4.2.1 Chemical Profiling

The chemical characterization of evidential materials and chemometrics[7] can be used to compare and assess the likelihood of a common source.

[7] Chemometrics is the application of mathematical methods to the solution of chemical problems, such as source attribution. The computing power now available allows the statistical analysis of large amounts of multivariate data.

Table 6.14 US Standards' Framework: BPA

Title	Body	Year	Ref
Guidelines for Proficiency Testing in Bloodstain Pattern Analysis	SWGSTAIN	2010	–
Guidelines for Report Writing in Bloodstain Pattern Analysis	SWGSTAIN	2010	QA.DOC4
Guidelines for Developing Standard Operating Procedures for Bloodstain Pattern Analysis Appendix	SWGSTAIN	2009	–
Recommended Terminology	SWGSTAIN	2009	–
Guidelines for the Minimum Education and Training Requirements For Bloodstain Pattern Analysts	SWGSTAIN	2008	–
Guidelines for a Quality Assurance Program in Bloodstain Pattern Analysis	SWGSTAIN	–	–
Guidelines for the Validation of New Procedures in Bloodstain Pattern Analysis	SWGSTAIN	–	–

SWGSTAIN—Scientific Working Group on Blood StainPattern Analysis (BPA). Replaced by the OSAC BPA Subcommittee which is part of the Physics/Pattern Interpretation Scientific Area Committee.

Perhaps the most extensive forensic application of chemical profiling has been in the area of drugs analysis. Heroin has been profiled in terms of composition, impurities, and trace elements and isotopic abundance (UNODC, 2005). The chemical profiling of drugs is discussed later in 6.4.3.1.

6.4.2.2 Fibers: Examination and Comparison

Like hair, fiber examination is a forensic discipline in decline (Coyle, 2015) and more rapidly as DNA-associated evidence is unlikely to be available. Again like hair, it is a highly specialized discipline requiring dedicated and experienced practitioners. It is therefore a costly capability to maintain and the sensitivity of DNA analysis has reduced demand.

Fig 6.3 makes clear the complexity of this evidence type and the variety of fibers that exist.

Recovery can be by a variety of means including lifting with adhesive tapes, hand picking, and vacuum sampling. It used to be a major evidence type linking people and objects in the overall process of incident reconstruction. Comparison is made by microscope and instrumental methods based on spectroscopy are employed.

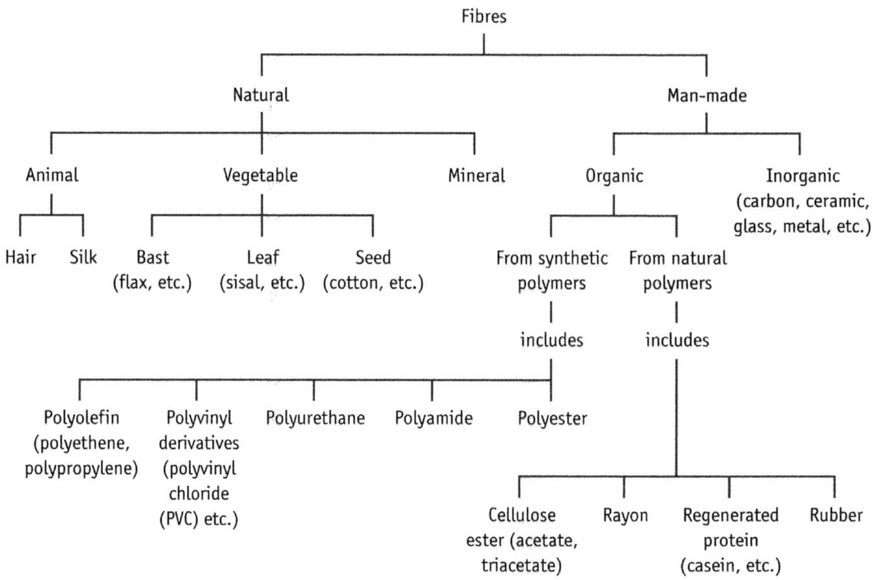

Figure 6.3 Complexity of fiber evidence. *(© Dr. Andrew Jackson & Dr. Julie Jackson, Fig 3.1 in Forensic Science 3rd Edition, Pearson Education Limited, reproduced with permission)*

Characteristics include the cross-sectional shape, dye, chemical composition; the latter two are determined using spectrophotometric[8] techniques.

The reliance on chemical analysis places this discipline within the field of forensic chemistry and is most appropriately accredited to ISO/IEC 17025 with comparison accredited to ISO/IEC 17020 as an extension to scope.

6.4.2.2.1 Australasia

In Australia, the comparison of fibers lies within the scope of AS5388 for ISO/IEC 17025 accredited laboratories.

In NZ, ESR provides a service accredited to ISO/IEC 17025 by ANAB. Therefore, ANAB supplemental Accreditation Requirements, introduced and detailed in 3.4.3.3, apply and also, presumably, the SWGMAT standards framework is described below and listed in Table 6.15 [US].

6.4.2.2.2 Europe

The ENFSI Textile and Hair Group has not published any standards or guidance documents.

[8] In spectrophotometry the interaction of light of various wavelengths, from ultraviolet to infrared, with the sample is measured. The wavelength and intensity of the reflected, absorbed or transmitted light are functions of the chemical composition of the fiber.

6.4.2.2.3 UK/E&W

The Forensic Science Regulator has yet to publish an appendix to the Codes of Practice and Conduct and, at the time of writing [2017], there are no published plans to do so.

6.4.2.2.4 US Table 6.15

As with other Scientific Working Groups Federal support for SWGMAT was withdrawn in 2013 and this discipline is now overseen by the Materials (Trace) subcommittee of the Chemistry/Instrumental Analysis SAC. Candidate standards and those under development by the SAC are listed at the SAC website (NIST 2017d).

Table 6.15 US Standards' Framework: Fibers

Title	Body	Year	Ref
Standard Terminology Related To Textiles	ASTM	2017	D123
Fabric and Cordage Examinations	SWGMAT	2015	–
Forensic Fiber Examination Guidelines	SWGMAT	2015	–
Infrared Analysis in Fiber Examinations	SWGMAT	2015	–
Standard Guide for Forensic Examination of Non-reactive Dyes in Textile Fibers by Thin-Layer Chromatography	ASTM	2013	E2227
Standard Guide for Forensic Analysis of Fibers by Infrared Spectroscopy	ASTM/ SWGMAT	2010	E2224
Standard Guide for Forensic Examination of Fabrics and Cordage	ASTM/ SWGMAT	2010	E2225
Standard Guide for Microscopic Examination of Textile Fibres	ASTM/ SWGMAT	2010	E2228
A Forensic Fiber Examiner Training Program	SWGMAT	2004	–
Trace Evidence Recovery Guidelines	SWGMAT	1999	–
Fiber Analysis for Investigative Leads	SWGMAT	–	–
UV-VIS Analysis in Fiber Examinations	SWGMAT	–	–

SWGMAT—Scientific Working Group for Materials Analysis—Fiber Subgroup. Note: At the time of writing [2017] SWGMAT Standards are hosted on the ASTEE (American Society of Trace Evidence Examiners) Website (ASTEE, 2017). accessed 2017-Sep-25 - http://www.asteetrace.org/

SWGMAT standards remain in force until replaced by standards approved and placed on the OSAC register.

6.4.2.3 Glass

Glass fragments are often created in the commission of a crime or other incident under investigation, e.g., a window or a container might have been broken.

In glass examination it is often the case that the questioned glass is recovered from clothing or other items associated with a suspect and reference glass recovered from the scene. The object of the examination in this discipline is to distinguish between fragments.

This approach, which is also shared with paint examination, of actively seeking differences rather than similarities raises again the issue of different standards for exculpatory and inculpatory evidence mentioned in 4.4.2. It does seem that the law accepts a lower standard for exculpatory evidence. As noted, this is an issue of interest that needs exploring but is beyond the scope of this work.

The examination of glass begins with two measurements: refractive index (RI) and density.

Glass RI measurement using GRIM[9] must meet the requirements of metrological traceability and measurement uncertainty, as explained in 1.4.6 and 1.4.7.1.

The reliance on instrumental techniques reduces the reliance on subjective judgment and the statistical analyses available to the examiner make this a highly scientific, objective, and therefore reliable evidence type Provided, of course, that the methods are valid and, ideally, fall within the scope of accreditation, which should be to ISO/IEC 17025.

However, as glass is a mass produced material, individual glass items do not possess characteristics or properties that would permit anything more than the broadest of classifications. Therefore, in the absence of any distinguishing features, the highest degree of association reported between questioned and reference materials is "indistinguishable" or "could be"; a possibility.

Compositional analysis often follows the measurements. The most common technique is X-ray spectroscopy using an instrument combining a scanning electron microscope (SEM), which produces the incident radiation that generates X-rays characteristic of changes induced in the atom of a molecule, and an energy dispersive X-ray spectroscope (EDS) that detects the X-rays emitted from the atom. The combined instrument is abbreviated as SEM-EDS (or EDX). This instrument will provide a profile of the major and minor elements present in glass, such as sodium, magnesium, silicon, aluminum, potassium, calcium, and sometimes boron or lead. However, major and minor elemental profiles lack discriminating power as these elements are present in many glasses. Standard methods exist for profiling trace elements using laser ablation—inductively coupled

[9] A commercial off-the-shelf instrument.

plasma–mass spectrometry abbreviated as LA-ICP-MS[10] or micro X-ray fluorescence (μ-XRF)[11]. Trace element profiling is usually sufficient to discriminate between glasses from different sources.

The reason SEM-EDS is used at all is that many forensic science laboratories will possess such instruments for other uses such as gunshot residue analysis for which, as explained earlier/later in 6.4.3.5, it is ideally suited.

Glass examiners usually report categorically and, as mentioned earlier, a positive report is that the questioned and reference materials "could have" a common source. Examiners do not usually offer a stronger positive opinion unless the questioned and known materials correspond in density, RI, and elemental profile and, most importantly, fit physically.

Less frequently used is classification relying chemometrics using the analytical and measurement data. With the availability of multivariate data from LA-ICP-MS and μ-XRF and computing power, a likelihood ratio approach to evaluation is possible. However, using a likelihood ratio approach to evaluate multivariate data is still in development (van Es et al., 2017).

Glass databases exist but do not seem to be supported by a quality standards framework; if so, evidential value would be weakened. However, the database is seen more as an investigational tool, to narrow the range that might be under consideration, rather than for the evaluation of evidence.

6.4.2.3.1 Australasia

In NZ ESR is accredited to ISO/IEC 17025 for the physical and chemical examination of glass. The service includes the measurement of RI.

The service is accredited by ANAB. Therefore, ANAB Accreditation Requirements, introduced and detailed in 3.4.2.3, apply and also, presumably, the applicable SWGMAT standards framework is described below and listed in Table 6.16 (US).

In Australia the examination of glass lies within the scope of AS5388 for provider's accredited to ISO/IEC 17025.

6.4.2.3.2 Europe

Despite the forensic utility of glass, the existence of an Expert Working Group, and the large body of research underpinning the evidence type, ENFSI publishes no discipline-specific standards.

[10] In LA-ICP-MS a laser vaporizes a small amount of the glass, the vapor is ionized in the plasma and the ions separated in the mass analyzer. The ions detected are characteristic of the glass.

[11] In μ-XRF a narrow beam of X-rays interacts with the sample and the resultant fluorescence is characteristic of the glass.

6.4.2.3.3 UK/E&W

The Regulator has published no annex to the Codes of Practice for this discipline and there are no published plans to do so.

6.4.2.3.4 US Table 6.16

In common with most other SWG, SWGMAT ceased to be federally supported in 2013 and responsibility for the discipline has been passed to the Materials (Trace) Subcommittee of the Chemistry/Instrumental Analysis SAC.

SWGMAT standards remain in force until replaced by standards approved and placed on the OSAC register.

Table 6.16 US Standards' Framework: Glass

Title	Body	Year	Ref
Standard Test Method for Forensic Comparison of Glass Using Micro X-ray Fluorescence Spectrometry	ASTM	2017	E2926
Standard Test Method for Determination of Trace Elements in Soda-Lime Glass Samples Using Laser Ablation Inductively Coupled Plasma Mass Spectrometry for Forensic Comparisons	ASTM	2016	E2927
Standard Test Method for Determination of Concentrations of Elements in Glass Samples Using Inductively Coupled Plasma Mass Spectrometry (ICP-MS) for Forensic Comparisons	ASTM	2012	E2330
Standard Test Method for the Automated Determination of Refractive Index of Glass Samples Using the Oil Immersion Method and a Phase Contrast Microscope	ASTM	2011	E1967
Forensic Glass Comparison: Background Information Used in Data Interpretation	SWGMAT	2009	FSC 2009 11.2
Collection, Handling, and Identification of Glass	SWGMAT	2005	FSC 2005 7.1

Table 6.16 US Standards' Framework: Glass—cont'd

Title	Body	Year	Ref
Elemental Analysis of Glass	SWGMAT	2004	—
Glass Density Determination	SWGMAT	2004	—
Glass Fractures	SWGMAT	2004	—
Glass Refractive Index Determination	SWGMAT	2004	—
Initial Examinations of Glass	SWGMAT	2004	—
Introduction to Forensic Glass Examination	SWGMAT	2004	—
Forensic Glass Training Program	SWGMAT	—	—

FSC—Forensic Science Communications, published by the US Federal Bureau of Investigation; *SWGMAT*—Scientific Working Group for Materials Analysis.

At the time of writing [December 2017], ASTM E2926 has been approved by OSAC and has been placed on the register of approved standards. Other ASTM International standards are progressing toward approval.

6.4.2.4 Paint

The ubiquity of painted surfaces makes paint an important evidential material. It is generally considered to fall into one of three source categories: automotive, architectural, and maintenance.

Paint essentially comprises pigments, a binder and a solvent. The solvent evaporates as the paint dries. In reality it is a complex mixture of chemical components and paint coatings are often multilayered. Therefore, there are many characteristics that might serve to classify paints.

Given the wide variety of colors and shades available and the numbers of layers, paints can often be discriminated using these features alone. Therefore, examiners usually begin with a side by side visual examination using a microscope. As mentioned earlier in 6.3.1.3, by not characterizing the questioned paint first, examiners risk cognitive bias infecting the process.

The examination procedure is set out in the SWGMAT Forensic Paint Analysis and Comparison Guidelines and ASTM E1610 listed in Table 6.17 (US). The procedure includes physical examination and physical matching, color examination using microspectrophotometry[12], spectroscopic examination with infra red[13] and analysis of the binder by pyrolyzing[14] the sample, separation using gas chromatography[15] and detection using mass spectrometry[16].

[12] A technique that measures the color of paint.
[13] A technique that characterizes paint by its interaction with infrared radiation.
[14] Causing the thermal decomposition of paint by heating in the absence of oxygen.
[15] A means of separating components in the gas phase.
[16] A means of detecting components according to mass.

As with glass, the object of the examination is to distinguish between questioned and reference materials, bearing in mind that paint samples from the same source may differ. If, by the tests applied, no significant difference is found then the examiner concludes that the questioned and reference materials "could have shared a common origin". To be clear, this is just a possibility. However, some examiners when unable to distinguish between the number of layers and the color of each layer may strengthen the opinion. For example, where paints are indistinguishable by the number of layers, the sequence of layers, the color of each layer and analytically, some examiners may offer the opinion that the chance that the paints are from different sources are "extremely remote". It should be noted that this is a categorical opinion with the weaknesses set out in 6.3.1.2, and what "extremely" means is unclear.

The RCMP (Royal Canadian Mounted Police) host and maintain the PDQ (Paint Data Query) database, the largest international automotive paint database. Each paint layer is separated and placed between two diamonds for infrared analysis. Each component has a characteristic fingerprint in the infrared spectrum. The comparison of the infrared spectrum of each paint layer in a paint system to the spectra in the paint database allows the paint system to be identified by manufacturing plant.

RCMP PDQ is being used by forensic scientists in Canada, the United States, Australia, NZ, Singapore, United Arab Emirates, South Africa, and 19 European countries.

It does not seem that the database is supported by a quality standards framework. If so, then that would weaken its evidential value. However, the database is used more as an investigational tool, to narrow the range of vehicles that might be under consideration, rather than for the evaluation of evidence.

6.4.2.4.1 Australasia

In NZ, ESR is accredited to ISO/IEC 17025 for the physical and chemical examination of paint. The service is accredited by ANAB. Therefore, ANAB's supplementary Accreditation Requirements, introduced and detailed in 3.4.2.3, apply and also, presumably, the applicable SWGMAT standards framework is described below and listed in Table 6.17 [US].

In Australia the examination of paint falls within the scope of AS5388 for ISO/IEC 17025 accredited laboratories.

6.4.2.4.2 Europe

ENFSI has published no guidance for this discipline in English.

6.4.2.4.3 UK/E&W

The Regulator has published no annex to the Codes of Practice for this discipline and there are no published plans to do so.

6.4.2.4.4 US Table 6.17

As already mentioned, SWGMAT ceased to be federally supported in 2013 and responsibility for the discipline has been passed to the Materials (Trace) subcommittee of the Chemistry/Instrumental Analysis SAC. SWGMAT standards remain in force until replaced by approved standards on the OSAC register.

Table 6.17 US Quality Standards Framework: Paint

Title	Body	Year	Ref
Standard Guide for Forensic Paint Analysis and Comparison	ASTM/ SWGMAT	2014	E1610
Standard Test Method for Determination of Concentrations of Elements in Glass Samples Using Inductively Coupled Plasma Mass Spectrometry (ICP-MS) for Forensic Comparisons	ASTM/ SWGMAT	2012	E2330
Standard Guide for Microspectrophotometry and Color Measurement in Forensic Paint Analysis	ASTM/ SWGMAT	2011	E2808
Standard Guide for Using Scanning Electron Microscopy/X-ray Spectrometry in Forensic Paint Examinations	ASTM/ SWGMAT	2013	E2937
Standard Guide for Using Scanning Electron Microscopy/X-ray Spectrometry in Forensic Paint Examinations	ASTM/ SWGMAT	2013	E2809
Forensic Paint Analysis and Comparison Guidelines	SWGMAT	2000	–
Forensic Paint Training Program	SWGMAT	2010	–
Standard Guide for Microspectrophotometry and Color Measurement in Forensic Paint Analysis	SWGMAT	2007	–

Continued

Table 6.17 US Quality Standards Framework: Paint—cont'd

Title	Body	Year	Ref
Standard Guide for using Infrared Spectroscopy in Forensic Paint Examinations	SWGMAT	2011	–
Standard Guide for Using Scanning Electron Microscopy/X-ray Spectrometry in Forensic Paint Examinations	SWGMAT	2002	–
Standard Guide for Using Pyrolysis Gas Chromatography 22 and Pyrolysis Gas Chromatography-Mass Spectrometry in Forensic Paint Examinations	SWGMAT	2014	–
Standard Terminology for Paint, Related Coatings, Materials and Applications	ASTM	2016	D16
Standard Practice for Specifying Color by the Munsell System	ASTM	2014	D1535
Standard Practice for Computing the Colors of Objects by Using the CIE[a] system	ASTM	2017	E308
Standard Practice for Receiving, Documenting, Storing and Retrieving Evidence in Forensic Science Laboratory	ASTM	2017	E1492

[a]Commission International de l'Eclairage (International Commission on Illumination). The CIE system links the human perception of color and the visible region of the electromagnetic spectrum. Numerical values are assigned to the red, green, and blue contributions to a particular color.

6.4.2.5 Tapes

This is very much a minor discipline. The US working group SWGMAT published standards and one ASTM standard are listed in Table 6.18. In Australia adhesive tape comparisons fall within the scope of AS5388.

6.4.3 Identification/Quantitation

6.4.3.1 The Analysis and Detection of Drugs/Controlled Substances/

This is by some margin the largest forensic science discipline relying on chemistry and that is reflected by the number of Level 3 standards applying in the United States and

Table 6.18 US Standards' Framework: Tapes

Title	Body	Year	Ref
Standard Guide for Using Pyrolysis Gas Chromatography and Pyrolysis Gas Chromatography/Mass Spectrometry in Forensic Tape Examinations	SWGMAT	2013	JASTEE 5.1
Guideline for Assessing Physical Characteristics in Forensic Tape Examinations Guideline	SWGMAT	2013	JASTEE 5.1
Guideline for Using Scanning Electron Microscopy/Energy Dispersive X-ray Spectroscopy in Forensic Tape Examinations	SWGMAT	2011	JASTEE 2.1
Guideline for Using Light Microscopy in Forensic Examinations of Tape Components	SWGMAT	2011	JASTEE 2.1
Guideline for Using Fourier Transform Infrared Spectroscopy in Forensic Tape Examinations	SWGMAT	2011	JASTEE 2.1
Guideline for Forensic Examination of Pressure Sensitive Tapes	SWGMAT	2011	JASTEE 2.1
Standard Guide for Using X-ray Fluorescence Spectrometry in Forensic Tape Examinations	SWGMAT	–	–
New Guide for Using Infrared Spectroscopy in Forensic Tape Examinations (under revision)	ASTM	–	WK50535

JASTEE—Journal of the American Society of Trace Evidence Examiners; *SWGMAT*—Scientific Working Group on Materials Analysis.

Europe (at the time of writing [December 2017] the United Kingdom is still part of the European Union). The most extensive quality standards framework is offered by the UNODC (United Nations Organization on Drugs and Crime).

The "war on drugs" is costly by any measure. According to Richard Saferstein more than 75% of the evidence evaluated in United States in crime laboratories is drugs related (Saferstein, 2015b). This is a function of illicit manufacturers making efforts to produce new products that do not contravene existing legislation and the number of offences that the detection of a drug might reveal:

- possession
- with intent to supply
- manufacture
- import/export
- being responsible for premises used for consumption or supply or production.

All these factors amount to a significant scientific challenge. Methods are needed to identify drugs and their precursors and also, in forensic medicine, their metabolites and to determine source and manufacturing process. The reliance on analytical testing is such that organizations providing drug analysis and detection should be accredited to ISO/IEC 17025. In the test methods employed, metrological traceability and uncertainty of measurement, introduced in 1.4.6 and 1.4.6.1, are particularly important. Lack of traceability or reporting a quantitative result without an uncertainly would render the reported result unreliable, if not meaningless.

This is a highly scientific field relying on complex and sophisticated instrumentation requiring scientific knowledge, skills, and experience particularly in analytical and synthetic chemistry. Therefore, the degree of technical competence required for both the organization and individuals is high with a significant risk of nonconformance with ISO/IEC 17025.

As novel materials will often be encountered in this discipline, having available valid methods will be a challenge. Therefore, flexible scope accreditation, discussed in 5.5, is recommended. Flexible scope accreditation should provide a sufficient quality standards framework to ensure the quality and therefore the reliability of quantitative and qualitative data derived from novel materials.

The components of the quality standards framework range widely, from recommended methods of analysis to guidance on the management a forensic science laboratory and include validation guidance and codes of conduct for individuals.

6.4.3.1.1 Australasia

As with other disciplines, the standard applying to this discipline in Australia is AS5388 for laboratories accredited to ISO/IEC 17025. The joint ENFSI/UNODC guide on representative sampling is referenced in AS5388. In addition to AS5388, AS/NZS4757 "Handling and destruction of drugs" provides a procedure for the seizure, handling, storage, disposal, and destruction of drugs and drug-related material for law enforcement purposes. AS/NZS4757 applies in both Australia and NZ.

In NZ, ESR is accredited to ISO/IEC 17025 by ANAB with flexible scope for quantitative and quantitative analyses of seized drugs. ESR is also accredited for the measurement of weight and volume with the requirements for metrolgiocal tracability and uncertainty of measurement introduced in 1.4 .6 and 1.4.6.1. ANAB's supplementary Accreditation Requirements will apply.

6.4.3.1.2 Europe Table 6.19

Standards are developed by the ENFSI Drugs Working Group and published by ENFSI. One standard is published jointly with UNODC.

6.4.3.1.3 UK/E&W

At the time of writing [December 2017] the Regulator has not published an annex to the Codes for this discipline.

6.4.3.1.4 US Table 6.20

In common with other SWGs, responsibility for the analysis and detection of seized drugs now rests with OSAC and the subcommittee on Seized Drugs part of the Chemistry/Instrumental Analysis SAC. Scientific Working Group for the Analysis of Seized Drugs

Table 6.19 European Standards' Framework: Drugs

Title	Body	Year	Ref
Guidelines on Representative Drug Sampling	ENFSI/ UNODC	—	—
Guidelines on Sampling of Illicit Drugs for Quantitative Analysis	ENFSI	2016	Drugs Working Group
Guidelines on the Use of Reference Materials in Forensic Drug Analysis	ENFSI	—	ENFSI/002
Hypergeometric Sampling Tool	ENFSI	—	—
Performance Based Standards for Forensic Science Practitioners	ENFSI	—	—
Validation and Implementation of Methods	ENFSI	—	—

ENFSI—European Network of Forensic Science Institutes; *UNODC*—United Nations Office on Drugs and Crime.

Table 6.20 US Standards' Framework: Drugs

Title	Body	Year	Ref
Recommendations Version 7.1	SWGDRUG	2016	–
• Part I—A Code of Professional Practice for Drug Analysts	SWGDRUG	2016	–
• Part II—Education and Training	SWGDRUG	2016	–
• Part III A—Methods of Analysis/Sampling Seized Drugs for Qualitative Analysis	SWGDRUG	2016	–
• Part III B—Methods of Analysis/Drug Identification	SWGDRUG	2016	–
• Part III C—Methods of Analysis/ Clandestine Laboratory Evidence	SWGDRUG	2016	–
• Part III D—Methods of Analysis/Analogue and Structural Class Determinations	SWGDRUG	2016	–
• Part IV A—Quality Assurance/General Practices	SWGDRUG	2016	–
• Part IV B—Quality Assurance/ Validation of Analytical Methods	SWGDRUG	2016	–
• Part IV C—Quality Assurance/ Uncertainty	SWGDRUG	2016	–
Supplemental Document SD-6[a] Examples of Measurement Uncertainty for Extrapolations of Net Weight and Unit Count	SWGDRUG	2016	–

Table 6.20 US Standards' Framework: Drugs—cont'd

Title	Body	Year	Ref
Standard Practice for Quality Assurance of Laboratories Performing Seized-Drug Analysis	ASTM	2015	E2327
Standard Practice for Identification of Seized Drugs[b]	ASTM	2014	E2329
Supplemental Document SD-4 For Part IV C Examples of Measurement Uncertainty for Purity Determinations	SWGDRUG	2013	–
Standard Guide for Analysis of Clandestine Drug Laboratory Evidence	ASTM	2012	E2882
Supplemental Document SD-5 For Part IV A Reporting Examples	SWGDRUG	2012	–
Supplemental Document SD-3 For Part IV C Examples of Measurement Uncertainty for Weight Determinations	SWGDRUG	2011	–
Standard Guide for Microcrystal Testing in the Forensic Analysis of Cocaine	ASTM	2011	E1968
Standard Guide for Microcrystal Testing in the Forensic Analysis of Phencyclidine and Its Analogues	ASTM	2011	E2125
Standard Guide for Sampling Seized Drugs for Qualitative and Quantitative Analysis	ASTM	2011	E2548

Continued

Table 6.20 US Standards' Framework: Drugs—cont'd

Title	Body	Year	Ref
Supplemental Document SD-1 For Part I A Code of Professional Practice for Drug Analysts	SWGDRUG	2006	–
Supplemental Document SD-2 For Part IV B Quality Assurance/ Validation of Analytical Methods	SWGDRUG	2006	–

SWGDRUG—Scientific Working Group for the Analysis of Seized Drugs.
[a]Apart from SD-6, the Supplemental Documents applied to earlier versions of the Recommendations Documents. They apply equally to the latest version, 7.1.
[b]At the time of writing [2017], this is under revision as ASTM WK53625.

standards will remain in existence until replaced by developed standards approved by OSAC and placed on the register of OSAC approved standards.

6.4.3.1.5 International Table 6.21A–C

The scale of the "war on drugs" is such that there are international standards development bodies, UNODC and IFSA (International Strategic Forensic Alliance), which have published standards for the identification and quantitation of drugs. The UNODC quality standards framework is so large that it is listed as three separate tables: that applying to seized drugs is a particularly a long list Tables 6.21A; 6.21B applies to the chemical profiling of seized drugs; 6.21.C applies to laboratory practice; and quality management, and 6.21.D applies to biological samples.

6.4.3.2 Toxicology

This subsection lists standards related to the analysis and detection of alcohol and drugs in biological samples. It does not include standards applying to postmortem/forensic medicine, which, as explained in the introduction, lies outside the scope of this work.

As this discipline relies heavily on analytical instrumentation, the providers should be accredited to ISO/IEC 17025 and test methods employed should lie within scope. Traceability and uncertainty will be important requirements for conformance.

6.4.3.2.1 Australasia

NATA (Australia) accredits some forensic science providers to ISO/IEC 17025 for "alcohol testing," "drugs in drivers," and "general toxicology". AS4760 "Procedures for specimen collection and the quantification of drugs in oral fluid" applies in Australia

Table 6.21.A International Standards Framework: Applying to Seized Materials

Title	Body	Year	Ref
Multilingual Dictionary of Narcotic Drugs and Psychotropic Substances Under International Control—Supplement	UNODC	2016	ST/NAR/1
Multilingual Dictionary of Narcotic Drugs and Psychotropic Substances Under International Control—Addendum	UNODC	2015	ST/NAR/1
Multilingual Dictionary of Precursors and Chemicals Frequently Used in the Illicit Manufacture of Narcotic Drugs and Psychotropic Substances Under International Control	UNODC	2015	ST/NAR/1A
Recommended methods for the Identification and Analysis of Synthetic Cathinones in Seized Materials	UNODC	2015	ST/NAR/49
Minimum Requirements for the Identification of Seized Drugs	IFSA	2014	MRD3
Recommended methods for the Identification and Analysis of Synthetic Cannabinoid Receptor Agonists in Seized Materials	UNODC	2013	ST/NAR/48
Recommended methods for the Identification and Analysis of Piperazines in Seized Materials	UNODC	2013	ST/NAR/47
Guidelines for the Safe Disposal of Chemicals Used in the Illicit Manufacture of Drugs	UNODC	2011	ST/NAR/36
Guidelines on Representative Drug Sampling	UNODC	2011	ST/NAR/38

Continued

Table 6.21.A International Standards Framework: Applying to Seized Materials—cont'd

Title	Body	Year	Ref
Recommended Methods for Testing Methaqualone/ Mecloqualone	UNODC	2010	ST/NAR/15
Screening Colour Test and Specific Colour Tests for the Detection of Methylenedioxyam-phetamine and Amphetamine Type Stimulants	UNODC	2009	SCITEC/16
Colour Tests for Precursor Chemicals of Amphetamine-Type Substances: Safrole and Safrole-rich Essential Oils	UNODC	2007	SCITEC/21
Multilingual Dictionary of Narcotic Drugs and Psychotropic Substances Under International Control	UNODC	2006	ST/NAR/1
Recommended Methods for the Identification and Analysis of Amphetamine, Methamphetamine and their Ring-Substituted Analogues in Seized Materials	UNODC	2006	ST/NAR/34
Colour Tests for Precursor Chemicals of Amphetamine-Type Substances: The Use of Colour Tests for Distinguishing between Ephedrine-Derivatives	UNODC	2005	SCITEC/20
Colour Tests for Precursor Chemicals of Amphetamine-Type Substances: Ephedrine Derivatives	UNODC	2005	SCITEC/20
	UNODC	2003	SCITEC/19

Table 6.21.A International Standards Framework: Applying to Seized Materials—cont'd

Title	Body	Year	Ref
Limited Opium Yield Assessment Surveys Technical Report: Observations and Findings; Guidance for Future Activities			
Guidelines for Yield Assessment of Opium Gum and Coca Leaf from Brief Field Visits	UNODC	2001	ST/NAR/33
Rapid On-site Screening of Drugs of Abuse: A Summary of Commercially Available Products and their Applications: Guidance for the Selection of Suitable Products Part I: Biological Specimens	UNODC	2001	SCITEC/18
Drug Characterization/ Impurity Profiling Background and Concepts	UNODC	2001	ST/NAR/32
Clandestine Manufacture of Substances under International Control	UNODC	1998	ST/NAR/10
Recommended Methods for Testing Opium, Morphine and Heroin	UNODC	1998	ST/NAR/29
Studies on Colour Tests for Field Detection of Narcotic Drugs and Psychotropic Substances under International Control (No. II). Screening Colour Test and Specific Colour Test for the Detection of Non-Barbiturate Sedatives and Hypnotics: Methaqualone/Mecloq	UNODC	1996	SCITEC/13
Rapid Testing Methods of Drugs of Abuse	UNODC	1994	ST/NAT/13

Continued

Table 6.21.A International Standards Framework: Applying to Seized Materials—cont'd

Title	Body	Year	Ref
Psychotropic Substances of the Amphetamine Type used by Drug Addicts in Bulgaria: Synthesis and Medicinal Forms Analytical Methods of Identification	UNODC	1994	SCITEC/10
Rapid Test Methods of Drugs of Abuse	UNODC	1994	ST/NAR/13
Recommended Methods for Testing Lysergide (LSD)	UNODC	1989	ST/NAR/17
Recommended Methods for Testing Peyote Cactus (Mescal Buttons) Mescaline and Psilocybin Mushrooms/ Psilocybin	UNODC	1989	ST/NAR/19
Chemistry and Reaction Mechanisms of Rapid Tests for Drugs of Abuse and Precursor Chemicals	UNODC	1989	SCITEC/6
Some Aspects of the Gas Chromatography Analysis of Heroin	UNODC	1989	SCITEC/5
Methods for Testing Benzodiazepine Derivatives Under International Control	UNODC	1988	ST/NAR/16
Recommended Methods for the Identification and Analysis of Cannabis and Cannabis Products	UNODC	–	ST/NAR/40

IFSA—International Strategic Forensic Alliance.

and AS/NZS4308 "Procedures for specimen collection and the detection and quantitation of drugs of abuse in urine" applies in both Australia and NZ. The methods are based on an immunoassay screen[17] and, if positive, confirmation by mass spectrometric detection with gas phase separation.

[17] Immunoassay is a method for detecting proteins.

Table 6.21.B International Standards Framework: Applying to Seized Materials—Chemical Profiling

Title	Body	Year	Ref
Methods for Impurity Profiling of Heroin and Cocaine	UNODC	2005	ST/NAR/35
Drug Characterization and Impurity profiling - Background and concepts	UNODC	2001	ST/NAR/32
A Practical Guide to Methamphetamine Characterization/Impurity Profiling	UNODC	2000	SCITEC/17
A Practical Guide to Methamphetamine Characterization/Impurity Profiling: Method Procedures, Mass Spectral Data of Selected Impurities, and Literature Reference	UNODC	2000	SCITEC/17

Table 6.21.C International Standards Framework: Applying to Laboratory Practice and Quality Management

Title	Body	Year	Ref
Guidance for the Implementation of a Quality Management System in Drug Testing Laboratories	UNODC	2009	ISBN 978-92-1-148239-3
Glossary of Terms for Quality Assurance and Good Laboratory Practices	UNODC	2009	ST/NAR/26
Guidance for the Validation of Analytical Methodology and Calibration of Equipment used for Testing of Illicit Drugs in Seized Materials and Biological Specimens	UNODC	2009	ST/NAR/41

Continued

Table 6.21.C International Standards Framework: Applying to Laboratory Practice and Quality Management—cont'd

Title	Body	Year	Ref
Recommended Guidelines for Quality Assurance and Good Laboratory Practices	UNODC	1995	ST/NAR/25

Table 6.21.D International Standards Framework: Applying to Biological Samples

Title	Body	Year	Ref
Guidelines for Testing Drugs under International Control in Hair, Sweat and Saliva Rapid On-site Screening of Drugs of Abuse	UNODC	2014	ST/NAR/30
Guidelines for Testing Drugs under International Control in Hair Sweat and Oral Fluid	UNODC	2014	ST/NAR/30
Guidelines for the Forensic analysis of drugs facilitating sexual assault and other criminal acts	UNODC	2011	ST/NAR/45
Recommended Methods for the Detection and Assay of Lysergide (LSD), Phencyclidine (PCP), Psilocybin and Methaqualone in Biological Specimens	UNODC	1999	ST/NAR/31

Table 6.21.D International Standards Framework: Applying to Biological Samples—cont'd

Title	Body	Year	Ref
Recommended Methods for the Detection and Assay of Barbiturates and Benzodiazepines in Biological Specimens	UNODC	1997	ST/NAR/28

6.4.3.2.2 Europe

There are many ENFSI members that offer a forensic toxicology service, but ENFSI does not have an Expert Working Group for this discipline nor does it publish any standards.

6.4.3.2.3 UK/E&W

In 2015 the Regulator consulted stakeholders on a plan to adopt the UK and Ireland Association of Forensic Toxicologists (UKIAFT) Laboratory Guidelines (Cooper et al., 2010), which as reported in 2.2.4.5.7 are adapted from the US SOFT (Society of Forensic Toxicologists) Laboratory guidelines listed in Table 6.22 (US) (SOFT/AAFS, 2006).

Therefore, at the time of writing [December 2017], the UKIAFT Laboratory Guidelines is the only published standard extant for this discipline. No doubt the Regulator will, in due course, publish a toxicology annex to the Codes.

6.4.3.2.4 US Table 6.22

As with other SWGs responsibility for the discipline has been transferred to OSAC. The relevant subcommittee is Toxicology of the Chemistry/Instrumental Analysis SAC. SWGTOX (SWG for Forensic Toxicology) standards will remain in effect until developed standards are approved by OSAC and placed on the register of approved standards.

Table 6.22 US Standards' Framework: Toxicology

Title	Body	Year	Ref
Sampling of Drugs	AOAC	2015	927.09–1927
Sympathomimetic drugs. Microchemical tests	AOAC	2015	960.55–1970
Standard for Breath Alcohol Personnel	SWGTOX	2014	005
Breath Alcohol Method Validation and Instrumentation Evaluation Standard (in draft)	SWGTOX	2014	—

Continued

Table 6.22 US Standards' Framework: Toxicology—cont'd

Title	Body	Year	Ref
Breath Alcohol QA Standard (in draft)	SWGTOX	2014	–
Standard for Laboratory Personnel	SWGTOX	2014	006
Guidelines for Research in Forensic Toxicology	SWGTOX	2014	002
Standard for a Quality Management System in Forensic Toxicology (in draft)	SWGTOX	2014	–
Standard for Identification Criteria for Forensic Toxicology (not yet drafted)	SWGTOX	2014	–
Standard for Mass Spectrometry Data Acceptance for Definitive Identification (in draft)	SWGTOX	2014	–
Standard for Measurement Traceability in Forensic Toxicology (not yet drafted)	SWGTOX	2014	–
Standard for Measurement Uncertainty in Forensic Toxicology (not yet drafted)	SWGTOX	2014	–
Standard for Proficiency Testing in Forensic Toxicology (in draft)	SWGTOX	2014	–
Standard for Quality Control in Forensic Toxicology Analytical Procedures (in draft)	SWGTOX	2014	–
Standard for Reporting Test Results in Forensic Toxicology (yet to be drafted)	SWGTOX	2014	–
Standard for Specimen Collection and Storage in Forensic Toxicology (in draft)	SWGTOX	2014	–
Standard for the Content in a Forensic Toxicology SOP (in draft)	SWGTOX	2014	–

Table 6.22 US Standards' Framework: Toxicology—cont'd

Title	Body	Year	Ref
Standard on the Accreditation of Forensic Toxicology Laboratories	SWGTOX	2014	004
Guideline for Developing a Code of Professional Conduct in Forensic Toxicology	SWGTOX	2014	001
Forensic Toxicology Laboratory Accreditation Manual	ABFT	2013	—
Standard Practices for Method Validation in Forensic Toxicology	SWGTOX	2013	003
ASCLD/LAB-International Supplemental Requirements for the Accreditation of Breath Alcohol Calibration Laboratories	ASCLD/ LAB	2011	AL-PD-3026-Ver 1.1
ASCLD/LAB-International Supplemental Requirements for the Accreditation of Forensic Science Testing Laboratories	ASCLD/ LAB	2011	AL-PD-3040-Ver 1.2
Forensic Toxicology Laboratory Guidelines 2006	AAFS/ SOFT	2006	—
Alkaloids and related amines in drugs. Microchemical tests	AOAC	—	930.40–1930
Amplification Document for the Auditing of Forensic Toxicology Laboratories Based on SWGTOX Standards (check lists published with appropriate standard)	SWGTOX	—	—

AAFS—American Academy of Forensic Sciences; *ABFT*—American Board of Forensic Toxicology; *AOAC*—Association of Official Analytical Chemists; *ASCLD/LAB*—American Society of Crime Laboratory Directors/Laboratory Accreditation Board; *SOFT*—Society of Forensic Toxicologists; *SWGTOX*—Scientific Working Group for Forensic Toxicology.

6.4.3.3 Ignitable Liquids—Analysis and Detection

The analysis and detection of ignitable liquids is conducted mainly in support of fire scene examination. The main sample type considered is fire debris.

As this discipline relies heavily on analytical instrumentation, providers should be accredited to ISO/IEC 17025 and test methods employed should lie within scope. Traceability and uncertainty will be important requirements for conformance.

6.4.3.3.1 Australasia

Standards Australia (SA) has published the standard AS5239:2011 "Examination of ignitable liquids in fire debris." This standard relies heavily on the ASTM International standards listed in the US Table 6.23. However, it adds sections on interpretation and reporting. At the time of writing [December 2017] NATA does not accredit to this standard even as an extension to scope for ISO/IEC 17025. Therefore, conformity to AS5239 is not assessed by an independent or third party and the standard is effectively a guidance document.

The analysis and detection of ignitable liquids falls squarely within the scope of ISO/IEC 17025 and if needed accreditation to AS5388 as an extension to scope for ISO/IEC 17025 accredited forensic science providers.

In NZ, ESR is accredited to ISO/IEC 17025 by ANAB for the examination of "fire scene debris." ANAB's supplementary Accreditation Requirements will apply.

6.4.3.3.2 Europe

The ENFSI guideline was published as a book by Elsevier entitled "Identifying Ignitable Liquids in Fire Debris: A Guideline for Forensic Experts," ENFSI, 2015, ISBN 9780128043165. According to the publisher, the guide is no longer available.

6.4.3.3.3 UK/E&W

At the time of writing [December 2017] the Regulator has not published an annex to the Codes for this discipline and there are no published plans to do so.

6.4.3.3.4 US Table 6.23

This table comprises standard operation procedures published by ASTM. The main method for analysis and detection is ASTM E1618.

Responsibility for this discipline now rests with the Fire Debris and Explosives subcommittee of the Chemistry/Instrumental Analysis SAC, which, at the time of writing [December 2017], is drafting and developing standards, including the ASTM standards listed, for eventual placement on the OSAC register of approved standards.

Table 6.23 US Standards Framework: Fires/Ignitable Liquids

Title	Body	Year	Ref
Standard Practice for Sampling of Headspace Vapors from Fire Debris Samples	ASTM	2017	E1388
Standard Practice for Separation of Ignitable Liquid Residues from Fire Debris Samples by Passive Headspace Concentration With Activated Charcoal	ASTM	2016	E1412
Standard Practice for Separation and Concentration of Ignitable Liquid Residues from Fire Debris Samples by Passive Headspace Concentration with Solid Phase Microextraction (SPME)	ASTM	2015	E2154
Standard Practice for Separation of Ignitable Liquid Residues from Fire Debris Samples by Solvent Extraction	ASTM	2015	E1386
Standard Test Method for Ignitable Liquid Residues in Extracts from Fire Debris Samples by Gas Chromatography- Mass Spectrometry	ASTM	2014	E1618
Standard Practice for Separation of Ignitable Liquid Residues from Fire Debris Samples by Dynamic Headspace Concentration	ASTM	2013	E1413
Standard Practice for Preserving Ignitable Liquids and Ignitable Liquid Residue Extracts from Fire Debris Samples	ASTM	2013	E2451
Standard Test Method for Extraction and Derivatization of Vegetable Oils and Fats from Fire Debris and Liquid Samples with Analysis by Gas Chromatography-Mass Spectrometry	ASTM	2013	E2881
Standard Test Method for Ignitable Liquid Residues in Extracts from Fire Debris Samples by Gas chromatography (withdrawn in 2010 without replacement)	ASTM	–	E1387

Note: E1387 withdrawn in accordance with Section 10.5.3.1 of the Regulations Governing ASTM Technical Committees, which requires that standards be updated by the end of the eighth year since the last approval date.

6.4.3.4 Explosives: The Analysis and Detection of

Forensic science providers will need to have facilities to offer analysis and detection at both trace and bulk levels. Trace level work will need to be conducted in a controlled environment in which contamination is avoided and monitored.

In most regions there are legal requirements governing the transport and storage of bulk explosives. Regulations related to transport are usually derived from the UN Transport of Dangerous Goods: Model Regulations. Each region will also have legal requirements concerning storage. In addition, there will be health and safety regulations applying to those working with explosives. Legal requirements will need to be taken into account when documenting procedures.

As this discipline relies heavily on analytical instrumentation, providers should be accredited to ISO/IEC 17025 and test methods employed should lie within scope. Traceability and uncertainty will be important requirements for conformance.

6.4.3.4.1 Australasia

In Australia, the quality standards framework applying to the analysis and detection of explosives is unclear. It seems that the identification of bulk explosives falls within the scope of AS5388 and Australian forensic science providers are accredited by NATA to ISO/IEC 17025 for "Fires and Explosions," which may limit the scope to traces.

In NZ, ESR possess flexible scope accreditation to ISO/IEC 17025 for qualitative analysis. ANAB's supplementary requirements will apply.

6.4.3.4.2 Europe

ENFSI has published a BPM for the Forensic Recovery, Identification and Analysis of Explosive Traces ENFSI-BPM-EXP-01 November 2015. As the title implies the analysis of bulk explosives lies outside the scope of this standard. Traces are defined as submicrogram quantities; a microgram is one-millionth of a gram. The standard specifies the technical and environmental requirements for the analysis and detection of explosives at trace level. It includes sections on interpretation and the presentation of evidence.

6.4.3.4.3 UK/E&W

As yet there are no published annexes to the FSR Codes of Practice for this discipline and there are no publically available plans at present [December 2017].

6.4.3.4.4 US Table 6.24

The standards listed are essentially SOPs that are under development by the Fire Debris and Explosives subcommittee of the Chemistry/Instrumental Analysis SAC. Under development/drafting/preparation are the following:

- Standard Guide for the Forensic Examination and Identification of Intact Explosives
- Standard Practice for Reporting Results and Opinions of Explosives Analysis

Table 6.24 US Standards' Framework: Explosives

Title	Body	Year	Ref
Recommended Guidelines for Forensic Identification of Post-Blast Explosive Residues	TWGFEX	2007	–
New Practice for Characterization of Smokeless Powder	ASTM	–	WK23817
New Test Method for Analysis of Smokeless Powder by Gas Chromatography-Mass Spectrometry and Fourier-Transform Infrared Spectroscopy	ASTM	–	WK35410
New Test Method for Analysis of Smokeless Powder by Gas Chromatography-Mass Spectrometry and Fourier-Transform Infrared Spectroscopy	ASTM	–	WK35410

TWGFEX—Technical Working Group for Fire and Explosion Analysis, the predecessor of SWGFEX (Scientific Working Group for Fire and Explosion Analysis). Note: the ASTM standards are under revision at the time of writing [2017].

- Terminology Relating to the Examination of Explosives

Once developed and approved standards will be placed on the OSAC register of approved standards.

6.4.3.5 Gunshot Residues—Analysis and Detection

Gunshot residues or GSR are post-explosion residues ejected from a discharging firearm hence alternative names are sometime used such as firearms discharge residue or cartridge discharge residue. GSR comprises inorganic residues originating from the ammunition's primer, metallic particles from the ammunition and weapon and organic residue from the propellant explosive that propels the bullet from in the ammunition casing. With the availability of off-the-shelf SEM-EDS instruments, referred to earlier in 6.4.2.3, the focus is on the detection of inorganic and metallic species, particularly the elements antimony, lead, and bismuth originating from the ammunition primer.

As this discipline relies heavily on analytical instrumentation, particularly SEM-EDS, providers should be accredited to ISO/IEC 17025 and test methods employed should lie within scope.

The main weakness of GSR evidence lies in its interpretation—the detection of characteristic GSR particles points to firearms involvement, but it is not yet possible to distinguish between a shooter and a bystander.

6.4.3.5.1 Australasia

The analysis and detection of GSR lie within the scope of AS5388. In addition, providers in Australia are accredited by NATA to ISO/IEC 17025 for the analysis and detection of GSR. In NZ ESR are not according to its scope.

6.4.3.5.2 Europe

The only extant standard is the BPM for Chemographic[18] Methods in Gunshot Residue Analysis ENFSI-BPM-FGR-01 November 2015. It does not apply to analysis and detection using SEM-EDS. Chemographic methods rely on the development of a color indicating the presence of GSR components. It can be used as a screening technique with conformation by SEM-EDS. It can also be used to visualize patterns and aid shooting distance estimations.

The following documents are no longer available:

- ENFSI Guide for Gunshot Residue Analysis by Scanning Electron Microscopy/Energy-Dispersive X-Ray Spectrometry|| ENFSI Working Group FIREARMS, Version 2, 2008.
- ENFSI Best Practice Manual in the Forensic Examination of Gunshot Residues|| ENFSI Working Group FIREARMS, 2003.

6.4.3.5.3 UK/E&W

At the time of writing [2017] the Regulator has not published an annex to the Codes of practice for this discipline and there are no published plans to do so.

6.4.3.5.4 US Table 6.25

Just two standards are listed and both apply to the use of SEM-EDS. As with other disciplines, responsibility for quality standards in this discipline now rests with the Gunshot Residue subcommittee of the Chemistry/Instrumental Analysis SAC. Among standards being developed are:

- ASTM E620-17 Standard Practice for Reporting Opinions of Scientific or Technical Experts, and a
- GSR Training Guide.

Once developed and approved standards will be placed on the OSAC register of approved standards.

[18] A method that uses chemical reagents to visualize particles that incorporate a selective element or component—not SEM-EDS.

Table 6.25 US Standards' Framework: Gunshot Residues

Title	Body	Year	Reference
Standard Practice for Gunshot Residue Analysis by Scanning Electron Microscopy/Energy Dispersive X-ray Spectrometry	ASTM	2017	E1588
Guide for Primer Gunshot Residue Analysis by Scanning Electron Microscopy/Energy Dispersive X-ray Spectrometry	SWGGSR	2011	11-29-11

SWGGSR—Scientific Working Group for Gunshot Residue.

6.5 FORENSIC BIOLOGY

6.5.1 Introduction

As with chemistry, the science of biology supports numerous fields and disciplines including identifying body fluids, DNA typing, and identifying the cause of ballistic trauma (gunshot wound). DNA analysis was discussed earlier and body fluid identification is mentioned below. Ballistic trauma falls into the category of forensic medicine and therefore falls outside the scope of this work.

6.5.2 Identification of Body Fluids

The body fluids in question include: blood, semen, and saliva. There are no discipline-specific quality standards frameworks supporting such identification. In forensic practice body fluid identification is a means of identifying stains suitable for DNA analysis. Therefore, this discipline is effectively a subdiscipline of DNA analysis. Accredited DNA methods often include the presumptive identification of a body fluid.

In the case of blood, a test for origin, human, or animal, may follow a positive presumptive test result. Such serological tests rely on antigen—antibody reactions to identify human-specific proteins.

Methods for identifying body fluids based on RNA (ribonucleic acid) are in development (Harbison and Flemming, 2016).

It should be recalled that, even when no discipline-specific standards framework exists, methods used must be validated and, ideally, fall within the scope of accreditation.

6.5.3 Other Applications of Biology

Forensic biology also includes palynology (the study of pollen), entomology (the study of insects), botany (the study of plants), and archaeology, sometimes referred to as the "ologies", that are used in the investigation of crime and can be helpful tools. However, scientific evidence gained by exploiting these essentially academic fields is unlikely to have much by way of a supporting quality standards framework and may be presented by an academic specialist with little knowledge of the competencies required to assure the quality of the scientific evidence offered. Therefore, such evidence should be treated with caution. The competence of the organization and individual regarding forensic science will need to be established as will the validity of methods used.

6.6 SCENE EXAMINATION

6.6.1 Introduction

As discussed in 3.1.3 scene examination is an inspection activity involving functional testing, i.e., comparisons. Organizations providing this service should be accredited to ISO/IEC 17020 with any analytical test methods accredited to ISO/IEC 17025 as an extension to scope.

As science and technology progresses equipment that facilitates analysis and detection at the scene becomes available. The use of such equipment at the scene must lie within the scope of accreditation of either the organization employing the operator or the organization responsible for scene examination treating the operator as a subcontractor and in conformance to ISO/IEC 17025 6.6 or ISO/IEC 17020 6.3. Even when sophisticated equipment offers high selectivity, defined in 3.4.2.3, any result obtained should be considered preliminary and require confirmation in a controlled laboratory environment before drawing conclusions.

As stated in 1.2.2, forensic science also serves noncriminal justice and aids the investigation of incidents where no crime has been committed; a good example is the investigation of "accidents" for the purpose of settling insurance claims. Therefore, where appropriate the adjective "crime" is omitted.

The scene is where evidence that might be relied on to determine facts in issue begins its journey. Mistakes made at the scene can rarely be undone. Suboptimal practice at the scene may contribute to a miscarriage of justice. Therefore, every effort should be made to ensure that scene examination is conducted in conformance to quality standards that will demonstrate competence and validity.

Scene examiners must be aware of the risk of cognitive bias, possibly amplified at harrowing or traumatic scenes. Cognitive bias might result in an examination strategy that aims to support a particular hypothesis to the exclusion of others that are reasonable and rational.

The risk of cognitive bias may deny a tribunal essential evidence to determine facts in issue. One practical example is choosing to sample certain items rather than others (Doyle and Doyle, 2012). Therefore, scene examiners must have in place procedures that recognize and reduce the risk of cognitive bias.

It is of concern that most of the standards specified in this subsection do not recognize the existence of cognitive bias and therefore lack bias avoidance measures.

Scenes are often uncontrolled environments where the risk of losing sample/evidence integrity, through contamination or disturbance, is high. Therefore, contamination avoidance and preserving and recording the scene are essential requirements. The risk of contamination is reduced by adequately packaging items of potential evidence and examining them in a laboratory where environmental conditions should be under control. Scene examiners, as a matter of course, should sample the scene environment to provide a background against which the significance of any positive results might be assessed.

Scene examination may be considered as two distinct activities: processing and investigation. Processing is governed by the principles of control, preserve, record, and recover. Investigation is directed toward answering questions such as what? and how? These activities are often inextricably linked, which is recognized in ILAC G19 08/2014. Therefore, the term scene examination can mean processing alone or processing and investigation.

The scope of scene examination varies by provider and the standards adopted to demonstrate competence. In this work, specialist disciplines that might be practiced at the scene are, and have been, considered separately.

The scene must first be brought under control to better avoid disturbance and contamination and facilitate recording and the recovery materials of potential evidential value. The integrity of recovered materials must be maintained and their continuity recorded. In addition, risks to the health and safety of those working at the scene must be managed.

As discussed in 3.3.2.2, ILAC Guide 19 08/2014 in addition to being a Level 2 standard contains sufficient prescriptive detail to also serve as a Level 3 standard for general scene examination.

In Section 4.4 of that guide, the main activities of scene examination are specified:

- the scene of crime is documented,
- the scene of crime is searched/examined,
- on-going interpretation of the scene of crime takes place,
- exhibits are recovered, labeled, documented, and collected,
- samples are taken, sampling is recorded,
- strategies and plans may be reviewed.

In addition, drawing a distinction between scene investigation and processing, processing in the guide is specified as:

- Search
- Locate
- Assess relevance
- Document
- Collect

- Identify (label)
- Preserve and protect
- Package
- Transport

However, as recognized in the guide, and more generally, scenes vary in type and complexity and require different approaches accordingly. Therefore, standards have been developed and published for a variety of scenes and they are introduced here.

6.6.2 General Scenes Examination

The scope of accreditation should be sufficiently broad to include the variety of scenes that might be encountered. As stated earlier in 6.6.1, forensic science providers offering crime scene examination services should be accredited to ISO/IEC 17020 with any analytical testing accredited to ISO/IEC 17025 as an extension to scope. Flexible scope accreditation to ISO/IEC 17025 might be needed for analytical tests.

6.6.2.1 Australasia

Crime scene examination lies within the scope of AS5388. Part 1: "Recognition, recording, recovery, transport and storage of material" specifically applies to crime scene examination. However, AS5388 assumes accreditation to ISO/IEC 17025. AS5388 is silent on ISO/IEC 17020, which implies that organizations undertaking crime scene examination can only be accredited to ISO/IEC 17025.

As set out in 3.1.3, ISO/IEC 17025 and ISO/IEC 17020 are different standards covering different activities: analytical testing and functional testing, respectively. An important element in ISO/IEC 17020 is the independence of the inspection body. This is not a requirement in ISO/IEC 17025. In addition, it is difficult to see how a standard applying to laboratories undertaking analytical testing can be accredited to ISO/IEC 17025 for scene activities that are essentially inspections involving functional testing and relying on professional judgment. Another factor that counts against accreditation to ISO/IEC 17025 for scene examinations is that scene examination has been deemed an inspection activity in Europe and the United States. Therefore, exclusion of ISO/IEC 17020 may be problematic. As stated earlier in 6.6.1, the optimal arrangement for a provider offering both testing and inspection services is to be accredited to one standard for its main activity and to the other standard as an extension to scope for its secondary activity.

AS5388 is a core standard and, as explained earlier in 6.1 and in 3.4, was intended to provide a framework for more discipline-specific standards. At the time of writing [2017], discipline-specific standards have yet to be developed. It is clear that AS5388 Part 1 is intended to apply to general scene examination. In addition, the specialist scenes, fires, explosions, and clandestine laboratories, which are discussed later, also appear to lie within scope. Applying ISO/IEC 17025 to the examination of these specialist scenes seems seem even more unlikely.

As discussed and reported earlier in 6.1, AS5388 is being developed as an ISO standard. Therefore, it seems certain that the relationship between AS5388 and ISO/IEC 17020 will be resolved in due course.

As discussed earlier in 6.1, in Australia crime scene examination services provided by police-based organizations are not accredited to an international standard such as ISO/IEC 17020. Individuals are "accredited" or, in this work, certified as competent by the AFFSAB, as discussed in 3.4.4.5.1.

The requirements for certification, are documented in 'Policy and Processes For Accreditation' which is currently [December 2017] under revision.

In NZ, ESR is accredited by ANAB to ISO/IEC 17025 and ANABs supplementary Accreditation Requirements apply. This seems odd, as ANAB also accredits forensic inspection agencies to ISO/IEC 17020. It is fair to say that accreditation processes are currently [December 2017] in transition and it may be that ESR's forensic inspection activities, in time, will be accredited to ISO/IEC 17020 as an extension to scope.

6.6.2.2 Europe Table 6.26

EA-5/03 Guidance for the Implementation of ISO/IEC 17020 in the field of crime scene investigation, mentioned in 3.1.3 and discussed briefly in 4.5.5, is a predecessor of ILAC Guide 19 08/2014, introduced in 3.3.2.2.

It is ENFSI policy[19] that all members that provide crime scene examination services should be accredited to ISO/IEC 17020 for those services or be working toward such accreditation. In addition, the BPM listed calls for ISO/IEC 17020 accreditation.

Table 6.26 European Standards' Framework: Scene Examination

Title	Body	Year	Ref
Scenes of Crime Examination Best Practice Manual	ENFSI EWG	2012	
Guidance for the Implementation of ISO/IEC 17020 in the field of crime scene investigation	EA	2008	EA-5/03

EA—European Accreditation Cooperation; *ENFSI*—European Network of Forensic Science Institutes; *EWG*—Expert Working Group—Scene of Crime.

19 Policy on standards for accreditation, 2016, QCC-ACR-001:006.

6.6.2.3 UK/E&W Table 6.27

At the time of writing [December 2017], the Forensic Science Regulator has yet to publish an appendix to the general Codes of Practice and Conduct for crime scene examination. The scope of the current Codes of Practice and Conduct, Issue 3 2016, relates mostly to laboratory-based activities. However, it includes a target date in which crime scene examination providers gain accreditation to ISO/IEC 17020. That date is October 2020. The target is also recorded in the Regulator's annual report (FSR, 2017). As reported in 3.1.3, accreditation to ISO/IEC 17020 for crime scene examination has been available since 2011.

In the absence of guidance from the Regulator, the UKAS guide RG201, discussed in 3.3.3 suffices. In effect, this is the standard UKAS uses for conformity assessment and accreditation.

Therefore, the UK quality standards framework for crime scene examination is, at the time of writing [December 2017], quite limited.

National Occupational Standards discussed in 3.4.3.5.2 may be of benefit to organizations preparing for accreditation or accredited to ISO/IEC 17020. As with all standards, compliance serves as a means of demonstrating competence.

6.6.2.4 US Table 6.28

The 2017 NIJ guide is the most comprehensive and detailed available.

OSAC have established a Crime Scene Investigation subcommittee as part of the Crime Scene/Death Investigation SAC. However, at the time of writing [December 2017], little progress on standards development has been made and the NIJ guide remains, for the time being, the effective standard for this discipline.

Table 6.27 UK Standards' Framework: Scene Examination

Title	Body	Year	Ref
The Control and Avoidance of Contamination in Crime Scene Examination involving DNA Evidence Recovery	FSR	2016	FSR-G-206
Codes of Practice and Conduct for forensic science providers in the Criminal Justice System	FSR	2016	
Accreditation of Bodies Carrying out Scene of Crime Examination	UKAS	2015	RG201
Undertake forensic examinations at scenes of incidents	SFJ	2008	NOS CN 403

FSR—Forensic Science Regulator; *NOS*—National Occupational Standards; *SFJ*—Skills for Justice; *UKAS*—UK Accreditation Service. Note: ILAC Guide-19-18/2014 is, in effect, a discipline-specific standard for crime scene examination.

Table 6.28 US Standards' Framework: Crime Scenes

Title	Body	Year	Ref
Crime Scene Investigation: Guides for Law Enforcement (Online publication)	NIJ	2017	–
Crime Scene Investigation Guide; A guide for law enforcement	NIST/NFSTC	2013	–
Crime Scene Investigation Guidelines	IAI	–	–

IAI—International Association of Identification; *NFSTC*—US National Forensic Science Technology Centre; *NIJ*—US National Institute of Justice.

As reported in 3.2.3 some US-based crime scene examination providers are accredited to ISO/IEC 17020 and both major accrediting bodies in the United States, ANAB and A2LA, accredit crime scene inspection activities to ISO/IEC 17020.

6.6.2.5 International

In 2014 IFSA (International Forensic Strategic Alliance) published "Minimum Requirements for Crime Scene Investigation Crime Scene Investigation." The standard is aimed at "emerging laboratories." As conformance to ISO/IEC 17025 or ISO/IEC 17020 are de facto minimum standards for forensic science providers, this document, and others in the IFSA "minimum requirements" series, focus on the essential elements of a QM system:

- Competence of Personnel.
- Equipment and Consumables.
- Collection, Analysis, Interpretation, Reporting.
- Procedures, Protocols, Validation.
- Qauality.

6.6.3 Explosions and Explosives

Essentially, there are two types of explosives scene:

- post-explosion, sometimes called post-blast, and
- those associated with the presence of explosives, their manufacture, storage, and/or transport.

The examination of scenes at which explosives or explosive devices have been manufactured is dealt with later at 6.6.5.2.

For suspected post-blast scenes, the initial purpose of scene examination will be to determine whether or not an explosion has taken place and, if so, what the cause was.

Not all scenes of violent destruction are caused by an explosion and, even if an explosion has occurred, it might not be the result of a criminal act. Those questions will need to be addressed as a matter of urgency.

The principles of control, preserve, record, and recover apply. Gaining control of a post-blast scene often takes some time during which there will be a risk, often realized, of disturbance and contamination.

There are some unique aspects to the investigation of explosives-related scenes. One of which is the involvement of bomb technicians (however named). Whose role it is to take control of the scene and make and declare it explosively safe before handing control back to the relevant authority.

Bomb technicians must be considered sources of contamination. The risk of contamination must be taken into account when planning scene examination and when interpreting the finding of explosives traces.

Post-blast scenes are often extremely hazardous environments in which to work. Therefore, in addition to the involvement of bomb technicians, other specialists may be required to help assess and manage the risk to the health and safety of forensic scientists, and others, working in the scene. Documented procedures for the examination of explosives scenes will need to include risk assessment and management.

In the investigation of explosives related crime, novel materials will be encountered and therefore flexible scope accreditation to ISO/IEC 17025, discussed in 5.5, would be of benefit.

Explosions often cause injury to those present at the time and therefore post-blast scenes are often compromised by disturbance and contamination as first responders treat and evacuate casualties and the dead are identified. All activity in the scene risks disturbance and contamination, which may compromise evidence integrity.

Religious observance often requires the dead to be buried within a short period of time limiting the opportunity for gathering evidence.

If analysis and detection equipment is used at the scene, then the points made earlier in 6.6.1 should be born in mind. The use of such equipment must lie within the scope of accreditation and any result obtained should be considered preliminary and require confirmation in a controlled laboratory environment before drawing conclusions.

In summary, the examination of explosives scenes is a complex process in which minimizing risks to health and safety, deconflicting priorities, and maintaining the integrity of evidence are major challenges. Demonstrating competence in the examination of explosives scenes is also a challenge. Accreditation to ISO/IEC 17020 seems most appropriate.

Regarding the analysis of explosive substances, validated methods and a suitable environment for the analysis and detection of explosives of both traces and bulks will be required. Optimally methods should lie within the scope of accreditation to ISO/IEC 17025. However, the examination of scenes is an inspection activity properly accredited to ISO/IEC 17020.

In addition, examiners will need skills and knowledge related to the construction and function of explosive devices.

6.6.3.1 Australasia

The examination of explosives scenes lies within the scope of AS5388 for ISO/IEC 17025 accredited providers. However, the examination of explosives scenes is an inspection activity properly accredited to ISO/IEC 17020. In AS5388 health and safety issues are addressed including the need for a bomb technician to make and declare a scene explosively safe. Nevertheless, there is little focus on scene control and preservation.

In NZ, ESR is not accredited for the examination of post-blast scenes.

6.6.3.2 Europe Table 6.29

There is no European standard written in English for the examination of post-blast scenes.

Guidance is available in Appendix C2 "Clandestine manufacture of home made explosives" of the ENFSI BPM for fire scene examination covers scenes of explosives manufacture and refers to the involvement of bomb technicians at the scene. However, this standard more appropriately applies to a scene of explosives manufacture discussed later in 6.6.5.2.

Also listed in the table is a BPM applying to the analysis and detection of traces. However, procedures applicable to explosives scenes are included in Section 5 of the document. A graphical representation of the approach described, including scene activities, is given by Fig. 6.4. In addition, Sections 8.1 and Appendix 2 specify scene procedures. In the absence of any further guidance on scene examination reference is made to ISO/IEC 17020.

Table 6.29 European Standards' Framework: Scenes—Explosions

Title	Body	Year	Ref
Best Practice Manual for the investigation of fire scenes: Appendix C2 Manufacture of Explosives	ENFSI	2017	ENFSI-BPM-FEI-01
Best Practice Manual for the Forensic Recovery, Identification and Analysis of Explosives Traces; Section 5 Methods	ENFSI	2015	ENFSI-BPM-EXP-01

ENFSI—European Network of Forensic Science Institutes.

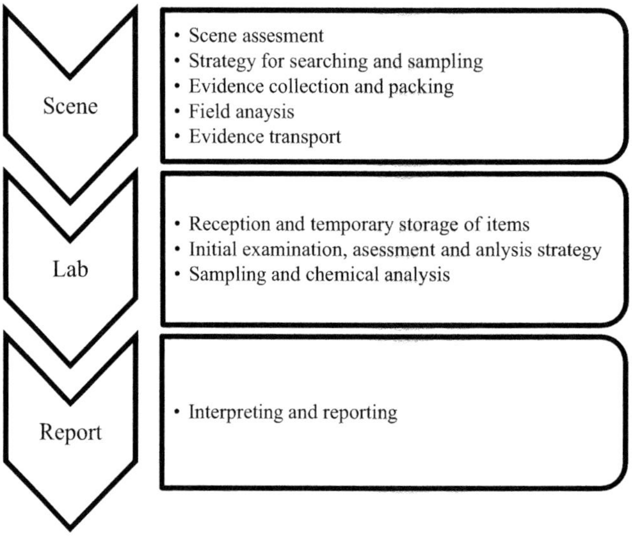

Figure 6.4 General approach to trace explosives investigation. *(Based on Figure 1 of ENFSI-BPM-EXP-01.)*

6.6.3.3 UK/E&W

At the time of writing [December 2017] there is no appendix to the Regulator's Codes for the examination of post-blast scenes, and there is no published plan to do so.

6.6.3.4 US Table 6.30

The most recent guide is the NIJ Guide for Investigating Bomb and Explosion Scenes. The 2009 NIJ guide is an excellent document offering sufficient scope and detail to be

Table 6.30 US Standard' Framework: Scenes—Explosions

Title	Body	Year	Ref
Guide for Fire and Explosion Investigations	NFPA	2017	921
A Guide for Investigating Bomb and Explosion Scenes (available on line)	NIJ	2009	(NIJ, 2009)
A Guide for Explosion and Bombing Scene Investigation	NIJ	2000	NCJ 181869
Instructors' Training Curriculum Guide to: A Guide to Explosion and Bombing scene Investigation	SWGFEX	—	—

NFPA—US National Fire Protection Association; *NIJ*—US National Institute of Justice; *SWGFEX*—Scientific Working Group for Fire and Explosion Analysis.

considered a comprehensive guide to post-blast scene examination; particularly scene management and processing. Conformance to this guide demonstrates competence and will ensure the safe recovery of evidence of sufficient quality to be relied on. It has five sections:

- Arriving at the scene,
- Evaluating the scene,
- Documenting the scene,
- Processing Evidence at the scene, and
- Completing and recording the scene investigation.

The guide applies the four principles of scene management: control, preserve, record, and recover. It also emphasizes the need to assess and manage risk and maintain the integrity of evidence. The guide requires first responders to be forensically aware and, as much as is practically possible, avoid contaminating and disturbing the scene.

OSAC have established a Crime Scene Investigation subcommittee as part of the Crime Scene/Death Investigation SAC. However, at the time of writing [December 2017] little progress on standards development has been made and the NIJ guide remains, for the time being, the effective standard for this discipline.

6.6.4 Fires

The initial purposes of scene examination are to determine the origin and cause of the fire and, in common with post-blast scenes, to determine whether or not the fire was the result of a criminal act. Until these questions have been answered, a fire scene should be processed as a crime scene. In common with post-blast scenes, fire scenes can be complex, hazardous, and a challenge to control and to maintain evidence integrity.

Validated test methods will be required for the analysis and detection of ignitable liquids and their vapors. Optimally, those methods should lie within the scope of accreditation to ISO/IEC 17025. However, the examination of scenes is an inspection activity properly accredited to ISO/IEC 17020.

If analysis and detection equipment is used at the scene, then the points made earlier in 6.6.1 should be born in mind. The use of such equipment must lie within the scope of accreditation, and any result obtained should be considered preliminary and require confirmation in a controlled laboratory environment before drawing conclusions.

6.6.4.1 Australasia

The examination of fire scenes lies within the scope of AS5388 Part 1 for ISO/IEC 17025 accredited providers. However, as crime scene examination is an inspection activity, it is properly accredited to ISO/IEC 17020.

According to its published scope, the NZ provider the ESR is not accredited for the examination of fire scenes.

6.6.4.2 Europe Table 6.31

The 2017 BPM incorporates the other two such that the BPM presents a comprehensive and detailed guide for all parties that might be involved in the examination of fire scenes. The BPM sees the object as establishing the cause and origin of the fire and, if required, subsequent fire development. The BPM considers scene examination as a sequence of events progressively involving first response, general examination, and finally specialist examination.

The BPM adheres to the principles of control, preservation, recording, and the recovery of potential evidence. Field detection of the vapors of ignitable liquids by canines and instruments is included, but items suspected of bearing ignitable liquids are collected at the scene and processed in a laboratory.

The BPM states that the scope does not include laboratory examination or individual competence and yet Section 4.1.2 mandates competence and lists the knowledge and skills required to demonstrate competence.

Although ISO/IEC 17020 is referenced in the BPM, accreditation is not mandated. However, it is ENFSI policy[20] that members providing crime scene examination services are accredited to ISO/IEC 17020 or "taking steps towards" such accreditation.

6.6.4.3 UK/E&W Table 6.32

There is only one extant standard applying to the examination of fire scenes, which is the first listed in the table. An earlier draft is also included as it overtly conforms to ISO/IEC

Table 6.31 European Standards' Framework: Scenes-Fires

Title	Body	Year	Ref
Best Practice Manual for the Investigation of Fire Scenes	ENFSI	2017	ENFSI-BPM-FEI-01
Practical Guide for Fire Investigators and Specialists (Appendix A2 to the BPM)	ENFSI	2017	FEIWGPG-001
Practical Guide for First Responders to Fire Scenes (Appendix A1 to BPM)	ENFSI	2008	F&EIWGBPM-001

ENFSI—European Network of Forensic Science Institutes.

[20] Policy on standards for accreditation, 2016, QCC-ACR-001:006.

Table 6.32 UK Standards' Framework: Scenes—Fires

Title	Body	Year
Code of Practice for Investigators of Fires and Explosions for the Criminal Justice Systems in the UK	CFOA | IFE | AFI	2017
Code of Practice for Investigators of Fires and Explosions for the Criminal Justice Systems in the UK (draft for consultation)	AFI	2014

AFI—Association of Fire Investigators; *CFOA*—Chief Fire Officers Association; *IFE*—Institute of Fire Investigators.

17020 and the Regulator's guidelines such that they are. The extant guide focuses mostly on the competence of the individual and does not conform to ISO/IEC 17020. The absence of accreditation will reduce the quality of evidence.

6.6.4.4 US Table 6.33

Fire investigation is part of the Fires and Explosion Investigation subcommittee of the Crime Scene/Death Investigation SAC. General crime scene examination is the responsibility of a different subcommittee.

The recently updated National Fire Protection Association Guide is being considered by the Forensic Science Standards Board, introduced in 3.4.6.3, for approval and placing on the OSAC register of approved standards.

The guide was prepared by a technical committee on fire investigations. Of the 30 chapters only one covers explosives scenes. Therefore, it cannot be considered a guide for the examination of such scenes, particularly where the criminal misuse of explosives is suspected.

The guide describes a process having seven steps, which is closely similar to the scientific method described in 1.2.1. The steps are:

1. Recognize the need
2. Define the problem
3. Collect data
4. Analyze data

Table 6.33 US Standards' Framework: Scenes-Fires

Title	Body	Year	Ref
Guide for Fire and Explosion Investigations	NFPA	2017	921
Fire and Arson Scene Evidence: A Guide for Public Safety Personnel	DOJ/NIJ	2000	NCJ 181584

DOJ—Department of Justice; *NFPA*—National Fire Protection Association; *NIJ*—National Institute of Justice.

5. Develop hypothesis
6. Test hypothesis
7. Select final hypothesis

6.6.5 Scenes at Which Illicit Substances Are Manufactured—"Clan Labs" and "Bomb Factories"

These scenes are often termed "clandestine laboratories" or "clan labs" in the case of drugs and "bomb factories" in the case of explosives and explosive devices.

There are many publications on the identification and investigation of clandestine laboratories of all types—biological, chemical, explosive, and drugs. One example is that published by the US Department of Homeland Security and the Los Angeles Joint Regional Intelligence Centre (DHS, 2008). However, many are informative and few are normative.

Such normative documents that do exist primarily focuses on the health and safety of those conducting the examination. The guidance presents likely scenarios including the materials that might be encountered at such scenes and the consequent risks, which must be assessed and managed. Despite the risks, the principles of control, preserve, record, and recover still apply.

Given the importance of this discipline, the limited number of standards is noteworthy and probably the result of the difficulty in arriving at a standardized approach to what will often be a unique situation.

As mentioned earlier in 6.6.3, explosives scenes are likely to require the involvement of a bomb technician. Such personnel must be considered sources of contamination, which should be taken into account when planning scene examination and interpreting results.

Scenes of this type lend themselves to the use of equipment that facilitates analysis and detection at the scene. As stated earlier in 6.6.1, the use of such equipment at the scene must lie within the scope of accreditation of either the organization employing the operator or the organization responsible for scene examination treating the operator as a subcontractor and in conformance to ISO/IEC 17025 6.6 or ISO/IEC 17020 6.3. Even when sophisticated equipment offering high selectivity, defined in 3.4.2.3, is employed any result obtained should be considered preliminary and require confirmation in a controlled laboratory environment before drawing conclusions.

6.6.5.1 Scenes at Which Illicit Drugs Are Manufactured

Scenes at which illicit drugs are manufactured are potentially hazardous. All materials present should be assumed to be hazardous and treated as such until proved otherwise. These scenes often afford the opportunity for careful planning prior to examination and processing. The principles of control, preservation, recoding, and recovery should be easily applicable. Examination of such scenes includes inspection that should be accredited to ISO/IEC 17020.

6.6.5.1.1 Europe

ENFSI guidance on the examinations of clandestine laboratories is given in Appendix C1 "Clandestine manufacture of controlled substances or clandestine drug laboratories (CDL)" of the BPM for the Investigation of Fire Scenes ENFSI-BPM-FEI-01 Version 02—June 2017.

As an aid to risk assessment this Appendix includes a list of precursors (substances from which drugs might be synthesized) and equipment likely to be encountered in a clan lab.

6.6.5.1.2 Australasia

The examination of clandestine laboratories lies within the scope of AS5388 Part 1 for ISO/IEC 17025 accredited providers. As stated earlier, the examination of crime scenes is an inspection activity and more appropriately accredited to ISO/IEC 17020.

It is not clear from its scope whether or not ESR is accredited to ISO/IEC 17025 for the examination of clandestine laboratories. If so ANAB's supplemental Accreditation Requirements apply.

6.6.5.1.3 UK

At the time of writing [December 2017] there is no annex to the Regulator's Codes on the examination of clandestine laboratories and there is no published plan to do so.

6.6.5.1.4 US Table 6.34

This discipline seems to lie within the remit of the Seized Drugs subcommittee of the Chemistry/Instrumental Analysis SAC. The discipline is not considered part of crime scene examination.

Table 6.34 US Standards Framework: Scenes—Clandestine Drug Laboratories

Title	Body	Year	Ref
Recommendations Version 7.1 • Part III C Methods of Analysis/Clandestine Laboratory Evidence	SWGDRUG	2016	
Standard Guide for Analysis of Clandestine Drug Laboratory Evidence (under revision as WK59310)	ASTM	2012	E2882

6.6.5.1.5 International UNODC Table 6.35

The document entitled "Clandestine Manufacture of Substances under International Control" is mainly informative. However, it does include relevant safety requirements and recommendations on legal and scientific issues related to the pretrial destruction of seized drugs, precursors, and essential chemicals, as well as to clandestine laboratory investigations.

6.6.5.2 Scenes at Which Explosives and/or Explosive Devices are Manufactured

These are among the most hazardous scenes. However, they often provide an opportunity for careful planning based on intelligence gathered. The principles of control, preserve, record, and recover should be easily applicable. An examination team, including bomb technicians and other specialists as required, can be assembled prior to examination. All materials at the scene should be assumed to be hazardous and treated accordingly until it is proved otherwise. When planning and interpreting trace evidence the potential for contamination by bomb technicians should be taken into consideration. In addition to the competencies necessary for the analysis and detection of explosives at both bulk and trace levels, scene examiners will also require the skills and knowledge necessary to assess equipment and components used to make explosive devices. The major activity is inspection involving functional testing that should be accredited to ISO/IEC 17020.

6.6.5.2.1 Australasia

The examination of scenes at which explosives and explosive devices are manufactured lies within the scope of AS5388 Part 1 for ISO/IEC 17025 accredited providers. However, as crime scene examination is an inspection activity it is properly accredited to ISO/IEC 17020.

In NZ the examination of these scenes lies outside the published scope of ESR's accreditation.

Table 6.35 UNODC Standards Framework: Scenes—Clandestine Drug Laboratories

Title	Body	Year	Ref
Guidelines for the Safe Disposal of Chemicals Used in the Illicit Manufacture of Drugs	UNODC	2011	ST/NAR/36
Clandestine Manufacture of Substances under International Control	UNODC	1998	ST/NAR/10

6.6.5.2.2 Europe Table 6.29

This table was produced for post-blast scenes discussed earlier in 6.6.3. The standards listed apply equally to scenes of explosives manufacture.

Guidance on the examination of scenes at which explosives and explosive devices are manufactured is given in Appendix C2 "Clandestine manufacture of homemade explosives" of the BPM for the Investigation of Fire Scenes ENFSI-BPM-FEI-01 Version 02—June 2017.

Also listed in the table is a BPM applying to the analysis and detection of traces. A trace is defined in this document as a submicrogram[21] quantity. The analyses of bulks and precursors are not within scope.

Surprisingly, Section 2 of the Appendix suggests that explosive might be individualized in terms of source attribution.

6.6.5.2.3 UK/E&W

At the time of writing [December 2017] there is no annex to the Regulator's Codes on the examination of scenes at which explosives or explosive devices are manufactured and there are no published plans to develop any.

6.6.5.2.4 US Table 6.24

This table was produced for post-blast scenes discussed earlier in 6.6.3. The three ASTM standards listed apply equally to scenes of explosives manufacture.

Responsibility for this discipline now rests with the Fire Debris and Explosives subcommittee of the Chemistry/Instrumental Analysis SAC and standards are progressing toward approval.

6.7 CONCLUDING REMARKS

It is clear from this section that the extent of the quality standards framework varies greatly from one discipline to another. The extent may be a measure of the evidential value of the evidence type and/or the frequency of use, e.g., fingerprint comparison, DNA and drug analysis have extensive frameworks, and the forensic application of the "ologies", see 6.5.3, is limited or nonexistent.

The quality standards themselves vary by discipline and region working against the objectives of standardization and harmonization and thwarts attempts to shape forensic science as a body of knowledge and method of enquiry in its own right. Furthermore, variation makes independent fourth party assessment of conformance more difficult and risks undetected nonconformances adversely affecting quality and therefore the reliability of scientific evidence.

[21] A µg (µg) is 10^{-6}, or one millionth, of a gram.

REFERENCES

ANZPAA NIFS, May 18, 2016. Deconvoluting Forensic Standards. ANZPAA NIFS.

ATFE, 2017. SWGGUN ARK. ATFE. https://afte.org/resources/swggun-ark.

Biedermann, A., Taroni, F., 2013. On the value of probability for evaluating results of comparative pattern analysis. Forensic Science International e44–e45.

Bird, C., Found, B., 2016. The modular forensic handwriting method. Journal of Forensic Document Examination 7–83.

Champod, C., 2015. Fingerprint identification: advances since the 2009 national research Council report. Philosophical Transactions of the Royal Society B 370.

Cole, S.A., 2014. Individualization is dead, long live individualization! Reforms of reporting practices for fingerprint analysis in the United States. Law, Probability and Risk 117–150.

Cooper, G.A., Paterson, S., David Osselton, M., 2010. The United Kingdom and Ireland association of forensic Toxicologists forensic toxicology laboratory guidelines (2010). Science & Justice 166–176.

Coyle, T., September 2015. News. The Justice Gap. http://thejusticegap.com/2015/09/forensics-in-crisis-why-are-vital-skills-being-allowed-to-die-out/.

DHS, February 14, 2008. Department of Homeland Security, Intelligence Fusion Centers. Public Intelligence. https://publicintelligence.net/ufouo-dhs-identifying-clandestine-biological-chemical-explosives-and-methamphetamine-laboratories/.

Dror, I.E., Thompson, W.C., Meissner, C.A., Kornfield, I., Krane, D., Saks, M., Risinger, M., 2015. Letter to the Editor— Context Management Toolbox: A Linear Sequential Unmasking (LSU) Approach for Minimizing Cognitive Bias in Forensic Decision Making. Journal of Forensic Sciences 1111–1112.

Doyle, S., Doyle, D., 2012. The AFSP Standard — a lesson for law enforcement agencie. Science & Justice 17–19.

FBI, Oien, C.T., 2009. Forensic hair comparison: background information for interpretation. Forensic Science Communications 1–14.

Forensic Science Regultor, 2017. Codes of Practice and Conduct – Fingerprint Comparison. The Forensic Regulator, Guidance, Birmingham.

FSR, 2017. Annual Report: November 2015 – November 2016. Annual Report. The Forensic Science Regulator, Birmingham.

Krane, D.E., Ford, S., Gilder, J.R., Inman, K., Jamieson, A., Koppl, R., Kornfield, I.L., Rissinger, D.M., Rudin, N., Taylor, M.S., Thompson, W.C., 2008. Sequential Unmasking: A Means of Minimizing Observer Effects in Forensic DNA Interpretation. Journal of Forensic Science 1006–1007.

Harbison, S.A., Flemming, R.I., 2016. Forensic body fluid identification: state of the art. Dovepress 11–23.

Hsu, S.S., April 18, 2015. FBI Admits Flaws in Hair Analysis over Decades. The Washington Post.

Jayaprakash, P.T., 2013. Practical relevance of pattern uniqueness in forensic science. Forensic Science International 403, e1–e16.

Morrison, G.S., et al., 2017. A comment on the PCAST report: skip the "match"/"non-match" stage. Forensic Science International e7–e9.

NIFS, March 27, 2007. Submission for AFFSAB Accreditation in the Field of Crime Scene Investigation. NIFS.

NIJ, June 1, 2009. Bomb and Explosion Scenes. National Institute of Justice. https://www.nij.gov/topics/law-enforcement/investigations/crime-scene/guides/explosion-bombing/pages/welcome.aspx#note1.

NIST. Forensic Science SAC Chemistry/Instrumental Analysis Materials (Trace) Subcommittee.

NIST, January 9, 2017b. Forensic Database Trace Evidence Table. NIST. https://www.nist.gov/oles/forensic-database-trace-evidence-table.

NIST, July 3, 2017a. Forensic Science: OSAC Catalog of External Standards and Guidelines. NIST. https://www.nist.gov/topics/forensic-science/osac-standards-and-guidelines.

NIST, July 3, 2017c. OSAC Research & Development Needs. https://www.nist.gov/topics/forensic-science/osac-research-development-needs.

NIST, September 20, 2017d. Forensic Science SAC Chemistry/Instrumental Analysis Materials (Trace) Subcommittee. https://www.nist.gov/topics/forensic-science/osac-subcommittees/materials-trace-subcommittee.

NRC, 2009. Strengthening Forensic Science in the United Sates: A Path Forward. The National Academies Press, Washington D.C.

OSAC, October 29, 2015. OSAC Research Needs Assessment Form. NIST. https://www.nist.gov/sites/default/files/documents/forensics/osac/FRS-Research-Need-Consistency-of-Markup.pdf.

Ottens, R., Taylor, D., Abarno, D., Linacre, A., 2013. Successful direct amplification of nuclear markers from a single hair follicle. Forensic Science, Medicine and Pathology 238–243.

PCAST, 2017. An Addendum to the PCAST Report on Forensic Science in Criminal Courts. Report. President's Council of Advisors on Science and Technology, Washington D.C.

PCAST, 2016. Forensic Science in Criminal Courts: Ensuring Scientific Validity of Feature-comparison Methods. Report. Presidents Council of Advisors on Science and Technology, Washington D.C.

Saferstein, R., 2015b. Drug abuse and drug evidence. In: Saferstein, R. (Ed.), Criminalistics: An Introduction to Forensic Science. Pearson Education Ltd., Harlow, England, p. 278.

Saferstein, R., 2015a. Evidentiary value of hair and Fibres. In: Saferstein, R. (Ed.), Criminalitics: An Introduction to Forensic Science. Pearson Education Ltd., Harlow, UK, p. 255.

SOFT/AAFS, 2006. Forensic Toxicology Laboratory Guidelines 2006 Version. Society of Forensic Toxicologists. http://www.soft-tox.org/files/Guidelines_2006_Final.pdf.

UNODC, 2005. Methods for – Impurity Profiling of Heroin and Cocaine. Methods of Analysis. United Nations, New York.

van Es, A., Wiarda, W., Hordijk, M., Alberink, I., Vergeer, P., 2017. Implementation and assessment of a likelihood ratio approach for the evaluation of LA-ICP-MS evidence in forensic glass analysis. Science & Justice 181–192.

SECTION 7

Current Issues

7.1 INTRODUCTION

Most of the issues discussed below have been touched on earlier in the work. In this section they are collected together and their impact on the quality of forensic science assessed. Risks are identified, and potential remedies suggested.

The coverage is not exhaustive. Only those issues considered to have a significant impact on the quality of forensic science are discussed. In some cases, a thorough analysis of the issue is beyond the scope of this work. External factors are considered first, followed by internal factors in no particular order.

7.2 EXTERNAL FACTORS: PHILOSOPHY, LOGIC, POLITICS, AND ECONOMICS

7.2.1 Philosophy

The debate as to what is and what is not science continues. However, whatever model applies, observation, theory, and experiment remain as elements of the scientific method of inquiry to which should be added peer review.

7.2.2 Logic: Bayesian Reasoning and the Likelihood Ratio

7.2.2.1 Subjectivity and Objectivity

Over recent decades the Bayesian model of probability and inference and the use of the likelihood ratio (*LR*) as a means of expressing the strength of scientific evidence has gained ground to the extent that most forensic scientists and mathematicians regard Bayesian reasoning and the *LR* as the only rational means of evaluating and presenting scientific evidence (Berger et al., 2011). The Bayesian notion of probability is as a degree of belief. The reliance on Bayesian reasoning and the LR has a basis in metrology and rationality.

In metrology, the classical or frequentist approach to obtaining a "true"[1] result lies in repeated measurements, calculating an average value, and determining some measure of the range in which the "true" result might lie. In the frequentist model, probability is defined in terms of the relative frequency of occurrence. The estimation of probabilities is based solely on statistical sampling.

[1] As explained in Chapter 1 the true result is unknowable, all that can be determined is the range in which the "true" result might lie.

Quality Management in Forensic Science
ISBN 978-0-12-805416-1, https://doi.org/10.1016/B978-0-12-805416-1.00007-4

As stated in 1.4.5, there are two types of measurement error, random and systematic. Random errors cause results to differ in an unpredictable way. Systematic error, also known as bias in the measurement sense, causes results to differ by some constant in magnitude and sign, producing a result that is consistently higher or lower than the expected result. The potential for systematic error in analytical science is significant and systematic errors are to be expected. The frequentist model deals adequately with random error but cannot make allowance for systematic error, only the Bayesian model can. Thus, measurement uncertainty requires a Bayesian approach. This is the metrological reason for adopting and applying Bayesian reasoning.

The second reason is rationality. Bayesian reasoning is subjective in nature and *LR*s are personal and subjective (Berger and Slooten, 2016). The process involves updating beliefs as new relevant information becomes available. Over time, and in the light of new information, beliefs converge toward the truth.

As recorded in 3.4, all the codes of conduct/ethics/practice, etc. call for forensic scientists to be objective and indeed objectivity is considered one of the hallmarks of scientific enquiry. In addition, ISO/IEC 17025 and ISO/IEC 17020 specify the requirement for impartiality in Section 4.1 and mandate objectivity.

The requirement for objectivity and the subjective nature of Bayesian reasoning and the *LR* might be reconciled by examining the Bayesian process in a little more detail. In doing so, the strength of the Bayesian model should become clearer.

The first point to bear in mind is that perfect objectivity, rationality, and accuracy/truth are illusory. Organizations and individuals will have beliefs and biases formed by knowledge, experience, values, environment, and perhaps even political and professional agendas. One of the strengths of the Bayesian model is that it makes allowance for prior beliefs and accepts that prior beliefs and biases will have an influence on results obtained and opinions expressed.

According to the Bayesian model, as the amount of information increases, subjective opinions will converge toward one another such that, based on the same information, competent forensic scientists will obtain similar results and arrive at similar conclusions. In effect the Bayesian approach reduces subjectivity and increases rationality and accuracy.

The convergence toward accuracy of the Bayesian model and its stepwise reduction in subjectivity satisfies the requirement for objectivity while accepting that perfect objectivity is unachievable.

Therefore, the central question is, has sufficient information, by way of foundational research, knowledge, and experience been gained such that results and opinions are of sufficient quality to be reliable. From the perspective of quality management, this will be demonstrated by accreditation to ISO/IEC 17025 and/or ISO/IEC 17020 assuring the competence of the organization and individual together with the validity of the method employed. Together with the proviso that evaluative opinions are arrived at in conformance to the AFSP Standard (Association of Forensic Science Providers, 2009) and the ENFSI guide (ENFSI, 2015).

7.2.2.2 Transposed Conditional

Transposing the conditional is a logical trap which is easily fallen into. The so-called prosecutor's fallacy appears to be the most common form with the potential to contribute to a wrongful conviction as this error strengthens the prosecution case (R v Deen 1993) (R v Doheny and Adams, 1996).

The reason that the prosecutor's fallacy is inviting is that, even though it gives a wrong answer, it purports to answer the question in which the court is really interested; given the evidence, what is probability of guilt?

Although what follows relates to the criminal justice system, it applies equally to all disputes decided by a tribunal of fact.

The *LR* approach to the evaluation of scientific evidence was introduced and discussed in 3.4.2.4.2 and 3.4.2.4.4.

It may be of value to reproduce a quote from one of the Royal Statistical Society Practitioner Guides discussed in 3.4.2.4.4:

> *Although likelihood ratios also feature in Bayes' Theorem, there is nothing inherently or distinctively 'Bayesian' about the use of likelihood ratios or the importance of considering the probability of evidence under competing propositions. It is simply a matter of elementary logic that evidence compatible with guilt could also be compatible with innocence, and one cannot, therefore, assess its relevance or probative value without first considering how a particular item of evidence might bear on both sides of the argument, for and against. This inquiry is inescapably probabilistic.*

Recalling the *LR*,

$$LR = \frac{(pE|H_p)}{(pE|H_d)}$$

where

$pE =$ the probability of the scientific evidence (finding, observation, or result)

$H_p =$ a proposition (or hypothesis) favorable to the prosecution, compatible with guilt

$H_d =$ a hypothesis favorable to the defense, compatible with not-guilt or innocence

The vertical line means "given", what lies to its right is the condition that applies, the conditional.

Therefore, the numerator, which is the expression above the line, is in effect the probability of the scientific evidence given guilt.

A forensic scientist using the LR as a means of assessing the strength of the evidence may report, for example, that the evidence is 100 times more likely if the prosecution hypothesis is true than if the defense hypothesis is true. In effect the evidence is 100 times more likely if the accused is guilty, although a forensic scientist should never put it that way.

The fallacy is committed by swapping the terms and stating that the probability of the proposition compatible with guilt is 100 times more likely given the evidence. That was not the evidence adduced and the practical effect of this error is to strengthen the evidence in favor of the prosecution.

The probability of the evidence given the hypothesis has become the probability of the hypothesis given the evidence and these are not the same; this is expressed mathematically as,

$$pE|H \neq pH|E$$

An easily understood example of this logical fallacy is as follows. Let H be "this animal is a cat" and E be "this animal has four legs." It should be immediately obvious that $pE|H$ is close to 1, if the animal is a cat then it is almost certain to have four legs. This is not the same as $pH|E$, which is the probability that the animal is a cat given, or knowing, that it has four legs. Thus, the two are not the same.

The pressure to commit this fallacy is significant as it is the role of the fact finder to determine the probability of guilt given all the evidence presented and to reach a verdict. Questions put to the forensic scientist acting as an expert witness may well be framed by this fallacy and a simple yes/no answer may mislead the court. The forensic scientist must be alert to the risk and careful to avoid it, as must advocates and judges.

The avoidance of this logical error is one of the many benefits of the LR approach, which, as discussed in 3.4.2.4.2, also include transparency, robustness, and balance. Focusing solely on the *LR* and reporting the probability of the evidence given hypotheses, also reduces the risk of cognitive bias.

7.2.2.3 Categorical Opinions

A categorical opinion is one with a limited and fixed number of categories. In feature-comparison disciplines such opinions are common and often take the form, match/no match/inconclusive. Such opinions have three major weaknesses.

Considering the likelihood of a common source given the degree of resemblance observed between the questioned and reference materials transfers the conditional and, as demonstrated above, is logically fallacious and usurps the role of the fact finder. In addition, with a probabilistic or *LR* approach those opinions falling into the inconclusive category could be given evidential weight.

Given the initiatives detailed in 6.3.1.1, the days of categorical opinions should be numbered to be replaced with a probabilistic approach to comparison disciplines such as fingerprints.

7.2.2.4 The Quality of Qualitative Results

Analytical chemistry offers forensic science many methods for the analysis and detection of substances of interest, as demonstrated in Section 3. An important measure of method performance is selectivity.

As discussed in 3.4.2.3.1, selectivity refers to the extent to which a method can detect the substance of interest without interference from other components present in the sample, components that might enhance or weaken the signal and bias the result.

Selectivity is a particularly important method performance measure in forensic science as samples are often complex mixtures.

The selectivity of methods available and in use varies considerably; high resolution and accuracy mass spectrometry at one end of the spectrum and a test relying on observing a color change at the other.

The ideal test method would be specific, i.e., only produce a signal in response to the substance of interest and no other. As explained in 3.4.2.3.1 and stated by International Union of Pure and Applied Chemistry specificity is an unachievable aim.

Using a less selective method when a more selective method is available might call into question competence. However, there are many rational reasons for the use of less selective methods. Cost is one; it is often the case that the more selective the method the greater the cost. Another is historical use; a forensic science provider may have a long history of using a method of proven worth.

In practice, methods of varying selectivity and in various combinations are used in the analysis and detection of substances of interest. An example of the methods of varying selectivity available and in use is given in Table 7.1, which is taken from TWGFEX (Technical Working Group for Fires and Explosions) guidelines for the "identification"

Table 7.1 Selectivity of methods used in the analysis and detection of explosives according to TWGFEX

Categories 1 and 2	Category 3	Category 4
Infrared spectroscopy (IR)	Gas chromatography (GC)	Burn test
Gas chromatography/Mass spectrometry (GC-MS)	Gas chromatography/Thermal energy analyzer (GC-TEA)	Flame test
Energy dispersive X-ray analyzer (EDX)	Liquid chromatography (LC)	Spot test
Raman spectroscopy	Liquid chromatography/Thermal energy analyzer (LC-TEA)	Melting point
X-ray diffraction (XRD)	Ion chromatography (IC)	
Liquid chromatography/Mass spectrometry (LC-MS)	Capillary electrophoresis (CE)	
	Thin-layer chromatography (TLC)	
	Ion mobility spectrometry (IMS)	
	Polarizing light microscopy (PLM)	
	Stereo light microscopy (SLM)	

Note: GC, LC, IC, and CE are all separatory techniques requiring a detector to complete an analytical system.

of explosives (TWGFEX n.d.). The higher the category the more selective the method. The guidance being that a positive result obtained using the most selective of methods is sufficient for "identification," and a positive result obtained using the least selective methods requires positive results to be obtained using up to three other methods for "identification."

The question arises, how can results obtained using methods of varying selectivity and in different combinations be evaluated and the strength of evidence conveyed to the fact finder?

What is required is a measure of the quality of the reported result. As discussed in Section 1, in the case of quantitative results this is expressed in the measurement uncertainty reported with the numerical result. Where the result is qualitative, e.g., that substance X is present, what might indicate the quality of the result? The LR has been identified as a candidate (Ellison et al., 1998; Berger and Slooten, 2016). It is the case that more selective methods will generate greater *LRs* than less selective methods. Therefore, the strength of evidence would be related to selectivity and the magnitude of the *LR* could be taken as a measure of the quality of the result. By using the *LR* as a measure of the quality of the result, methods of different selectivity could be used, and the relative strength of the test result obtained conveyed to the court. The current weakness in this approach is the general lack of reliable and relevant data[2] that would allow a numerical value to be assigned to the *LR*. This would be remedied by research.

However, if it is for the fact finder to consider the probability of the hypothesis (compatible with guilt or not-guilt) given the evidence then, even when there is insufficient relevant and reliable data to allow a numerical value to be assigned, reporting the test result in the form of an *LR*, i.e., the test result is more likely given that it is substance X (H_p) rather than something other than X (H_d), is preferable to risking usurping the role of the fact finder or reporting "it could be substance X" with all the inherent risks of that illogical and potentially misleading statement (Redmayne et al., 2011).

There is now a considerable body of scholarship that supports the use of the *LR*, whether expressed numerically or qualitatively, as a means of indicating to the fact finder the strength of the scientific evidence (Berger et al., 2011; Kaye, 2012).

It should be noted that the issues of varying selectivity and the quality of qualitative results are currently [December 2017] beyond the scope of accreditation.

7.2.2.5 Advantages of the Likelihood Ratio

As stated above, and as evidenced throughout this work, there is considerable support for using the *LR* as a means of assessing the strength of scientific evidence and the Bayesian

[2] It is likely that numerical data has been generated and is available but not utilized.

model of updating subjective belief as new information becomes available. However, there are still pockets of resistance, to the approach in general and particularly where a numerical value cannot be assigned to the *LR* (Bodziak, 2012; R v T, 2010).

At this point the advantages of the *LR* approach should be considered. In addition to ensuring that the evidence is balanced, logical, robust, and transparent, as specified in the AFSP Standard (Association of Forensic Science Providers, 2009); assessing the strength of evidence in this way also reduces the risk of cognitive bias by focusing solely on the scientific evidence and ensures that the role of the fact finder is not usurped. These advantages are considerable, and all contribute to improving the quality of the scientific evidence making it more reliable than it otherwise would be.

7.2.3 Politics and Economics

Politics and economics are closely related and are considered together under one heading.

The amount of resources allocated, and priority afforded to forensic science are decided by politicians. In democracies decisions made should reflect the will of the people and/or the political climate at the time.

The replacement of the Obama administration with that of Trump in the United States is an example of political change resulting in a reallocation of recourses and changed priorities. Under Obama the NCFS (National Commission on Forensic Sciences) and OSAC (Organization of Scientific Area Committees), discussed in 4.3.2, were established with the aim of improving standards. With the change in administration the NCFS charter was not renewed and resources redirected, prioritizing the conviction the guilty (Hsu, 2017).

7.2.3.1 The Market in England and Wales

According to one author, "market exchange is superior to public ownership in promoting quality and efficiency" (Roberts, 1996)

However, the market in forensic science in England and Wales (E&W) directly lead to the closure of the Forensic Science Service (FSS) in March 2012. The FSS was a world leading forensic science provider and a pioneer in the development in forensic science and quality management.

More recently [October 2017], LGC Forensics, after around two decades of operation, has been sold to the European company Eurofins (Eurofins, 2017). The sale may not be market related. However, as many of the 43 police forces of E&W continue to take forensic science provision in-house, the size of the market shrinks making it more difficult for commercial providers to turn a profit. In-house provision also results in customers competing with suppliers.

The market is distorted in other ways (House of Commons Science and Technology Committee, 2013). The tendering process is biased in favor of the police customer. This might be argued away as securing value for money for the taxpayer. However, to win contracts providers might reduce the level of service by employing more junior staff. In-house provision by police forces also distorts the market. Some police-based providers are unaccredited and are competing with commercial providers that are and carrying the additional cost of maintaining an accredited quality management system. In addition, short-term contracts awarded to providers militate against investing in innovation and research (Governement Chief Scientific Advisor, 2015).

The trend is toward police provision. However, history suggests that police providers do not consider accreditation essential or even necessary (UK Home Office, 2016) (House of Commons Science and Technology Committee, 2016). In addition, the cost of quality might be considered prohibitive, particularly in times of austerity. If the quality of forensic science falls such that scientific evidence becomes unreliable, we may come full circle with politicians requiring forensic science provision to be removed from police control echoing the recommendation by the US 2009 National Research Council report (NRC, 2009). At the time of writing [December 2017], there is little sign of progress toward implementation.

To add some balance, the market resulted in the creation of the Forensic Science Advisory Council and the office and role of the Forensic Science Regulator.

7.2.3.2 The Equality of Arms

There appears to be a trend in criminal justice systems toward the efficient conviction of the guilty being prioritized over the acquittal of the innocent and more generally reducing the risk of wrongful convictions.

Blackstone's adage, that 10 guilty persons go free rather than one innocent person wrongfully convicted and the presumption of innocence, if not under threat are certainly in question; particularly when it comes to terrorism and the security of the law-abiding citizen (Van Sliedregt, 2009).

Forensic scientists have a clear duty to report their evidence fairly and play their part in ensuring judicial processes that rely on their expertise are fair and the decision reached is safe.

However, the pressure to secure the conviction of those charged with serious offences, particularly terrorist related, which are in effect crimes against the state or society, impact on all the ethical dilemmas a forensic scientist faces. The following are circumstances in which such dilemmas might arise:

- assessing the competence of a fellow professional
- selecting items for examination[3]
- selecting which tests to apply[4]
- selecting which method to employ[5]

[3,4,5] Where commercial pressures exist these may not be decided by the forensic scientist.

- selecting propositions for consideration
- selecting information to include in a report
- being considered a "soldier" in the war on drugs, terrorism, or crime
- advising on tactics and strategy
- being considered a member of the prosecution team.

The ethical duty of forensic scientists and law enforcement/prosecution agents differ and should be recognized. The duty of a forensic scientist is to be impartial.

However, the reality is that forensic science providers are either part of law enforcement or financially dependent on those agencies and therefore must be influenced by the objectives of law enforcement and prosecution agencies.

It is a requirement of ISO/IEC 17025 and ISO/IEC 17020 that any risk to impartiality must be identified and the risk eliminated or minimized (see 4.1.4 of both standards). The focus on impartiality will require careful management of the relationship between forensic science providers and other stakeholders. The requirement may also focus more attention on recommendation 4 of 2009 NRC Report discussed in 4.3.2.2.3 (NRC 2009).

7.2.3.3 Legal Aid

Legal aid is the provision of financial assistance to those who would otherwise be unable to afford legal representation. It provides access to justice helping to ensure equality before the law and ultimately a fair trial and a safe verdict. Most, if not all, jurisdictions have some system in place. Legal representation under legal aid includes public defenders and court-appointed lawyers.

Eligibility criteria differ and provisions are, of course, resource-dependent leaving some parties too "rich" to qualify for legal aid and too "poor" to cover the cost themselves. However, in most jurisdictions legal aid is provided to those accused of serious crimes such as murder, fraud, and terrorism.

Law enforcement agencies and prosecuting authorities have at their disposal forensic science providers that are funded by the state at the point of delivery. The argument that an equal resource should be available to the defense is often met with the response that state or major providers are accredited, and this provides an assurance that scientific evidence is reliable and, where it lies within the scope of accreditation, it should be.

With time, science advances and standards improve. What might have been considered reliable evidence yesterday might not be today. The innocence project and issues with the bullet lead analysis, disused in 4.3.2.2.2, and hair comparison (FBI National Press Office, 2015) demonstrate that accreditation is not always the assurance of quality that it might be. In addition, in their duty to secure the conviction of the accused, law enforcement and prosecuting authorities are often willing to use novel science and technology. Methods based on novel science and technology might not be fully validated and/or consensus has yet to emerge in the relevant scientific community. Such methods will not lie within the scope of accreditation. The use of methods that lie outside the scope of accreditation might not be disclosed. Therefore, defense review of scientific evidence should be undertaken as it makes an important contribution to equality before the law, a fair trial and a safe verdict.

Given the aim of universal mandatory accreditation and the fact that most forensic science laboratories used by law enforcement agencies and prosecuting authorities are accredited, there are now calls for organizations normally instructed by the defense to review scientific evidence to be accredited.

Many of the organizations that conduct defense review are small, perhaps even just one or two practitioners, and as such find it difficult to make a business case for accreditation.

If organizations that conducted defense review are to be accredited, then this needs to be recognized in the provision of legal aid so that small organizations can afford to acquire and maintain accreditation.

In 2013 the UK government implemented a major reduction in legal aid provision leading to the closure of criminal law firms (Marsden, 2013). Helpfully, in 2017 the Regulator called for more legal aid funding for reviewing digital evidence (Bowcott, 2017).

7.3 FOCUS ON LABORATORY ACTIVITIES

One of the models of the forensic science process is:

$$\text{Crime scene} \Rightarrow \text{Laboratory} \Rightarrow \text{Court}$$

As emphasized in 6.6, mistakes made at the crime scene are hard to rectify and may render scientific information unreliable or unusable. In addition, the evaluation and communication of scientific evidence remain developmental areas at present [December 2017].

Readers of substantial parts of this work will notice the focus on the quality of laboratory-based forensic science provision. The development of quality management systems (QMSs) has mainly applied to laboratory-based activities and conformance to ISO/IEC 17025. Accreditation for crime scene activities has been available since 2011; to date [December 2017] there has been little uptake. In addition, Australasian providers have rejected ISO/IEC 17020 as a crime scene standard militating against international harmonization.

A harmonized approach to the quality management of crime scene activities and the evaluation and communication of scientific evidence is required.

7.4 INDEPENDENCE

7.4.1 The Assessment of Individual Competence

As discussed in 4.3.1, the responsibility for the competence of staff in an organization accredited to ISO/IEC 17025 and/or 17020 lies with the management. This does not represent independent 3rd party assessment of the competence of the individual forensic scientist. The initiative taken by the US Forensic Specialties Accreditation Board (FSAB), reported in 3.4.4.3, of conforming to ISO/IEC 17011 and accrediting certification bodies to ISO/IEC 17024, if it comes to fruition, will be a major advance. It will be interesting to see if the UK, Europe or Australasia follow suit to further the aim of international harmonization.

The case of *R v T* (R v T, 2010) is relevant. A forensic scientist giving footwear mark evidence was found by the appellate court to have used an *LR* approach in forming an evaluative opinion and had not disclosed that fact at trial. The appellate court found that the process by which the evidence was adduced lacked transparency. The court was not critical of the forensic scientist as "he was simply following practice" but concluded that the lack of transparency was "wrong in principle." The quality issue is that the evidence was given by an employee of an accredited forensic science provider and that employee was considered an experienced expert by the court. In this case conformance to ISO/IEC 17025 was insufficient to assure the competence of the organization in training its staff. As recommend in 3.2.5 assessment of competence by an independent body accredited to ISO/IEC 17024 "Conformity assessment—General requirements for bodies operating certification of persons," discussed in 2.3 and 3.4.4.3, is the optimal solution. As reported above, a solution now adopted by the FSAB.

7.4.2 Independence of the Forensic Science Provider

The separation between law enforcement and forensic science provision has been discussed frequently in this work and earlier in this section. As reported in 4.3.2.2.3, the 2009 NRC Report (NRC, 2009) recommendation 4 calls for the removal of forensic science provision from the administrative control of law enforcement agencies and/or prosecuting authorities. The NRC thought that forensic investigations should be independent of law enforcement and that forensic scientists should function independently of law enforcement administrators. This recommendation is remarkable given that three major federal law enforcement agencies, the FBI, Bureau of Alcohol Tobacco and Firearms, and Drugs Enforcement Agency are also forensic science providers and all part of the Department of Justice. Nevertheless, to date [December 2017], and as reported earlier, there has been little progress toward implementation. Outside the US, some forensic science providers are one step removed from the law enforcement/prosecution environment in which case, separation might be easier to achieve.

Although the separation of forensic science provision from law enforcement, particularly where it is firmly entrenched, would face considerable political and cultural challenges, such a separation would go a long way to reducing the risk of cognitive bias resulting from a prosecution mindset; i.e., only considering propositions relating to the prosecution case.

The challenge to change is perhaps exemplified by the fate of the Department of Forensic Sciences (Washington DC), which tried to implement a degree of separation (Thompson, 2015).

As mentioned earlier in 3.2.2, the 2017 edition of ISO/IEC 17025 will call into question the relationship between law enforcement and forensic science provision. The requirement for impartiality was already present in ISO/IEC 17020:2012 as the same clause, 4.1. The requirement includes an absence of conflicts-of-interest. Such conflicts where they do exist must be resolved to avoid adversely affecting the activities of the provider. Relationships are specifically identified as a potential threat to impartiality, and where a risk is identified, the provider is required to demonstrate that the risk is managed. As mentioned earlier in 7.2.3.2, the new edition of ISO/IEC 17025 may well provide some impetus to the process of separating forensic science provision from law enforcement agencies and prosecuting authorities.

7.4.3 Independence in Standard Development/Setting, Conformity Assessment, and Service Provision

One organization, or closely related organisations exercising the roles of standards development, conformity assessment and service provision is another independence issue that has been raised in this work, see 3.1. This is a situation where the same organization (or closely related organizations) provides forensic science, sets standards, and assesses conformity to those standards. Optimally the three roles should be separate and independent. This is remedied by ensuring as much separation and independence of the three roles as is reasonably practicable.

The current OSAC model described in 4.3.2.2.3, has the relevant community identifying needs and the American Academy of Forensic Sciences Standards Board developing standards that, once registered by OSAC, will be used by accreditation bodies for conformance assessment. This model is optimal, and it includes sufficient independence to reduce the risk of a conflict-of-interest.

7.5 FRAGMENTATION, DISHARMONY, AND NONSTANDARDIZATION

Level 1 standards such as ISO/IEC 17025 and ISO/IEC 17020 are international consensus standards and represent a common approach that demonstrates that providers operate a management system, are technically competent, and can generate technically valid results. ISO expects the use of international standards to facilitate international harmonization of standards and procedures. As made clear in Section 3, below Level 1 there is a plethora of standards and standards setting/development bodies all contributing to variation in the management, practice, and delivery of forensic science. These factors represent a significant barrier to standardization and harmonization.

Although each accredited provider may argue that accreditation is a sufficient assurance of quality, which it is, the utility of the science depends on the level of service provided. Accreditation bodies can only accredit the service provided. A provider relying on tandem mass spectrometry, a highly selective technique, to generate results is operating at a higher standard than a provider relying on thin layer chromatography, a far less selective technique. The more selective the method the more weight that can be attached to the results obtained and the stronger the evidence.

For the sake of justice, harmonization should be the goal. Justice systems should be offered the same level of service and quality of forensic science irrespective of jurisdiction. Clearly there are cost implications. However, in Australasia, Europe, and North America forensic science provisions should be sufficiently resourced to facilitate the development of global standards and promote harmonization, a role perhaps for the International Forensic Science Alliance, see 2.5.5.

7.6 THE IMPACT OF SCIENTIFIC AND TECHNOLOGICAL DEVELOPMENTS

Forensic scientists should not be relying on courts of law and their admissibility criteria to determine the validity of methods used. It has been argued in this work that courts are not competent to make such determinations, notwithstanding US Federal Rule 702, which makes judges gatekeepers. Forensic scientists should consider it their duty to fully validate novel methods, ideally prior to use, and certainly before evidence based on results obtained is reported. Full validation should include an interlaboratory comparison exercise.

The habit of seizing novel methods with the aim of strengthening evidence only to find out at a later date that the evidence adduced is not as strong as first thought is not in the interests of justice. The premature use of novel methods to obtain an advantage for the prosecution is perhaps another example of the trend toward prioritizing the conviction of the guilty over the acquittal of the innocent.

It is right and proper for forensic science to adopt and apply scientific and technological advances but in a way that serves justice and is not partisan. It is certainly not the role of the forensic scientist to expend every effort to help secure a conviction. In addition to being ethically questionable, such behaviour might not conform to the review of requests, tenders and contracts section of ISO/IEC 17025.

Developments in science and technology are to be expected and must be accommodated in a quality standards framework to ensure reliability. Standards setting bodies such as ISO are not able to respond quickly. In the case on the application of novel science and technology OSAC in the United States, the Regulator in E&W and National Institute of Forensic Science in Australasia should make it a priority to develop relevant standards in a timely fashion.

7.7 ACCESS TO DOCUMENTED STANDARDS AND TRANSPARENCY

Transparency is a specified requirement of the AFSP Standard (Association of Forensic Science Providers, 2009) and the ENFSI Guidelines (ENFSI, 2015) both discussed in Section 3.

The requirement is described in the AFSP Standard as:

Transparency—The expert will be able to demonstrate how he [sic]

came to his conclusion. He will set out in the statement or report the basis of his opinion viz.:

- *Propositions addressed.*
- *Test or examination results.*
- *The background information he has used in arriving at his conclusion.*
- *He will be able, if required, to provide the data he has used and its provenance.*

And in the ENFSI Guidelines

Transparency—The reported conclusions should be derived from a demonstrable process in both the case file and the report .... The report should be written in such a way that it is suitable for a wide audience of readers (i.e., participants in the justice system). It may include supplements explaining the technical background.

Transparency as required by these standards echoes the legal requirement for transparency specified in Davie v Magistrates of Edinburgh (1953) and the Ikarian Reefer (1993) discussed in 4.3.3.2.1.

In addition, as reported in 1.2.1, peer review is an essential part of the scientific method that depends on the availability of accurate, comprehensive, and accessible records of methods used, results obtained, and their interpretation, i.e., transparency. Transparency, therefore, is an essential requirement in forensic science.

One major issue is that many reports do not satisfy the requirement for transparency. They provide insufficient detail to enable the reader to know how the conclusions contained in the report were arrived at.

The simple remedy would be to include the necessary detail in the report. However, most providers instead rely on accreditation and the assurance it gives that the conclusions reported can be relied on. Accreditation to either ISO/IEC 17025 or ISO/IEC 17020 does provide an assurance that scientific evidence is of sufficient quality to be relied on. However, when accreditation is claimed and there is evidence that competence or validity may be in question, review of the relevant parts of the documented QMS and the methods used is necessary. Access to the documented QMS of providers including accredited methods then becomes an issue. As stated in 1.3.1, the quality of scientific evidence is dependent on the competence of the organization, the competence of the individual, and the validity of methods.

In restricting access, providers sometimes claim that such documentation represents intellectual property that must be protected. Access to inspect documents is granted, but the inspection must take place at the provider's premises, which delays justice and adds to the cost. The remedy is to defeat the intellectual property argument and place the entire documented QMS, including accredited and nonaccredited methods, online.

One of the unforeseen consequences of creating the market in E&W was providers charging for the time and effort involved in facilitating defense examinations. Again, placing the QMS and methods online would reduce costs.

The recommendation by the NCFS and implemented by the US Attorney General that the QMS of providers should be available online, discussed in 4.3.2, is the remedy. Such documentation including methods has been paid for by the taxpayer, directly or indirectly, and access should be freely available to all stakeholders, citizens, and others. Indeed, the entire case file, redacted as necessary, could be made available online bringing significant savings in time, effort, and cost.

The availability to all stakeholders of the documented QMS, including methods, would also promote standardization and harmonization. A provider would be better able to benchmark its service against others. Variation in methods would reduce, and in time industry standard methods, would be developed supporting international harmonization.

Access and transparency would decrease the cost of justice and increase its efficiency, supporting the overriding objective of the E&W Crown Prosecution Service specified in Part 1 of the Criminal Procedure Rules.

Another transparency issue is the limited amount of information given in the publicly available scope of accreditation. A simple but vital question is, does the method used by the provider lie within the scope of accreditation? Some accrediting bodies, such as UKAS (UK Accreditation Service), provide sufficient detail others, such as NATA (the Australian national accreditation body), provide very little, making it impossible to answer that question. Accreditation bodies should include sufficient detail in the scope of accreditation to enable stakeholders to determine whether or not a method used to produce scientific information or evidence lies within the scope of the provider's accreditation.

A further transparency issue is that most documented standards lie behind a pay wall. This is a barrier to conformance and the promotion of good practice and harmonization. Stakeholders should not have to pay to find out what standard the provider is meant to be conforming to and whether it is conforming to that standard. The organizational infrastructure, the generalist nature, and the scope of Level 1 international standards justifies the cost of access. However, a charge for access to lower level standards is harder to justify. In addition, as they apply to the nuts and bolts of forensic science and conformance is required as standard practice, forensic science providers and all stakeholders should have unrestricted access to any and all relevant standards.

In the interests of justice, promoting good practice and ensuring the quality and reliability of forensic science access should be free.

It is relevant to note that the OSAC has negotiated free access to all forensic (E30 Committee) ASTM International standards for SAC members and affiliates (NIST, 2017).

Except for Level 1 ISO standards, forensic science providers, and indeed all stakeholders, should have unrestricted access to standards applying to the management practice and delivery of forensic science. Such access would promote a better understanding of quality management in forensic science among all the stakeholders: law enforcers, defenders, prosecutors, the judiciary, providers, academics, and interested citizens. Better understanding can only positively contribute to the efficient delivery of justice.

The development of AS5388:2012 "Forensic Analysis" into an ISO Standard, which as discussed in 3.4.2 and covers the nuts and bolts of forensic practice, is a particular threat to greater transparency, unless ISO makes the standards freely available which is unlikely.

Transparency and the development of quality management in forensic science requires that stakeholders have unrestricted access to the standards to which forensic science providers must conform.

7.8 STREAMLINED FORENSIC REPORTING

At present [December 2017] the issues discussed here relate only to the jurisdiction of E&W. Streamlined forensic reporting (SFR) is employed in other jurisdictions, e.g., the state of Victoria in Australia, but not to the same degree as in E&W or with the same risks.

SFR is part of a case management process that aims to achieve an early identification of the key issues in a case and to reduce costs and delays associated with the use of scientific evidence in criminal proceedings. In the first instance reports served on the defense contain only selected results on which the prosecution proposes to rely often reported by a nonscientist (CPS n.d.). The defense is then expected either to accept or contest the results. If the defense wishes to contest, then reasons must be given. If issues are raised the prosecution will then serve a second stage SFR addressing only the issues raised by the defense. If the defense requires further scientific work, then it must again explain why. A full evaluative report by an expert instructed by the prosecution is very much a last resort.

To identify issues and explain why further work and reports are required, the defense must instruct their own expert. Given the pressures on legal aid the defense might decide not to do so, potentially allowing unreliable scientific evidence to go unchallenged.

According to Keith Borer Consultants, a forensic science provider based in England:

> *In simple terms, SFR means that the prosecution undertake just enough forensic work to support a charge/secure a guilty plea.*
>
> **Bloor (2013)**

Although there is little doubt that SFR reduces costs and provides a swift and sure route to the conviction of the guilty, it seriously hampers the defense of the innocent as is made plain by Sallavaci in her thorough review (Sallavaci, 2016). SFR is more evidence of the political trend, discussed earlier in 7.2.3.2, toward weakening the presumption of innocence, strengthening the hand of the prosecution and reversing Blackstone's adage in an attempt to reduce the risk of acquitting the guilty.

If the defense has the resources to instruct its own expert and successfully argues for an expert's report from the prosecution, that report will presumably be based on work undertaken by an accredited forensic science provider and prepared by an expert.

Initial SFR reports do not conform to the Criminal Practice Rule 19 or the requirements of ISO/IEC 17020 or ISO/IEC 17025. Stage 1 reports are not intended to be adduced as evidence, but they are (R v Abraham Ghebre-Amlak, 2014). When the defense does not contest the scientific evidence there seems no alternative. In which case the quality implication is that the interpretation of the results will be left to the fact finder or interpreted in the witness box but outside any quality standards framework.

To give an example, a partial Y-STR DNA profile is obtained from a vaginal swab. The work is done in an accredited laboratory and the profile passed to the police. The police interrogate the national DNA database and get a "hit" for the accused. The Stage 1 SFR is prepared by the police and contains the information that a match has been found between the DNA of the accused and the DNA on the vaginal swab. The accused accepts that it is his DNA, but, importantly, may not be guilty of the offense. No further scientific work is done and the evidence that the accused's DNA is on the vaginal swab is adduced at trial. Apart from the "match" between questioned Y-STR profile and the reference profile on the database and perhaps the fact that the questioned profile is partial, the fact finder is left to determine the strength of the evidence and interpret it in the context of the case; activities that now lie outside the quality standards framework of ISO/IEC 17025/17020 and the Regulator's Codes.

Quality failures in the SFR process have already contributed to a miscarriage justice; a plea of guilty to an offense not committed (R v Lawrence (Nyira), 2013).

As stated earlier, SFR is an efficient and effective way of securing the conviction of the guilty but seems to be based on a presumption of guilt and places significant barriers in the way of acquitting the innocent. Acquitting the innocent is part of the "overriding objective" of the Crown Prosecution Service, as specified in Part 1 of the Criminal Procedure Rules.

From the perspective of quality management, it is hard to see how a forensic science provider accredited to ISO/IEC 17025/17020 and compliant with the Regulator's codes could support such a scheme.

All reports issued should conform to a quality standards framework that assists fact finders assess scientific evidence and tribunals make safe decisions based on a fair process.

7.9 CONCLUDING REMARKS

This section has highlighted some of the issues that still face forensic science and put at risk the quality and reliability of scientific information. The major risks arise from;

- the relationship between forensic science providers and law enforcement/prosecuting agencies,
- the premature use of novel science and technology which lies outside a quality standards framework,
- errors in reasoning,
- lack of standardization and harmonization,
- lack of resources, and
- lack of transparency.

REFERENCES

Association of Forensic Science Providers, 2009. Standards for the formulation of evaluative forensic science expert opinion. Science and Justice 49, 161–164.
Berger, C.E.H., Buckleton, J., Champod, C., Evett, I.W., Jackson, G., 2011. Response to Faigman et al. Science and Justice 215.
Berger, C.E.H., Slooten, K., 2016. The LR does not exist. Science and Justice 388–391.
Bloor, J., March 2013. Streamlined Forensic Reporting - The Forensic Expert Perspective. Keith Borer Consultants. http://www.keithborer.co.uk/news/view-article/streamlined-forensic-reporting-the-forensic-expert-perspective.
Bodziak, W.J., 2012. A Final Comment. Law, Probabaility and Risk, pp. 363–364.
Bowcott, O., May 3, 2017. Official Forensic Regulator Calls for Increase to Legal Aid Funding. The Gaurdian.
CPS., n.d. Streamlined Forensic Reporting Guidance and Toolkit, CPS. http://www.cps.gov.uk/legal/s_to_u/scientific_evidence/sfr_guidance_and_toolkit/.
Davie v Magistrates of Edinburgh, 1953. 34 (Court of Sessions).
Ellison, S.L.R., Gregory, S., Hardcastle, W.A., 1998. Quantifying Uncertainty in Qualitative Analysis. Analyst, pp. 1155–1161.
ENFSI, 2015. ENFSI Guideline for Evaluative Reporting in Forensic Science. Guide. ENFSI, Wiesbaden.
Eurofins, 2017. News. Business Wire. October 12. http://www.businesswire.com/news/home/20171011006395/en/Eurofins-reinforce-Forensic-services-portfolio-footprint-acquisition.
FBI National Press Office, 2015. FBI Testimony on Microscopic Hair Analysis Contained Errors in at Least 90 Percent of Cases in Ongoing Review. Press Release. FBI, Washington, DC.
Governement Chief Scientific Advisor, 2015. Annual Report: Forensic Science and beyond: Authenticity, Provenance and Assurance. Government Office for Science, London.
House of Commons Science, Technology Committee, 2016. Forensic Science Strategy. House of Commons, London.
House of Commons Science and Technology Committee, 2013. Forensic science: second report of the session 2013-14. In: Parliamentary Committee, vol. 1. The Sationery Office, London.
Hsu, S.S., 2017 10 April. Sessions Orders Justice Dept. To End Forensic Science Commission, Suspend Review Policy. The Washington Post.
Ikarian Reefer, 1993. 68 (2 Lloyds Law Report).
Kaye, D.H., 2012. Likelihoodism, Bayesianism, and a pair of shoes. Jurimetrics 1–9.
Marsden, S., 23 September, 2013. Michael Mansfield QC's chambers to close over 'devastating' legal aid changes. The Telegraph. https://www.telegraph.co.uk/news/uknews/law-and-order/10328955/Michael-Mansfield-QCs-chambers-to-close-over-devastating-legal-aid-changes.html.
NIST, October 2, 2017. ASTM Standards Access. National Institute of Standards and Technology. https://www.nist.gov/topics/forensic-science/organization-scientific-area-committees-osac/astm-standards-access.
NRC, 2009. Strengthening Forensic Science in the United Sates: A Path Forward. The National Academies Press, Washington, DC.
R v Abraham Ghebre-Amlak, 2014. 1670 (EWCA).

R v Deen CADC 21 Dec 1993
R v Doheny and Adams, 1996. Crim 728 (EWCA).
R v Lawrence (Nyira), 2013. Crim 1054 (EWCA).
R v T, 2010. Crim 2439 (EWCA).
Redmayne, M., Roberts, P., Aitkin, C., Jackson, G., 2011. Forensic Science Evidence in Question. Criminal Law Review, pp. 347–356.
Roberts, P., 1996. What price a free market in forensic science Services? The organization and regulation of science in the criminal process. British Journal of Criminology 37–60.
Sallavaci, O., 2016. Streamlined reporting of forensic evidence in England and Wales: is it the way forward? The International Journal of Evidence and Proof 235–249.
Thompson, W.C., May 8, 2015. A Setback for Forensic Science. The Washington Post.
TWGFEX., n.d. Recommended Guidelines for Forensic Identification of Intact Explosives, SWGFEX. https://docs.wixstatic.com/ugd/4344b0_48a898605b19408d9e0b649afc5febbe.pdf.
UK Home Office, 2016. Forensic Science Strategy: A National Approach to Forensic Science Delivery in the Criminal Justice System. HMSO Cm9271, London.
Van Sliedregt, E., 2009. A Contemporary Reflection on the Presumption of Innocence. Revue internationale de droit pénal, pp. 247–267.

APPENDIX A

International Association for Identification: Code of Ethics and Standards of Professional Conduct

The ethical and professionally responsible International Association for Identification (IAI) member or certificant:

1. PROFESSIONALISM

1.01 Is unbiased, and objective, approaching all assignments and examinations with due diligence and an open mind.

1.02 Conducts full and fair examinations in which conclusions are based on the evidence and reference material relevant to the evidence, not on extraneous information, political pressure, or other outside influences.

1.03 Is aware of his/her limitations and only renders conclusions that are within his/her area of expertise and about matters for which he/she has given careful consideration.

1.04 Truthfully communicates with all parties (i.e., the investigator, prosecutor, defense, and other expert witnesses) about information related to his/her analyses, when communications are permitted by law and agency practice.

1.05 Maintains confidentiality of restricted information obtained in the course of professional endeavors.

1.06 Reports to appropriate officials any conflicts between his/her ethical/professional responsibilities and applicable agency policy, law, regulation, or other legal authority.

1.07 Does not accept or participate in any case in which he/she has any personal interest or the appearance of such an interest and shall not be compensated based upon the results of the proceeding.

1.08 Conducts oneself personally and professionally within the laws of his/her respective jurisdiction and in a manner that does not violate public trust.

1.09 Reports to the appropriate legal or administrative authorities unethical, illegal, or scientifically questionable conduct of other practitioners of which he/she has knowledge.

1.10 Does not knowingly make, promote, or tolerate false accusations of a professional or criminal nature.

1.11 Supports sound scientific techniques and practices and does not use his/her position to pressure a practitioner to arrive at conclusions or results that are not supported by reliable scientific data.

2. COMPETENCY AND PROFICIENCY

2.01 Is committed to career-long learning in the forensic disciplines in which he/she practices, and stays abreast of new technology and techniques while guarding against the misuse of methods that have not been validated.

2.02 Expresses conclusions and opinions that are based on generally accepted protocols and procedures. New and novel techniques must be validated prior to implementation in case work.

2.03 Is properly trained and determined to be competent through relevant testing prior to undertaking the examination of the evidence.

2.04 Gives utmost care to the treatment of any samples or items of potential evidentiary value to avoid tampering, adulteration, loss, or unnecessary consumption.

2.05 Uses controls and standards, including reviews and verifications appropriate to his/her discipline, when conducting examinations and analyses.

3. CLEAR COMMUNICATIONS

3.01 Accurately represents his/her education, training, experience, and area of expertise.

3.02 Presents accurate and complete data in reports, testimony, publications, and oral presentations.

3.03 Makes and retains full, contemporaneous, clear, and accurate records of all examinations and tests conducted, and conclusions drawn, in sufficient detail to allow meaningful review and assessment of the conclusions by an independent person competent in the field.

3.04 Does not falsify or alter reports or other records, or withhold relevant information from reports for strategic or tactical litigation advantage.

3.05 Testifies to results obtained and conclusions reached only when he/she has confidence that the opinions are based on good scientific principles and methods. Opinions are to be stated so as to be clear in their meaning.

3.06 Attempts to qualify his/her responses while testifying when asked a question with the requirement that a simple "yes" or "no" answer be given, if answering "yes" or "no" would be misleading to the judge or the jury.

The ethical and professionally responsible International Association for Identification (IAI) member.

4. ORGANIZATIONAL RESPONSIBILITY

4.01 Does not misrepresent his/her affiliation with the IAI.

4.02 Does not issue any misleading or inaccurate statement that gives the appearance of representing the official position of the IAI.

4.03 Reports violations of this code of which he/she knows to the President of the IAI.

4.04 Cooperate fully with any official investigation by the IAI.

APPENDIX B

Forensic Science Regulator: Code of Conduct for Forensic Science Practitioners

The Forensic Science Regulator (the Regulator) sets out for all practitioners, whether instructed by the prosecution or defence, the values and ideals the profession stands for. This Code of Conduct provides a clear statement to customers and the public of what they have a right to expect.

As a practitioner you must

1. Recognise your overriding duty is to the court and to the administration of justice.
2. Act with honesty, integrity, objectivity and impartiality.
3. Comply with the legal obligations imposed on practitioners (and specifically expert witnesses) in the jurisdiction(s) in which you practice.
4. Declare, at the earliest opportunity, any personal, business, financial and/or other interest that could be perceived as a potential conflict of interest.
5. Act, and in particular provide expert advice and evidence, only within the limits of your professional competence.
6. Take all reasonable steps to maintain and develop your professional competence, taking account of material research and developments within the relevant field.
7. Inform those instructing you, in writing, of any information which may reasonably be considered to undermine your credibility as a practitioner or the reliability of the material you produce and include this information with/within any written report provided to those instructing you.
8. Establish the integrity and continuity of items as they come into your possession and ensure these are maintained whilst in your possession.
9. Seek access to exhibits/productions/information that may have a significant impact on the output from your work9 and record both the request for material and the result of that request.
10. Conduct casework using methods of demonstrable validity and comply with the quality standards set by the Regulator10 relevant to the area in which you work.
11. Be prepared to review any casework if any new information or developments are identified that would significantly impact on the output from your work9.

12. Ensure that the relevant instructing party is informed where you have good grounds for believing a situation may result in a miscarriage of justice, either by (a) invoking the appropriate organisational processes for addressing potential miscarriages of justice or (where you do not operate as part of an organisation or the organisation does not have appropriate procedures) (b) by informing the party directly.
13. Preserve confidentiality unless the law obliges, a court/tribunal orders, or a customer explicitly authorises disclosure.

APPENDIX C

The National Code of Professional Responsibility for Forensic Science and Forensic Medicine Service Providers (USA)

The National Code of Professional Responsibility ("Code") defines a framework for promoting integrity and respect for the scientific process and encouraging a research-based culture. To increase public confidence in the quality of forensic services, each forensic science and forensic medicine service provider must meet the requirements enumerated below:

1. Accurately represent his/her education, training, experience, and areas of expertise.
2. Pursue professional competency through training, proficiency testing, certification, and presentation and publication of research findings.
3. Commit to continuous learning in the forensic disciplines and stay abreast of new findings, equipment, and techniques.
4. Promote validation and incorporation of new technologies, guarding against the use of non-valid methods in casework and the misapplication of validated methods.
5. Avoid tampering, adulteration, loss, or unnecessary consumption of evidentiary materials.
6. Avoid participation in any case where there are personal, financial, employment-related, or other conflicts of interest.
7. Conduct full, fair, and unbiased examinations, leading to independent, impartial, and objective opinions and conclusions.
8. Make and retain full, contemporaneous, clear, and accurate written records of all examinations and tests conducted and conclusions drawn, in sufficient detail to allow meaningful review and assessment by an independent person competent in the field.
9. Base conclusions on generally accepted procedures supported by sufficient data, standards, and controls, not on political pressure or other outside influence.
10. Do not render conclusions that are outside one's expertise.
11. Prepare reports in unambiguous terms, clearly distinguishing data from interpretations and opinions, and disclosing all known associated limitations that prevent invalid inferences or mislead the judge or jury.
12. Do not alter reports or other records, or withhold information from reports for strategic or tactical litigation advantage.

13. Present accurate and complete data in reports, oral and written presentations and testimony based on good scientific practices and validated methods.
14. Communicate honestly and fully, once a report is issued, with all parties (investigators, prosecutors, defense attorneys, and other expert witnesses), unless prohibited by law.
15. Document and notify management or quality assurance personnel of adverse events, such as an unintended mistake or a breach of ethical, legal, scientific standards, or questionable conduct.
16. Ensure reporting, through proper management channels, to all impacted scientific and legal parties of any adverse event that affects a previously issued report or testimony.

APPENDIX D

American Academy of Forensic Sciences: Code of Ethics and Conduct

As a means to promote the highest quality of professional and personal conduct of its members and affiliates, the following constitutes the Code of Ethics and Conduct which is endorsed by all members and affiliates of the American Academy of Forensic Sciences:

1. Every member and affiliate of the Academy shall refrain from exercising professional or personal conduct adverse to the best interests and objectives of the Academy. The objectives stated in the Preamble to these bylaws shall be to promote professionalism, integrity, and competency in the membership's actions and associated activities; to promote education for and research in the forensic sciences; to encourage the study, improve the practice, elevate the standards and advance the cause of the forensic sciences; to promote interdisciplinary communications; and to plan, organize and administer meetings, reports and other projects for the stimulation and advancement of these and related purposes.
2. No member or affiliate of the Academy shall materially misrepresent his or her education, training, experience, area of expertise, or membership status within the Academy.
3. No member or affiliate of the Academy shall materially misrepresent data or scientific principles upon which his or her conclusion or professional opinion is based.
4. No member or affiliate of the Academy shall issue public statements that appear to represent the position of the Academy without first obtaining specific authority from the Board of Directors.

APPENDIX E

Australia and New Zealand Forensic Science Society: Code of Professional Practice

1. OBLIGATIONS TO SOCIETY

1.1 Be informed of legal, social, environmental, economic and other possible consequences. Forensic practitioners must take reasonable steps to be informed, and to inform clients and employees, of legal, social, environmental, economic and other possible consequences that might arise from professional forensic services.

1.2 Act with honesty, integrity, fairness and without discrimination. Forensic practitioners must act with honesty, integrity, fairness and without unlawful discrimination.

1.3 Take reasonable steps to safeguard health, welfare and public safety.

Forensic practitioners must take reasonable steps to safeguard the health, welfare and safety of the public in the exercise of their roles and duties.

2. OBLIGATIONS TO CLIENTS AND EMPLOYERS

2.1 Act truthfully, objectively, and not mislead people, nor engage in misrepresentation, including through omission.

Forensic practitioners must act truthfully and objectively, and not knowingly provide misleading information, statements, reports, opinions or evidence, nor knowingly misrepresent a situation. Forensic practitioners must never misrepresent credentials, education, training, experience or membership status.

2.2 Disclosure obligations

Forensic practitioners must disclose actual or possible conflicts of interest to a client or employer upon discovery of that actual, potential or perceived, conflict of interest. Conflicts of interest will include any financial or other interest that is likely to affect, or appear to affect, the forensic practitioner's judgement.

Conflicts of interest may include:

- accepting instructions or assignments that would knowingly create a possible conflict of interest between themselves and their clients or employees
- where a forensic practitioner reasonably believes they have been subject to undue pressure or influence to obtain a specific outcome which may not be impartial

Disclosure includes:

- forensic practitioners have an overriding duty to the court and justice system for disclosure. Client confidentiality is important but should not to be an excuse for nondisclosure. Where a forensic practitioner believes they are being inhibited from appropriate disclosure they should:
  - seek explicit authorisation by the client to disclose specified information,
  - advise the client of any requirements by the law or court ordered process to disclose specified information, and,
  - endeavour to advise their client or employer that information that could identify the complainant/s and or their personal details may be contained within the practitioner's court report.

Notwithstanding the above, a forensic practitioner must not disclose commercially sensitive or proprietary technology information of an employer or client without the written agreement of that employer or client.

2.3 Examinations and analyses

A forensic practitioner must:

- examine and analyse the evidence in a case provided to them in a manner proportionate to the nature of the case,
- conduct and document all examinations and analysis using established protocols and fit-for-purpose or validated methods,
- render opinions having a basis that is demonstratively valid,
- not withhold any findings, where inculpatory or exculpatory, that would cause the facts of a case to be misrepresented or distorted, and,
- disclose or make available test methods if requested.

3. GENERAL PROFESSIONAL OBLIGATIONS

3.1 Apply knowledge, skill and judgement

Forensic practitioners must bring knowledge, skill, judgement and care that are of a standard which might reasonably be expected by the public by relevant professional peers, or as determined by formal standards.

3.2 Not engage in professional misconduct, fraudulent, or dishonest behaviour.

Forensic practitioners must not:

- engage in misconduct in a professional respect, or,
- engage in fraudulent or dishonest behaviour in their forensic practice.

3.3 Communicate with fairness, honesty, and adequate knowledge.

Forensic practitioners must, both orally and in writing, express opinions, make statements, or give evidence with fairness, honesty, and only on the basis of adequate knowledge.

3.4 Not promise, accept or give inducements Forensic practitioners must not:

- promise to give, or give to any person, anything intended to improperly influence that person's decisions as they relate to the forensic practitioner's services or to secure work, or,
- accept from any person anything intended to improperly influence the forensic practitioner's decisions.

3.5 Work within areas of competence and not misrepresent competence.

Forensic practitioners must:

- undertake forensic services only within their area of competence,
- not misrepresent their competence, and,
- not knowingly permit forensic practitioner's whose work they are responsible for to breach the above obligations.

Examples of competence in an area of practice include:

- formal training in that area
- previous relevant experience
- consultation with or reference to a person competent in the area to supervise the task
- participation in appropriate proficiency tests or competency based assessment.

Examples of not misrepresenting competence in an area of practice include:

- fully informing the client as to any limitations or legitimate concerns that a forensic practitioner might have with regard to their competence relevant to the client's specific instructions, and/or,
- if competence is not fully established organising for a person competent in the area to provide supervision of or advice to the forensic practitioner in relation to the task.

3.6 Supervision

If a forensic practitioner supervises a person in the carrying out of forensic services the forensic practitioner in the role of supervisor, must:

- have sufficient knowledge of the forensic service carried out,
- sufficient control over any outputs of the forensic services to reasonably form the view that the standard of the forensic services meets relevant standards, and,
- take full professional responsibility for the forensic services provided by the supervised person.

3.7 Continue to develop knowledge, skills and expertise.

Forensic practitioners must:

- continue to develop relevant knowledge, skills, and expertise throughout their careers,
- actively assist and encourage those with whom they are associated to do likewise, and,
- seek to meet Continuing Professional Development (CPD) requirements appropriate to their discipline and role.

APPENDIX F

The Criminal Procedure Rules Part 19 (Applying in England and Wales)

1. EXPERT'S DUTY TO THE COURT

Rule 19.2.

1. An expert must help the court to achieve the overriding objective—
   a. by giving opinion which is—
      i. objective and unbiased, and
      ii. within the expert's area or areas of expertise; and
   b. by actively assisting the court in fulfilling its duty of case management under rule 3.2, in particular by—
      i. complying with directions made by the court, and
      ii. at once informing the court of any significant failure (by the expert or another) to take any step required by such a direction.

2. This duty overrides any obligation to the person from whom the expert receives instructions or by whom the expert is paid.
3. This duty includes obligations—
   a. to define the expert's area or areas of expertise—
      i. in the expert's report, and
      ii. when giving evidence in person;
   b. when giving evidence in person, to draw the court's attention to any question to which the answer would be outside the expert's area or areas of expertise; and
   c. to inform all parties and the court if the expert's opinion changes from that contained in a report served as evidence or given in a statement.

2. CONTENT OF EXPERT'S REPORT

Rule 19.4. … an expert's report must

1. give details of the expert's qualifications, relevant experience and accreditation;
2. give details of any literature or other information which the expert has relied on in making the report;

3. contain a statement setting out the substance of all facts given to the expert which are material to the opinions expressed in the report, or upon which those opinions are based;
4. make clear which of the facts stated in the report are within the expert's own knowledge;
5. where the expert has based an opinion or inference on a representation of fact or opinion made by another person for the purposes of criminal proceedings (for example, as to the outcome of an examination, measurement, test or experiment)—
   a. identify the person who made that representation to the expert,
   b. give the qualifications, relevant experience, and any accreditation of that person, and
   c. certify that that person had personal knowledge of the matters stated in that representation;
6. where there is a range of opinion on the matters dealt with in the report—
   a. summarise the range of opinion, and
   b. give reasons for the expert's own opinion;
7. if the expert is not able to give an opinion without qualification, state the qualification;
8. include such information as the court may need to decide whether the expert's opinion is sufficiently reliable to be admissible as evidence;
9. contain a summary of the conclusions reached;
10. contain a statement that the expert understands an expert's duty to the court, and has complied and will continue to comply with that duty; and
11. contain the same declaration of truth as a witness statement.

APPENDIX G

Council for the Registration of Forensic Practitioners: Required Competencies

1. Knowing the hypothesis or question to be tested
2. Establishing that items submitted are suitable for the requirements of the case
3. Confirming that the best type of examination has been selected
4. Conforming that the examination was carried out competently
5. Recording, summarizing, and collating the results of the examination
6. Interpreting the results in accordance with established scientific principles
7. Considering alternative hypotheses
8. Preparing a report based on the findings
9. Presenting oral evidence to court and at case conferences
10. Ensuring all documentation is fit for purpose

APPENDIX H

UK Forensic Science Liaison Group: Code of Practice

1. Confine themselves to the areas of their professional competence
2. Ensure that they possess the skills and knowledge required for any task they undertake
3. Employ procedures which prevent the corruption or contamination of evidence
4. Only employ methods of demonstrable validity
5. Make a full, contemporaneous and accurate record of all work undertaken, in a form which can readily be reviewed for reliability and accuracy
6. Review the results of their examinations critically, ensuring that any limitations are clearly stated
7. Set out their conclusions clearly, giving details of any limitations or other possible explanations
8. Make available all information to any person having a legal entitlement to receive it, and also protect such information from improper disclosure
9. Conduct all their professional activities in a manner which protects the health and safety of themselves, their colleagues and the public
10. Draw the attention of their line management to any substantive failure to observe the above principles

APPENDIX I

New Zealand Code of Conduct for Expert Witnesses

DUTY TO THE COURT

1. An expert witness has an overriding duty to assist the court impartially on relevant matters within the expert's area of expertise.
2. An expert witness is not an advocate for the party who engages the witness.

EVIDENCE OF EXPERT WITNESS

3. In any evidence given by an expert witness, the expert witness must—
   a. acknowledge that the expert witness has read this code of conduct and agrees to comply with it:
   b. state the expert witness' qualifications as an expert:
   c. state the issues the evidence of the expert witness addresses and that the evidence is within the expert's area of expertise:
   d. state the facts and assumptions on which the opinions of the expert witness are based:
   e. state the reasons for the opinions given by the expert witness:
   f. specify any literature or other material used or relied on in support of the opinions expressed by the expert witness:
   g. describe any examinations, tests, or other investigations on which the expert witness has relied and identify, and give details of the qualifications of, any person who carried them out.
4. If an expert witness believes that his or her evidence or any part of it may be incomplete or inaccurate without some qualification, that qualification must be stated in his or her evidence.
5. If an expert witness believes that his or her opinion is not a concluded opinion because of insufficient research or data or for any other reason, this must be stated in his or her evidence.

DUTY TO CONFER

6. An expert witness must comply with any direction of the court to—
   a. confer with another expert witness:
   b. try to reach agreement with the other expert witness on matters within the field of expertise of the expert witnesses:
   c. prepare and sign a joint witness statement stating the matters on which the expert witnesses agree and the matters on which they do not agree, including the reasons for their disagreement.
7. In conferring with another expert witness, the expert witness must exercise independent and professional judgment, and must not act on the instructions or directions of any person to withhold or avoid agreement.

APPENDIX J

Criminal Practice Directions Parts 19A and B (Applying in England and Wales)

1. 19A EXPERT EVIDENCE

1.1 19A.5

Therefore, factors which the court may take into account in determining the reliability of expert opinion, and especially of expert scientific opinion, include:

1. the extent and quality of the data on which the expert's opinion is based, and the validity of the methods by which they were obtained;
2. if the expert's opinion relies on an inference from any findings, whether the opinion properly explains how safe or unsafe the inference is (whether by reference to statistical significance or in other appropriate terms);
3. if the expert's opinion relies on the results of the use of any method (for instance, a test, measurement, or survey), whether the opinion takes proper account of matters, such as the degree of precision or margin of uncertainty, affecting the accuracy or reliability of those results;
4. the extent to which any material upon which the expert's opinion is based has been reviewed by others with relevant expertise (for instance, in peer-reviewed publications), and the views of those others on that material;
5. the extent to which the expert's opinion is based on material falling outside the expert's own field of expertise;
6. the completeness of the information which was available to the expert, and whether the expert took account of all relevant information in arriving at the opinion (including information as to the context of any facts to which the opinion relates);
7. if there is a range of expert opinion on the matter in question, where in the range the expert's own opinion lies and whether the expert's preference has been properly explained; and
8. whether the expert's methods followed established practice in the field and, if they did not, whether the reason for the divergence has been properly explained.

1.2 19A.6

In addition, in considering reliability, and especially the reliability of expert scientific opinion, the court should be astute to identify potential flaws in such opinion which detract from its reliability, such as:

1. being based on a hypothesis which has not been subjected to sufficient scrutiny (including, where appropriate, experimental or other testing), or which has failed to stand up to scrutiny;
2. being based on an unjustifiable assumption;
3. being based on flawed data;
4. relying on an examination, technique, method, or process which was not properly carried out or applied, or was not appropriate for use in the case; or
5. relying on an inference or conclusion which has not been properly reached.

2. 19B STATEMENTS OF UNDERSTANDING AND DECLARATIONS OF TRUTH IN EXPERT REPORTS

2.1 19B.1

The statement and declaration required by CrimPR 19.4(j), (k) should be in the following terms, or in terms substantially the same as these:

"I (name) DECLARE THAT:

1. I understand that my duty is to help the court to achieve the overriding objective by giving independent assistance by way of objective, unbiased opinion on matters within my expertise, both in preparing reports and giving oral evidence. I understand that this duty overrides any obligation to the party by whom I am engaged or the person who has paid or is liable to pay me. I confirm that I have complied with and will continue to comply with that duty.
2. I confirm that I have not entered into any arrangement where the amount or payment of my fees is in any way dependent on the outcome of the case.
3. I know of no conflict of interest of any kind, other than any which I have disclosed in my report.
4. I do not consider that any interest which I have disclosed affects my suitability as an expert witness on any issues on which I have given evidence.
5. I will advise the party by whom I am instructed if, between the date of my report and the trial, there is any change in circumstances which affect my answers to points 3 and 4 above.
6. I have shown the sources of all information I have used.
7. I have exercised reasonable care and skill to be accurate and complete in preparing this report.

8. I have endeavoured to include in my report those matters, of which I have knowledge or of which I have been made aware, that might adversely affect the validity of my opinion. I have clearly stated any qualifications to my opinion.
9. I have not, without forming an independent view, included or excluded anything which has been suggested to me by others including my instructing lawyers.
10. I will notify those instructing me immediately and confirm in writing if for any reason my existing report requires any correction or qualification.
11. I understand that:
    a. my report will form the evidence to be given under oath or affirmation;
    b. the court may at any stage direct a discussion to take place between experts;
    c. the court may direct that, following a discussion between the experts, a statement should be prepared showing those issues which are agreed and those issues which are not agreed, together with the reasons;
    d. I may be required to attend court to be cross-examined on my report by a cross-examiner assisted by an expert;
    e. I am likely to be the subject of public adverse criticism by the judge if the Court concludes that I have not taken reasonable care in trying to meet the standards set out above.
12. I have read Part 19 of the Criminal Procedure Rules and I have complied with its requirements.
13. I confirm that I have acted in accordance with the Code of Practice for Experts.
14. [For Experts instructed by the Prosecution only] I confirm that I have read guidance contained in a booklet known as Disclosure: Experts' Evidence and Unused Material which details my role and documents my responsibilities, in relation to revelation as an expert witness. I have followed the guidance and recognise the continuing nature of my responsibilities of disclosure. In accordance with my duties of disclosure, as documented in the guidance booklet, I confirm that:
    a. I have complied with my duties to record, retain and reveal material in accordance with the Criminal Procedure and Investigations Act 1996, as amended;
    b. I have compiled an Index of all material. I will ensure that the Index is updated in the event I am provided with or generate additional material;
    c. In the event my opinion changes on any material issue, I will inform the investigating officer, as soon as reasonably practicable and give reasons.

I confirm that the contents of this report are true to the best of my knowledge and belief and that I make this report knowing that, if it is tendered in evidence, I would be liable to prosecution if I have wilfully stated anything which I know to be false or that I do not believe to be true."

APPENDIX K

A Selection of Important Works Recommended for Further Reading

Short Title	Authors	Year	ISBN
Interpretation			
Interpreting Evidence	Robertson, B., Vignaux, G.A., and Berger, C.E.H.	2016	9781118492482
Misleading DNA Evidence	Gill, P.	2014	9780124172142
Statistics and the Evaluation of Evidence for Forensic Scientists	Aitkin, C. and Taroni, F.	2004	0470843675
The Use of Statistics in Forensic Science	Aitkin, C.G.C. and Stoney, D.A.	1991	0139337482
Quality Assurance			
Quality Assurance and Quality Control in The Analytical Chemical Laboratory	Konieczka, P. and Namiesnik, J.	2009	9781420087208
Quality Assurance in Analytical Chemistry	Pritchard, E. and Barwick, V.	2008	9780470012048
Quality Assurance for The Analytical Chemistry Laboratory	Hibbert, D.B.	2007	9780195162134
Statistics			
Statistics and Chemometrics for Analytical Chemistry	Miller, J.N., Miller, J.C., and Miller, R.D.	2018	9781292186719
Statistical Analysis in Forensic Science	Zadora, G., Martyna, A., Ramos, D., and Aitkin, C.	2014	9780470972106
Practical Statistics for the Analytical Scientist	Ellison, S., Barwick, V.J., and Farrant, T.J.D.	2009	9780854041312
Introduction to Statistics for Forensic Scientists	Lucy, D.	2007	9780470022016
General Practice			
Criminalistics	Saferstein, R.	2018	9780134477596
Forensic Science	Jackson, A.R.W. and Jackson, J.M.	2016	9781292088181
Professional Issues in Forensic Science	Houck, M. (Ed)	2015	9780128005675
Fundamentals of Forensic Science	Houck, M.M. and Siegel, J.A.	2015	9780128000373
Forensic Chemistry	Bell, S.	2014	9781292020440

Key Quality Standards Applying to the Management and Delivery of Forensic Science

General Management	
ISO 9001	Quality management systems— requirements
Testing Laboratories	
ISO/IEC 17025	General requirements for the competence of testing and calibration laboratories
ISO/IEC Guide 98-3	Uncertainty of measurement—Part 3: Guide to the expression of uncertainty in measurement (GUM:1995)
ISO/IEC Guide 99	International vocabulary of metrology—Basic and general concepts and associated terms
UKAS M3003	The Expression of Uncertainty and Confidence in Measurement
ISO/IEC 17034	General requirements for the competence of reference material producers
ISO/IEC 17043	Conformity assessment—General requirements for proficiency testing
AS5388	Forensic Analysis—in four parts **1.** Recognition, recording, recovery, transport and storage of material **2.** Analysis and examination of material **3.** Interpretation **4.** Reporting
ANAB 3028	ISO/IEC 17025:2005—FORENSIC SCIENCE TESTING LABORATORIES Accreditation Requirements
NATA	ISO/IEC 17025 Standard Application Document for accreditation of testing and calibration facilities
ILAC G19 2002	Guidance for Forensic Science Laboratories
EA-2/15 M2008	Requirements for the Accreditation of Flexible Scopes
Inspection Bodies	
ISO/IEC 17020	Conformity assessment—Requirements for the operation of various types of bodies performing inspection
ILAC P15 07/2016	Application of ISO/IEC 17020:2012 for the Accreditation of Inspection Bodies
EA-5/03 M2008	Guidance for the implementation of ISO/IEC 17020 in the field of crime scene investigation
ILAC G19 08/2014	Modules in a Forensic Science Process

Continued

General Management

ANAB 3055	ISO/IEC 17020:2012—FORENSIC INSPECTION BODIES Accreditation Requirements
UKAS RG201	Accreditation of Bodies Carrying out Scene of Crime Examination

Others

ISO/IEC 17024	Conformity assessment—General requirements for bodies operating certification of persons
ISO/IEC 17011	Conformity assessment—General requirements for accreditation bodies accrediting conformity assessment bodies

INDEX

'*Note*: Page numbers followed by "f" indicate figures, "t" indicate tables.'

A

E

F

V

9780128054161